Modeling and
Measuring
Natural Resource
Substitution

Modeling and Measuring Natural Resource Substitution

Edited by
Ernst R. Berndt
Barry C. Field

The MIT Press
Cambridge, Massachusetts
London, England

This book was set in Times New Roman by Asco Trade Typesetting Ltd., Hong Kong, and printed and bound by Murray Printing Co. in the United States of America.

Library of Congress Cataloging in Publication Data
Main entry under title:
Modeling and measuring natural resource substitution.

Revisions of papers originally presented at a conference held in Key Biscayne, Fla., Dec. 13–14, 1979.
Bibliography: p.
Includes index.
1. Costs, Industrial—Mathematical models—Congresses. 2. Materials—Costs—Mathematical models—Congresses. 3. Substitute products—Costs—Mathematical models—Congresses. 4. Conservation of natural resources—Economic aspects—Mathematical models—Congresses. I. Berndt, Ernst R.
II. Field, Barry C.
HC79.C7M62   333.7′0724   81-15673
ISBN 0-262-06078-7   AACR2

Contents

List of Contributors

Richard G. Anderson, Department of Economics, Ohio State University

Ernst R. Berndt, Sloan School of Management, Massachusetts Institute of Technology

Gardner M. Brown, Department of Economics, University of Washington

Randall S. Brown. Mathematica Policy Research, Princeton, New Jersey

Laurits R. Christensen, Department of Economics, University of Wisconsin

Michael Denny, Institute for Policy Analysis, University of Toronto

Barry C. Field, Department of Agricultural and Resource Economics, University of Massachusetts

Barbara M. Fraumeni, Department of Economics, Tufts University

Melvyn Fuss, Institute for Policy Analysis, University of Toronto

James M. Griffin, Department of Economics, University of Houston

Michael J. Harper, Division of Productivity Research, Bureau of Labor Statistics

Dale W. Jorgenson, Department of Economics, Harvard University

Heejoon Kang, School of Business, University of Indiana

Raymond J. Kopp, Resources for the Future, Washington, D.C.

John R. Moroney, Department of Economics, Texas A & M University

Catherine J. Morrison, Department of Economics, NewYork University

J. Randolph Norsworthy, Division of Productivity Research, Bureau of Labor Statistics

V. Kerry Smith, Department of Economics, University of North Carolina

David C. Stapleton, Department of Economics, University of British Columbia

John M. Trapani, Department of Economics, Tulane University

C. Campbell Watkins, Data Metrics, Limited, and Department of Economics, University of Calgary

Leonard Waverman, Institute for Policy Analysis, University of Toronto

Foreword

The chapters in this volume, with the exception of the introductory chapter, are revisions of papers presented at a conference funded by the National Science Foundation, December 13 and 14, 1979. The conference was organized by Barry C. Field, coeditor of this volume, and was held in Key Biscayne, Florida.

The objective of the conference was to provide an intensive and closely focused setting in which recent research efforts on natural resource substitution could be presented and vigorously critiqued. By all accounts the conference was a tremendous success, both in terms of the quality of the papers presented and, in that salubrious setting, the vigor with which discussion was pursued by conference participants.

It is particularly appropriate therefore that these papers be made available to a wider group of scholars. By doing so, we hope also to kindle additional interest in the important and critical study of natural resource substitution.

We wish to express our deep gratitude to the NSF and especially our project manager Lynn Pollnow, whose encouragement and managerial efforts were critical to the success of the project. That success would have been fundamentally impossible of course, without the creativity, cooperations, and diligence of the authors. Thanks are also due to the discussants, who ably focused the critiques of the individual papers, and to general conference attendees, whose active participation contributed to the revision process that has led to this book. Our thanks go to the officials of the University of Miami who helped in smoothing logistical problems of the conference and especially to Debbie Rogers, for her superlative administrative assistance throughout the conference. Finally, thanks to Connie Ballou and Kathi Smith for typing services throughout the complicated task of handling the revised papers.

Ernst R. Berndt
Barry C. Field

Modeling and Measuring Natural Resource Substitution

1

An Introductory Review of Research on the Economics of Natural Resource Substitution

Barry C. Field and Ernst R. Berndt

Popular and professional concern with the adequacy of natural resources to permit sustained economic growth has been an important issue at least since the early work of Malthus and Jevons. Much more recently Barnett and Morse published *Scarcity and Growth*, which emphasized that the 'doomsday' predictions of Malthus and Jevons had been invalidated largely as a result of natural resource-saving technical progress. By the time that book was published in 1963, the attention of many economists was already shifting away from issues of resource adequacy to newer problems of environmental quality. Traditional natural resource scarcity issues reappeared in the public arena in the 1970s, no doubt due primarily to OPEC energy market developments but also to substantial price increases in other commodity markets. The immensely popular book *Limits to Growth* converted these specific natural resource issues into a generalized concern over exhaustion of natural resource stocks but failed to address important scientific issues of possibilities for resource conservation. Economists typically pointed out that *Limits to Growth* type simulation models do not address the role of substitution and technical progress in mitigating growth impacts of depleting resources. Since increased scarcity of a natural resource is signaled by a rise in its price, a variety of substitution phenomena come into play: substitution to other inputs in the production sectors and to less resource-intensive goods in the consumption sector. These responses are not accounted for by *Limits to Growth* type models. The ultimate extent of these adjustments depends of course on the magnitudes of the substitution parameters underlying consumers' utility functions and producers' production functions. If substitution possibilities are meager, and technological progress is sluggish, the economic pressures from resource scarcity are likely to be substantial; however, if possibilities for natural resource substitution are considerable, and technological progress is brisk, then that ultimate day of resource reckoning can continue to be postponed indefinitely. Hence the extent of substitutability and technological progress is an extremely important empirical issue.

The chapters in this book focus on the empirical issues of measuring resource substitutability and/or technological change. Although much of the applied research of the 1970s is typified by these studies, they also provide important ideas for the research agenda of the 1980s, a decade in which concern over natural resource economics will likely become more pervasive. Hence these studies not only survey recent work but provide the basis for the next generation of research on natural resource substitution and technical change as well.

A decade ago it would have been impossible to publish such a book, despite the critical importance of the natural resource conservation issue, since the necessary developments in the economic theory of cost and production had not yet taken place. A bit of intellectual history may help illustrate this point.

While at Stanford University in the early 1960s, Marc Nerlove became interested in modeling both returns to scale and substitution possibilities among capital, labor, and fuel inputs in the electricity-generating sector of the U.S. economy. Nerlove's 1963 paper was innovative and seminal, particularly his use of a dual cost function with nonconstant returns to scale rather than a production function. Unsatisfied with the rather restrictive Cobb-Douglas form, but excited with the possibilities of using dual cost functions in estimating substitution possibilities, Nerlove directed his research assistant, Daniel McFadden, to examine both further use of duality theory and the problem of generating flexible functional forms with three or more inputs, forms that were less restrictive than the *CES* or Cobb-Douglas functions. McFadden focused most of his attention on the theory and applications of duality in production. It was left to a student of McFadden's at the University of California-Berkeley, W. Erwin Diewert, to solve this problem of developing flexible functional forms with three or more inputs. Diewert's 1969 Ph.D. dissertation at Berkeley and his subsequent 1971 article, "An Application of the Shephard Duality Theorem: A Generalized Leontief Production Function," made widely available to applied economists functional forms that placed no a priori restrictions on substitution elasticities yet could be consistent with the constraints typically assumed by economic theory.

Diewert's work was the first in a series of developments in the theory of dual cost and production, most of them emanating from the Berkeley campus. At the 1970 World Congress Meetings of the Econometric Society, for example, a combination of Berkeley faculty and graduate students, L. R. Christensen, D. W. Jorgenson, and L. J. Lau presented a paper entitled, "Conjugate Duality and the Transcendental Logarithmic Function," which introduced the translog functional form for production, cost, and profit functions with multiple inputs and multiple outputs, a form that also placed no prior restrictions on substitution elasticities.

Although the important work of Nerlove, McFadden, Diewert, Christensen, Jorgenson, and Lau is now well known, many of the flexible functional form developments were actually predated by the innovative and ingenious contributions of agricultural economists, advances that have been woefully neglected outside of the agricultural economics profession. For example, already in 1961 Earl Heady and John Dillon published *Agricultural Production Functions*, a book summarizing their research results of the previous decade. In it they discussed using various Taylor series expansions as polynomial approximations to unknown algebraic forms and noted that (p. 204) "while the approximation will differ in algebraic form from the true functions, its implications will be quite similar over the relevant range." Heady and Dillon explicitly considered the second-degree polynomial in logarithms (called the translog form almost a decade later by Christensen, Jorgenson and Lau), and provided least squares regression estimates of a square root transformation which took on as a special case the generalized linear production function introduced by Diewert in 1971.[1] Apparently later researchers were unaware of the functional form developments by Heady and Dillon. In any event, while Heady and Dillon focused on direct estimation of production function parameters and plotted production function contours, others worked from the vantage of the dual cost function and typically estimated parameters from the system of derived demand equations rather than the cost function itself.

For applied economists interested in estimating demand elasticities based on cost and production functions, the 1970s was a very exciting decade filled with significant developments. Important applications of these developments often involved estimating substitution elasticities for resources, especially energy. The studies presented in this volume represent the conjunction of the concern over resource scarcity, resource substitutability, and technological progress, along with developments of the last decade in production function modeling. They address general issues of measuring and modeling substitutability among inputs, assessing the bias of technological change, and focus in particular on natural resource conservation.

1.1 General Considerations

To a strict believer in laissez faire and perfect markets, the pursuit of measuring resource substitution parameters might seem unnecessary; for such believers the market presumably will make whatever adjustments are appropriate, as long as markets are made to operate smoothly.[2] It is quite important, however, and indeed imperative, that analysts address themselves to the issue of assessing the magnitude of natural resource substitution possibilities. Even if markets were perfect, and there were no cartels, the growth prospects of individual countries would be linked to the uneven geographical distribution of natural resources. National policies for technology development will reflect this distributional problem, and intelligent policies require some knowledge of substitution and innovation prospects. It is clear that a nation's short-, medium-, and long-run vulnerability to resource price or quantity shocks depends on, among other matters, possibilities for resource substitution and resource-saving technological change.

A more analytical reason for concern over measuring resource substitution possibilities is the growth viability question. When convex isoquants do not cross the nonresource input axes, continued growth is possible only if the elasticity of substitution between these other inputs and natural resources is greater than or equal to unity (Dasgupta and Heal, Stiglitz). This conclusion abstracts of course from technological change. More important, these elasticities need not be constant; indeed we would expect that price elasticities would eventually increase (in absolute value) as scarcity increased, or else budget shares on resources would ultimately exceed unity.

Stated in this way, the growth viability matter is a very long-run question. Econometric studies based only on post-World War II, or only twentieth-century data, are unlikely to shed a great deal of light on such apocalyptic issues, and critics (Meadows, Georgescu-Roegen) of this use of econometrics are justified in stating this objection clearly. Some have argued that such very long-run perspectives on resource adequacy may best be obtained from an economic-engineering approach, where future patterns are not necessarily mechanically limited to anything that has happened in the past but rely only on physical and chemical laws which tend to change less frequently than the parameter estimates of econometricians. But physical laws often tend to provide only asymptotic guidance; for example, it is doubtful that actual energy efficiency will ever closely approach the technical limits demonstrated by the second law of thermodynamics. The present state of the art in such engineering-economic modeling is such that exceedingly wide ranges of results are admissible; for two studies with contrasting conclusions regarding the distant future, see Brobst and Goeller. Hence the hard intellectual problem remains of understanding and measuring, as best as possible, substitution and technical change in the short, intermediate, and long run.

Apart from the long-run growth viability question there are numerous shorter-run problems for which the understanding of natural resource substitution processes is quite critical. Foremost among these is the prediction of economic dislocation in sectors exposed to rapid rises in resource prices. In the face of such increases, costs will rise by the greatest amount in those sectors that are most resource intensive and where substitution parameters are the lowest. Even if markets were perfect and yielded efficient resource and market adjustments, the speed and extent of the adjustments would be matters of public concern. Estimation of industry, sector, and regional elasticities of substitution should allow us to anticipate and prepare for adjustment problems of this type.

1.2 Previous Empirical Studies

From an econometric standpoint interest in natural resource substitution is very recent. In the seminal work by Cobb and Douglas inputs other than capital and labor were not mentioned, even though the output variable was gross physical output. Frisch's fascinating study on cocoa substitution in the production of ordinary nut chocolate is perhaps the first empirical study of substitution possibilities using intermediate or raw material inputs. In the major work by Arrow et al. in which the *CES* function was introduced, inputs other than capital and labor are first mentioned in the last sentence: "How about natural resources and purchased material inputs?" This question was presumably meant to generate interest in extending the analysis of production functions to a wider array of inputs. But in Nerlove's lengthy and exhaustive review of empirical work done with the *CES* function, in the six years after the original paper, natural resources are not mentioned, as none of the papers reviewed dealt with this input.[3]

Perhaps the first series of studies to include natural resource inputs were those of agricultural economists, based upon input usage data from farm management surveys conducted in pre-World War I decades and for sometime thereafter.[4] The search for optimal resource patterns was typically an inductive pursuit, based on generalizations from a large number of such surveys. The primary difficulties encountered with this approach were to account properly for quality differences among enterprises, for example, in management inputs (Griliches, Mundlak) and meteorological and soil conditions (Plaxico). It is perhaps for this reason that in the 1950s agricultural economists began to cooperate with agronomists and other physical scientists in using experimental data in production research. Such experimental research was pioneered at Iowa State University by Earl O. Heady and his associates.

In recent years there have been several econometric studies of the agricultural sector using the cost function approach and flexible functional forms. For example, an aggregate study of Binswanger featured not only the measurement of input substitution parameters among capital, labor, and other agricultural inputs but also the assessment of technical-change biases. In this volume Brown and Christensen (chapter 9) undertake an aggregate analysis of the agricultural sector.

In the nonagricultural sector the first steps beyond capital-labor models were to include inputs of diverse intermediate goods without regard to their natural resource content. One motivation for this extension was the desire to check on possible bias of estimated capital-labor substitutability in models that omitted all intermediate inputs.[5] Moreover the validity of the value-added specification rests on the separability of capital and labor from other inputs. Parks examined the Swedish manufacturing sector from 1870 to 1950 using a generalized Leontief function in which, besides capital and labor, inputs included materials from the agricultural sector, imported materials and commercial services, and transportation services. He found that the conditions for capital-labor separability were not satisfied, primarily because labor-intermediate input substitutability was greater than capital-intermediate input substitutability. Parks's results also showed that agricultural inputs in manufacturing were substitutable with labor but complementary with capital. By contrast, a study by Humphrey and Wolkowitz concluded that capital and labor were separable from intermediate inputs in a number of U.S. industries.

Studies of the manufacturing sector examining the role of natural resources are quite recent.[6] One of the first was the study of two-digit U.S. manufacturing sectors by Humphrey and Moroney, who concluded that natural resources were substitutable with both capital and labor, but that there was "somewhat higher labor-resource substitutability than capital-resource substitutability."

Moroney and Toevs estimated substitution elasticities among aggregate capital, labor, and natural resources in seven natural resource intensive industries. Several results were prominent. Capital and natural resource inputs were complementary in flour milling and cereal. Labor and natural resources appeared to be complements in gypsum products—one of the few known instances of labor and natural resource complementarity.

More recent work has often focused on energy substitution. Six chapters of this volume focus on energy use, mostly in manufacturing sectors (chapters 2, 4, 7, 10, 11, and 12). Studies of the substitutability among energy and other inputs have been carried out for U.S. manufacturing by Berndt and Wood (1975), Field and Grebenstein, Halvorsen and Ford, and Berndt and Jorgenson.[7] Research analyzing international cross-section data has been carried out by Griffin and Gregory, Pindyck, and Ozatalay et al. Several studies have also been completed on other countries, including those on Canada by Fuss, the Netherlands by Magnus, and the United Kingdom by Peterson. Studies of energy use in specific sectors have been done by a number of authors, including Christensen and Greene, and Wills.

Perhaps such an outburst of research will provide a building up of classic empirical results, but as yet the studies apparently lack unanimity. The most prominent difference seems to be in estimates of the elasticity of substitution between capital and energy. Some researchers find these two inputs to be complements, while others find them to be substitutes. A number of reasons have been put forward for this discrepancy. In chapter 4 Griffin attempts to assess their plausibility. Interpretations of energy-capital complementarity are also discussed by Berndt-Morrison-Watkins in chapter 12.

Greater agreement exists regarding the labor-energy relationship—at least here most everyone has found that the two inputs are substitutes, or essentially independent as in the case of Pindyck. The estimated elasticities vary considerably, however. Substitutability between energy and other nonenergy intermediate inputs remains also an unsettled question. The widest area of agreement seems to be in the capital-labor substitutability, most estimates of which are reasonably close to unity (with the exception of the Griffin-Gregory study).

Several studies have focused on substitution among different energy forms: see Atkinson and Halvorsen, Duncan and Binswanger, Halvorsen, and Peterson. Here there are even wider variations among results. This may be due to the general vagaries of disaggregated data, but it is also undoubtedly traceable to the fact that nearly every study examines different sectors or countries, uses different definitions of inputs, and computes elasticities holding different variables fixed. Considerably more effort will be required before these findings can be reconciled.

A number of recent articles have examined substitutability of the land resource with nonland inputs in the production of housing (Muth 1969, 1971, Koenker, Clapp, Sirmans and Redman, and Field). Another important natural resource, water, has been studied by Grebenstein and Field, and Hexem and Heady. In chapter 3 Moroney and Trapani examine models featuring inputs of nonfuel minerals.

1.3 Conceptual and Analytical Problems

The surge of work in natural resource substitution based on flexible production function forms, while providing insight into the role of natural resources in the production process, has also pinpointed more clearly numerous theoretical and empirical problems that remain.

Previous value-added studies have assumed, either implicitly or explicitly, that primary inputs of capital and labor are separable from other inputs such as materials and energy. Griliches and Ringstad have summarized why most production function investigations have omitted materials as inputs; the same arguments presumably could be used to justify omitting natural resources. Value-added studies, they say, (1) facilitate comparisons among firms or industries that differ in terms of the extent of vertical integration; such differences could lead to erroneous conclusions regarding the role of materials inputs, since, for example, one vertically integrated firm could appear to have highly productive materials inputs compared to the situation where the same production stages were divided into two firms, the first of which sold its output as intermediate goods to the second; (2) facilitate the adding together of output measures across industries by avoiding the double counting of embodied materials; (3) avoid problems of estimation that might be encountered when the same variables, materials, are added to both sides of a production function equation; and (4) avoid possible problems that might be caused if materials inputs are used in fixed proportions to output.

These reasons for the focus on value-added studies are not persuasive. The first two problems may be avoided by careful choice of industries, in particular by including in each estimation procedure only those industry observations that are comparable; cross-section studies, even in value-added approaches, have usually been limited to specific industries.[8] Estimation problems referred to in the third argument may be handled by employing sufficiently rich production function forms as well as more sophisticated econometric techniques. Alternatively, this argument can be reversed by noting that the same data have been subtracted from both sides of the equation in value-added studies.

The assumption of fixed proportions has a seductive appeal, but on reflection it does not appear to be the most obvious a priori belief on which to structure a model. Although there is, for example, an absolute minimum amount of yarn required to manufacture some quantity of cloth, most production processes utilize larger quantities of cloth. Capital equipment and operating procedures are likely to differ in the amounts of raw materials required to produce specified levels of final product. Thus raw material requirements may be varied by changing the quantities of other inputs; moreover there will usually be some degree of substitutability among different types of materials. Whether this amount of substitutability is sufficient to invalidate the assumption of fixed proportions is an empirical matter.

There is one final reason why intermediate goods may have been omitted in past studies. In some cases the prices of intermediate inputs may not be independent of the prices of primary factors used in the same sector. These issues are the subject of chapter 7 by Richard Anderson. Anderson examines the recent work of Berndt and Wood to test for exogeneity of input prices and determine the effect on measured substitution elasticities of adjusting for interindustry, interfirm shipments of traded intermediate products.

A different issue emerging from recent research concerns the appropriate measure of factor substitutability. Disparate results on substitutability may in fact be consistent, if common measures of substitutability are applied in comparing results.

To date most investigators have presented their substitution results in terms of Allen-Uzawa elasticities of substitution. These are essentially non-normalized own and cross-price elasticities of input demand. If the production function is $Y = f(X_i, \ldots, X_n)$, then these elasticities are

$$AES_{ij} = \frac{\partial \ln X_i}{\partial \ln P_j} \cdot \frac{1}{W_j}\bigg|_{Y=\bar{Y}},$$

where P_i is the piece of the ith input and W_i its cost share. Some analysts use normalized elasticities (conventional price elasticities), that is, $AES_{ij} \cdot W_j$, since these have a more straightforward economic interpretation. In both measures the quantities of all inputs are allowed to adjust to a change in P_j, output fixed.

An alternative notion is that elasticities of substitution have something to do with changing factor proportions. A very simple concept would be the percentage change in the ratio of two input quantities in response to a change in the price of some other input, or

$$\sigma_{ij} = \frac{\partial \ln (X_i/X_j)}{\partial \ln P_k}\bigg|_{Y=\bar{Y}, k \neq i,j}.$$

Mundlak has shown that these two elasticity notions are related according

$$\sigma_{ij} = w_k(AES_{ik} - AES_{jk}).$$

In chapter 5, Heejoon Kang and Garhner Brown show that the two elasticity measures can give entirely different impressions of the extent and direction of input responses, because different phenomena are being measured. They further show that σ_{ij}, which they call full elasticities of substitution, have properties that could recommend them for wider use.

Few people have bothered to calculate direct elasticities of substitution, which hold output and all other input quantities constant. These can be interpreted as short-run elasticities and presumably would be useful for assessing the relationship between two easily varied inputs, say, energy and materials, under the assumption that capital and labor were held constant. But the direct elasticity may be too inflexible to be of wide usefulness. Elasticities from restricted cost functions in which a subset of variables (the quasi-fixed inputs) are held constant might be more useful. This approach could be applied to a wide variety of production processes, each characterized by a unique partition of inputs into fixed and variable categories. Among other things this would place more emphasis on the economics of the sectors being examined and thus on the most relevant types of substitution parameters given the policy objectives of the study.

Virtually all elasticity estimates to date have been of the output-constant type. Presumably these measures offer the best means of sorting out patterns of input substitutability and complementarity in a given production situation. For policy purposes, however, such as predicting the change on an industry's input demand resulting from an increase in its price of energy, output-variable elasticities might be more useful. Output effects can emerge because of downward sloping demand functions and/ or because of short-run nonconstant returns to scale. Field and Allen have shown that

$$\left.\frac{\partial \ln X_i}{\partial \ln P_j}\right|_{P_k=\bar{P}_k, k \neq j} = \eta_{ij} = W_j(AES_{ij} + \eta\phi),$$

where η is the price elasticity of demand for output and ϕ is a function of returns to scale, such that $CRTS$ implies $\phi = 1$ (giving the expression derived by Allen, p. 508) and fixed output implies $\phi = 0$ (giving the familiar constant-output measure). To date the use of output variable elasticities of substitution has been limited to the measurement of gross and net elasticities for inputs in separable subfunctions of overall production functions. Here the required measures of η are estimated as part of the analysis; the barrier to using net elasticities more generally for inputs is the lack of estimated output elasticities.

Another important problem is that of aggregation. Most studies to date have been carried out at a rather high level of aggregation, such as all manufacturing or the two-digit industrial sector level. This is due primarily to data constraints. Widespread agreement exists that lower levels of aggregation would be useful, provided that reliable data were available. However, the previously mentioned experience with agricultural economic research might be kept in mind. Griliches and Ringstad encountered difficulties in obtaining clear and substantive results, even with a level of microdata rarely encountered by economists. Aggregation is not necessarily bad.

Chapter 8 of this volume specifically addresses several parts of the aggregation problem. Using data obtained from a large-scale process model of iron and steel production, Ray Kopp and V. Kerry Smith examine the ability of neoclassical models to yield accurate estimates of substitution parameters at different levels of input and technology aggregation. This approach to the data problem, sometimes called the pseudodata approach, has also been widely used by Griffin. Surprisingly, the experimental data generated in agricultural economics research has not been used to examine this issue.

One matter not yet mentioned is the problem of regional disaggregation of national production functions. This would be particularly useful in energy research, since the political-economic struggle over energy policy occurs within an arena of strong regional interests. In this context it is a matter of critical importance to identify any regional differences that may exist in energy use and adjustment patterns.

A still different issue is that of static and dynamic specifications. Most of the innovative empirical studies of the 1970s on resource substitution assumed, either implicitly or explicitly, that all inputs could adjust to their long-run equilibrium levels within one time period (such as within one year). This assumption is clearly inappropriate for much of natural resource demand; for example, a great deal of energy use is tied to the characteristics of long-lived energy-using equipment, and it will take some time before the old energy inefficient capital stock is replaced entirely with new energy efficient models. Adjusting capital input is a costly process, and thus such investments are typically not undertaken all at once. Marshall recognized this distinction between short and long run decades ago, but dynamic empirical models of demand for natural resources are a relatively recent development.

For quite some time a number of analysts have argued that it is not even necessary to have explicit dynamic models to obtain long-run substitution elasticity estimates; rather, provided that relative prices have remained stable for some time in each region, cross-sectional data can be used to obtain long-run elasticity estimates. Time-series data, the argument goes, will tend to yield short-run elasticity estimates. This argument has been advanced, for example, as a possible reason for differing estimates of energy-capital substitution elasticities (Griffin and Gregory, Pindyck). In chapter 6 David Stapleton examines cross-section, long-run, and the time-series, short-run arguments analytically, and concludes otherwise. According to Stapleton, reliable estimates of short- and long-run elasticities cannot depend only on whether the data base is cross section or time series but also on the underlying model.

A more direct approach to obtaining short- and long-run elasticity estimates is to employ models in which only a subset of the inputs are adjusted instantaneously, the rest being fixed in the short run. Pioneering theoretical work on such variable cost or variable profit functions has been undertaken by McFadden and Lau, among others. Surprisingly it is possible to obtain estimates of both short- and long-run elasticities, using a model of static optimization. In chapter 10 Randy Brown and Laurits Christensen apply such an approach to data from the U.S. agricultural sector. They provide estimates of short-run elasticities—elasticities among variable inputs conditional on the current (perhaps nonequilibrium) quantities of the quasi-fixed inputs—and long-run elasticities based on the assumption that eventually the quasi-fixed inputs adjust to their long-run equilibrium levels.

An alternative approach to dynamic models is that illustrated by J. R. Norsworthy and Michael J. Harper. In chapter 9, they specify a cost function in such a way that the derived demand equations include lagged values of the factor demands.

A more explicit dynamic approach is that adopted in chapter 11 by M. Denny, M. A. Fuss, and Leonard Waverman who specify a model that distinguishes between variable and quasi-fixed inputs, the latter being characterized by increasing internal marginal adjustment costs. Demand equations for the variable inputs (conditional on current levels of quasi-fixed factors) and optimal adjustment paths for the quasi-fixed factors are derived as a simultaneous system of demand equations. This innovative approach is illustrated using two-digit data for various Canadian and U.S. manufacturing industries.

The introduction of adjustment costs into dynamic models of natural resource substitution is a very recent innovation and promises to open up numerous interesting and difficult issues in the measurement and modeling of resource substitution. In the last chapter of this volume, E. R. Berndt, C. J. Morrison, and G. C. Watkins survey three generations of dynamic models—from the single-equation Balestra-Nerlove type models to the complex multiple-equation models incorporating adjustment costs and explicit dynamic optimization—and assess them in terms of consistency with economic theory and empirical applicability. The survey also suggests numerous issues on dynamic models that should be addressed in the 1980s.

Finally, there is the issue of modeling technical change. In *Scarcity and Growth* Barnett and Morse list technological progress as the most important determinant of the secular decline in natural resource extraction costs and prices. Regrettably very little is known about factors altering the rate and bias of technological change. Although the theoretical literature on induced innovation is substantial, to the best of our knowledge this type of framework has not yet been amenable to empirical implementation.

Until recently almost all empirical work on multifactor technological progress has assumed that improvements in technology are disembodied and exogenous. In chapter 2 Dale Jorgenson and Barbara Fraumeni relax this assumption, specifying that, while the bias of technological change is exogenous and constant, the rate of multifactor productivity growth depends on the particular mix of inputs purchased and thus is price responsive. Hence the rate of multifactor productivity growth depends on relative prices, but the bias of technological change is independent of relative price movements. Jorgenson-Fraumeni estimate a translog model using annual data from 1958 to 1974 from thirty-five sectors of the U.S. economy and find that in twenty-nine of them the constant bias of technical change has been energy using; this provocative result implies that the rate of multifactor productivity growth declines with increases in energy prices, thereby suggesting a rather different version of the doomsday story.

A somewhat similar framework is employed in the essay by John Moroney and John Trapani in chapter 3, except that these authors focus on nonfuel minerals rather than energy. Moroney-Trapani report a similar finding, however, in that in five of the six resource-intensive industries examined the exogenous bias of technical progress has been resource using.

Whether such biases are immutably fixed or subject to changes in relative prices or policy is an extremely important problem that requires extensive theoretical underpinnings and empirical examination.

Notes

We wish to thank V. Kerry Smith and David Wood for comments on an earlier draft of this chapter, and acknowledge informative discussions with Earl 0. Heady and Harold Carter.

1. See Heady and Dillon, equations (6.16) to (6.18), pp. 205–206. Heady and Dillon's equation (6.21) reduces to Diewert's generalized linear production function when the restrictions $B_1 = B_2 = 0$ are imposed. Heady and Dillon provide numerous regression estimates based on (6.21) in subsequent chapters of their book.

2. "When the raw materials market system is functioning smoothly and adjusting ideally, there are no long-run economic raw material problems." See Gander, p. 2.

3. See also the earlier survey by Walters of empirical research based on the Cobb-Douglas function.

4. For a recent historical view of agricultural production function research, see Woodworth and Jensen.

5. At the same time several other studies were published in which the capital and labor inputs were disaggregated to determine whether the conditions necessary for aggregation were satisfied by the data. See Berndt and Christensen (1973, 1974).

6. Actually the earliest production studies that isolated energy inputs were those of specific industries, such as Klein's model of railroads, Ferguson's study of Northeast Airlines, and Nerlove's analysis of electric utilities.

7. For a review of these and other studies, see Berndt and Wood (1977).

8. The first problem is also less severe if establishment rather than firm data are employed.

I
**Results from Recent
Research on Resource
Substitution and
Technological Progress**

Introduction to Part I

The first four chapters interpret important empirical results on resource substitution and resource-saving technological progress. In chapter 2 Dale Jorgenson and Barbara Fraumeni present a framework for measuring and interpreting the rate and bias of technological progress (unit cost diminution), based on recent developments in the theory of cost and production, and then produce empirical estimates for thirty-six sectors of the U.S. economy, using annual data for 1958 to 1974. The provocative finding reported by Jorgenson-Fraumeni is that in almost all sectors, technological change has been energy using, which implies that multifactor productivity (technological progress) falls as the price of energy increases, *ceteris paribus*. The bias of technological progress is also estimated in the third chapter by John Moroney and John Trapani, using 1954 to 1974 data on six resource-intensive American industries. Unlike Jorgenson-Fraumeni, Moroney-Trapani focus particular attention on nonfuel mineral resources; however, Moroney-Trapani obtain the related empirical result that in five of the six industries examined technological progress was significantly resource using. Moroney-Trapani also note that estimated substitution elasticities are frequently quite sensitive to model specification.

In chapter 4 James Griffin comments on his assessment of the energy-capital complementarity or substitutability controversy. It might be recalled that Berndt-Jorgenson and Berndt-Wood (1975) reported energy-capital complementarity, while Griffin-Gregory and Pindyck found substitutability between these two inputs. Here Griffin describes why in his judgment the reconciliation of empirical results by Berndt-Wood (1979) is less than completely convincing and what additional research will be necessary to resolve this important issue. In chapter 5 Heejoon Kang and Gardner Brown note that numerous definitions of elasticity of substitution are possible, and reasonable, and that a certain degree of dispersion in empirical results among studies is due to use of alternative elasticities and/or separability assumptions. They note that one elasticity notion, the full elasticity of substitution, is numerically invariant to the choice of omitted inputs and thus is particularly attractive in comparing alternative empirical estimates. Kang-Brown illustrate this elasticity discussion by providing alternative estimates of full elasticities of substitution between energy and capital based on published estimates by, among others, Berndt-Wood, Hudson-Jorgenson, Griffin-Gregory, and Fuss, and find that substantial dispersion still remains.

2

**Relative Prices and
Technical Change**

Dale W. Jorgenson and
Barbara M. Fraumeni

Our objective is to analyze technical change and the distribution of the value of output for thirty-six industrial sectors of the U.S. economy. Our most important conceptual innovation is in determining the rate of technical change and the distributive shares of productive inputs simultaneously as functions of relative prices. We show that the effects of technical change on the distributive shares are precisely the same as the effects of relative prices on the rate of technical change.

2.1 Methodology

Our methodology is based on a model of production that treats substitution among inputs and changes in technology symmetrically. The model includes a production function for each industrial sector, giving output as a function of time and of capital, labor, energy, and materials inputs. Necessary conditions for producer equilibrium in each sector are given by equalities between the distributive shares of the four productive inputs and the corresponding elasticities of output with respect to each of these inputs.

Producer equilibrium under constant returns to scale implies that the value of output is equal to the sum of the values of capital, labor, energy, and materials inputs into each sector. Given this identity and the equalities between the distributive shares and the elasticities of output with respect to each of the inputs, we can express the price of output as a function of the prices of capital, labor, energy, and materials inputs, and time. We refer to this function as the sectoral price function.

Given sectoral price functions for all thirty-six industrial sectors, we can generate econometric models that determine the rate of technical change and the distributive shares of the four productive inputs endogenously for each sector. The distributive shares and the rate of technical change, like the price of sectoral output, are functions of relative prices and time. We assume that the prices of sectoral outputs are transcendental logarithmic or, more simply, translog functions of the prices of the four inputs and time.

While technical change is endogenous in our models of production and technical change, these models must be carefully distinguished from models of induced technical change, such as those analyzed by Hicks (1963), Kennedy, Samuelson (1965), van Weizsäcker, and many others.[1] In those models the biases of technical change are endogenous and depend on relative prices. In our models the biases of technical change are fixed, while the rate of technical change is endogenous and depends on relative prices.

As Samuelson (1965) has pointed out, models of induced technical change require intertemporal optimization, since technical change at any point of time affects future production possibilities. In our models myopic decision rules are appropriate, even though the rate of technical change is endogenous, provided that the price of capital input is treated as a rental price for capital services.[2] The rate of technical change at any point of time is a function of relative prices but does not affect future production possibilities. This vastly simplifies the modeling of producer behavior and greatly facilitates the implementation of our econometric models.

Given myopic decision rules for producers in each industrial sector, we can describe all of the implications of the theory of production in terms of the sectoral price functions. The sectoral price functions must be homogeneous of degree one in the prices of the four inputs, symmetric in the input prices and time, and nondecreasing and concave in the input prices. A novel feature of our econometric methodology is to fit econometric models of sectoral production and technical change that incorporate all of these implications of the theory of production.

The translog price functions that we employ to generate our econometric models cannot be monotone and concave for all possible input prices. However, we can assure concavity of these functions for any prices that result in nonnegative distributive shares for all four inputs, so that price effects on demands for productive inputs are nonpositive wherever the inputs themselves are nonnegative. This new methodology is based on the Cholesky factorization of a matrix of constant parameters in our econometric models associated with price effects. We have fitted these matrices subject to the condition that they must be negative semidefinite.

Under constant returns to scale the rate of technical change for each sector can be expressed as the negative of the rate of growth of the price of output, plus a weighted average of the rates of growth of the prices of the four inputs. We employ indexes of the rate of technical change and the four input prices that are exact for translog price functions. This important innovation assures consistency between the representations of technology that underly our measures of technical change and input prices and the representations that underly our econometric models.

Our most striking empirical finding is that the rate of technical change is predominately decreasing in the prices of capital, labor, and energy and increasing in the price of materials. This pattern characterizes nineteen of the industries included in our study. The rate of technical change decreases with the price of capital in twenty-five industries, decreases with the price of labor in thirty-one industries, decreases with the price of energy in twenty-nine industries, and increases with the price of materials in thirty-three industries.

Our econometric models have been fitted to annual data for the period 1958–1974. Since 1973 the relative prices of capital, labor, energy, and materials in the United States have been altered radically as a consequence of the increase in the price of energy relative to the prices of other productive inputs. The sharp increase in the price of energy began with the run-up of world petroleum prices in late 1973 and early 1974 in the aftermath of the Arab Oil Embargo. Our econometric models reveal that slower productivity growth at the sectoral level after 1973 is associated with higher energy prices.

Our empirical findings on patterns of substitution are almost as clearcut as our findings on patterns of technical change. We find that the elasticities of the shares of capital with respect to the price of labor are nonnegative for thirty-three of our thirty-six industries, so that the shares of capital are nondecreasing in the price of labor for thirty-three sectors. Similarly, elasticities of the share of capital with respect to the price of energy are nonnegative for thirty-four industries and elasticities with respect to the price of materials are nonnegative for all thirty-six industries. We find that the share elasticities of labor with respect to the prices of energy and materials are nonnegative for nineteen and for all thirty-six industries, respectively. Finally, we find that the share elasticities of energy with respect to the price of materials are nonnegative for thirty of the thirty-six industries.

2.2 Econometric Models

Our econometric model of production and technical change proceeds through two stages. We first specify a functional form for the sectoral price functions, say, $\{P^i\}$, taking into account restrictions on the parameters implied by the theory of production.[3] Then we formulate an error structure for the econometric model and discuss procedures for estimation of the unknown parameters.

In formulating an econometric model of production and technical change, the specific forms we consider for the sectoral price functions $\{P^i\}$ are

$$
q_i = \exp \left[\alpha_0^i + \alpha_K^i \ln p_K^i + \alpha_L^i \ln p_L^i + \alpha_E^i \ln p_E^i + \alpha_M^i \ln p_M^i + \alpha_T^i \cdot T \right.
$$

$$
+ \frac{1}{2}\beta_{KK}^i(\ln p_K^i)^2 + \beta_{KL}^i \ln p_K^i \ln p_L^i + \beta_{KE}^i \ln p_K^i \ln p_E^i
$$

$$
+ \beta_{KM}^i \ln p_K^i \ln p_M^i + \beta_{KT}^i \ln p_K^i \cdot T + \frac{1}{2}\beta_{LL}^i(\ln p_L^i)^2
$$

$$
+ \beta_{LE}^i \ln p_L^i \ln p_E^i + \beta_{LM}^i \ln p_L^i \ln p_M^i + \beta_{LT}^i \ln p_L^i \cdot T
$$

$$
+ \frac{1}{2}\beta_{EE}^i(\ln p_E^i)^2 + \beta_{EM}^i \ln p_E^i \ln p_M^i + \beta_{ET}^i \ln p_E^i \cdot T
$$

$$
\left. + \frac{1}{2}\beta_{MM}^i(\ln p_M^i)^2 + \beta_{MT}^i \ln p_M^i \cdot T + \frac{1}{2}\beta_{TT}^i \cdot T^2 \right],
$$

for $i = 1, 2, \ldots, n$. For these price functions the prices of outputs are transcendental or, more specifically, exponential functions of the logarithms of the prices of inputs. We refer to these forms as transcendental logarithmic price functions or, more simply, translog price functions,[4] indicating the role of the variables that enter into the price functions.

The price functions $\{P^i\}$ are homogeneous of degree one in the input prices. The translog price function for an industrial sector is characterized by homogeneity of degree one if and only if the parameters for that sector satisfy the conditions:

$$
\alpha_K^i + \alpha_L^i + \alpha_E^i + \alpha_M^i = 1,
$$

$$
\beta_{KK}^i + \beta_{KL}^i + \beta_{KE}^i + \beta_{KM}^i = 0,
$$

$$
\beta_{LK}^i + \beta_{LL}^i + \beta_{LE}^i + \beta_{LM}^i = 0,
$$

$$
\beta_{EK}^i + \beta_{EL}^i + \beta_{EE}^i + \beta_{EM}^i = 0,
$$

$$
\beta_{MK}^i + \beta_{ML}^i + \beta_{ME}^i + \beta_{MM}^i = 0,
$$

$$
\beta_{KT}^i + \beta_{LT}^i + \beta_{ET}^i + \beta_{MT}^i = 0,
$$

for $i = 1, 2, \ldots, n$.

For each sector the value shares of capital, labor, energy, and materials inputs, say, $\{v_K^i\}$, $\{v_L^i\}$, $\{v_E^i\}$, and $\{v_M^i\}$, can be expressed in terms of logarithmic derivatives of the sectoral price function with respect to the logarithms of price of the corresponding input:

$$v_K^i = \alpha_K^i + \beta_{KK}^i \ln p_K^i + \beta_{KL}^i \ln p_L^i + \beta_{KE}^i \ln p_E^i + \beta_{KM}^i \ln p_M^i + \beta_{KT}^i \cdot T,$$

$$v_L^i = \alpha_L^i + \beta_{KL}^i \ln p_K^i + \beta_{LL}^i \ln p_L^i + \beta_{LE}^i \ln p_E^i + \beta_{LM}^i \ln p_M^i + \beta_{LT}^i \cdot T,$$

$$v_E^i = \alpha_E^i + \beta_{KE}^i \ln p_K^i + \beta_{LE}^i \ln p_L^i + \beta_{EE}^i \ln p_E^i + \beta_{EM}^i \ln p_M^i + \beta_{ET}^i \cdot T,$$

$$v_M^i = \alpha_M^i + \beta_{KM}^i \ln p_K^i + \beta_{LM}^i \ln p_L^i + \beta_{EM}^i \ln p_E^i + \beta_{MM}^i \ln p_M^i + \beta_{MT}^i \cdot T,$$

for $i = 1, 2, \ldots, n$.

Finally, for each sector the rate of technical change, say, $\{v_T^i\}$, can be expressed as the negative of the rate of price growth of sectoral output with respect to time, holding the prices of capital, labor, energy, and materials inputs constant. The negative of the rate of technical change takes the following form:

$$-v_T^i = \alpha_T^i + \beta_{KT}^i \ln p_K^i + \beta_{LT}^i \ln p_L^i + \beta_{ET}^i \ln p_E^i + \beta_{MT}^i \ln p_M^i + \beta_{TT}^i \cdot T,$$

for $i = 1, 2, \ldots, n$.

Given the sectoral price functions $\{P^i\}$, we can define the share elasticities with respect to price as the derivatives of the value shares with respect to the logarithms of the prices of capital, labor, energy, and materials inputs.[5] For the translog price functions the share elasticities with respect to price are constant. We can also characterize these forms as constant share elasticity or CSE price functions, indicating the interpretation of the fixed parameters that enter the price functions.[6] The share elasticities with respect to price are symmetric, so that the parameters satisfy the conditions:

$$\beta_{KL}^i = \beta_{LK}^i, \qquad \beta_{LE}^i = \beta_{EL}^i,$$

$$\beta_{KE}^i = \beta_{EK}^i, \qquad \beta_{LM}^i = \beta_{ML}^i,$$

$$\beta_{KM}^i = \beta_{MK}^i, \qquad \beta_{EM}^i = \beta_{ME}^i,$$

for $i = 1, 2, \ldots, n$.

Similarly, given the sectoral price functions $\{P^i\}$, we can define the biases of technical change with respect to price as derivatives of the value shares with respect to time.[7] Alternatively, we can define the biases of technical change with respect to price as derivatives of the rate of technical change with respect to the logarithms of the price of capital, labor, energy, and materials inputs.[8] Those two definitions of biases of technical change are equivalent. For the translog price functions the biases of technical change with respect to price are constant; these parameters are symmetric and satisfy the conditions:

$$\beta_{ET}^i = \beta_{TE}^i,$$

$$\beta_{LT}^i = \beta_{TL}^i,$$

$$\beta_{ET}^i = \beta_{TE}^i,$$

$$\beta_{MT}^i = \beta_{TM}^i,$$

for $i = 1, 2, \ldots, n$.

Finally, we can define the rate of change of the negative of the rate of technical change, $\beta_{TT}^i (i = 1, 2, \ldots, n)$, as the derivative of the negative of the rate of technical change with respect to time.[9] For the translog price functions these rates of change are constant.

Our next step in considering specific forms of the sectoral price functions $\{P^i\}$ is to derive restrictions on the parameters implied by the fact that the price functions are increasing in all four input prices and concave in the four input prices. First, since the price functions are increasing in each of the four input prices, the value shares are nonnegative:

$$v_K^i \geqq 0,$$

$$v_L^i \geqq 0,$$

$$v_E^i \geqq 0,$$

$$v_M^i \geqq 0,$$

for $i = 1, 2, \ldots, n$. Under homogeneity these value shares sum to unity:

$$v_K^i + v_L^i + v_E^i + v_M^i = 1,$$

for $i = 1, 2, \ldots, n$.

Concavity of the sectoral price functions $\{P^i\}$ implies that the matrices of second-order partial derivatives $\{\mathbf{H}^i\}$ are negative semidefinite, so that the matrices $\{\mathbf{U}^i + \mathbf{v}^i \mathbf{v}^{i'} - \mathbf{V}^i\}$ are negative semidefinite, where:[10]

$$\frac{1}{q_i} \cdot \mathbf{N}^i \cdot \mathbf{H}^i \cdot \mathbf{N}^i = \mathbf{U}^i + \mathbf{v}^i \mathbf{v}^{i'} - \mathbf{V}^i,$$

for $i = 1, 2, \ldots, n$, where

$$
\mathbf{N}^i = \begin{bmatrix} p_K^i & 0 & 0 & 0 \\ 0 & p_L^i & 0 & 0 \\ 0 & 0 & p_E^i & 0 \\ 0 & 0 & 0 & p_M^i \end{bmatrix},
$$

$$
\mathbf{V}^i = \begin{bmatrix} v_K^i & 0 & 0 & 0 \\ 0 & v_L^i & 0 & 0 \\ 0 & 0 & v_E^i & 0 \\ 0 & 0 & 0 & v_M^i \end{bmatrix},
$$

$$
\mathbf{v}^i = \begin{bmatrix} v_K^i \\ v_L^i \\ v_E^i \\ v_M^i \end{bmatrix},
$$

for $i = 1, 2, \ldots, n$, and $\{\mathbf{U}^i\}$ are matrices of constant share elasticities, defined previously.

Without violating the nonnegativity restrictions on value shares, we can set the matrices $\{\mathbf{v}^i \mathbf{v}^{i'} - \mathbf{V}^i\}$ equal to zero, for example, by choosing the value shares:

$$
v_K^i = 1,
$$

$$
v_L^i = 0,
$$

$$
v_E^i = 0,
$$

$$
v_M^i = 0.
$$

Necessary conditions for the matrices $\{\mathbf{U}^i + \mathbf{v}^i \mathbf{v}^{i'} - \mathbf{V}^i\}$ to be negative semidefinite are that the matrices of share elasticities $\{\mathbf{U}^i\}$ must be negative semidefinite. These conditions are also sufficient, since the matrices $\{\mathbf{v}^i \mathbf{v}^{i'} - \mathbf{V}^i\}$ are negative semidefinite for all nonnegative value shares summing to unity and the sum of two negative semidefinite matrices is negative semidefinite.

To impose concavity on the translog price functions, the matrices $\{\mathbf{U}^i\}$ of constant share elasticities can be represented in terms of their Cholesky factorizations shown in figure 2.1.

Under constant returns to scale the constant share elasticities satisfy symmetry restrictions and restrictions implied by homogeneity of degree one of the price function. These restrictions imply that the parameters of

$$
\begin{bmatrix}
\beta^i_{KK} & \beta^i_{KL} & \beta^i_{KE} & \beta^i_{KM} \\
\beta^i_{KL} & \beta^i_{LL} & \beta^i_{LE} & \beta^i_{LM} \\
\beta^i_{KE} & \beta^i_{LE} & \beta^i_{EE} & \beta^i_{EM} \\
\beta^i_{KM} & \beta^i_{LM} & \beta^i_{EM} & \beta^i_{MM}
\end{bmatrix}
=
\begin{bmatrix}
1 & 0 & 0 & 0 \\
\lambda^i_{21} & 1 & 0 & 0 \\
\lambda^i_{31} & \lambda^i_{32} & 1 & 0 \\
\lambda^i_{41} & \lambda^i_{42} & \lambda^i_{43} & 1
\end{bmatrix}
\begin{bmatrix}
\delta^i_1 & 0 & 0 & 0 \\
0 & \delta^i_2 & 0 & 0 \\
0 & 0 & \delta^i_3 & 0 \\
0 & 0 & 0 & \delta^i_4
\end{bmatrix}
\begin{bmatrix}
1 & \lambda^i_{21} & \lambda^i_{31} & \lambda^i_{41} \\
0 & 1 & \lambda^i_{22} & \lambda^i_{42} \\
0 & 0 & 1 & \lambda^i_{43} \\
0 & 0 & 0 & 1
\end{bmatrix}
$$

$$
=
\begin{bmatrix}
\delta^i_1 & \lambda^i_{21}\delta^i_1 & \lambda^i_{31}\delta^i_1 & \lambda^i_{41}\delta^i_1 \\
\lambda^i_{21}\delta^i_1 & \lambda^i_{21}\lambda^i_{21}\delta^i_1 + \delta^i_2 & \lambda^i_{21}\lambda^i_{31}\delta^i_1 + \lambda^i_{32}\delta^i_2 & \lambda^i_{41}\lambda^i_{21}\delta^i_1 + \lambda^i_{42}\delta^i_2 \\
\lambda^i_{31}\delta^i_1 & \lambda^i_{31}\lambda^i_{21}\delta^i_1 + \lambda^i_{32}\delta^i_2 & \lambda^i_{31}\lambda^i_{31}\delta^i_1 + \lambda^i_{32}\lambda^i_{32}\delta^i_2 + \delta^i_3 & \lambda^i_{41}\lambda^i_{31}\delta^i_1 + \lambda^i_{42}\lambda^i_{32}\delta^i_2 + \lambda^i_{43}\delta^i_3 \\
\lambda^i_{41}\delta^i_1 & \lambda^i_{41}\lambda^i_{21}\delta^i_1 + \lambda^i_{42}\delta^i_2 & \lambda^i_{41}\lambda^i_{31}\delta^i_1 + \lambda^i_{42}\lambda^i_{32}\delta^i_2 + \lambda^i_{43}\delta^i_3 & \lambda^i_{41}\lambda^i_{41}\delta^i_1 + \lambda^i_{42}\lambda^i_{42}\delta^i_2 + \lambda^i_{43}\lambda^i_{43}\delta^i_3 + \delta^i_4
\end{bmatrix},
$$

for $i = 1, 2, \ldots, n$.

Figure 2.1

the Cholesky factorizations $\{\lambda_{21}^i, \lambda_{31}^i, \lambda_{41}^i, \lambda_{32}^i, \lambda_{42}^i, \lambda_{43}^i, \delta_1^i, \delta_2^i, \delta_3^i, \delta_4^i\}$ must satisfy the following conditions:

$$1 + \lambda_{21}^i + \lambda_{31}^i + \lambda_{41}^i = 0,$$

$$1 + \lambda_{32}^i + \lambda_{42}^i \qquad\quad = 0,$$

$$1 + \lambda_{43}^i \qquad\qquad\quad = 0,$$

$$\delta_4^i \qquad\qquad\qquad\quad = 0,$$

for $i = 1, 2, \ldots, n$. Under these conditions there is a one-to-one transformation between the constant share elasticities $\{\beta_{KK}^i, \beta_{KL}^i, \beta_{KE}^i, \beta_{KM}^i, \beta_{LL}^i, \beta_{LE}^i, \beta_{LM}^i, \beta_{EE}^i, \beta_{EM}^i, \beta_{MM}^i\}$ and the parameters of the Cholesky factorizations. The matrices of share elasticities are negative semidefinite if and only if the diagonal elements $\{\delta_1^i, \delta_2^i, \delta_3^i\}$ of the matrices $\{\mathbf{D}^i\}$ are nonpositive. This completes the specification of our model of production and technical change.

The negative of the average rates of technical change in any two points of time, say, T and $T - 1$, can be expressed as the difference between successive logarithms of the price of output, less a weighted average of the differences between successive logarithms of the prices of capital, labor, energy, and materials inputs, with weights given by the average value shares:

$$-\bar{v}_T^i = \ln q_i(T) - \ln q_i(T - 1) - \bar{v}_K^i[\ln p_K^i(T) - \ln p_K^i(T - 1)]$$

$$- \bar{v}_L^i[\ln p_L^i(T) - \ln p_L^i(T - 1)] - \bar{v}_E^i[\ln p_E^i(T) - \ln p_E^i(T - 1)]$$

$$- \bar{v}_M^i[\ln p_M^i(T) - \ln p_M^i(T - 1)],$$

for $i = 1, 2, \ldots, n$, where

$$\bar{v}_T^i = \tfrac{1}{2}[v_T^i(T) + v_T^i(T - 1)],$$

for $i = 1, 2, \ldots, n$, and the average value shares in the two periods are given by

$$\bar{v}_K^i = \tfrac{1}{2}[v_K^i(T) + v_K^i(T - 1)],$$

$$\bar{v}_L^i = \tfrac{1}{2}[v_L^i(T) + v_L^i(T - 1)],$$

$$\bar{v}_E^i = \tfrac{1}{2}[v_E^i(T) + v_E^i(T - 1)],$$

$$\bar{v}_M^i = \tfrac{1}{2}[v_M^i(T) + v_M^i(T - 1)],$$

for $i = 1, 2, \ldots, n$. We refer to the expressions for the average rates of technical change $\{\bar{v}_T^i\}$ as the translog price indexes of the sectoral rates of technical change.

Similarly we can consider specific forms for prices of capital, labor, energy, and materials inputs as functions of prices of individual capital, labor, energy, and materials inputs into each industrial sector.

We assume that the price of each input can be expressed as a translog function of the price of its components. Accordingly, the difference between successive logarithms of the price of the input is a weighted average of differences between successive logarithms of prices of its components. The weights are given by the average value shares of the components. We refer to these expressions of the input prices as translog indexes of the price of sectoral inputs.

To formulate an econometric model of production and technical change, we add a stochastic component to the equations for the value shares and the rate of technical change. We assume that each of these equations has two additive components.[12] The first is a nonrandom function of capital, labor, energy, and materials inputs and time; the second is an unobservable random disturbance that is functionally independent of these variables. We obtain an econometric model of production and technical change corresponding to the translog price function by adding random disturbances to all five equations:

$$v_K^i = \alpha_K^i + \beta_{KK}^i \ln p_K^i + \beta_{KL}^i \ln p_L^i + \beta_{KE}^i \ln p_E^i + \beta_{KM}^i \ln p_M^i + \beta_{KT}^i \cdot T + \varepsilon_K^i,$$

$$v_L^i = \alpha_L^i + \beta_{KL}^i \ln p_K^i + \beta_{LL}^i \ln p_L^i + \beta_{LE}^i \ln p_E^i + \beta_{LM}^i \ln p_M^i + \beta_{LT}^i \cdot T + \varepsilon_L^i,$$

$$v_E^i = \alpha_E^i + \beta_{KE}^i \ln p_K^i + \beta_{LE}^i \ln p_L^i + \beta_{EE}^i \ln p_E^i + \beta_{EM}^i \ln p_M^i + \beta_{ET}^i \cdot T + \varepsilon_E^i,$$

$$v_M^i = \alpha_M^i + \beta_{KM}^i \ln p_K^i + \beta_{LM}^i \ln p_L^i + \beta_{EM}^i \ln p_E^i + \beta_{MM}^i \ln p_M^i + \beta_{MT}^i \cdot T + \varepsilon_M^i,$$

$$-v_T^i = \alpha_T^i + \beta_{KT}^i \ln p_K^i + \beta_{LT}^i \ln p_L^i + \beta_{ET}^i \ln p_E^i + \beta_{MT}^i \ln p_M^i + \beta_{TT}^i \cdot T + \varepsilon_T^i,$$

for $i = 1, 2, \ldots, n$, where $\{\alpha_K^i, \alpha_L^i, \alpha_E^i, \alpha_M^i, \alpha_T^i, \beta_{KK}^i, \beta_{KL}^i, \beta_{KE}^i, \beta_{KM}^i, \beta_{KT}^i, \beta_{LL}^i, \beta_{LE}^i, \beta_{LM}^i, \beta_{LT}^i, \beta_{EE}^i, \beta_{EM}^i, \beta_{ET}^i, \beta_{MM}^i, \beta_{MT}^i, \beta_{TT}^i\}$ are unknown parameters and $\{\varepsilon_K^i, \varepsilon_L^i, \varepsilon_E^i, \varepsilon_M^i, \varepsilon_T^i\}$ are unobservable random disturbances.

Since the value shares sum to unity, the unknown parameters satisfy the same restrictions as before and the random disturbances corresponding to the four value shares sum to zero:

$$\varepsilon_K^i + \varepsilon_L^i + \varepsilon_E^i + \varepsilon_M^i = 0,$$

for $= 1, 2, \ldots, n$, so that these random disturbances are not distributed independently.

We assume that the random disturbances for all five equations have expected value equal to zero for all observations:

$$
E \begin{pmatrix} \varepsilon_K^i \\ \varepsilon_L^i \\ \varepsilon_E^i \\ \varepsilon_M^i \\ \varepsilon_T^i \end{pmatrix} = 0,
$$

for $i = 1, 2, \ldots, n$. We also assume that the random disturbances have a covariance matrix that is the same for all observations; since the random disturbances corresponding to the four value shares sum to zero, this matrix is positive semidefinite with rank at most equal to four.

We assume that the covariance matrix of the random disturbances corresponding to the first three value shares and the rate of technical change, say $\mathbf{\Sigma}^i$, has rank four, where

$$
V \begin{pmatrix} \varepsilon_K^i \\ \varepsilon_L^i \\ \varepsilon_E^i \\ \varepsilon_T^i \end{pmatrix} = \mathbf{\Sigma}^i,
$$

for $i = 1, 2, \ldots, n$, so the $\mathbf{\Sigma}^i$ is a positive definite matrix. Finally, we assume that the random disturbances corresponding to distinct observations in the same or distinct equations are uncorrelated. Under this assumption the matrix of random disturbances for the first three value shares and the rate of technical change for all observations has the Kronecker product form,

$$
V \begin{pmatrix} \varepsilon_K^i(1) \\ \varepsilon_K^i(2) \\ \vdots \\ \varepsilon_K^i(N) \\ \varepsilon_L^i(1) \\ \vdots \\ \varepsilon_T^i(N) \end{pmatrix} = \mathbf{\Sigma}^i \otimes I,
$$

for $i = 1, 2, \ldots, n$.

Since the rates of technical change $\{v_T^i\}$ are not directly observable, the equation for the rate of technical change can be written:

$$
-\bar{v}_T^i = \alpha_T^i + \beta_{KT}^i \overline{\ln p_K^i} + \beta_{LT}^i \overline{\ln p_L^i} + \beta_{ET}^i \overline{\ln p_E^i} + \beta_{MT}^i \overline{\ln p_M^i} + \beta_{TT}^i \cdot \overline{T} + \bar{\varepsilon}_T^i,
$$

for $i = 1, 2, \ldots, n$, where $\bar{\varepsilon}_T^i$ is the average disturbance in the two periods:

$$\bar{\varepsilon}_T^i = \tfrac{1}{2}[\varepsilon_T^i(T) + \varepsilon_T^i(T - 1)],$$

for $i = 1, 2, \ldots, n$. Similarly the equations for the value shares of capital, labor, energy, and materials inputs can be written:

$$\bar{v}_K^i = \alpha_K^i + \beta_{KK}^i \overline{\ln p_K^i} + \beta_{KL}^i \overline{\ln p_L^i} + \beta_{KE}^i \overline{\ln p_E^i} + \beta_{KM}^i \overline{\ln p_M^i} + \beta_{KT}^i \cdot \overline{T} + \bar{\varepsilon}_K^i,$$

$$\bar{v}_L^i = \alpha_L^i + \beta_{KL}^i \overline{\ln p_K^i} + \beta_{LL}^i \overline{\ln p_L^i} + \beta_{LE}^i \overline{\ln p_E^i} + \beta_{LM}^i \overline{\ln p_M^i} + \beta_{LT}^i \cdot \overline{T} + \bar{\varepsilon}_L^i,$$

$$\bar{v}_E^i = \alpha_E^i + \beta_{KE}^i \overline{\ln p_K^i} + \beta_{LE}^i \overline{\ln p_L^i} + \beta_{EE}^i \overline{\ln p_E^i} + \beta_{EM}^i \overline{\ln p_M^i} + \beta_{ET}^i \cdot \overline{T} + \bar{\varepsilon}_E^i,$$

$$\bar{v}_M^i = \alpha_M^i + \beta_{KM}^i \overline{\ln p_K^i} + \beta_{LM}^i \overline{\ln p_L^i} + \beta_{EM}^i \overline{\ln p_E^i} + \beta_{MM}^i \overline{\ln p_M^i} + \beta_{MT}^i \cdot \overline{T} + \bar{\varepsilon}_M^i,$$

where

$$\bar{\varepsilon}_K^i = \tfrac{1}{2}[\varepsilon_K^i(T) + \varepsilon_K^i(T - 1)],$$

$$\bar{\varepsilon}_L^i = \tfrac{1}{2}[\varepsilon_L^i(T) + \varepsilon_L^i(T - 1)],$$

$$\bar{\varepsilon}_E^i = \tfrac{1}{2}[\varepsilon_E^i(T) + \varepsilon_E^i(T - 1)],$$

$$\bar{\varepsilon}_M^i = \tfrac{1}{2}[\varepsilon_M^i(T) + \varepsilon_M^i(T - 1)],$$

for $i = 1, 2, \ldots, n$. As before, the average value shares $\{\bar{v}_K^i, \bar{v}_L^i, \bar{v}_E^i, \bar{v}_M^i\}$ sum to unity, so that the average disturbances $\{\bar{\varepsilon}_K^i, \bar{\varepsilon}_L^i, \bar{\varepsilon}_E^i, \bar{\varepsilon}_M^i\}$ sum to zero:

$$\bar{\varepsilon}_K^i + \bar{\varepsilon}_L^i + \bar{\varepsilon}_E^i + \bar{\varepsilon}_M^i = 0,$$

for $i = 1, 2, \ldots, n$.

The covariance matrix of the average disturbances corresponding to the equation for the rate of technical change for all observations, say, $\boldsymbol{\Omega}$, is a Laurent matrix:

$$V\begin{pmatrix} \bar{\varepsilon}_T^i(2) \\ \bar{\varepsilon}_T^i(3) \\ \vdots \\ \bar{\varepsilon}_T^i(N) \end{pmatrix} = \boldsymbol{\Omega},$$

where

$$\boldsymbol{\Omega} = \begin{bmatrix} \tfrac{1}{2} & \tfrac{1}{4} & 0 & \cdots & 0 \\ \tfrac{1}{4} & \tfrac{1}{2} & \tfrac{1}{4} & \cdots & 0 \\ 0 & \tfrac{1}{4} & \tfrac{1}{2} & \cdots & 0 \\ \vdots & \vdots & \vdots & & \vdots \\ 0 & 0 & 0 & \cdots & \tfrac{1}{2} \end{bmatrix}$$

The covariance matrix of the average disturbance corresponding to each equation for the four value shares is the same, so that the covariance matrix of the average disturbances for the first three value shares and the rate of technical change for all observations has the Kronecker product form:

$$V \begin{pmatrix} \bar{\varepsilon}_K^i(2) \\ \bar{\varepsilon}_K^i(3) \\ \vdots \\ \bar{\varepsilon}_K^i(N) \\ \bar{\varepsilon}_L^i(2) \\ \vdots \\ \bar{\varepsilon}_T^i(N) \end{pmatrix} = \Sigma^i \otimes \Omega,$$

for $i = 1, 2, \ldots, n$.

Although disturbances in equations for the average rate of technical change and the average value shares are autocorrelated, the data can be transformed to eliminate the autocorrelation. The matrix Ω is positive definite, so that there is a matrix T such that

$$T\Omega T' = I,$$

$$T'T = \Omega^{-1}.$$

To construct the matrix T, we can first invert the matrix Ω to obtain the inverse matrix Ω^{-1}, a positive definite matrix. We then calculate the Cholesky factorization of the inverse matrix Ω^{-1}:

$$\Omega^{-1} = LDL',$$

where L is a unit lower triangular matrix and D is a diagonal matrix with positive elements along the main diagonal. Finally, we can write the matrix T in the form

$$T = D^{1/2}L',$$

where $D^{1/2}$ is a diagonal matrix with elements along the main diagonal equal to the square roots of the corresponding elements of D.

We can transform the equations for the average rates of technical change by the matrix $T = D^{1/2}L'$ to obtain equations with uncorrelated random disturbances:[13]

$$\mathbf{D}^{1/2}\mathbf{L}'\begin{pmatrix}\bar{v}_T^i(2)\\\bar{v}_T^i(3)\\\vdots\\\bar{v}_T^i(N)\end{pmatrix} = \mathbf{D}^{1/2}\mathbf{L}'\begin{pmatrix}1 & \overline{\ln p_K^i(2)} & \cdots & 2-\frac{1}{2}\\1 & \overline{\ln p_K^i(3)} & \cdots & 3-\frac{1}{2}\\\vdots & & & \vdots\\1 & \overline{\ln p_K^i(N)} & \cdots & N-\frac{1}{2}\end{pmatrix}\begin{pmatrix}\alpha_T^i\\\beta_{KT}^i\\\vdots\\\beta_{TT}^i\end{pmatrix}$$

$$+ \mathbf{D}^{1/2}\mathbf{L}'\begin{pmatrix}\bar{\varepsilon}_T^i(2)\\\bar{\varepsilon}_T^i(3)\\\vdots\\\bar{\varepsilon}_T^i(N)\end{pmatrix},$$

for $i = 1, 2, \ldots, n$, since

$$\mathbf{T\Omega T}' = (\mathbf{D}^{1/2}\mathbf{L}')\mathbf{\Omega}(\mathbf{D}^{1/2}\mathbf{L}')' = \mathbf{I}.$$

The transformation $\mathbf{T} = \mathbf{D}^{1/2}\mathbf{L}'$ is applied to data on the average rates of technical change $\{\bar{v}_T^i\}$ and data on the average values of the variables that appear on the right-hand side of the corresponding equation.

We can apply the transformation $\mathbf{T} = \mathbf{D}^{1/2}\mathbf{L}'$ to the first three equations for average value shares to obtain equations with uncorrelated disturbances. As before, the transformation is applied to data on the average values shares and the average values of variables that appear in the corresponding equations. The covariance matrix of the transformed disturbances from the first three equations for the average value shares and the equation for the average rate of technical change has the Kronecker product form:

$$(\mathbf{I} \otimes \mathbf{D}^{1/2}\mathbf{L}')(\mathbf{\Sigma}^i \otimes \mathbf{\Omega})(\mathbf{I} \otimes \mathbf{D}^{1/2}\mathbf{L}')' = \mathbf{\Sigma}^i \otimes \mathbf{I},$$

for $i = 1, 2, \ldots, n$.

To estimate the unknown parameters of the translog price function we combine the first three equations for the average value shares with the equation for the average rate of technical change to obtain a complete econometric model of production and technical change. We estimate the parameters of the equations for the remaining average value shares, using the restrictions on these parameters discussed earlier. The complete model involves fourteen unknown parameters. A total of sixteen additional parameters can be estimated as functions of these parameters, given the restrictions. Our estimate of the unknown parameters of the econometric model of production and technical change is based on the nonlinear, three-stage, least squares estimator introduced by Jorgenson and Laffont.

2.3 Empirical Results

To implement the econometric models of production and technical change developed in section 2.2 we assembled a data base for thirty-six industrial sectors of the U.S. economy listed in table 2.1. For capital and labor inputs we first compiled data by sector on the basis of the classification of economic activities employed in the U.S. National Income and Product Accounts. We then transformed these data into a format appropriate for the classification of activities employed in the U.S. Interindustry Transactions Accounts. For energy and materials inputs we compiled data by sector on interindustry transactions among the thirty-six industrial sectors. For this purpose we used the classification of economic activities employed in the U.S. Interindustry Transactions Accounts.[14]

For each sector we compiled data on the value shares of capital, labor, energy, and materials inputs, annually, for the period 1958 to 1974. We also compiled indexes of prices of sectoral output and all four sectoral inputs for the same period. Finally, we compiled translog indexes of sectoral rates of technical change. For the miscellaneous sector the rate of technical change is equal to zero by definition, so that the econometric model for the sector does not include an equation for the sectoral rate of technical change. There are sixteen observations for each behavioral equation, since two-period averages of all data are employed.

The parameters $\{\alpha_K^i, \alpha_L^i, \alpha_E^i, \alpha_M^i\}$ can be interpreted as average value shares of capital input, labor input, energy input, and materials input for the corresponding sector. Similarly the parameters $\{\alpha_T^i\}$ can be interpreted as averages of the negative of rates of technical change. The parameters $\{\beta_{KK}^i, \beta_{KL}^i, \beta_{KE}^i, \beta_{KM}^i, \beta_{LL}^i, \beta_{LE}^i, \beta_{LM}^i, \beta_{EE}^i, \beta_{EM}^i, \beta_{MM}^i\}$ can be interpreted as constant share elasticities with respect to price for the corresponding sector. Similarly the parameters $\{\beta_{KT}^i, \beta_{LT}^i, \beta_{ET}^i, \beta_{MT}^i\}$ can be interpreted as constant biases of technical change with respect to price. Finally, the parameters $\{\beta_{TT}^i\}$ can be interpreted as constant rates of change of the negative of the rates of technical change.

In estimating the parameters of our sectoral models of production and technical change, we retain the average of the negative of the rate of technical change, biases of technical change, and the rate of change of the negative of the rate of technical change as parameters to be estimated for thirty-five of the thirty-six industrial sectors. For the miscellaneous sector the rate of technical change is equal to zero by definition, so that these parameters are set equal to zero. Estimates of the share elasticities with respect to price are obtained under the restrictions implied by the necessary and sufficient conditions for concavity of the price functions presented in

Table 2.1
Parameter estimates for sectoral models of production and technical change

Parameter	Industry			
	Agriculture forestry and fisheries	Metal mining	Coal mining	Crude petroleum and natural gas
α_K^i	0.186 (0.00620)	0.232 (0.0113)	0.248 (0.0135)	0.486 (0.0136)
α_L^i	0.295 (0.0122)	0.314 (0.0139)	0.515 (0.0110)	0.113 (0.00377)
α_E^i	0.026 (0.000718)	0.0398 (0.00301)	0.125 (0.00636)	0.0579 (0.00190)
α_M^i	0.492 (0.0173)	0.414 (0.0135)	0.112 (0.0288)	0.343 (0.0182)
α_T^i	−0.00949 (0.0637)	−0.00306 (0.0605)	0.0323 (0.0872)	0.000985 (0.0837)
β_{KK}^i				
β_{KL}^i				
β_{KE}^i				
β_{KM}^i	0.00418 (0.000778)	0.00268 (0.0142)	0.00954 (0.00169)	0.00342 (0.00170)
β_{KT}^i	−0.970 (0.0683)	−1.44 (0.151)		
β_{LL}^i	−0.0415 (0.00593)	0.0168 (0.0254)		
β_{LE}^i	1.01 (0.0671)	1.42 (0.133)		
β_{LM}^i	0.0353 (0.00302)	0.0432 (0.00401)	0.00971 (0.00138)	0.000277 (0.00047)
β_{LT}^i	−0.00178 (0.000553)	−0.000195 (0.000578)	−0.137 (0.00862)	
β_{EE}^i	0.0433 (0.00647)	−0.0166 (0.0249)	0.137 (0.00862)	
β_{EM}^i	0.00177 (0.000235)	0.000243 (0.000688)	−0.00433 (0.000808)	0.000979 (0.00023)
β_{ET}^i	−1.05 (0.0662)	−1.405 (0.119)	−0.137 (0.00862)	
β_{MM}^i	−0.0413 (0.00334)	−0.0461 (0.00360)	−0.0149 (0.00360)	−0.00468 (0.00228)
β_{MT}^i				
β_{TT}^i	0.000200 (0.00803)	−0.00120 (0.00757)	0.00426 (0.0110)	0.000491 (0.0105)

Table 2.1 (continued)

Parameter	Industry			
	Nonmetallic mining	Construction	Food and kindred products	Tobacco manufacturers
α_K^i	0.290 (0.0135)	0.0735 (0.00350)	0.0595 (0.00234)	0.179 (0.00719)
α_L^i	0.333 (0.0337)	0.469 (0.0185)	0.167 (0.00623)	0.144 (0.00686)
α_E^i	0.0798 (0.00214)	0.0256 (0.000905)	0.0116 (0.000746)	0.00383 (0.000404)
α_M^i	0.297 (0.0447)	0.432 (0.0228)	0.761 (0.00910)	0.673 (0.0135)
α_T^i	0.0633 (0.0347)	0.0502 (0.00809)	0.0106 (0.0142)	0.0772 (0.141)
β_{KK}^i				
β_{KL}^i				
β_{KE}^i				
β_{KM}^i				
β_{KT}^i	0.00403 (0.00169)	0.000853 (0.000438)	-0.000718 (0.000294)	0.00289 (0.000901)
β_{LL}^i		-0.448 (0.0483)		-0.0709 (0.0168)
β_{LE}^i		-0.0517 (0.00602)		0.00281 (0.00158)
β_{LM}^i		0.500 (0.0526)		0.0681 (0.0163)
β_{LT}^i	0.000724 (0.00422)	-0.00579 (0.00290)	-0.000548 (0.000781)	0.00794 (0.00125)
β_{EE}^i		-0.00597 (0.00106)		-0.000112 (0.000118)
β_{EM}^i		0.0577 (0.00697)		-0.00270 (0.00146)
β_{ET}^i	0.00225 (0.000268)	-0.00142 (0.000246)	0.000133 (0.0000935)	-0.0000257 (0.0000995)
β_{MM}^i		-0.558 (0.0577)		-0.0654 (0.0159)
β_{MT}^i	-0.00700 (0.00560)	0.00636 (0.00343)	0.00113 (0.00114)	-0.0108 (0.00191)
β_{TT}^i	0.00610 (0.00429)	0.00379 (0.00108)	0.00132 (0.00176)	0.0140 (0.0177)

Table 2.1 (continued)

Parameter	Industry			
	Textile mill products	Apparel and other fabricated textile products	Lumber and wood products	Furniture and fixtures
α_K^i	0.0739 (0.00232)	0.0446 (0.00131)	0.166 (0.00506)	0.0704 (0.00299)
α_L^i	0.221 (0.00650)	0.324 (0.00819)	0.295 (0.0134)	0.411 (0.0122)
α_E^i	0.0164 (0.000675)	0.00657 (0.000231)	0.0193 (0.00113)	0.0106 (0.000486)
α_M^i	0.689 (0.00936)	0.625 (0.00956)	0.519 (0.0175)	0.507 (0.0155)
α_T^i	−0.0133 (0.0147)	−0.00745 (0.0347)	0.00408 (0.0412)	−0.00687 (0.0233)
β_{KK}^i			−0.0896 (0.0196)	
β_{KL}^i			−0.178 (0.0301)	
β_{KE}^i			−0.0127 (0.00418)	
β_{KM}^i			0.280 (0.0474)	
β_{KT}^i	0.000457 (0.000291)	0.000693 (0.000164)	0.0145 (0.00162)	0.000122 (0.000375)
β_{LL}^i		−0.230 (0.0257)	−0.353 (0.0819)	−1.56 (0.0643)
β_{LE}^i		−0.00880 (0.00202)	−0.0253 (0.00768)	−0.0625 (0.00323)
β_{LM}^i		0.239 (0.0272)	0.556 (0.108)	1.62 (0.0645)
β_{LT}^i	0.00114 (0.00178)	0.00552 (0.00116)	0.0184 (0.00367)	0.0328 (0.00196)
β_{EE}^i		−0.000336 (0.00130)	−0.00181 (0.00112)	−0.00251 (0.000276)
β_{EM}^i		0.00913 (0.00214)	0.0398 (0.0126)	0.0650 (0.00348)
β_{ET}^i	0.000366 (0.000217)	0.000479 (0.0000517)	0.00197 (0.00380)	0.00143 (0.0000851)
β_{MM}^i		−0.248 (0.0288)	−0.876 (0.146)	−1.69 (0.0648)
β_{MT}^i	−0.00197 (0.00208)	−0.00669 (0.00133)	−0.0349 (0.00497)	−0.0344 (0.00230)
β_{TT}^i	−0.000516 (0.00187)	−0.00162 (0.00436)	0.00384 (0.00517)	0.000417 (0.00292)

Table 2.1 (continued)

Parameter	Industry			
	Paper and allied products	Printing publishing and allied industries	Chemicals and allied products	Petroleum refining
α_K^i	0.119 (0.00504)	0.114 (0.00412)	0.138 (0.00508)	0.116 (0.00583)
α_L^i	0.276 (0.0150)	0.398 (0.0152)	0.218 (0.00596)	0.0792 (0.00330)
α_E^i	0.0328 (0.00114)	0.00857 (0.000312)	0.0945 (0.00348)	0.638 (0.00600)
α_M^i	0.572 (0.0210)	0.479 (0.0195)	0.549 (0.0138)	0.167 (0.0107)
α_T^i	0.298 (0.0371)	-0.0124 (0.0289)	0.00607 (0.0242)	0.0203 (0.0432)
β_{KK}^i				
β_{KL}^i				
β_{KE}^i				
β_{KM}^i				
β_{KT}^i	-0.00101 (0.000632)	0.00154 (0.000517)	-0.00399 (0.000637)	0.00131 (0.000731)
β_{LL}^i		-0.402 (0.0713)	-0.102 (0.0406)	-0.312 (0.0624)
β_{LE}^i		-0.0268 (0.00436)	0.00183 (0.0133)	0.00205 (0.0167)
β_{LM}^i		0.429 (0.0741)	0.101 (0.0474)	0.310 (0.0764)
β_{LT}^i	0.00154 (0.00188)	0.0157 (0.00304)	0.00253 (0.00157)	-0.0000384 (0.000593)
β_{EE}^i		-0.00179 (0.000452)	-0.0000330 (0.000483)	-0.0000135 (0.000221)
β_{EM}^i		0.0286 (0.00475)	-0.00180 (0.0128)	-0.00203 (0.0164)
β_{ET}^i	0.000767 (0.000143)	0.00121 (0.000152)	0.00232 (0.000640)	0.00593 (0.000764)
β_{MM}^i		-0.457 (0.0772)	-0.0989 (0.0562)	-0.308 (0.0910)
β_{MT}^i	-0.00130 (0.00264)	-0.0185 (0.00347)	-0.000867 (0.00237)	-0.00721 (0.00145)
β_{TT}^i	0.00826 (0.00463)	-0.00188 (0.00363)	0.00337 (0.00304)	0.00272 (0.00542)

Table 2.1 (continued)

Parameter	Industry			
	Rubber and miscellaneous plastic products	Leather and leather products	Stone, clay, and glass products	Primary metal industries
α_K^i	0.106 (0.00225)	0.0507 (0.00160)	0.128 (0.00520)	0.0940 (0.00446)
α_L^i	0.283 (0.00452)	0.372 (0.0105)	0.416 (0.0117)	0.301 (0.0172)
α_E^i	0.0250 (0.000427)	0.00837 (0.000523)	0.0472 (0.00130)	0.0432 (0.00270)
α_M^i	0.586 (0.00678)	0.569 (0.0116)	0.409 (0.0173)	0.562 (0.0241)
α_T^i	0.0232 (0.0437)	−0.00966 (0.0275)	0.00972 (0.0255)	−0.00869 (0.0302)
β_{KK}^i				
β_{KL}^i				
β_{KE}^i				
β_{KM}^i				
β_{KT}^i	−0.00245 (0.000282)	0.0000824 (0.000201)	−0.00279 (0.000652)	−0.00157 (0.000559)
β_{LL}^i	−0.658 (0.0301)	−0.215 (0.0627)	−2.06 (0.122)	
β_{LE}^i	−0.134 (0.00505)	−0.0142 (0.00279)	−0.108 (0.0200)	
β_{LM}^i	0.792 (0.0316)	0.229 (0.0653)	2.17 (0.136)	
β_{LT}^i	0.0144 (0.000832)	0.00832 (0.00214)	0.0568 (0.00329)	0.00435 (0.00215)
β_{EE}^i	−0.0274 (0.00216)	−0.000936 (0.000155)	−0.00562 (0.00189)	
β_{EM}^i	0.162 (0.00694)	0.0151 (0.00291)	0.113 (0.0219)	
β_{ET}^i	0.00359 (0.000122)	0.000685 (0.0000997)	0.00287 (0.000512)	−0.0000721 (0.000339)
β_{MM}^i	−0.954 (0.0337)	−0.244 (0.0680)	−2.28 (0.152)	
β_{MT}^i	−0.0155 (0.00106)	−0.00908 (0.00228)	−0.0568 (0.00393)	−0.00271 (0.00302)
β_{TT}^i	0.00585 (0.00548)	−0.00188 (0.00343)	0.00158 (0.00319)	−0.00123 (0.00379)

Table 2.1 (continued)

Parameter	Industry			
	Fabricated metal products	Machinery except electrical	Electrical machinery	Motor vehicles and equipment
α_K^i	0.0969 (0.00338)	0.107 (0.00194)	0.102 (0.00344)	0.121 (0.00403)
α_L^i	0.370 (0.00999)	0.332 (0.00442)	0.362 (0.00851)	0.204 (0.00618)
α_E^i	0.0129 (0.000308)	0.0119 (0.000227)	0.0107 (0.000414)	0.00773 (0.000201)
α_M^i	0.520 (0.0135)	0.549 (0.00604)	0.525 (0.111)	0.667 (0.0102)
α_T^i	0.0224 (0.0252)	0.000389 (0.0156)	0.0113 (0.0420)	0.00787 (0.0386)
β_{KK}^i				
β_{KL}^i				
β_{KE}^i				
β_{KM}^i				
β_{KT}^i	0.00126 (0.000424)	−0.000343 (0.000244)	0.000801 (0.000431)	0.000981 (0.000505)
β_{LL}^i	−0.602 (0.0240)	−2.05 (0.111)	−0.616 (0.191)	−0.350 (0.0655)
β_{LE}^i	−0.0431 (0.00218)	−0.120 (0.00831)	−0.0276 (0.0103)	−0.00435 (0.00316)
β_{LM}^i	0.645 (0.0245)	2.17 (0.118)	0.643 (0.201)	0.354 (0.0666)
β_{LT}^i	0.0169 (0.00134)	0.0446 (0.00243)	0.0150 (0.00457)	0.0174 (0.00248)
β_{EE}^i	−0.00309 (0.000315)	−0.00699 (0.000715)	−0.00124 (0.000575)	−0.0000541 (0.0000760)
β_{EM}^i	0.0462 (0.00248)	0.127 (0.00899)	0.0289 (0.0108)	0.00441 (0.00324)
β_{ET}^i	0.00104 (0.0000570)	0.00289 (0.000178)	0.000901 (0.000244)	0.000330 (0.000117)
β_{MM}^i	−0.691 (0.0251)	−2.30 (0.125)	−0.672 (0.211)	−0.359 (0.0679)
β_{MT}^i	−0.192 (0.00176)	−0.0471 (0.00262)	−0.0167 (0.00487)	−0.0187 (0.00272)
β_{TT}^i	0.00407 (0.00314)	0.000205 (0.00196)	0.00244 (0.00525)	0.00235 (0.00482)

Table 2.1 (continued)

Parameter	Industry			
	Transportation equipment and ordinance	Instruments	Miscellaneous manufacturing industries	Transportation
α_K^i	0.0411 (0.00291)	0.139 (0.00515)	0.0995 (0.00339)	0.184 (0.00670)
α_L^i	0.396 (0.00882)	0.349 (0.00729)	0.350 (0.00561)	0.457 (0.0126)
α_E^i	0.00993 (0.000352)	0.00668 (0.000151)	0.0115 (0.000290)	0.0561 (0.00304)
α_M^i	0.553 (0.0109)	0.505 (0.0122)	0.539 (0.00747)	0.303 (0.0222)
α_T^i	−0.0153 (0.0333)	0.0191 (0.0459)	0.0123 (0.0715)	−0.0357 (0.0138)
β_{KK}^i				
β_{KL}^i				
β_{KE}^i				
β_{KM}^i				
β_{KT}^i	−0.00119 (0.000365)	0.000381 (0.000646)	0.00114 (0.000425)	0.000922 (0.000839)
β_{LL}^i		−1.21 (0.0336)	−1.02 (0.076)	
β_{LE}^i		−0.0230 (0.00181)	−0.0750 (0.00635)	
β_{LM}^i		1.24 (0.0335)	1.10 (0.0774)	
β_{LT}^i	0.00104 (0.00111)	0.0217 (0.00105)	0.0244 (0.00177)	0.00252 (0.00158)
β_{EE}^i		−0.000434 (0.0000704)	−0.00549 (0.000950)	
β_{EM}^i		0.0234 (0.00188)	0.0804 (0.00723)	
β_{ET}^i	0.000197 (0.0000441)	0.000460 (0.0000332)	0.00199 (0.000140)	0.000845 (0.000381)
β_{MM}^i		−1.26 (0.0335)	−1.18 (0.0791)	
β_{MT}^i	−0.0000465 (0.00136)	−0.0225 (0.00161)	−0.0276 (0.00190)	−0.000429 (0.00278)
β_{TT}^i	−0.00164 (0.00417)	0.00369 (0.00575)	0.00354 (0.00895)	−0.00243 (0.00174)

Table 2.1 (continued)

Parameter	Industry			
	Communications	Electric utilities	Gas utilities	Trade
α_K^i	0.403 (0.0185)	0.352 (0.00940)	0.229 (0.00428)	0.158 (0.00996)
α_L^i	0.431 (0.0181)	0.244 (0.0114)	0.192 (0.00218)	0.627 (0.0357)
α_E^i	0.0121 (0.00118)	0.259 (0.0150)	0.579 (0.00582)	0.0247 (0.000658)
α_M^i	0.154 (0.0357)	0.144 (0.0330)	0.000 (0.000)	0.190 (0.0456)
α_T^i	−0.0109 (0.0344)	0.0252 (0.0251)	−0.0133 (0.0155)	−0.00386 (0.0171)
β_{KK}^i	−0.757 (0.109)			
β_{KL}^i	−1.08 (0.109)			
β_{KE}^i	0.0568 (0.00728)			
β_{KM}^i	1.78 (0.213)			
β_{KT}^i	0.00397 (0.00251)	−0.00246 (0.00118)	−0.00453 (0.000666)	0.00135 (0.00125)
β_{LL}^i	−1.55 (0.106)			−1.48 (0.120)
β_{LE}^i	0.0813 (0.00811)			−0.0207 (0.0119)
β_{LM}^i	2.55 (0.207)			1.50 (0.125)
β_{LT}^i	0.00802 (0.00279)	−0.00460 (0.00143)	0.00883 (0.000475)	0.0492 (0.00557)
β_{EE}^i	−0.00427 (0.000849)			−0.000290 (0.000325)
β_{EM}^i	−0.134 (0.0144)			0.0210 (0.0122)
β_{ET}^i	−0.000350 (0.000172)	0.00999 (0.00188)	0.00621 (0.00103)	0.000192 (0.000345)
β_{MM}^i	−4.20 (0.409)			−1.52 (0.131)
β_{MT}^i	−0.116 (0.00512)	−0.00294 (0.00414)	−0.0105 (0.00151)	−0.0508 (0.00667)
β_{TT}^i	0.00116 (0.00432)	0.00702 (0.00315)	−0.000823 (0.00233)	0.00116 (0.00207)

Table 2.1 (continued)

Parameter	Industry			
	Finance insurance and real estate	Services	Government enterprises	Miscellaneous
α_K^i	0.258 (0.00971)	0.106 (0.00552)	0.112 (0.00755)	0.595 (0.00227)
α_L^i	0.241 (0.00886)	0.558 (0.0258)	0.619 (0.0405)	0.350 (0.00210)
α_E^i	0.0164 (0.00102)	0.0214 (0.000719)	0.0332 (0.00187)	0.0000739 (0.000007)
α_M^i	0.485 (0.0172)	0.315 (0.0312)	0.236 (0.0405)	0.0556 (0.000661)
α_T^i	−0.0198 (0.0346)	−0.0307 (0.0502)	−0.0106 (0.0593)	
β_{KK}^i	−0.0304 (0.0178)			
β_{KL}^i	−0.0561 (0.0160)			
β_{KE}^i	−0.00682 (0.00186)			
β_{KM}^i	0.0934 (0.0324)			
β_{KT}^i	0.00215 (0.00201)	0.00154 (0.000691)	0.00689 (0.000947)	
β_{LL}^i	−0.104 (0.0489)		−0.511 (0.927)	
β_{LE}^i	−0.0126 (0.00598)		0.0338 (0.0425)	
β_{LM}^i	0.172 (0.0624)		0.477 (0.890)	
β_{LT}^i	0.00954 (0.0212)	0.00877 (0.00324)	0.0373 (0.0484)	
β_{EE}^i	−0.00153 (0.000783)		−0.00223 (0.00271)	−0.000154 (0.0000474)
β_{EM}^i	0.0210 (0.00764)		−0.0315 (0.0406)	0.000154 (0.0000474)
β_{ET}^i	0.000942 (0.000247)	0.000238 (0.0000901)	−0.00202 (0.00222)	
β_{MM}^i	−0.287 (0.0821)		−0.446 (0.853)	−0.000154 (0.0000474)
β_{MT}^i	−0.0126 (0.00368)	−0.0105 (0.00391)	−0.0421 (0.0464)	
β_{TT}^i	0.00118 (0.00433)	−0.00374 (0.00635)	−0.00171 (0.00787)	

section 2.2. Under these restrictions the matrices of constant share elasticities $\{\mathbf{U}^i\}$ must be negative semidefinite for all industries. To impose the concavity restrictions, we represent the matrices of constant share elasticities for all sectors in terms of their Cholesky factorizations. The necessary and sufficient conditions are that the diagonal elements $\{\delta_1^i, \delta_2^i, \delta_3^i\}$ of the matrices $\{\mathbf{D}^i\}$ that appear in the Cholesky factorizations must be nonpositive. The estimates presented in table 2.1 are subject to these restrictions for all thirty-six industrial sectors.

Our interpretation of the parameter estimates reported in table 2.1 begins with an analysis of the estimates of the parameters $\{\alpha_K^i, \alpha_L^i, \alpha_E^i, \alpha_M^i, \alpha_T^i\}$. The average value shares are nonnegative for all thirty-six sectors included in our study. The negative of the estimated average rate of technical change is negative in sixteen sectors, positive in nineteen sectors, and zero, by definition, in the miscellaneous sector. Negative signs predominate only in transportation, communications, utilities, trade, and services. Positive signs predominate in the extractive industries and durable goods manufacturing industries. Nondurable goods manufacturing industries are almost evenly divided between positive and negative signs.

The estimated share elasticities with respect to price $\{\beta_{KK}^i, \beta_{KL}^i, \beta_{KE}^i, \beta_{KM}^i, \beta_{LL}^i, \beta_{LE}^i, \beta_{LM}^i, \beta_{EE}^i, \beta_{EM}^i, \beta_{MM}^i\}$ describe the implications of patterns of substitution among capital, labor, energy, and materials inputs for the relative distribution of the value of output among these four inputs. Positive share elasticities imply that the corresponding value shares increase with an increase in price; negative share elasticities imply that the value shares decrease with an increase in price; share elasticities equal to zero imply that the value shares are independent of price. It is important to keep in mind that we have fitted these parameters subject to the restrictions implied by concavity of the price function. These restrictions require that all the share elasticities be set equal to zero for eleven of the thirty-six industries. For these eleven industries the share elasticities for all inputs with respect to the prices of energy and materials inputs are set equal to zero. For thirteen of the thirty-six industries the share elasticities with respect to the price of labor input are set equal to zero. Finally, for thirty-three of the thirty-six industries the share elasticities for all inputs with respect to the price of capital input are set equal to zero. Of the three hundred and sixty share elasticities for the thirty-six industries included in our study, two hundred and four are set equal to zero and one hundred and fifty-six are fitted without constraint.

Our interpretation of the parameter estimates given in table 2.1 continues with the estimated elasticities of the share of each input with respect to the price of the input itself $\{\beta^i_{KK}, \beta^i_{LL}, \beta^i_{EE}, \beta^i_{MM}\}$. Under the necessary and sufficient conditions for concavity of the price function for each sector, these share elasticities are nonpositive. The share of each input is nonincreasing in the price of the input itself. This condition together with the condition that the sum of all the share elasticities with respect to a given input is equal to zero implies that only two of the elasticities of the shares of each input with respect to the prices of the other three inputs $\{\beta^i_{KL}, \beta^i_{KE}, \beta^i_{KM}, \beta^i_{LE}, \beta^i_{LM}, \beta^i_{EM}\}$ can be negative. All six of these share elasticities can be nonnegative, and this condition holds for twelve of the thirty-six industries.

The share elasticity of capital with respect to the price of labor $\{\beta^i_{KL}\}$ is nonnegative for thirty-three of the thirty-six industries. By symmetry this parameter can also be interpreted as the share elasticity of labor with respect to the price of capital. The share elasticity of capital with respect to the price of energy $\{\beta^i_{KE}\}$ is nonnegative for thirty-four of the thirty-six industries. Finally, the share elasticity of capital with respect to the price of materials $\{\beta^i_{KM}\}$ is nonnegative for all thirty-six industries. These parameters can also be interpreted as the share elasticities of energy and materials with respect to the price of capital. Comparing the elasticities of the share of labor with respect to the prices of energy and materials inputs, we find that the share elasticity with respect to the price of energy is nonnegative for nineteen of the thirty-six industries, while the share elasticity with respect to the price of materials is nonnegative for all thirty-six industries. These parameters can also be interpreted as share elasticities of energy and materials with respect to the price of labor. Finally, the share elasticity of energy with respect to the price of materials input is nonnagative for thirty of the thirty-six industries. This parameter can also be interpreted as the share elasticity of materials with respect to the price of energy.

We continue the interpretation of parameter estimates given in table 2.1 with the estimated biases of technical change with respect to the price of each input $\{\beta^i_{KT}, \beta^i_{LT}, \beta^i_{ET}, \beta^i_{MT}\}$. These parameters can be interpreted as the change in the negative of the rate of technical change with respect to the price of each input or, alternatively, as the change in the share of each input with respect to time. The sum of the four biases of technical change with respect to price is equal to zero, so that we can rule out the possibility that all four biases are either all negative or all positive. Of the fourteen remaining logical possibilities, only eight actually occur among the results presented in table 2.1. Of these, only three patterns occur for more than one industry. Most important the biases of technical change are not affected by the concavity of the price function, so that all four parameters are fitted for thirty-five industries. For the miscellaneous sector the rate of technical change is zero by definition, so that all biases of technical change are set equal to zero.

We first consider the bias of technical change with respect to the price of capital input. If the estimated value of this parameter is positive, technical change is capital using. Alternatively the rate of technical change decreases with an increase in the price of capital. If the estimated value is negative, technical change is capital saving, and the rate of technical change increases with the price of capital. Technical change is capital using for twenty-five of the thirty-five industries included in our study of the biases of technical change; it is capital saving for ten of these industries. We conclude that the rate of technical change decreases with the price of capital for twenty-five industries and increases with the price of capital for ten industries.

The interpretation of the biases of technical change with respect to the prices of labor, energy, and materials inputs is analogous to the interpretation of the bias with respect to the price of capital input. If the estimated value of the bias is positive, technical change uses the corresponding input; alternatively the rate of technical change decreases with an increase in the input price. If the estimated value is negative, technical change saves the corresponding input; alternatively the rate of technical change decreases with the input price. Considering the bias of technical change with respect to the price of labor input, we find that technical change is labor using for thirty-one of the thirty-five industries included in our study and labor saving for only four of these industries. The rate of technical change decreases with the price of labor for thirty-one industries and increases with the price of labor for four industries.

Considering the bias of technical change with respect to the price of energy input, we find that technical change is energy using for twenty-nine of the thirty-five industries included in our study and energy saving for only six of these industries. The rate of technical change decreases with the price of energy for twenty-nine industries and increases for six industries. Finally, technical change is materials using for only two of the thirty-five industries included in our study and materials saving for the remaining thirty-three. We conclude that the rate of technical change increases with the price of materials for thirty-three industries and decreases with the price of materials for two industries.

A classification of industries by patterns of the biases of technical change is given in table 2.2. The pattern that occurs with greatest frequency is capital-using, labor-using, energy-using, and materials-saving technical change. This pattern occurs for nineteen of the thirty-five in-

Table 2.2
Classification of industries by biases of technical change

Pattern of biases	Industries
Capital using, labor using, energy using, material saving	Agriculture, metal mining, crude petroleum and natural gas, nonmetallic mining, textiles, apparel, lumber, furniture, printing, leather, fabricated metals, electrical machinery, motor vehicles, instruments, miscellaneous manufacturing, transportation, trade, finance, insurance and real estate, services
Capital using, labor using, energy saving, material saving	Coal mining, tobacco manufactures, communications, government enterprises
Capital using, labor saving, energy using, material saving	Petroleum refining
Capital using, labor saving, energy saving, material using	Construction
Capital saving, labor saving, energy using, material saving	Electric utilities
Capital saving, labor using, energy saving, material saving	Primary metals
Capital saving, labor using, energy using, material saving	Paper, chemicals, rubber, stone, clay and glass, machinery except electrical, transportation equipment and ordnance, gas utilities
Capital saving, labor saving, energy using, material using	Food

dustries included in our study. For this pattern the rate of technical change decreases with increases in the prices of capital, labor, and energy inputs and increases with the price of materials input. The pattern that occurs next most frequently is capital-saving, labor-using, energy-using, and materials-saving technical change. This pattern occurs for seven industries. The third most frequently occurring pattern is capital-using, labor-using, energy-saving, and materials-saving technical change. This pattern occurs for four industries. No other pattern occurs for more than one industry.

Our interpretation of the parameter estimates given in table 2.1 concludes with rates of change of the negative of the rate of technical change $\{\beta_{TT}^i\}$. If the estimated value of this parameter is positive, the rate of technical change is decreasing; if the value is negative, the rate is increasing. For twenty-four of the thirty-five industries included in our study of the rate of change of the rate of technical change the estimated value is positive; for eleven industries, the value is negative; for the remaining industry, this parameter is set equal to zero, since the rate of technical change is zero by definition. We conclude that the rate of technical change is decreasing with time for twenty-four industries and increasing with time for eleven industries.

2.4 Conclusion

Our empirical results for sectoral patterns of production and technical change are very striking and suggest a considerable degree of similarity across industries. However, it is important to emphasize that these results have been obtained under strong simplifying assumptions. First, for all industries we have employed conditions for producer equilibrium under perfect competition; we have assumed constant returns to scale at the industry level; finally, we have employed a description of technology that leads to myopic decision rules. These assumptions must be justified primarily by their usefulness in implementing production models that are uniform for all thirty-six industrial sectors of the U.S. economy.

The most important simplification of the theory of production and technical change employed in the specification of our econometric models is the imposition of concavity of the sectoral price functions. By imposing concavity on the sectoral price functions, we have reduced the number of share elasticities to be fitted from three hundred sixty, or ten for each of our thirty-six industrial sectors, to one hundred fifty-six, or less than five per sector on average. All share elasticities are constrained to be zero for eleven of the thirty-six industries. The concavity constraints contribute to the precision of our estimates but require that the share of each input be nonincreasing in the price of the input itself.

Although it might be worthwhile to weaken each of the assumptions we have enumerated here, a more promising direction for further research appears to lie within the framework provided by these assumptions. First, we can provide a more detailed model for allocation among productive inputs. We have disaggregated energy and materials into thirty-six groups —five types of energy and thirty-one types of materials—by constructing a hierarchy of models for allocation within the energy and materials aggregates. For this purpose we have assumed that each aggregate is homogeneously separable within the sectoral production function. We assume, for example, that the share of energy in the value of sectoral output depends on changes in technology, while the share of, say, electricity in the value of energy input does not.

The second research objective suggested by our results is to incorporate the production models for all thirty-six industrial sectors into a general equilibrium model of production in the U.S. economy. An econometric general equilibrium model of the U.S. economy has been constructed for nine industrial sectors by Hudson and Jorgenson. This model is currently being disaggregated to the level of the thirty-six industrial sectors included in our study. A novel feature of the thirty-six sector general equilibrium model will be the endogenous treatment of the rate of technical change for thirty-five of the thirty-six industries we have analyzed. A general equilibrium model will make it possible to analyze the implications of sectoral patterns of substitution and technical change for substitution and technical change for the U.S. economy as a whole.

Notes

We are indebted to Peter Derksen for development of the software for transformation of the data to eliminate autocorrelation in the disturbances, as described in section 2.2. We are grateful to Thomas Stoker for development and Christopher Holsing for implementation of the software used in obtaining the estimates presented in section 2.3. All of the estimation was carried out by Holsing. We are indebted to Denise Gaudet and Nelda Hoxie for very able assistance in preparation of the data for estimation. Finally, we are grateful to Ernst Berndt, Frank Gollop, William Hogan, Edward Hudson, Lawrence Lau, and James Sweeney for valuable advice. Financial support for this research was provided by the Federal Emergency Management Agency and the U.S. Department of Energy.

1. A review of the literature on induced technical change is given by Binswanger (1978c). Binswanger distinguishes between models, like ours and those of Ben-Zion and Ruttan, Lucas (1967b) and Schmookler with an endogenous rate of technical change and models, like those of Hicks (1963), Kennedy, Samuelson (1965), von Weizsäcker, and others, with an endogenous bias of technical change. Additional references are given by Binswanger (1978c).

2. For further discussion of myopic decision rules, see Jorgenson (1973).

3. The price function was introduced by Samuelson (1953).

4. The translog price function was introduced by Christensen, Jorgenson, and Lau (1971, 1973). The translog price function was first applied at the sectoral level by Berndt and Jorgenson and Berndt and Wood (1975a). References to sectoral production studies incorporating energy and materials inputs are given by Berndt and Wood (1979).

5. The share elasticity with respect to price was introduced by Christensen, Jorgenson, and Lau (1971, 1973) as a fixed parameter of the translog price function. An analogous concept was employed by Samuelson (1973). The terminology is due to Jorgenson and Lau (1980).

6. The terminology "constant share elasticity price function" is due to Jorgenson and Lau (1981), who have shown that constancy of share elasticities with respect to price, biases of technical change with respect to price, and the rate of change of the negative of the rate of technical change are necessary and sufficient for representation of the price function in translog form.

7. The bias of technical change was introduced by Hicks (1963). An alternative definition of the bias of technical change is analyzed by Burmeister and Dobell. Binswanger (1974a) has introduced a translog cost function with fixed biases of technical change. Alternative definitions of biases of technical change are compared by Binswanger (1978b).

8. This definition of the bias of technical change with respect to price is due to Jorgenson and Lau (1981).

9. The rate of change of the negative of the rate of technical change was introduced by Jorgenson and Lau (1981).

10. The following discussion of share elasticities with respect to price and concavity follows that of Jorgenson and Lau (1981). Representation of conditions for concavity in terms of the Cholesky factorization is due to Lau (1978b). The discussion of concavity for the translog price function is based on that of Jorgenson and Lau (1981).

11. The price indexes were introduced by Fisher and have been discussed by Törnqvist, Theil (1965), and Kloek. These indexes were first derived from the translog price function by Diewert (1976). The corresponding index of technical change was introduced by Christensen and Jorgenson (1970). The translog index of technical change was first derived from the translog price function by Diewert (1980) and by Jorgenson and Lau (1980). Earlier Diewert (1976) had interpreted the ratio of translog indexes of the prices of input and output as an index of productivity under the assumption of Hicks neutrality.

12. The formulation of an econometric model of production and technical change is based on that of Jorgenson and Lau (1981).

13. The Cholesky factorization is used to obtain an equation with uncorrelated random disturbances by Jorgenson and Lau (1981).

14. Data on energy and materials are based on annual interindustry transactions tables for the United States, from 1958 to 1974, compiled by Jack Faucett Associates (1977) for the Federal Preparedness Agency. Data on labor and capital are based on estimates by Fraumeni and Jorgenson (1980).

3

Alternative Models of Substitution and Technical Change in Natural Resource Intensive Industries

John R. Moroney and John M. Trapani

We describe changes in the costs and use of capital, labor, and nonfuel mineral resources in six U.S. manufacturing industries during the period 1954 to 1974 and propose two models of substitution and technological change for analyzing the observed changes in input use. The models are based on identical assumptions save one: the more general formulation allows for nonneutral, price-induced technological progress, while the other imposes Hicks-neutral technical progress a priori.

Most attempts to estimate substitution elasticities using translog dual cost functions have assumed constant returns to scale and either Hicks-neutral technical change (Berndt and Wood 1975a) or factor-augmenting technical change (Binswanger 1974b, Berndt and Wood 1975b). A recent study by Berndt and Khaled relaxed the assumptions of homothetic production technology and its more restrictive subsets—homogeneity and linear homogeneity, neutral technological change, and the translog functional form. Nonetheless, the pure effects of alternative specifications of technical change were not analyzed. If the estimated substitution elasticities vary considerably according to these specifications, estimates based on the Hicks-neutral model may be misleading indicators of technical substitutability.

The role of technical progress as a means to extend exhaustible resource supplies has been emphasized by Barnett and Morse, Nordhaus and Tobin, Stiglitz, and others. The idea is straightforward: gains in the efficiency of services obtained from a declining stock of resources will prolong the effective life of the remaining stock. Binswanger (1974b), Berndt and Wood (1975b), and Wills have estimated models of input-augmenting technical change. Employing a four-input (capital, labor, energy, material), constant-returns-to-scale translog cost model, Berndt and Wood could not reject the hypothesis of Hicks-neutral (equal rates of factor augmenting) technical change in the aggregate U.S. manufacturing sector. Wills applied a similar model to the U.S. primary metals sector and found strong evidence of Hicks-biased technical change. Likewise Binswanger (1974b) found evidence of biased technological progress in his five-input translog cost study of American agriculture. Neither Berndt-Wood nor Wills find evidence of energy-saving innovations, and Binswanger finds no support for land-saving innovations; all three studies conclude that technical change has been relatively labor saving.[1]

3.1 Trends in Input Costs and Input Use

For empirical purposes we examine industries that use primarily one exhaustible resource to produce a reasonably homogeneous output or output mix. The natural resource inputs and the four-digit manufacturing industries in which they are processed are

Resource input	Resource-using industry (SIC code)
Crude iron ore and scrap	Blast furnaces and basic steel (3312)
Refined copper and copper scrap	Copper rolling and drawing (3351)
Bauxite	Primary aluminum (3334)
Lead	Storage batteries (3691)
Gypsum (uncalcined)	Hydraulic cement (3241)
Gypsum (calcined)	Gypsum products (3275)

We construct annual series on the current-dollar value of net output attributable to the use of capital, labor, and natural resource inputs by adding annual purchases of the natural resource input (plus scrap in industries 3312 and 3351) to value added. We then construct for each of these industries a yearly Törnqvist aggregate input price index by which the current-dollar value of net output is deflated. Details are discussed in appendix 3.1.

The estimated cost of capital is calculated here as a residual: current-dollar value added minus current-dollar labor costs yields gross quasi rent, which includes capital consumption allowances and indirect business taxes. These taxes could not be netted out because they are not recorded by four-digit industry.

The price of capital is computed by dividing gross quasi rent by the estimated constant-dollar capital stock. Hence by definition this price of capital is the average rate of return (inclusive of indirect business taxes) on the constant-dollar capital stock. If these taxes remain a roughly constant fraction of gross quasi rent, the price of capital calculated in this way overstates the true cost of capital but does not distort any trend in the true series.[2] Nonetheless, this residual price of capital exhibits random year-to-year fluctuations for the following reason: the random and cyclical variability in value added exceeds that in labor costs, so there is a relatively large random component in gross quasi rents. Hence our residual price of capital is likely to show greater cyclical variance than the rental price of capital suggested by Jorgenson and Griliches. For further discussion see Moroney (pp. 79 ff.). We analyze trends in the unadjusted residual price of capital, but, for purposes of estimating parameters, we use an instrumental variable for the price of capital.

Perhaps the best descriptive measure of changes in input prices is the estimated trend coefficient from the regression:

$$\ln P_{i(t)} = a + bt + e_{i(t)},$$

for $i = K, L, N, S$, where $\hat{b}$ is an estimate of the proportional rate of change of P_i. In this regression P_K is the cost of constant-dollar capital, P_L, the cost of labor per manhour, P_N, the price of natural resources, and P_S, the price of scrap. These prices are not deflated by industry output prices. We recognize that the estimated trend coefficients are only a summary and incomplete description of the actual movements in factor costs. Indeed this regression, estimated by ordinary least squares, consistently produces a low Durbin-Watson statistic, a striking indication that the assumption of smooth proportional change misspecifies the actual pattern of input prices. However, we are interested here only in descriptive trends, not in a structural explanation.

The estimated coefficients and their standard errors appear in table 3.1. The sample period is 1954 to 1974 for all industries except copper rolling and drawing, for which it is 1958 to 1974. The cost of capital was trendless in all industries except storage batteries, where it displayed a significant positive trend. Hourly labor costs are quite a different story: all industries experienced average annual increases in the range of 4.5 to 6 percent. The price of natural resource inputs increased in a statistically significant sense in all industries except storage batteries and aluminum. The broad patterns of factor price change are clear: labor cost increased relative to the cost of capital in every industry except storage batteries; similarly labor became increasingly expensive relative to natural resources in all industries except copper rolling and drawing.

Such changes in factor costs should induce responses in relative input use. The trends in manhours of labor, real capital stocks, and natural resources are shown in table 3.2. All industries expanded their stocks of real capital assets, typically at average annual rates between 3 and 5 percent. Manhours were remarkably stable in three industries, expanding at roughly 2 percent per year in storage batteries and aluminum and

Table 3.1
Annual percentage changes in the costs of capital, labor, and natural resource inputs in manufacturing industries

Industry	ΔP_K	ΔP_L	ΔP_N	ΔP_S
Blast furnaces and steel (3312)	-0.00367 (0.01217)	0.05137 (0.00429)	0.01722 (0.00460)	0.01196 (0.01811)
Copper rolling and drawing (3351)	0.02138 (0.01857)	0.04599 (0.00368)	0.05643 (0.00744)	0.05904 (0.01050)
Aluminum (3334)	0.01237 (0.00991)	0.05385 (0.00440)	0.01068 (0.00549)	
Storage batteries (3691)	0.05363 (0.00778)	0.04808 (0.00280)	0.01231 (0.00931)	
Hydraulic cement (3241)	-0.00268 (0.00802)	0.06115 (0.00363)	0.01498 (0.00229)	
Gypsum products (3275)	-0.01283 (0.00890)	0.05038 (0.00349)	0.02649 (0.00366)	

Note: Estimated standard errors are listed in parentheses beneath the estimated regression coefficients. All regressions were characterized by positively autocorrelated residuals, according to a Durbin-Watson test. The first-order autocorrelation coefficient, ρ, was estimated, and the original estimated standard errors were adjusted upward (multiplied) by the factor $(1 + 2\hat{\rho})^{\frac{1}{2}}$. For the rationale of this adjustment see Wold, p. 44.

Table 3.2
Annual percentage changes in employment of capital, labor, and natural resource inputs in manufacturing industries

Industry	ΔK	ΔL	ΔN	ΔS
Blast furnaces and steel (3312)	0.03501 (0.00250)	-0.00588 (0.00423)	0.02425 (0.00554)	0.02180 (0.00603)
Copper rolling and drawing (3351)	0.03556 (0.00230)	-0.00333 (0.00215)	0.03575 (0.00626)	0.05143 (0.00575)
Aluminum (3334)	0.04666 (0.00652)	0.01873 (0.00654)	0.06220 (0.00257)	
Storage batteries (3691)	0.03039 (0.00324)	0.02329 (0.00212)	0.04397 (0.00576)	
Hydraulic cement (3241)	0.03245 (0.00797)	-0.02029 (0.00184)	0.03165 (0.00163)	
Gypsum products (3275)	0.02570 (0.00620)	-0.00569 (0.00230)	0.01442 (0.00495)	

Note: Estimated standard errors are listed in parentheses beneath the estimated regression coefficients. All regressions were characterized by positively autocorrelated residuals, according to a Durbin-Watson test. The first-order autocorrelation coefficient, ρ, was estimated, and the original estimated standard errors were adjusted upward (multiplied) by the factor $(1 + 2\hat{\rho})^{\frac{1}{2}}$. For the rationale of this adjustment see Wold, p. 44.

decreasing on the average by 2 percent annually in hydraulic cement. Every industry substantially increased its use of natural resource inputs. Comparison of the trend coefficients shows that each industry was characterized by the joint substitution of capital and natural resources against labor, a pattern entirely compatible with the evolution of relative factor costs. The observed evolution in factor proportions could be attributable to either pure factor substitution with Hicks-neutral technological change or a combination of factor substitution and Hicks-biased technological change.

3.2 Transcendental Logarithmic Cost Models

The models that follow are based on three assumptions:

1. Input prices are predetermined variables for entrepreneurs.
2. Industry production functions exhibit constant returns to scale.
3. Entrepreneurs minimize cost, subject to 1 and 2.

A reasonably general, constant-returns-to-scale translog cost function is given by

$$\ln C(P_i, q, t) = \alpha_0 + \ln q + \sum_i \alpha_i \ln P_i$$

$$+ \frac{1}{2} \sum_i \sum_j \gamma_{ij} \ln P_i \ln P_j + \beta t + \sum_i \beta_i t \ln P_i, \tag{3.1}$$

where α_0, α_i, γ_{ij}, β, and β_i are technological parameters, C is total cost, q is physical output, t is an index of technology, and P_i and P_j are input prices. Subscripts i and j index the inputs capital K, labor, L, natural resources N, and, in two industries, scrap, S. If technological progress is assumed to be neutral and to occur at a constant proportional rate, (3.1) takes the simpler form

$$\ln C(P_i, q, t) = \alpha_0^* + \ln q + \sum \alpha_i^* \ln P_i$$

$$+ \frac{1}{2} \sum_i \sum_j \gamma_{ij}^* \ln P_i \ln P_j + \beta^* t. \tag{3.2}$$

Assumption 3 requires that (3.1) and (3.2) be linearly homogeneous in factor prices. The necessary and sufficient restrictions on the parameters of (3.1) and (3.2) are, respectively,

$$\sum \alpha_i = 1,$$

$$\sum \beta_i = 0,$$

$$\gamma_{ij} = \gamma_{ji}, \quad \text{for } i \neq j,$$

$$\sum_i \gamma_{ij} = \sum_j \gamma_{ji} = \sum_i \sum_j \gamma_{ij} = 0, \tag{3.3}$$

$$\sum \alpha_i^* = 1,$$

$$\gamma_{ij}^* = \gamma_{ji}^*, \quad \text{for } i \neq j,$$

$$\sum_i \gamma_{ij}^* = \sum_j \gamma_{ji}^* = \sum_i \sum_j \gamma_{ij}^* = 0. \tag{3.4}$$

The rate of technological progress is conceptually the rate of reduction in the unit cost function when factor prices are constant. If (3.1) is expressed as a unit cost function, the rate of technological progress is

$$-\frac{\partial \ln (C/q)}{\partial t} = -(\beta + \sum_i \beta_i \ln P_i). \tag{3.5}$$

The term $-\beta$ is the autonomous part of the overall rate, and the other terms are the price-induced components. Note that the overall rate of technical change is variable and that it varies directly with P_i if $\beta_i < 0$.

From equation (3.2) the proportional rate of Hicks-neutral technological progress is

$$-\frac{\partial \ln (C/q)}{\partial t} = -\beta^*. \tag{3.6}$$

In principle the rates of technical progress can be estimated from equations (3.5) and (3.6). In practice, however, our method of constructing an index of physical output prevents the reliable estimation of these rates. The basic problem is this: there is not any identifiable (countable) physical output, such as tons of homogeneous steel or number of physically homogeneous storage batteries, ascribable strictly to the limited subset of inputs in our analysis. Accordingly we must estimate in each industry an index of physical output attributable to our particular input subsets. To do so, using the maintained hypothesis of translog cost technology, as we do, we should properly deflate current-dollar expenditures by an appropriate Törnqvist index of input prices (cf., Diewert 1976).

The theoretically correct index of output would be $q_{T(t)} = C_{(t)}/P_{T(t)}$, where $q_{T(t)}$ is the output index in year t, $C_{(t)}$ is current-dollar expenditure on the relevant input subset, and $P_{T(t)}$ is the Törnqvist input price index based on the prevailing technology T in period t. In the absence of any exogenous estimate of the true technology T, we must resort to a Törnqvist index of current-dollar input prices, $P_{(t)}$, as the deflator for $C_{(t)}$. This procedure yields an estimated index of output, $q_{(t)}^* = C_{(t)}/P_{(t)}$, that generally differs from the true index. Specifically $q^*_{(t)} \gtreqless q_{T(t)}$ as $P_{(t)} \lesseqgtr P_{T(t)}$. The substantive point is that the use of $q^*_{(t)}$ instead of $q_{T(t)}$ causes the estimate of β in (3.5) or β^* in (3.6) to be biased toward zero. Thus the overall rates of technological change cannot reliably be estimated. But statistical estimation based on the use of $q^*_{(t)}$, nonetheless, yields consistent estimates of the coefficients of biased technical change (β_i in 3.2) and of the slope coefficients α^*_i and γ^*_{ij} ($i, j = K, L, N, S$).[3]

The assumption of cost minimization yields an explicit set of factor demand equations. In particular the Samuelson-Shephard lemma ensures that at a point of cost minimization the demand for the ith factor is

$$\hat{X}_i = \frac{\partial C(\cdot)}{\partial P_i}, \tag{3.7}$$

for $i = K, L, N, S$. Thus the equilibrium cost share of the ith factor is

$$\hat{M}_i = \frac{P_i \hat{X}_i}{\sum P_i \hat{X}_i} = \frac{\partial \ln C(\cdot)}{\partial \ln P_i}. \tag{3.8}$$

We can differentiate (3.1) with respect to $\ln P_i$ to obtain the minimum-cost input share equations

$$\hat{M}_i = \alpha_i + \sum_i \gamma_{ij} \ln P_i + \beta_i t, \tag{3.9}$$

for $i, j = K, L, N, S$. Differentiation of (3.2) yields the alternative minimum-cost input share equations

$$\hat{M}^*_i = \alpha^*_i + \sum_i \gamma^*_{ij} \ln P_i, \tag{3.10}$$

for $i, j = K, L, N, S$.

Notice that relative input cost shares in (3.9) respond to changes in technology: technological change is factor using or factor saving as $\beta_i \lesseqgtr 0$.[4] Relative shares in (3.10) depend only on factor prices.

For the purpose of estimation disturbance terms are added to the cost equations (3.1) and (3.2) and to the factor demand equations (3.9) and (3.10). Equations (3.1) and (3.9) and equations (3.2) and (3.10) are then estimated as separate simultaneous systems. The disturbances associated with these equations are attributable chiefly to managerial errors. Since the disturbances in each system are contemporaneously correlated across equations, we take this into account by using the iterative Zellner efficient estimation method. Parameter estimates obtained by this method have been shown to be equivalent to maximum likelihood estimates (Kmenta and Gilbert).

The central purpose of estimating the parameters of the cost functions (3.1) and (3.2) is to estimate the direction of factor-saving bias, and technical input substitutability. The most widely used measure of input substitutability is the Allen partial elasticity of substitution. Uzawa (1962) has shown that this elasticity may be obtained from the derivatives of a total cost function:

$$\sigma_{ij} = \frac{CC_{ij}}{C_i C_j}, \tag{3.11}$$

where $C_i = (\partial C / \partial P_i)$ with q and technology constant and $C_{ij} = (\partial^2 C / \partial P_i \partial P_j)$ with q and technology constant. Substituting these derivatives from equations (3.1) or (3.2) into (3.11), we obtain the cross elasticities of substitution

$$\sigma_{ij} = \left(\frac{\gamma_{ij}}{M_i M_j}\right) + 1, \tag{3.12}$$

for $i \neq j$, and own elasticities of substitution

$$\sigma_{ii} = \frac{\gamma_{ii} + M_i^2 - M_i}{M_i^2}. \tag{3.13}$$

The cross elasticities indicate which inputs are substitutes or complements of each other. This is intuitively more clear if we substitute the optimal factor demands from (3.7) into (3.11). Thus $\sigma_{ij} = C(\partial \hat{X}_i / \partial P_j) / \hat{X}_i \hat{X}_j$. A positive (negative) value of $\partial \hat{X}_i / \partial P_j$ is an intuitively sensible definition of a substitute (complement). If $\sigma_{ij} = 0$, inputs i and j are independent.

For other purposes it is important to know the change in factor use in response to a change in its own price, when output and other factor prices are constant. This response is measured by the own price elasticity of demand.

$$e_{ii} = \frac{\partial \ln X_i}{\partial \ln P_i}, \tag{3.14}$$

with q, P_j, and technology constant. This elasticity may be estimated immediately from the translog cost parameters and relative input shares, since $e_{ii} = M_i \sigma_{ii}$. Stable (cost-minimizing) input demand equations require that each σ_{ii} be nonpositive. Embedded in the value of the own elasticity of demand is the complete set of complementarity and substitution relationships between the ith input and all others. For example, Allen (p. 504) has shown that

$$-e_{ii} = \sum_j M_j \sigma_{ij} \geq 0, \qquad (3.15)$$

for $i \neq j$ and $i, j = 1, \ldots, n$. It follows that in a three-input model there can be at most one pair of complementary inputs and that in a four-input model there can be at most three pairs of complements.

From a policy viewpoint the own price elasticity of demand is of vital importance. It shows the proportionate reduction in factor use in response to a given proportionate increase in that factor's price, when output is constant. The greater the (weighted) substitutability of other factors for the input in question, the greater the opportunity for resource conservation.

There are two other potentially important avenues for resource conservation. First, the neutral component of technological progress, β in equation (3.5) and β^* in equation (3.6), shows the autonomous rate of reduction in unit input requirements in response to improved technology. Second, the price-induced components, β_i in equation (3.5), show the reduction in unit input requirements of the specific factors in response to factor-saving technological change. This is clear if we write an input cost share equation (3.9) as

$$M_i = \frac{P_i X_i}{pq} = \alpha_i + \sum_i \gamma_{ij} \ln P_i + \beta_i t,$$

where p is product price. If for the moment we hold (P_i/p) constant, then $\partial M_i/\partial t = (P_i/p)\partial(X_i/q)/\partial t = \beta_i$.

The three potential sources of input conservation may be developed in an alternative way. To begin, write the cost-minimizing, constant-output input demand as

$$X_i = X_i(P_L, P_K, P_N, P_S, t). \qquad (3.16)$$

By differentiating (3.16) totally with respect to time and using the relations $e_{ij} = \partial \ln X_i/\partial \ln P_j$, for i and $j = K, L, N$, and S, we obtain

$$\frac{\dot{X}_i}{X_i} = e_{iL}\left(\frac{\dot{P}_L}{P_L}\right) + e_{iK}\left(\frac{\dot{P}_K}{P_K}\right) + e_{iN}\left(\frac{\dot{P}_N}{P_N}\right) + e_{iS}\left(\frac{\dot{P}_S}{P_S}\right) + \frac{\partial \ln X_i}{\partial t}, \qquad (3.17)$$

for $i = K, L, N, S$, where $\dot{X}_i/X_i = (dX_i/dt)/X_i$ and a similar interpretation applies to factor price changes. Now substitute $M_j \sigma_{ij}$ for e_{ij} to obtain

$$\frac{\dot{X}_i}{X_i} = M_L \sigma_{iL}\left(\frac{\dot{P}_L}{P_L}\right) + M_K \sigma_{iK}\left(\frac{\dot{P}_K}{P_K}\right) + M_N \sigma_{iN}\left(\frac{\dot{P}_N}{P_N}\right) + M_S \sigma_{iS}\left(\frac{\dot{P}_S}{P_S}\right)$$
$$+ \frac{\partial \ln X_i}{\partial t}. \qquad (3.18)$$

The proportional change in factor demand is thus expressed in terms of relative shares, substitution elasticities, relative variation in factor prices, and technological change. Equation (3.18) could be used to simulate the relative change in input usage in response to alternative paths of factor prices, given econometric estimates of σ_{ij} and the technical change parameters embedded in $\partial \ln X_i / \partial t$. One special case of (3.18) is of interest: if $\dot{P}_i / P_i = \dot{P}_j / P_j$ for all i and j, there is no conventional factor substitution, and (3.18) reduces to

$$\frac{\dot{X}_i}{X_i} = \frac{\partial \ln X_i}{\partial t}. \tag{3.19}$$

The components of technological change in (3.18) of course depend on whether the cost function has the form (3.1) or (3.2): If (3.1), $\partial \ln X_i / \partial t = \beta^*$, and, if (3.2), $\partial \ln X_i / \partial t = (\beta_i / M_i) + (\beta + \sum_j \beta_j \ln P_j)$.

3.3 Parameter Estimates

Equations (3.1) and (3.2) are expressed as unit cost functions, with unit cost deflated by P_N. All factor price terms on the right-hand side of these equations are also deflated by P_N. The unit cost function associated with (3.1) is estimated simultaneously with the input demand equations (3.9), and that associated with (3.2) is estimated simultaneously with equations (3.10).

Since the calculated cost of capital contains some error attributable to cyclical disturbances, an instrumental variable for P_K is constructed. The calculated cost of capital is first regressed on a time trend and current-year capacity utilization. The least squares estimate of P_K thus obtained is then used in the regression systems (3.1) and (3.9) and (3.2) and (3.10). These systems are estimated by the iterative Zellner efficient method, with restrictions (3.3) and (3.4) imposed. The sample period is 1954 to 1974, except in copper rolling and drawing for which the sample period is 1958 to 1974.

The partial elasticities of substitution, evaluated at sample means, appear in table 3.3. Asymptotic standard errors are listed in parentheses below the estimated substitution elasticities.[5]

Consider first the stability conditions. The primary criterion we adopt is that the own elasticities of substitution, evaluated at sample means, must be nonpositive. This criterion is satisfied statistically in eight of the twelve sets of estimated elasticities. It is violated in copper rolling and drawing under the specification of neutral technological change ($\hat{\sigma}_{SS}$ is positive and statistically significant), storage batteries under the specification of

Table 3.3
Partial elasticities of substitution between capital, labor, natural resources, and scrap in U.S. four-digit manufacturing industries

	Copper rolling and drawing		Blast furnaces and basic steel	
	Nonneutral	Neutral	Nonneutral	Neutral
σ_{KL}	−2.08	2.46	0.50	0.95
	(0.36)	(1.48)	(0.05)	(0.04)
σ_{KN}	1.06	0.18	1.16	1.08
	(0.10)	(0.30)	(0.17)	(0.19)
σ_{KS}	−1.52	−3.51	−0.33	−0.90
	(0.40)	(0.59)	(0.08)	(0.08)
σ_{LN}	0.42	0.43	1.61	1.14
	(0.15)	(0.35)	(0.41)	(0.13)
σ_{LS}	0.97	−2.55	−0.08	0.20
	(0.38)	(1.13)	(0.06)	(0.10)
σ_{NS}	−0.34	0.54	−0.14	0.39
	(0.10)	(0.26)	(0.22)	(0.21)
σ_{KK}	−0.92	0.09	−1.01	−1.24
	(0.33)	(0.85)	(0.09)	(0.08)
σ_{LL}	−0.85	−1.39	−0.85	−1.15
	(0.63)	(3.63)	(0.12)	(0.05)
σ_{SS}	0.03	3.53	0.80	0.72
	(0.50)	(0.78)	(0.14)	(0.29)
σ_{NN}	−0.25	−0.27	−7.28	−6.41
	(0.03)	(0.16)	(1.38)	(1.25)
	Primary aluminum		Storage batteries	
	Nonneutral	Neutral	Nonneutral	Neutral
σ_{KL}	0.45	−0.13	1.18	0.60
	(0.17)	(0.08)	(0.22)	(0.24)
σ_{KN}	0.31	0.47	−0.70	0.02
	(0.11)	(0.16)	(0.14)	(0.09)
σ_{LN}	−0.36	1.33	0.03	0.63
	(0.27)	(0.17)	(0.14)	(0.11)
σ_{KK}	−0.34	−0.12	−0.59	−0.74
	(0.11)	(0.07)	(0.27)	(0.24)
	Primary aluminum		Storage batteries	
	Nonneutral	Neutral	Nonneutral	Neutral
σ_{LL}	−0.65	−0.79	−1.02	−1.13
	(0.33)	(0.16)	(0.24)	(0.26)
σ_{NN}	−0.36	−2.90	0.55	−0.65
	(0.38)	(0.46)	(0.15)	(0.11)

Table 3.3 (continued)

	Hydraulic cement		Gypsum products	
	Nonneutral	Neutral	Nonneutral	Neutral
σ_{KL}	0.18	0.65	0.47	0.83
	(0.13)	(0.02)	(0.21)	(0.07)
σ_{KN}	0.24	−0.38	1.40	0.08
	(0.32)	(0.23)	(0.35)	(0.12)
σ_{LN}	−1.02	1.08	−0.67	−0.18
	(0.62)	(0.18)	(0.15)	(0.14)
σ_{KK}	−0.10	−0.33	−1.35	−0.49
	(0.07)	(0.01)	(0.28)	(0.12)
σ_{LL}	−0.30	−1.30	0.11	−1.35
	(0.24)	(0.05)	(0.41)	(0.13)
σ_{NN}	11.94	−7.40	−1.34	0.01
	(10.39)	(12.23)	(0.40)	(0.17)

Note: K = capital, L = labor, N = natural resources, and S = scrap.

nonneutral technological change ($\hat{\sigma}_{NN}$ is positive and significant), and blast furnaces and basic steel under both the neutral and nonneutral specifications ($\hat{\sigma}_{SS}$ is positive and significant). The positive estimates of the own elasticity for scrap in basic steel is a puzzling result, which may suggest an absence of cost-minimizing behavior in that industry. During the past two decades this industry has been affected by environmental legislation more than most others. It has also experienced more dramatic changes in the mix of underlying production methods. These responses to legislative constraints may well have dominated any tendency to minimize pure and simple production costs. Kopp and Smith (1981) have in fact demonstrated that legislated emissions constraints in the iron and steel industry may affect perceived patterns of factor substitution.

Our secondary criterion for stability is the sufficiency conditions themselves: for an n-input model the determinants of the matrix of substitution elasticities should alternate in sign, the first-order determinant being negative. Accordingly we compute these determinants at each input sample point in all industries. Under the Hicks-neutral specification these conditions are satisfied at either all or all but two or three sample points in those industries including only three inputs. The conditions are obviously not satisfied in copper rolling and drawing or basic steel. By contrast, the full sufficiency conditions are violated at almost all sample points in industries using the more general model with Hicks neutrality not imposed. We are unable to explain this troublesome result, which seems to merit further study.[6]

Note that ten of twelve estimated σ_{KL} are positive and eight of the positive estimates are significant at the 95 percent significance level. In every industry except primary aluminum and storage batteries the estimated σ_{KL} obtained from the model based on neutral technical change exceeds the estimate obtained from the more general model. This suggests that some of the observed capital deepening vis-à-vis labor has been attributable to capital-using and/or labor-saving technological change. As we shall see, all industries except primary aluminum and gypsum products display a relatively labor-saving bias. The overall impression is that capital and labor are substitutes, a finding that accords closely with the earlier work of Moroney and Toevs (1977, 1979).

Capital and nonrenewable natural resource inputs show mixed patterns of substitutability. Six of the estimated σ_{KN} are positive and highly significant. Capital and iron ore are plainly substitutes in the production of basic steel products, and capital and bauxite are substitutes in aluminum production. In the other four industries, however, the estimates of σ_{KN} are sensitive to the underlying model specified. If we allow for nonneutral technical change, for example, capital and refined copper appear to be reasonably good substitutes in copper rolling and drawing ($\hat{\sigma}_{KN} = 1.06$) as do capital and gypsum in the production of gypsum products ($\hat{\sigma}_{KN} = 1.40$). If we impose neutral technological change, however, the estimated elasticities are much lower ($\hat{\sigma}_{KN} = 0.18$ in copper rolling and drawing and $\hat{\sigma}_{KN} = 0.08$ in gypsum products) and not statistically different from zero.

Labor and natural resources also display a mixed pattern. Six of the estimated σ_{LN} are positive and significant, but five are not statistically different from zero. It is striking that in four industries—primary aluminum, storage batteries, hydraulic cement, and gypsum products—the σ_{LN} estimate obtained under the restriction of neutral technical change is substantially larger than that obtained from the more general model. Thus some of the apparently price-induced substitution of natural resources for labor may in fact be attributable to natural resource-using and/or labor-saving technological change. Each of these industries experienced significant natural resource-using and labor-saving technological change.

Capital and scrap appear to be complementary both in the copper rolling and drawing and in the basic steel industries, regardless of model specification. By contrast, the technical input relation between scrap and natural resources is quite sensitive to model specification. In the copper rolling and drawing industry $\hat{\sigma}_{NS}$ is positive and significant if neutral technical change is imposed, but negative and significant when estimated from the more general model. The estimates of σ_{NS} also switch signs in the basic steel industry.

To test the restrictiveness of the Hicks-neutral specification, we calculate the difference between the weighted sum of squared residuals in this system and the nonneutral system. We then divide this number by the weighted error sum of squares in the nonneutral system. Dividing numerator and denominator by their appropriate degrees of freedom, we obtain a test statistic asymptotically distributed as F. In all industries except gypsum products the calculated F is significant at the 1 percent level of significance; in the gypsum products industry the calculated F is significant at the 5 percent significance level.

Thus there is a basic conflict between the criteria for choice of models. On purely statistical grounds these F-tests indicate that the more general model, unrestricted by Hicks neutrality, is preferable. On economic grounds, however, the Hicks-neutral specification is superior. Recall that the latter model yields estimates that satisfy the sufficient conditions for stability in four of the six industries; but the model with unrestricted technical change produces estimates that consistently violate these sufficiency conditions.

Given this conflict, and if forced to choose between criteria, we lean toward the economic grounds, but hesitantly for several reasons. First, the numerical solutions for the second- and third-order determinants do not themselves have confidence bands; indeed their finite sample distributions are not known, and we have not attempted to estimate their asymptotic variances. Second, even if their (asymptotic) statistical significance could be established, the weight to be accorded the higher-order stability conditions would remain unclear. After all, the data are generated by globally stable economic processes, so violation of these conditions at a sample point may not be much to worry about. If, however, these conditions are not satisfied over a broad range of the sample, there are probably basic problems in model specification and/or measurement errors. Two things are clear: the economic and statistical criteria for model selection are discordant, and the grounds for choice are infirm.

The estimated biases in technical change appear in table 3.4. The annual rates of bias are small but are estimated with high precision: eighteen of the twenty estimates are approximately three or more times their asymptotic standard errors. All six industries display labor-saving technological change (statistically significant in five). Five industries display natural resource-using technological change. Both the copper rolling and drawing and the blast furnace and basic steel industries adopted more scrap-intensive technologies. Both the blast furnace and basic steel and the hydraulic cement industries adopted capital-using innovations. The dominant patterns of labor-saving and natural resource-using innovations

Table 3.4
Estimates of biased technological change in U.S. four-digit manufacturing industries

Industry	Bias			
	β_L	β_K	β_N	β_S
Copper rolling and drawing	−0.00680 (0.00029)	−0.00077 (0.00021)	0.00529 (0.00030)	0.00228 (0.00029)
Blast furnace and basic steel	−0.00273 (0.00058)	0.00174 (0.00030)	−0.00075 (0.00076)	0.00174 (0.00026)
Primary aluminum	−0.00098 (0.00063)	−0.00467 (0.00074)	0.00565 (0.00068)	
Storage batteries	−0.00346 (0.00074)	−0.00202 (0.00064)	0.00548 (0.00057)	
Hydraulic cement	−0.00431 (0.00093)	0.00352 (0.00097)	0.00079 (0.00017)	
Gypsum products	−0.00303 (0.00117)	−0.00543 (0.00177)	0.00846 (0.00185)	

are consistent with the movements in relative input prices described in table 3.1.

3.4 Conclusions

We determined trends in relative costs and relative use of capital, labor, and natural resources in six industries that process nonfuel mineral resources. During the period 1954 to 1974, hourly labor costs in most industries increased by roughly 5 percent per year. Capital costs, on the other hand, were practically trendless in all industries except storage batteries (3691). Natural resource prices typically increased by 1.5 to 2.5 percent annually. These changes in relative costs (table 3.1) induced a pervasive substitution of capital and natural resources against labor (table 3.2).

We then analyzed the trends in input use by means of a neoclassical economic framework. Assuming that entrepreneurs minimize cost, subject to predetermined factor prices and constant-returns-to-scale production functions, we posited two translog cost systems: one is based on the assumption that technological change is Hicks neutral; the other allows for biased technical change.

The estimated partial elasticities of substitution are generally sensitive to the alternative model specifications. Using either model, capital and labor are substitutes in most industries. Half of the estimated elasticities between capital and natural resources are positive and significant, as are half of the estimates between labor and natural resources. Both the Cobb-

Douglas and the fixed-coefficient models inadequately describe production technologies in these mineral-processing sectors.

Our findings provoke a substantive methodological question, since our inferences concerning substitution are often sensitive to model specification. For example, using the criteria "significantly positive," "not significantly different from zero," and "significantly negative" as boundaries defining input relations, the two models yield different inferences concerning σ_{KL} in three industries, σ_{KN} in three industries, and σ_{LN} in five industries. In these instances the implications concerning input use depend essentially on specification, and estimates based on an incorrect prior specification could be seriously misleading.

How should one choose the correct prior specification? If economic criteria, such as correctly signed own elasticities and the sufficient conditions for cost function concavity, are satisfied by both models, the customary F test should usually be a reliable guide. We are not so fortunate. In each industry the more general model always yields a lower asymptotic system variance but also produces substitution estimates that violate the concavity conditions. The dilemma is clear, but its solution is not. Ours is a specific instance of a more general problem requiring much further study, particularly in the context of systems estimation.

Appendix 3.1 Measurement of Variables

In this section we describe the procedures employed to measure each variable to be used in the analysis. Data are developed for the years 1954 to 1974.

Value of Output

The value-of-output variable, VO, is conceptually the contribution to the nominal value of production of capital, labor, and the natural resource input, s, employed by the industry. We have deliberately selected industries that make comparatively intensive use of labor, reproducible capital, and homogeneous natural resource inputs. We assume that the economic contributions of these agents are separable from those of other intermediate inputs. Value of output is measured here as the sum of value added, VA, and the total cost of the natural resource, $P_n N$. For industries 3312 (steel and blast furnaces) and 3351 (copper rolling and drawing) the total cost of scrap, $P_s \cdot S$, is also added, since in these two cases scrap and the natural resource inputs can be substituted in the production of output. That is, (1) $VO = VA + P_n \cdot N$ or (2) $VO = VA + P_n \cdot N + P_s \cdot S$, when scrap and the natural resource input are conceptually separate inputs.

Value Added

Value added, *VA*, is reported for the four-digit industries in the *Census of Manufactures* and *Annual Survey of Manufactures* for the years under review. The measurement of natural resource price and input series will be discussed.

Price Deflator for Value of Output

For each industry we construct a Törnqvist discrete approximation to a Divisia aggregate input price index. Under the assumptions of constant returns to scale and cost minimization for the industry, an aggregate input price index is the appropriate deflator for the nominal value of output (Arrow), and, if the underlying production technology is consistent with a translog cost function (either homothetic or nonhomothetic but characterized by Hicks-neutral technological change), the Divisia input price index is an exact deflator for the nominal value of output (Diewert 1976). It appears to be a reasonably accurate deflator for a wide range of production technologies.

The aggregate Törnqvist input price in period t relative to that in period $t - 1$ is

$$\frac{P_{(t)}}{P_{(t-1)}} = \Pi \left[\frac{P_i(t)}{P_i(t - 1)} \right]^{1/2\,(S_i(t)+S_i(t-1))},$$

for $t = 1, \ldots, 20$ and $i = K, L, N$ (and S in industries 3312 and 3351). The index is defined such that $P_i(0) \equiv 1$, and each year's index is linked to the base year (1954) through chain multiplication. The nominal value of output in each year is deflated by the aggregate input price index, thereby yielding a time series of real output expressed in 1954 dollars.

Real Capital Stock

The nominal capital stock is measured as gross book value of capital assets when reported by *Census of Manufactures* and *Annual Survey of Manufactures*. For several years (1954–56, 1958–61, 1965–66) these figures were not reported and had to be approximated. Data on new capital expenditures, available in the *Annual Survey of Manufactures*, and an adjustment for fully depreciated capital, permitted the approximation of gross book value in all of these years for the industries under study.

To deflate gross book value of assets we employed a composite price deflator which adjusts for the price of structures and the price of durable equipment. That is, the gross book value for an industry is separated into two components: structures (plant and structures) and nonstructures (machinery and equipment). This disaggregation permits the consideration of the separate price movements in new structural additions and in new nonstructural investments. In addition structures have substantially longer useful lives than nonstructures, so it is necessary to employ a different deflator for each type of asset.

Consider first the method used to obtain a gross book value deflator for nonstructures in a specific manufacturing industry. A nonstructure that is in service less than n years is included in gross book value, where n is the average useful life of a nonstructure. (These life expectancies, which average twelve years, are obtained from the U.S. Department of Treasury publication, *Tax Information on Depreciation*.) The formula used to calculate the deflator for the nonstructure component of gross book value in year T, D_{nT} is:

$$D_{nT} = \sum_{t=T-n}^{T} \frac{NI_t d_{nt}}{\sum\limits_{t=T-n}^{T} NI_t},$$

where d_{nt} is the implicit price deflator for producers' durable equipment in year t (compiled and reported by the Department of Commerce in the Survey of Current Business) and NI_t is constant dollar nonstructure investment in year t. Thus the weights are determined by the relative importance of each year's investment in total nondepreciated investment of nonstructures.

Since nonstructure investment is reported for four-digit manufacturing industries beginning in 1947, a less precise method of computing d_{nt} for the years 1954 to $1947 + (n - 1)$ was employed. It is assumed that the annual industry investment in nonstructures for years prior to 1947 is in the same proportion to total manufacturing investment in nonstructures as its average for the years 1947 through 1965. Total manufacturing investment in nonstructures is known for the years prior to 1947. It is computed as the sum of lines 8, 9, 10, 15, 16, 17, 20, 21, 23, 29, and 30 in tables 5.4 of Office of Business Economics, *National Income and Product Accounts of the United States, 1929–1965*. With this information we can approximate industry-specific investment for these years.

Consider now the structures component of gross book value. We assume that structures have a useful life of forty years. A deflation procedure similar to that just developed is unfruitful because yearly investment in structures is reported for four-digit industries only since the year 1947. The only workable alternative is to assume that for each industry the ratio of investment in structures has been constant since 1913. This assumption, although somewhat restrictive, has a precedent in the literature. For example, George J. Stigler (1963) and Daniel Creamer et al. used it to derive gross book value deflators for specific industries.

The construction price index, d_S, used to build a deflator for the gross book value of structures is the Boeckh's Price Index of Commercial Construction. The measure used for total manufacturing investment in structures is the "Industrial and Commercial Construction Put in Place" series. Both are reported in the *Statistical Abstract of the United States*. The deflator for gross book value of structures in year T, D_{ST}, is:

$$D_{ST} = \sum_{t=T-n}^{T} \frac{SI_t d_{St}}{\sum\limits_{t=T-n}^{T} SI_t},$$

where SI_t is the constant dollar investment in structures undertaken by all manufacturing industries in year t. Given this assumption, the resulting deflator will be applicable to all the sample industries.

The two components of gross book value cannot be individually deflated because reported gross book value is not always disaggregated into structures and nonstructures. Therefore a composite deflator is calculated as a weighted average of the nonstructures deflator and the structures deflator. In each manufacturing industry the weights are the average relative shares of structures and nonstructures in gross book value during the period 1967 to 1974. The resulting figures are used industry by industry to deflate the series on the gross book value of capital assets, forming the constant dollar gross book value series that serve as our measures of capital stocks.

Cost of Capital
The cost of capital, P_K, is computed as a residual rate of return to capital.

$$P_K = \frac{VA - P_L \cdot L}{K},$$

where $P_L \cdot L$ represents total labor costs.

Labor Input
Labor input, L, is measured as the sum of total man hours of production employees plus 2,000 man hours per nonproduction employee per year. Data required for this computation are reported in the *Census of Manufactures* and *Annual Survey of Manufactures*.

Cost of Labor
The cost of labor, P_L, is computed as the sum of total payroll plus total supplements divided by total man hours, L. Supplemental labor costs are

divided into legally required expenditures and payments for voluntary programs. The legally required portion consists primarily of federal old age and survivors' insurance, unemployment compensation, and workman's compensation. Payments for voluntary programs include those not specifically required by legislation, whether they are employee initiated or the result of collective bargaining (employer portion of insurance premiums, pension plans, stock purchase plans on which the employer payment is not subject to withholding tax, and so on).

Total supplements were not reported for the years 1954 to 1956 and 1958 to 1966 and were therefore approximated. The procedure was to estimate the rate of growth, g, of the ratio of total supplements to total payroll, R, and apply this ratio to total payroll. For example the rate of growth of R between 1958 and 1966 was estimated by

$$R_{67} = R_{57}(1 + g)^9.$$

Data required for the cost of labor computation are reported in *Census of Manufactures* and the *Annual Survey of Manufactures*.

Natural Resource Inputs and Prices
The data on resource input, N^*, and resource input prices, P_n, are taken from the *Minerals Yearbook* unless otherwise noted.

1. Uncalcined gypsum to hydraulic cement (SIC 3241): consumption of uncalcined gypsum (in short tons) as cement retarder is the resource input series employed. The price is computed as the average value (dollars per short ton) of uncalcined gypsum sold for portland cement retarder.
2. Calcined gypsum to gypsum products (SIC 3275): total calcined gypsum produced (short tons) is used as the resource input series. Commodity experts at the Bureau of Mines stated that essentially all calcined gypsum is for use in gypsum products, so the industrial disposition of this natural resource is known with accuracy. The price series is computed as average value of calcined gypsum at the processing plant. Since the calcining of gypsum and its subsequent use in gypsum products is almost always a continuous process in a common production site, the computed price series reflects with accuracy the unit cost to the input purchaser.
3. Bauxite to primary aluminum (SIC 3334): Bauxite consumed in the production of aluminum is not reported directly by the Bureau of Mines. It can be approximated by use of available series on bauxite used in the production of alumina and alumina used in the production of aluminum. The procedure is to sum consumption of domestic and foreign bauxite used in the production of alumina to develop for each year a bauxite to

alumina input-output ratio. We then calculate for the corresponding year the input-output ratio of alumina to aluminum produced in the United States. The product of these two ratios yields the bauxite to aluminum input-output ratio for the United States. This latter ratio is then applied to total production of aluminum to obtain the bauxite input series. The price of bauxite (dollars per long ton) is computed as a weighted average of foreign and domestic bauxite where the weights are the percentages of foreign and domestic bauxite used in the production of alumina.

4. Refined lead to storage batteries (SIC 3691): consumption of lead (short tons) in the production of storage batteries is reported directly by the Bureau of Mines. The price series is the average price per short ton of common lead.

5. Refined copper and copper scrap to copper rolling and drawing (SIC 3351): The consumption of refined copper by brass and wire mills is used as the natural resource input series. Since scrap copper is a separate input and potentially a substitute for refined copper, its use in brass and wire mills was also compiled. Copper wire mills do not make use of scrap, however, whereas brass mills use copper scrap extensively. Scrap is the primary resource input used by brass mills, and they use refined copper as a secondary raw material. The price of refined copper (dollars per short ton) is measured by the average price of electrolytic copper reported by the Bureau of Mines. The price of copper scrap is measured by the average price of no. 2 wire and heavy copper scrap reported by the American Metal Market's, *Metal Statistics.*

6. Iron ore and iron and steel scrap to blast furnaces and basic steel (SIC 3312): iron ore consumed by blast furnaces and steel furnaces is reported by the Bureau of Mines. Since the average iron content of ore increased during the sample period, this series was adjusted to correct for variation in the quality of ore consumed, by multiplying the series by the average iron content of U.S. ore. The resulting natural resource input series is iron consumption in the form of iron ore. Since iron and steel scrap is a separate input to this industry, and is potentially a substitute for iron ore, its use was also compiled. The scrap-use series is net scrap consumption by blast and steel furnaces. For iron ore the average value at the mine is reported by the Bureau of Mines. To this series we added shipping cost (per long-ton) from Mesabi Range to lower lake ports rail or vessel. The resulting figure is divided by the average yield of iron from domestic ore, thereby producing an average delivered price of iron ore. The price of iron and steel scrap is measured by the average composite price for no. 1 heavy melting scrap.

Notes

We are pleased to acknowledge the helpful comments of Ernst Berndt, John Krutilla, and V. Kerry Smith on earlier versions of this chapter. Richard L. Dennis provided invaluable research assistance. This research was supported by the National Science Foundation, RANN Program Grant AER 77-14568.

1. In a two-input model incorporating capital and labor, technical change that is labor augmenting is labor saving (in Hicks' classification) if the substitution elasticity between capital and labor is less than one. For elaboration, see David and Van de Klundert or Moroney. The classification of biased technical change in multi-input models is analyzed most easily with reference to changes in relative cost shares. See Binswanger (1974b).

Several studies have been published recently about some of the industries analyzed here, (such as the world copper market model by Fisher, Cootner, and Baily, lineaı programming models of steel production by Russell and Vaughan, and the review of innovations in the U.S. steel industry by Gold. But they have not been concerned with modeling neoclassical substitution and biased technical change, which are our focal points.

2. In the aggregate U.S. economy indirect business taxes increased slightly in comparison with proprietary income, corporate profits, and net interest payments during the period 1954 to 1974. But it is not possible to read much into individual industries from this economy-wide trend.

3. All coefficients are obtained by estimating simultaneously the unit cost function (based on the use of $q_{(t)}^*$) and the minimum-cost input share equations. This procedure generally gives rise to measurement error in the dependent variable, since $C_{(t)}/q_{(t)}^* \neq C_{(t)}/q_{T(t)}$ in general. But it does not impart measurement errors to the regressors, so the estimated slope coefficients remain consistent estimators of the true parameters.

4. This classification of the bias in technical change is equivalent to that introduced by Binswanger (1974b) and adopted by Jorgenson and Fraumeni. Thus $\partial M_i/\partial t = \beta_i > 0$ identifies factor-using technical change as one that increases the cost share of the ith factor and, conversely, for factor-saving technical change. If $\partial M_i/\partial t = 0$, technical change is Hicks-neutral.

5. The asymptotic standard errors are estimated by treating the mean cost shares in equations (3.12) and (3.13) as nonstochastic constants (which of course they are not). Thus asym. var $(\hat{\sigma}_{ij}) = (\overline{M_i M_j})^{-2}$ asym. var $(\hat{\gamma}_{ij})$, for $i \neq j$, and asym. var $(\hat{\gamma}_{ii}) = (\overline{M_i})^{-4}$ asym. var $(\hat{\gamma}_{ii})$, for $i = j$. In a few cases we estimated the asymptotic variances in equations (3.12) and (3.13) by expressing the mean cost shares in terms of the parameter estimates and the sample mean values of the regressors and then evaluating the Taylor's series expansion. This method yielded estimates that were equivalent (to three significant digits) to the simpler method, so the latter was employed.

6. Wills in his study based on translog cost functions also found that concavity conditions were usually violated under nonneutral technical change but were satisfied when neutrality was imposed.

4

The Energy-Capital Complementarity Controversy: A Progress Report on Reconciliation Attempts

James M. Griffin

Ernst Berndt and David Wood's 1975 finding that energy, E, and capital, K, are complements in the U.S. manufacturing sector has stimulated research in the policy significance of E/K complementarity and its empirical validity. Even though the Berndt-Wood results are entirely partial equilibrium, describing the manufacturing sector's demand for factor inputs, the sign and magnitude of the elasticity of substitution between E and K has important policy implications for a world in which energy is becoming increasingly scarce. William Hogan and John Solow have recast the problem in a general equilibrium framework, emphasizing the role of supply as well as demand elasticities. If we assume a very inelastic supply of labor, energy-labor substitutions will be quite limited, leaving only the possibility of substituting materials and capital for energy.

As Hogan and Manne demonstrate, the ability of the macroeconomy to increase output and at the same time cope with limited available energy resources depends critically on the extent of substitution possibilities. Since policies to stimulate capital investment to improve productivity may conflict with energy conservation goals, E/K complementarity is important to the productivity problem. Whether substitutes or complements in a partial equilibrium sense, E and K are likely to have important macroeconomic consequences.

At the same time the policy significance of the E/K complementarity finding was being established, the Berndt-Wood study evoked a number of empirical attempts to reconcile this finding with the more traditional view that E and K are substitutes.[1] To date research has tended to offer three alternative explanations:

1. E and K are complements or substitutes depending on whether a short- or long-run production relationship is being measured. In the short run energy inputs per unit of machine hours tend to be fixed. To the extent

that other inputs (maintenance labor) can be substituted against the capital-energy aggregate, capital and energy can be short-run complements. Since in the long run the energy input per unit of capital can be varied substantially, we can expect energy and capital to be long-run substitutes.[2]

2. In contrast to the studies showing energy-capital complementarity, those studies finding E/K substitution measure only a gross elasticity because one or more factors have been omitted from the production function. Moreover the empirical results are consistent with energy and capital being gross substitutes but net complements.[3]

3. Capital is itself not a weakly separable aggregate. Rather it should be disaggregated into working capital and physical capital, which consists of equipment and structures. Energy acts as a complement against physical capital or a substitute against working capital, and vice versa, depending on the study.[4]

This chapter reviews the plausibility of these three viewpoints in the light of extant research and offers suggestions for future research.

4.1. The Short-Run, Long-Run Dichotomy

Griffin and Gregory first exposited the view that the Berndt-Wood results probably reflect a short-run relationship because the specification is static, based on annual time-series data. The period 1947 to 1971 was one of relatively small variations in the price of energy relative to other inputs. This fact combined with the observation that energy consumption is closely tied to the technical characteristics of the stock of energy-using equipment suggests that an instantaneous adjustment (one-year) to a long-run equilibrium is not plausible. Rather the Berndt-Wood E/K complementarity result should be interpreted as a short-run relationship since in the short run energy and capital tend to enter the production process in roughly fixed proportions, with some substitution of other inputs against the E/K aggregate.

Empirical support for the proposition that E and K are long-run substitutes is found in the pooled intercountry studies by Griffin and Gregory and by Pindyck (1979). Halvorsen and Ford employed cross-sectional data for states within the United States at a two-digit industry level and obtained similar findings of E/K substitution. For example, the estimates of the Allen elasticity of substitution between energy and capital range from 1.07 in Griffin-Gregory and 0.8 in Pindyck to -1.01 to 2.0 in

Halvorsen and Ford. These estimates stand in sharp contrast to the Berndt-Wood estimate of $\sigma_{EK} = -3.2$.

The rationale for attaching long-run interpretations to these results rests on the propositions that relative factor price variation tends to be much greater in these pooled intercountry or cross-sectional samples and that these differentials have tended to persist for substantial time periods, so that adjustment to a long-run equilibrium is possible.[5] The intercountry pooled samples such as Griffin-Gregory's sample of nine industrialized countries with time-series observations for 1955, 1960, 1965, and 1969 contain two major sources of variation—between country, or intercountry variation, and within country, or intracountry time-series variation. Intercountry variation in factor prices is particularly large owing in part to differing labor costs and long standing energy tariff and tax policy differences among countries. Even the intracountry variation is appreciable owing to changing relative factor prices over time in the nine countries. Halvorsen and Ford's use of state cross-sectional data relies on interstate variation in factor prices. Between states, energy and labor prices differ substantially, providing a well-identified production structure. Here again, since these interstate differentials have tended to persist for some period, a long-run equilibrium may be observed.

To illustrate the magnitude of the relative price differentials observed in U.S. annual time-series and intercountry pooled data, we contrast the relative price variation in the Berndt-Wood data sample to pooled intercountry data used by Griffin-Gregory. Table 4.1 reports the ratio of the highest to the lowest relative price over the sample period. For example, the pooled intercountry ratio for P_K/P_E is 4.12 obtained by dividing the highest relative price for P_K/P_E of 3.37 for Denmark in 1969 by the lowest relative price of 0.819 for Belgium in 1955. Table 4.1 indicates the maximum extent of relative price variation occurring in the sample. Since the remaining data will fall between these limits, the bulk of relative price variation tends to be considerably smaller than these ratios.

Table 4.1
The extent of relative price variation (ratio of maximum to minimum relative price)

Relative price	Berndt-Wood U.S. time series (1947–1971)	Griffin-Gregory pooled intercountry data (1955–1969)
P_K/P_E	1.68	4.12
P_L/P_E	2.03	9.42
P_K/P_L	2.30	7.24

Table 4.1 shows that for the three relative price ratios P_K/P_E, P_L/P_E, and P_K/P_L the pooled intercountry data offer substantially greater relative price variation than U.S. annual time-series data. In both samples the range of P_K/P_E variation, which is essential to the E/K complementarity question, is small relative to variation in P_L/P_E and P_K/P_L. The U.S. time-series data are particularly troublesome since the highest relative price ratio exceeds the lowest relative price ratio by only 68 percent. Most of the relative price variation is much smaller of course. Therefore, even putting aside the question of instantaneous adjustment, the range of the production surface observed in E/K space appears rather limited.

The generality of the pooled international and U.S. cross-sectional results has been questioned in view of Fuss's pooled Canadian results which found $\sigma_{KE} = -0.21$, indicating weak complementarity. Pooled data are not a sufficient condition for observing long-run phenomena. Fuss employed an analysis of covariance pooling method which resulted in an analysis of deviations about interprovincial means. The inter province variation, which is likely to reflect substantial P_K/P_E variation between western and eastern provinces, is completely omitted. With a model entirely dependent on intraprovince variation, the extent of relative price variation over time within a province is critical. If this time-series variation is similar in range to U.S. experience, as seems likely, we can conjecture that short-run phenomena dominate the regression. Even if we accept the Fuss results as indicative of a long-run relationship, a substitution elasticity of -0.21 is a great deal smaller than the Berndt-Wood estimate of -3.2 and numerically closer to the estimates cited here.

This potential problem of intra and inter variation does not appear to materialize in the pooled intercountry sample or in state cross-sectional studies. Clearly Halvorsen and Ford's cross-sectional study is entirely dependent on interstate variation. In the pooled international samples Griffin and Gregory demonstrate that the OLS and covariance model yields reasonably similar elasticities.[6] Pindyck's (1979b) estimates from an analysis of a covariance model solely dependent on intracountry variation probably conform to a long-run interpretation.

In sum econometric evidence to date clearly does not reject the short- and long-run dichotomy interpretation. This interpretation contains a plausible technical explanation for the divergence in econometric results. Nevertheless, there remain two valid objections to these results. First, pooled international data are subject to greater measurement error than found in the aggregate time-series analysis. Intercountry differentials in labor quality require imperfect adjustments to reflect these phenomena. The user cost of capital employed by Griffin and Gregory does not incorporate intercountry differences in depreciation guidelines, tax rates, investment tax credits, and so on. Even in state cross-sectional data Halvorsen and Ford face the problem of obtaining capital and labor price series that reflect true interstate quality-adjusted price differences. The second limitation of these studies is that they do not describe the dynamic adjustment path to the long-run production structure.

As a research priority the measurement error problem seems likely to be of minor consequence especially in its relation to the substantial inter-country price variation, although it cannot be ruled out as potentially important. The application of a dynamic model to pooled intercountry data would appear a logical next step.[7] It would be particularly significant if the short- and long-run dichotomy could be reconciled in a single model. Ultimately resolution of the short- and long-run question may require an approach differentiating capital by vintages.

4.2 The Omitted Factor Story

Berndt and Wood (1979) point out that energy and capital can be gross substitutes in a production subfunction and yet net complements in the aggregate production function. Using this theoretical proposition, they attempt to reconcile the econometric findings of energy-capital com-plementarity with other studies finding energy-capital substitutability. Their reconciliation rests on the finding that those studies finding energy-capital substitutability considered only capital, labor, and energy (*KLE*). By omitting materials, *M*, only a gross elasticity is obtained. The net elasticity, which allows for the additional substitution between the *KLE* aggregate and *M*, can indicate energy-capital complementarity. In fact *KLEM* studies generally find energy-capital complementarity.

While this explanation probably tends to reduce the disparity between the original Berndt-Wood estimate $[\sigma_{KE} = -3.2]$ and Griffin-Gregory $[\sigma_{KE} = 1.07]$, three independent sources of evidence suggest that the omission of *M* is not a sufficient explanation. In fact it may not even be an empirically important explanation for the disparity of findings.

First, the difference between the gross elasticity in a *KLE* submodel and the net elasticity in a *KLEM* model depends critically on the elasticity of substitution between *M* and *KLE*. Let us adopt the Berndt-Wood notation and consider their mathematical example which demonstrates the possi-bility of gross capital energy substitutability as in the Griffin-Gregory study with net capital-energy complementarity:

$$Y = F(K, L, E, M) = F^*[(K, L, E), M] = F^{**}(V, M), \tag{4.1}$$

where

$$V = v(K, L, E).$$

To be estimable, studies based on the output of V such as Griffin-Gregory must assume separability with respect to M. Consequently KLE studies measure only gross price elasticities (ε_{ij}^*). Following equation (27) in Berndt-Wood, we note that the net price elasticity between energy and capital (ε_{EK}) depends on the gross price elasticity (ε_{EK}^*), the cost share of capital in the V aggregate (S_{KV}), and the own price elasticity of the V aggregate (ε_{VV}) in the $F^{**}(\quad)$ aggregate function:

$$\varepsilon_{EK} = \varepsilon_{EK}^* + S_{KV}\varepsilon_{VV}. \tag{4.2}$$

From equation (4.2) it is apparent that in terms of elasticities the gross elasticity measured by Griffin-Gregory will tend to overstate the substitutability between E and K. Furthermore, based on the Griffin-Gregory finding that $\varepsilon_{EK}^* = 0.15$ and their 1965 data showing $S_{KV} = 0.14$, a price elasticity for V slightly in excess of unity is sufficient to yield energy-capital complementarity in the net elasticity,

$$\varepsilon_{EK} \leq 0 \quad \text{if} \quad \varepsilon_{VV} \leq -1.07. \tag{4.3}$$

This seemingly plausible result is not so plausible when we consider the conditions under which ε_{VV} is price elastic. By recasting equation (4.2) in terms of Allen partial elasticities of substitution, we can explore the implications of assuming $\varepsilon_{VV} = -1.07$. Since $F^{**}(\quad)$ is linearly homogeneous, we require that $\varepsilon_{VV} = -\varepsilon_{VM}$, so that equation (4.2) can be rewritten as

$$\varepsilon_{EK} = \varepsilon_{EK}^* - S_{KV}\varepsilon_{VM}. \tag{4.4}$$

Next, utilizing the facts that $\varepsilon_{ij} = S_{jY}\sigma_{ij}$ and $\varepsilon_{ij}^* = S_{jV}\sigma_{ij}^*$, we re-express equation (4.4) as follows:

$$\sigma_{EK} = \frac{S_{KV}}{S_{KY}}\sigma_{EK}^* - \frac{S_{KV}}{S_{KY}}S_{MY}\sigma_{VM}. \tag{4.5}$$

Equation (4.5) is useful in several respects. First, it demonstrates that the bias in interpreting a gross partial elasticity of substitution as a net partial elasticity of substitution is not necessarily toward substitutability as in the case of simple cross-price elasticities. In fact σ_{EK} can exceed σ_{EK}^* in a variety of circumstances. Second, this formulation enables us to consider the partial elasticity of substitution necessary to obtain net complementarity. For 1965, $S_{KV} = 0.144$, $S_{KY} = 0.055$, and the cost share of materials relative to total output, $S_{MY} = 0.619$. Taking the Griffin-Gregory estimate, $\sigma_{EK}^* = 1.07$, we find

$$\sigma_{EK} \leq 0 \quad \text{if} \quad \sigma_{VM} \geq 1.73. \tag{4.6}$$

Thus the Berndt-Wood reconciliation rests on an elasticity of substitution between materials and KLE of 1.7 just to obtain a zero net elasticity of substitution. To justify Berndt-Wood's original point estimate $\sigma_{KE} = -3.22$, the elasticity of substitution between materials and non-materials would have to be 3.7. The fundamental fallacy of the gross/net elasticity reconciliation is that there is simply no empirical support for materials/nonmaterials substitution elasticities of this magnitude (or equivalently an elastic own price elasticity of demand for V, the KLE aggregate). The more common wisdom would follow Leontief and place σ_{VM} well below unity. Paradoxically, if $\sigma_{VM} < 1$, $\sigma_{EK} > \sigma_{EK}^*$, suggesting Griffin-Gregory underestimated the extent of E/K substitution measured by the Allen partial elasticity, even though in terms of the cross-price elasticity $E_{EK}^* > E_{EK} > 0$. Irrespective of the choice of elasticity, E and K are clearly substitutes under these conditions.

The second piece of disquieting evidence leading as to question the Berndt-Wood reconciliation is the following proposition. Barring problems of specification error, due to failure of M separability with KLE, wouldn't we expect to find σ_{EK}^* to be substitutes in their data sample? If the explanation is simply that KLE studies left out M, then shouldn't dropping out M from a $KLEM$ model yield results more or less consistent with gross substitutability between energy and capital? Using the Berndt-Wood data, a KLE model was estimated treating prices as exogenous. The results for 1971 indicate gross energy-capital complementarity ($\sigma_{EK}^* = -1.31$, with a standard error of 0.19). While this result does tend to reduce the disparity between the two sets of results, it is hardly consistent with other KLE studies, nor does it support the assumption that $\sigma_{VM} > 1.7$.

Finally, to the extent that recent additional studies including all four factors, $KLEM$, find E/K substitutability, the gross/net elasticity distinction cannot offer a complete explanation. In studies of four key energy-consuming industries using a pseudodata approach, Griffin has found energy-capital substitutability in two of the four industries (electricity generation, and petrochemicals).[8] Petroleum refining exhibited energy-capital complementarity while the iron and steel industry revealed approximately a zero partial elasticity of substitution. These results are interesting because they avoid the short-run, long-run controversy that exists between time-series and cross-sectional or pooled data sets. These are long-run responses based on an approximation to engineering process models for these industries. In sum substantial differences persist among econometric studies of energy-capital substitution even after allowing for differences between net and gross elasticities.

4.3 E/K Substitution between Working and Physical Capital

Two studies have attempted to explain the divergent E/K substitution results by positing that capital must be disaggregated into physical and working capital. If indeed capital must be disaggregated, the Berndt-Wood study and all other studies considering only physical capital are subject to misspecification for omitting working capital. In addition other studies that include working capital in the capital aggregate are likewise mis-specified because capital is not disaggregated.

Before addressing the empirical results, it is useful to ask under what conditions does working capital belong in the production function. If we adopt the view that the production function is intended to describe only the relationship between physical inputs and outputs, the production process ends with the emanation of output from the assembly line. Following this view, the choice of inventory levels, accounts payable and receivable, cash and securities on hand, and so on, belongs to a separable sales/financial activity of the firm. If indeed the production and sales/ financial activities are separable, there is no need to include working capital in the production function, although it may be necessary to exclude the value of financial services included in the output measure. Conversely, if we can postulate conditions under which weak separability would not hold, there may be good reasons for the inclusion of working capital. It would appear that a precondition for an empirical study including working capital would be a well-developed theoretical model that would provide certain a priori expectations on substitution relationships. Unfortunately empirical work has proceeded without the benefit of such a model.

Field and Grebenstein use cross-section state data to estimate a four-factor translog model for ten two-digit industries. The four factors considered are labor, energy, working capital, and physical capital. Physical capital is obtained by independently calculating the stock of capital structures and equipment. The expenditures on physical capital were then estimated by the product of the user cost times the capital stock. The cost of working capital is obtained by subtracting the cost of physical capital from the cost of all capital, which is obtained by subtracting labor costs from value added. In effect working capital is obtained as a residual.

Field and Grebenstein found energy and physical capital tend to behave or balance as complements as they reject E/K substitution in four of the ten industries and cannot reject E/K complementarity in all ten industries. In contrast, the relationship between energy and working capital tends toward substitution. In five of the ten industries E/K complementarity is rejected. But E/K substitution cannot be rejected in all ten industries. While the power of these tests is by no means conclusive, the tendency is for energy and physical capital to act as complements while energy and working capital tend to be substitutes.

In contrast to these results, Kopp and Smith (1978) find energy and working capital to be complements while energy and physical capital are substitutes. They utilize a truncated version of the Berndt-Wood annual time-series data covering the period 1947 to 1970. Working capital is simply appended as a fifth input onto the $KLEM$ model. Working capital is measured much differently than in Field and Grebenstein, however, as working capital is estimated directly. For the manufacturing sector Kopp and Smith obtain data for cash balances, U.S. government securities, accounts receivable, and inventories. These four components were then aggregated to determine a working capital index.

Casual observation might suggest that the Kopp-Smith data are superior to Field-Grebenstein data, since working capital is measured directly. Kopp and Smith face several conceptual problems in the measurement of working capital. The first is definitional. The rationale for treating accounts receivable as a component of working capital and excluding accounts payable as a negative asset is less than transparent.[9] Does the firm with offsetting accounts payable and receivable of $100 million have more working capital or access to financial markets than a firm with offsetting accounts payable and receivable of $1? If the relevant concept is the net difference between accounts receivable and payable, accounts receivable no longer receives the dominant weight in the working capital index, and cash and inventories become more important components in the index.

The price of working capital appears subject to bias arising from errors in measuring the opportunity cost of holding the various forms of working capital. Normally, we think of the rental cost on cash balances as simply the short-term interest rate, yet Kopp and Smith use a rental price consisting of the nominal interest rate plus an inflation rate adjustment. In fact for all working assets the inflation rate is added to the nominal interest rate to obtain the price of capital inputs. Inventories, form of working capital for which inflation tends to reduce the cost of holding, is treated like cash and other liquid assets. In sum both the resulting working capital aggregate and its price appear subject to such serious conceptual difficulties that we must question the credibility of the Kopp-Smith results.

A subtle difference in the definition of value added poses a problem of similar gravity for the Field-Grebenstein attempt at measuring working capital.[10] Based on the reported estimated mean cost shares, Field and Grebenstein's results indicate that physical capital constitutes an average of only 30 percent of the cost of capital for the ten industries. The remaining 70 percent is attributed to the cost of working capital. Such a result should appear implausible since the stock of physical capital (equipment and structures) exceeds working capital (cash, inventories, accounts receivable less accounts payable). Furthermore the rental cost is much higher on the stock of physical capital owing to depreciation. Casual empiricism would suggest that Field and Grebenstein have their percentages reversed.

The error arises because the census of manufactures concept of value added differs from the notion of income used in the national income accounts. Value added, as measured by the census of manufactures, is merely the value of shipments less the purchase of physical materials. Included in value added are purchases of services from nonmanufacturing enterprises (such as consultants, advertising, telephone, insurance, royalties, patent fee) in addition to state and local taxes, depreciation and other costs of capital. The U.S. Office of Business Economics estimated that in 1967 this definition of value added in manufacturing exceeded national income originating in manufacturing by 34 percent.[11] Unfortunately the additional 34 percent becomes included in the expenditure on capital since Field and Grebenstein estimate the expenditure on working capital as a residual (value added minus the costs of labor and physical capital). Thus in actuality they are measuring an amorphous set of inputs that has little to do with working capital. Despite these measurement difficulties their choice of cross-sectional data at a microeconomic level offers numerous attractive advantages for unraveling the role of working capital. Perhaps future research in this area will use the Field-Grebenstein data base coupled with an adequate measure of working capital as a point of departure.

4.4 Conclusions

The issue of energy-capital complementarity remains an unanswered but important policy question. Nevertheless, empirical research over the last five years has offered some insights. Annual time-series studies using a static *KLEM* model strongly support E/K complementarity, although probably not of the magnitude of the original Berndt-Wood estimate ($\sigma_{EK} = -3.2$).[12] Whether or not this relationship holds in the long run is unclear. Pooled intercountry and state cross-sectional results offer considerable support that E/K are long-run substitutes. The distinction between gross and net substitution elasticities arising from the omission of materials does not appear of empirical importance even though it represents an important conceptual distinction. Differential substitution relationships between energy and working as opposed to physical capital remain an interesting but relatively unexplored theoretical and empirical consideration.

Academics seem to prefer a varied diet, opting to move on to new questions even if the old ones are not resolved. Will this be the fate of the energy-capital complementarity issue? Numerous interesting research directions exist. Particularly important is the issue of how inputs adjust over time. Dynamic production structures offer numerous attractive possibilities. In addition a vintage approach to capital may offer insights not obtained through the standard capital aggregate, which assumes similar substitution possibilities across vintages.

Notes

I am particularly indebted to Paul Gregory for several insightful comments. I also wish to thank Ernst Berndt and the conference participants for their useful comments.

1. Prior to the introduction of generalized functional forms, all multi-input production functions utilizing the Cobb-Douglas or CES functions implicitly assumed all inputs were substitutes. In these cases, the cross-price elasticity of energy with respect to capital (ε_{EK}) is greater than or equal to zero.

2. This view is set forth in Griffin and Gregory.

3. See Berndt and Wood (1979).

4. See Kopp and Smith (1978) and Field and Grebenstein.

5. For an interesting examination of this question, see chapter 6.

6. For example, maximum likelihood estimates of σ_{EK} are 1.07 for the OLS and 1.92 for the covariance model. The standard errors are 0.95 and 0.81, respectively.

7. See chapter 11.

8. See Griffin (1979).

9. See Kopp and Smith (1978), p. 5

10. I wish to thank Paul Gregory for pointing out this problem.

11. See U.S. Bureau of Census (1976), pp. 653–654.

12. For an extensive review, see Berndt and Wood (1979).

5

**Partial and Full
Elasticities of Substitution
and the Energy-Capital
Complementarity
Controversy**

Heejoon Kang and
Gardner M. Brown

Since Joan Robinson introduced the concept of elasticity of substitution to measure the ease of substitutability between two inputs (with constant output), the definition has been the derivative of the ratio of two input levels with respect to the ratio of two input prices. For a production function $Y = f(X_1, X_2)$, where Y is output and X_1 and X_2 are inputs, with prices W_1 and W_2, respectively, $\sigma_{12} = d\ln(X_1/X_2)/d\ln(W_2/W_1)$, and σ grows larger as the substitution becomes easier between the two inputs. Furthermore, if $\sigma_{12} > 1 \,(<1)$, the share of input 1 becomes larger (smaller) relative to the share of input 2 as the price of input 1 becomes relatively cheaper. When there are only two inputs, there is only one relative price between the two inputs. Thus there is no ambiguity in the meaning of a price change. In this case $\sigma_{12} = \sigma_{21}$, and one measure of σ is sufficient to describe the substitutability.

When there are more than two inputs, however, even defining an elasticity is not a simple matter. Since any definition of elasticities necessarily involves various partial derivatives, there may be infinitely many different definitions depending on the *ceteris paribus* conditions under which partial derivatives are obtained. Hicks's and Allen's definitions are ones that are more widely used in the field, the latter far more so than the former. These definitions are not comparable to Joan Robinson's in that they are not the elasticity of substitution proper but the price elasticity, $d\ln X_i/d\ln P_j$ weighted by shares.

In the many input case the direct elasticity of substitution introduced by McFadden (1963) is definitionally akin to Robinson's definition, but the ceteris paribus conditions are critically different. With the direct elasticity, all inputs other than the two inputs directly involved are held constant. That is, for m inputs the direct elasticity of substitution between input i and j is $d\ln(X_i/X_j)/d\ln(W_j/W_i)$, under the condition that all $X_k\ (k \neq i,j)$

are held constant. Output also is held constant. The conditions seem to be too inflexible to apply except in the short run.

The full elasticity of substitution, F_{ij}, developed in this chapter for the many input case, has the same qualitative implications as Robinson's definition. Namely, it measures the ease of substitution between two inputs when prices change. When $F_{ij} > 1$ (< 1), the share of ith input grows relatively larger (smaller) than that of the jth input, as the price of the jth input becomes relatively cheaper. Moreover the use of the full elasticity of substitution makes comparisons straightforward among various empirical works while that of the partial elasticity of substitution does not.

Recently, there has been a controversy about whether two inputs are complements or substitutes. For instance, Griffin and Gregory obtained a positive partial elasticity of substitution, A_{KE}, between capital K and energy, E in their three input, KLE, production function (L being labor), whereas Berndt and Wood (1975b) obtained negative A_{KE} in their four imput model with K, L, E, and materials, M. Griffin and Gregory assumed that materials were weakly separable from the three inputs studied. Griffin and Gregory concluded that capital and energy were substitutes while Berndt and Wood concluded they were complements.

Recent research by Berndt and Wood (1979) indicates that A_{KE} in the three-input study is not comparable with A_{KE} in the four-input case even if the fourth input, material, is separable. In general partial elasticities of substitution yield different values between a three-input study and a four-input study, with the fourth input separable. In contrast, the values of full elasticities of substitution are numerically the same in the two cases. Therefore the values of F_{ij} in the two different studies are immediately comparable. As we shall show, calculation of full elasticities does not require data for the input omitted by the separability assumption. We believe this fact can enhance our knowledge about ease of substitution when there are various competing studies.

5.1 Definitions

When output Y is related to inputs X_1, X_2, and X_3 by a positive, twice differentiable, strictly quasi-concave linearly homogeneous production function

$$Y = f(X_1, X_2, X_3),$$

and when all input prices are denoted as W_1, W_2, and W_3, an Allen partial elasticity of substitution is defined as (Allen, p. 564)

$$A_{ij} = \frac{X_1 f_1 + X_2 f_2 + X_3 f_3}{X_i X_j} \frac{\tilde{F}_{ij}}{\tilde{F}}, \tag{5.1}$$

for $i, j = 1, 2, 3$, where $f_i = \partial Y/\partial X_i$, and $\tilde{F}_{ij}$ denotes the cofactor of f_{ij} in $\tilde{F}$, and where

$$\tilde{F} = \begin{vmatrix} 0 & f_1 & f_2 & f_3 \\ f_1 & f_{11} & f_{12} & f_{13} \\ f_2 & f_{21} & f_{22} & f_{23} \\ f_3 & f_{31} & f_{32} & f_{33} \end{vmatrix}.$$

In this definition of A_{ij} all inputs are free to vary. There is a more transparent way to write A_{ij}, one more readily susceptible to economic interpretation. Let

$$k_i = \frac{X_i f_i}{X_1 f_1 + X_2 f_2 + X_3 f_3} = \frac{X_i W_i}{Y}, \tag{5.2}$$

where Y is output whose normalized price is 1. The last equality in (5.2) is obtained if at an equilibrium position f_i is assumed equal to input price W_i. Along an isoquant the cross-demand elasticities are expressed as (Allen, p. 508),

$$\frac{\partial \ln X_i}{\partial \ln W_j} = k_j A_{ij}, \tag{5.3}$$

for $i, j = 1, 2, 3$. Thus $A_{ij} = (\partial \ln X_i/\partial \ln W_j)/k_j$ is a compensated (Y constant), share-weighted, Allen cross-elasticity of demand, E_{ij}. Naturally the own elasticity of demand is the special case of $i = j$.

The generalization of Robinson's definition in the case of more than two variables, $F_{ij} = d \ln (X_i/X_j)/d \ln (f_j/f_i)$, is ambiguous because the partial derivatives can be evaluated under various conditions, each set of which gives rise to different values of F_{ij}.[1] However, F_{ij} can be defined for the three (or more) input cases in the spirit of Allen's demand elasticities by permitting all inputs to vary, but restricting $d(f_3/f_1) = 0$ or $d(W_3/W_1) = 0$, while f_2 changes. This definition of the full elasticity of substitution can be credited to Morishima.[2] Since output is constant, $f_1 dX_1 + f_2 dX_2 + f_3 dX_3 = 0$. When f_2 or W_2 changes, then

$$F_{12} = \frac{d \ln (X_1/X_2)}{d \ln (f_2/f_1)} \bigg|_{\substack{Y \text{ const.} \\ (f_3/f_1) \text{ const.}}}, \tag{5.4}$$

More generally

$$F_{ij} = \frac{d \ln (X_i/X_j)}{d \ln (f_j/f_i)} \bigg|_{\substack{Y \text{ const.} \\ (f_k/f_i) \text{ const.} \\ k \neq i,j}} \tag{5.5}$$

for $i \neq j$, and

$$F_{ij} = k_j(A_{ij} - A_{jj}) = E_{ij} - E_{jj}, \tag{5.6}$$

where each A_{ij} is an AES depicted in (5.1). Although $A_{ij} = A_{ji}$ when there are more than two inputs, $F_{ij} \neq F_{ji}$.[3] Furthermore F_{ii} is not defined, although A_{ii} is a well-defined own elasticity.[4]

5.2 Properties and Interpretations of the Full Elasticities of Substitution

When there are only two inputs in a production function, $Y = f(X_1, X_2)$, the partial and full elasticities A_{ij} and F_{ij} are the same as Mundlak showed. To see this,

$$A_{12} = A_{21} = \frac{X_1 f_1 + X_2 f_2}{X_1 X_2} \frac{f_1 f_2}{\Delta},$$

where

$$\Delta = 2f_1 f_2 f_{12} - f_2^2 f_{11} - f_1^2 f_{22}$$

and

$$A_{11} = \frac{X_1 f_1 + X_2 f_2}{X_1^2} \frac{-f_2^2}{\Delta},$$

$$A_{22} = \frac{X_1 f_1 + X_2 f_2}{X_2^2} \frac{-f_1^2}{\Delta}.$$

From these equations

$$\begin{aligned} F_{21} &= \frac{X_1 f_1}{X_1 f_1 + X_2 f_2}(A_{21} - A_{11}) \\ &= \frac{X_1 f_1}{\Delta} \left(\frac{f_1 f_2}{X_1 X_2} + \frac{f_2^2}{X_1^2} \right) \\ &= \frac{f_1 f_2}{\Delta X_1 X_2}(X_1 f_1 + X_2 f_2) = A_{21}. \end{aligned}$$

From similar reasoning, $F_{12} = A_{12}$.

Hence, when there are only two inputs, the partial elasticity of substitution, *AES*, and the full elasticity of substitution, *FES*, between two inputs are the same and symmetrical.

Suppose there are m inputs which are homothetically weakly separable from $n - m$ inputs. For this general production function, $Y = F(V(X_1, X_2, \ldots, X_M), X_{M+1}, \ldots, X_N)$. As shown by Berndt and Wood (1979), the net cross-elasticity of demand between inputs i and j among N inputs $E_{ij}(i, j \in M)$ is

$$
E_{ij} = \frac{d \ln X_i}{d \ln W_j}\bigg|_{Y=Y_0} = \frac{\partial \ln X_i}{\partial \ln W_j}\bigg|_{V=V_0}
$$
$$
+ \frac{\partial \ln X_i}{\partial \ln V}\frac{\partial \ln V}{\partial \ln W^V} \cdot \frac{\partial \ln W^V}{\partial \ln W_j}\bigg|_{Y=Y_0},
$$
(5.7)

and

$$
E_{jj} = \frac{d \ln X_j}{d \ln W_j}\bigg|_{Y=Y_0} = \frac{\partial \ln X_j}{\partial \ln W_j}\bigg|_{V=V_0}
$$
$$
+ \frac{\partial \ln X_j}{\partial \ln V}\frac{\partial \ln V}{\partial \ln W^V} \cdot \frac{\partial \ln W^V}{\partial \ln W_j}\bigg|_{Y=Y_0},
$$
(5.8)

where W^V is the price index of the subfunction V, $\partial \ln X_i/\partial \ln W_j\big|_{V=V_0}$ and $\partial \ln X_j/\partial \ln W_j\big|_{V=V_0}$ are respectively E_{ij}^* and E_{jj}^*, and these are the gross price elasticities (to use Berndt and Wood's terminology) between inputs i and j in the subfunction V.

Since a weakly separable subfunction V can be transformed into a homothetic function (see Blackorby, Primont, and Russell, p. 266),

$$
\frac{\partial \ln X_i}{\partial \ln V} = \frac{\partial \ln X_j}{\partial \ln V}.
$$

Therefore from (5.6), (5.7), and (5.8), $F_{ij} = E_{ij} - E_{jj} = F_{ij}^* = E_{ij}^* - E_{jj}^*$. In short F_{ij} remains the same both in the entire production function and the separable subfunction. It follows from this that $F_{ij} = A_{ij}$ for all i and j, if the function is completely separable. Examples would be the Cobb-Douglas and *CES* functions.

Appendix 5.1 illustrates this major result for two cases. In the first, X_1 and X_2, weakly separable from X_3, are inputs in a *CES* production function, while X_3 enters in a Cobb-Douglas form. In the second, X_1 and X_2 are inputs in a transcendental logarithmic production function, while X_3 enters in a *CES* form.

Expressing the invariant property of F_{ij} another way, we note that, when a group of inputs is weakly separable from other inputs present, this separability indicates the neutrality of all other inputs as long as substitutions among separable inputs are concerned. As has been indicated, when X_3 is separable from X_1 and X_2, say, in a Cobb-Douglas production function, the share of input 3 is constant. A price change in any input does not change the fixed share of input 3. The substitution between inputs 1 and 2 should not depend on the actual value of the share of input 3. This attractive property is embodied in the full elasticity of substitution. In contrast, the magnitude of A_{ij} or E_{ij}, reported in contemporary studies on resource substitution, is a function of parameters of the production function explicitly excluded by the separability assumption.

The elasticity of substitution originally was developed as a summary measure of the implications of an input price change for its share, as we pointed out in the introduction. This condition is satisfied by F_{ij}. The ratio of the shares of two inputs i and j is $W_i X_i / W_j X_j$. Thus

$$\frac{d\ln(W_i X_i / W_j X_j)}{d\ln(W_j / W_i)} = -1 + \frac{d\ln(X_i / X_j)}{d\ln(W_j / W_i)} = -1 + F_{ij}.$$

Hence the right-hand side is positive (negative) if and only if $F_{ij} > 1 (<1)$. Put differently, when the relative price of the jth input increases, the share of ith input becomes relatively larger (smaller) than the share of jth input, if and only if F_{ij} is greater (smaller) than 1.[5]

5.3 Application

The application of the *FES* can most easily be illustrated by calculating them from readily available E_{ij}. Estimates reported in this section are derived from translog models using either time-series or cross-section data. The elasticities between capital and energy and between capital and labor are given in table 5.1.

The values of E_{KE} and E_{EK} are all negative in the four input models while they are positive in the three input model of Griffin and Gregory, where materials, M, is assumed to be weakly separable from K, L, and E. The discrepancies among the estimates do not provide any further information. By comparing F_{KE} and F_{EK}, the differences and similarities can yield useful information. Due to the positive value of E_{EE} in Hudson and Jorgenson (1974), we discard their F_{KE} from further discussion. Then all F_{KE} (or F_{EK}) are between 0 and 1, and with the exception of F_{KE} in Griffin and Gregory and F_{EK} in Fuss (1977) they are very similar in magnitude.

One important difference in these estimates is that F_{KE} and F_{EK} are smaller than F_{KL} and F_{LK}. Roughly speaking, capital and energy are less substitutable than capital and labor. The exception to this rule is found

Table 5.1
Comparisons of price elasticities of demand and full elasticities of substitution

Study	Capital-energy				Capital-labor				Own elasticities		
	F_{KE}	F_{EK}	E_{KE}	E_{EK}	F_{KL}	F_{LK}	E_{KL}	E_{LK}	E_{KK}	E_{LL}	E_{EE}
GG	0.92	0.33	0.13	0.15	0.17	0.19	0.05	0.01	−0.18	−0.12	−0.79
BW	0.31	0.32	−0.14	−0.18	0.75	0.56	0.29	0.06	−0.50	−0.46	−0.45
HJ	−0.09	0.24	−0.02	−0.18	0.74	0.56	0.29	0.14	−0.42	−0.45	0.07
FUSS	0.436	0.758	−0.050	−0.004	0.689	0.960	0.198	0.198	−0.762	−0.491	−0.486

Note: GG = Griffin and Gregory in *KLE* model, with pooled international data for 1955, 1960, 1965, and 1969; BW = Berndt and Wood (1975b) in *KLEM* model, with U.S. manufacturing time-series data for 1947 to 1971; HJ = Hudson and Jorgenson (1974) in *KLEM* model, with U.S. inter-industry time-series data for 1947 to 1971; $FUSS$ = Fuss (1977) in *KLEM* model, with Canadian times series for 1961 to 1971 and cross-section manu-facturing data evaluated at Ontario values. The values of E_{ij} in BW and HJ were obtained from the Griffin and Gregory paper.

in the Griffin and Gregory estimates. It would be interesting to test the hypothesis that substitutability between capital and energy is indeed smaller than that between capital and labor, using the *FES* concept.

The concept of full elasticities of substitution is the direct extension of the traditional concept of elasticity of substitution between two inputs for general cases where there are more than two inputs. Full elasticities of substitution have the attractive property that they are invariant to the separability assumption often made and therefore do not depend on the unestimated excluded characteristics of the function.

Appendix 5.1

We compute F_{ij} and A_{ij} for two different production functions involving three inputs, where the third input is separable from the other two. F_{12} or F_{21} are shown to be independent of X_3, and A_{12} or A_{21} are shown to depend on parameters of the overall production function which are veiled from view by the separability assumption.

First, consider a homogeneous production function with three inputs, inputs X_1 and X_2 being weakly separable from X_3. Let the first two inputs take a *CES* form, while the third input enters in a Cobb-Douglas form:

$$Y = G(H(X_1, X_2), X_3),$$

with

$$G = A_0 H^\alpha X_3^{1-\alpha},$$

$$H = (cX_1^{-\rho} + (1 - c)X_2^{-\rho})^{-1/\rho},$$

where $0 < \alpha, c < 1$, $A_0 > 0$, and $-1 < \rho < \infty$, for $\rho \neq 0$. For the H function $A_{12} = A_{21} = F_{12} = F_{21} = 1/1 + \rho$. For the G function $F_{12} = F_{21} = 1/1 + \rho$ as before, but $A_{12} = A_{21} = 1 + \rho/\alpha(1 + \rho)$.

Now consider a function when X_1 and X_2 are in a transcendental logarithmic form while X_3 enters in a *CES* form:

$$Y = W(Z(X_1, X_2), X_3),$$

with

$$W = B_0(dZ^{-\rho} + (1 - d)X_3^{-\rho})^{-1/\rho},$$

$$Z = \exp\left[\ln A_0 + \beta \ln X_1 + (1 - \beta)\ln X_2 + \tfrac{1}{2}\delta(\ln X_1 - \ln X_2)^2\right].$$

Let $\eta \equiv \beta + \delta(\ln X_1 - \ln X_2)$ and $\varepsilon \equiv (1 - \beta) - \delta(\ln X_1 - \ln X_2)$. Then for Z

$$A_{12} = A_{21} = F_{12} = F_{21} = \frac{\eta\varepsilon}{\eta\varepsilon - \delta}.$$

On the other hand, for the W function

$$A_{12} = A_{21} = \frac{1}{(1 + \rho)(\eta\varepsilon - \delta)}$$

$$\left[(1 + \rho)\eta\varepsilon + \frac{1 - d}{d} Z^{+\rho} X_3^{-\rho}(+\rho\eta\varepsilon + \delta) \right],$$

but

$$F_{12} = F_{21} = \frac{\eta\varepsilon}{\eta\varepsilon - \delta}.$$

Notes

We express our gratitude to the National Science Foundation (Grant AER77-06507 ACI) for support of this research and to Ernst R. Berndt for helpful comments.

1. We adopt the covention that j, the second subscript, denotes the price that has changed.

2. Six years after initial publication the concept appeared in English in Kuga and Murota.

3. The asymmetry of F_{ij} and F_{ji} is the substance of Koizumi's paper. Murota proves that $F_{ij} = F_{ji}$ when there is complete strong separability of the production function. Blackorby and Russell extend Murota's result to n-dimensional nonhomothetic production functions.

4. This is true for all Hicks's (1970) conditions on computing an elasticity of subtitution. Hicks let all inputs change fully, subject to holding X_3/X_1 and output constant. See Kang and Brown. Mundlak also discussed the Hicksian elasticity of substitution for the many factor case.

5. Samuelson's (1968) n-dimensional generalization of Hicks's partial elasticity of substitution possesses the same property. That is $\partial k_i/\partial X_i \gtreqless 0$ if $1 \gtreqless -E_{ii}(1 - k_i)$. The last expression is Samuelson's definition of the partial elasticity of substitution.

6. The fact that F_{ij} is not symmetric ($F_{ij} \neq F_{ji}$ in general) should not deter us in making use of them. If a single value for substitutability between two inputs is desired, we perhaps can use $\bar{F}_{ij}$ which is an arithmetic mean of F_{ij} and F_{ji}.

II
**Problems Arising from
Recent Research**

Introduction to Part II

The three chapters in this section focus on important problems that have emerged out of recent empirical research on resource substitutability. Chapter 6 by David Stapleton contributes importantly to the interpretation of results from cross-section and time-series data. Specifically Stapleton carefully examines the oft-heard argument that cross-section data are likely to yield long-run elasticity estimates, while time-series data yield short-run elasticities. After examining this view analytically, Stapleton concludes that it is not always true and that in many cases both time-series and cross-section estimates will fall between short- and long-run elasticities.

In chapter 7 Richard Anderson argues that including intermediate inputs as factors of production is eminently sensible at the firm level but that at the industry level within-industry sales should be excluded, with only inter-industry sales considered as intermediate inputs. Anderson notes that substitution elasticity estimates are affected by this change in definition of output and intermediate input and that the alternative elasticity estimates correspond with different derivatives. Anderson thus reminds us that elasticity estimates must be interpreted carefully.

In chapter 8 Raymond Kopp and V. Kerry Smith address issues of aggregation over diverse inputs and technologies. Using data from a detailed process model of three technologies in the steel industry, Kopp-Smith optimize the model, given alternative prices, and then generate pseudodata which are used in estimating parameters of a neoclassical translog cost function. Kopp-Smith find that at the most disaggregated level the translog function provides a remarkably good description of each of the three technologies. When material inputs are aggregated, the translog loses some ability in describing input associations precisely, although it seldom generates incorrect input associations. Aggregation over diverse technologies, however, raises much greater difficulties. Kopp-Smith conclude by presenting tentative guidelines for using neoclassical models to estimate the features of production technologies.

6

Inferring Long-Term Substitution Possibilities from Cross-Section and Time-Series Data

David C. Stapleton

While it is commonplace to investigate production function characteristics by estimating factor demand equations (or transformations of these equations) derived under the assumption that relative factor prices are equated to relative marginal products, a well-known difficulty is that observed input levels may not reflect fully optimal input levels.[1] This would be the case, for instance, if some fixed inputs could not be immediately adjusted to their optimal values without incurring adjustment costs or if expected prices on which input decisions are based differ from realized prices. In either case, the firm can be expected to adjust inputs toward their long-run optimum values if its environment remains constant over a long period. To make any inferences about long-run elasticities of substitution and factor demands, their relation to observed short-run disequilibrium demands must be specified.[2]

It is often claimed that, if adjustment to long-run equilibrium is slow, estimates of demand function parameters based on cross-section data are likely to reflect long-run adjustments of inputs to changes in factor and output prices while estimates based on time-series data reflect only partial adjustments. This claim is frequently used to explain differences between estimates of demand functions using the two data types.[3] While I am uncertain of the origin of this claim, early statements of it are found in Edwin Kuh and John R. Meyer in the context of consumer demand and Kuh in the context of input demand.[4] Regarding cross-section data, Kuh makes the following argument:

Because disequilibrium among firms tends to be synchronized in response to common market forces and the business cycle, many disequilibrium effects wash out (or appear in the regression intercept) so that the higher cross-section slope estimates can be interpreted as long-run coefficients. The fully adjusted response will typically show a higher coefficient than an incompletely adjusted response. Since the cross-section data will also contain some short-run disturbances, however, these coefficients will only approximate fully adjusted long-run coefficients (p. 208).

Kuh also argues that cross-section data that are averages of time-series data for the individual cross-section observations are more likely to yield long-run estimates than data based on a single year. The argument is that if averages are taken over a period that is sufficiently long relative to the speed of adjustment, deviations around equilibrium values will be cancelled out in the averaging. This argument is also made by Hendrik Houthakker (1965). Both Kuh and Houthakker present evidence from pooled cross-section time-series data that coefficients from a single cross-section may vary considerably from values based on intertemporal averages. This seems to be ignored, however, in later claims about the consistency of cross-section estimates for long-run parameters.[5]

Kuh's argument regarding time-series estimates is:

Suppose that the explanatory variable operates according to a pattern of distributed lags:

(10) $I_t = a + b_0 x_t + b_1 x_{t-1} + \cdots + b_n x_{t-n} + c k_{t-1} + \varepsilon_t$

[I may be interpreted as investment, x as the price of capital and k as the capital stock]. If, for example, terms beyond b_0 are neglected, b_0, which represents only a part of the reaction, will be a small number compared to the total, long-run reaction coefficient. Least-square bias, which arises from high partial correlations between the excluded and included variables, should not ordinarily be large, since the x_{t-i} are likely to have almost equally strong simple correlations with x_t and k_{t-1} (p. 208).

My interpretation of this statement is that b_0 is the short-run effect of a change in price on investment and that a regression of investment on the lagged capital stock and the current price alone will result in estimates that are not substantially biased for b_0 and c, the coefficient of capital. However the reasoning behind the statement is unclear. First, why should the correlations of x_{t-i} with k_{t-1} and x_t be equal? Second, even if they were, why would this lead to small biases for both coefficients?[6]

Discussions of times-series analysis sometimes refer to detrended data or deviations of the first differences around their means (cf., Houthakker 1965). While correlations between the included and omitted variables will be smaller after removing trends, in general there are no grounds for expecting them to be zero.

Since the assumptions underlying the various claims of consistency are not clear, particularly regarding time-series estimates, the first objective of this chapter is to derive specific assumptions under which the claims will hold. This is done in the context of a model in which firms are assumed to minimize costs in every period subject to one factor being fixed, gradually adjusting to the unconstrained minimum over time. Assuming the resulting short-run factor demand equations hold for every observation, the consistency of estimates of the related long-run specifications are examined. After assumptions under which estimates will be consistent for long-run or short-run demand parameters are obtained, we consider whether the assumptions are likely to hold in cross-section or time-series data. It is concluded that while cross-section estimates are likely to be closer to long-run coefficients than time-series estimates, both are likely to be between the long- and short-run coefficients in many circumstances. Further an examination of the histories of factor prices may suggest the extent of the bias.

An obvious question is, If there is thought to be only incomplete adjustment, why not specify a model that allows for this? For instance in time series we might specify a long-run equation and then a Koyck adjustment mechanism that gives a relation that may be assumed to hold in every period. Alternatively we might specify a short-run equilibrium model, such as short-run profit maximization subject to fixed input constraints, which would hold in every period and from which long-run parameters could be inferred.

In fact there are numerous examples of the first type of specification in the time-series literature. Many are ad hoc, such as the Koyck mechanism, but more recently adjustments based on dynamic optimization models have been considered.[7] Very few examples of the second type of specification are to be found.[8] A difficulty is that data are often poor or unavailable. This is particularly a problem in single cross-sections, since dynamic adjustment mechanisms generally require data from more than one period. Frequently measures of fixed factors are not available or are poor, with capital service measures being a primary example. If such a problem arises, the question of consistency of estimates when long-run equations are specified becomes important.

The second objective of the chapter is to develop methods to deal with the problem of insufficient data. The approach is to consider estimation by unobserved variable techniques applied to the short-run equations from the cost minimization model previously mentioned, viewing the single fixed factor as being unobserved or measured with error. Recently substantial progress has been made in identifying and estimating linear models in which some variables are unobserved. Identification may often be achieved if the variables are imbedded in a system of equations; it is further facilitated by cross-equation restrictions on parameters in the system. Since usually many restrictions are imposed on demand systems, it seems likely that useful results will be obtained. The three examples considered in the chapter support this optimism.

6.1 A Cost Minimization Model with One Fixed Input

Consider a firm that is a price taker in input markets and operates under long-run constant returns to scale.[9] Assume that in a single period one input is fixed. Further assume that the firm takes output as being fixed and minimizes variable costs in each period, subject to the fixed output level, a production function constraint, and a fixed factor constraint. If the production function satisfies standard regularity conditions, solution of the short-run cost minimization problem will yield a variable cost function that will be linearly homogeneous, nondecreasing, and concave in variable input prices and nonincreasing and convex in the fixed factor. In the special case of constant returns to scale variable unit costs are a linearly homogeneous, nondecreasing, concave function of the variable input prices and a nonincreasing, convex function of the fixed factor-output ratio.[10] Hence the general specification of the variable unit cost function to be considered here is

$$c = g(\mathbf{p}, f), \tag{6.1}$$

where c is unit variable cost, $\mathbf{p}$ is the vector of prices for the variable inputs, and f is the input-output ratio for the fixed input. The properties of the function of interest are

i. $\partial g/\partial \mathbf{p} \geq \mathbf{0}$ (nondecreasing in variable input prices),

ii. $\partial g/\partial f \leq 0$ (nonincreasing in the fixed factor output ratio),

iii. $\mathbf{a}'(\partial^2 g/\partial \mathbf{p}\partial \mathbf{p})\,\mathbf{a} \leq 0$ for arbitrary vector $\mathbf{a}$ (concavity in variable input prices),

iv. $g(\lambda\mathbf{p}, f) = \lambda g(\mathbf{p}, f)$ for any scalar λ (linear homogeneity in variable prices),

v. $\partial^2 g/\partial f^2 > 0$ (convexity in the fixed factor-output ratio).

The short-run factor-output ratio for a variable input is the function of $\mathbf{p}$ and f given by the first partial derivative of the variable unit cost function with respect to the factor's price.[11] Letting $\mathbf{y}$ be the vector of short-run variable factor-output ratios, we obtain:

$$\mathbf{y} = \frac{\partial g}{\partial \mathbf{p}}(\mathbf{p}, f). \tag{6.2}$$

A quadratic approximation to the variable unit cost function will be considered henceforth. While this implies that unit costs are not homogeneous of degree one in prices, it greatly simplifies the analysis of specification error and the development of unobserved variable techniques. The problem is taken up again in the concluding section.

The quadratic unit cost function is

$$c = \theta + \boldsymbol{\mu}_p'\mathbf{p} + \mu_f f + \frac{1}{2}(\mathbf{p}'\mathbf{B}\mathbf{p} + \boldsymbol{\alpha}'\mathbf{p}f - \gamma^{-1}f^2). \qquad (6.3)$$

The parameter matrix $\mathbf{B}$ is symmetric and negative semidefinite to satisfy property iii, and γ is negative to satisfy property v.[12] The input-output ratios for the variable inputs are obtained from the first partial derivatives of (6.3) with respect to $\mathbf{p}$:

$$\mathbf{y} = \boldsymbol{\mu}_p + \mathbf{B}\mathbf{p} + \boldsymbol{\alpha} f. \qquad (6.4)$$

Hereafter the intercept vector, $\boldsymbol{\mu}_p$, will be suppressed on the assumption that the data are in deviation form. We also add on a disturbance vector, $\boldsymbol{\varepsilon}$, assumed to be independent of $\mathbf{p}$ and f and independent across observations:

$$\mathbf{y} = \mathbf{B}\mathbf{p} + \boldsymbol{\alpha} f + \boldsymbol{\varepsilon}. \qquad (6.5)$$

In general covariances among the elements of $\boldsymbol{\varepsilon}$ are not zero but constant across observations. The equations of (6.5) will hereafter be referred to as the short-run equations.

In the long run the firm chooses all factor-output ratios to minimize total cost. Long-run variable unit costs will be given by the short-run functions evaluated at the optimal fixed factor-output ratio. Hence the problem is to choose f to minimize

$$g(\mathbf{p}, f) + qf, \qquad (6.6)$$

where q is the rental price of the fixed factor. The first-order condition is

$$\frac{\partial g}{\partial f}(\mathbf{p}, f^*) = -q, \qquad (6.7)$$

where the star of f^* indicates the long-run optimal value. Apply condition (6.7) to the quadratic cost function to obtain (after suppressing the intercept):

$$f^* = \gamma\boldsymbol{\alpha}'\mathbf{p} + \gamma q. \qquad (6.8)$$

To complete the stochastic specification, we add on a disturbance, w, that is independent of $\mathbf{p}$, q, and ε; the reason for assuming independence of w and ε will become evident in the next section:

$$f^* = \gamma\boldsymbol{\alpha}'\mathbf{p} + \gamma q + w. \tag{6.9}$$

The long-run factor-output ratios for the variable factors are obtained by substitution of (6.9) into (6.5):

$$\mathbf{y}^* = (\mathbf{B} + \gamma\boldsymbol{\alpha}\boldsymbol{\alpha}')\mathbf{p} + \gamma\boldsymbol{\alpha} q + \boldsymbol{\varepsilon} + \boldsymbol{\alpha} w. \tag{6.10}$$

The equations of (6.10) will hereafter be called the long-run equations.

The long-run equations include only one coefficient parameter, γ, which does not appear in the short-run equations. Hence estimation of the short-run functions would tell us almost everything about the long-run functions. If the variable unit cost function were also included in the estimation procedure, an estimate of γ could be obtained. In fact, since the long-run functions are obtained by minimizing (6.6), they can be derived at least implicitly for any choice of functional form. This illustrates a statement made in the introduction: in general, if adjustment is slow, a fully specified and estimated short-run equilibrium model will yield all of the information required for the long run. While this proposition is by no means new, it does not seem to be fully appreciated in the literature.

The symmetric coefficient matrix of $\mathbf{p}$ in the long-run equations has two components: $\mathbf{B}$ indicates the effect on $\mathbf{y}$ of a change in $\mathbf{p}$, holding f fixed, and $\gamma\boldsymbol{\alpha}\boldsymbol{\alpha}'$ indicates the additional effect when f is allowed to adjust optimally. The diagonal elements of $\mathbf{B}$ are nonpositive by property iii of the variable unit cost function. Further $\gamma < 0$ by property v while the diagonals of $\boldsymbol{\alpha}\boldsymbol{\alpha}'$ are necessarily nonnegative. Hence the own price coefficients in the long-run equations are no smaller in absolute value than the same coefficients in the short run. This important property is not a result of the assumed linearity; rather it reflects the general Le Chatelier principle.[13]

To investigate the effect of mistakenly specifying the long-run variable factor-output functions using data that do not represent long-run equilibria, it is necessary to specify the short-run relation between the fixed factor and all factor prices. As a first step toward this end a Koyck adjustment scheme is specified for the fixed factor-output ratio. Specification of an adjustment process will also aid identification when the fixed factor is unobserved. Letting d be the one-period change in the fixed factor, we specify

$$d = f - f_{-1} = (1 - \lambda)(f^* - f_{-1}), \quad 0 \le \lambda < 1. \tag{6.11}$$

Upon substitution for f^* from (6.8), (6.10) becomes

$$d = (1 - \lambda)\gamma\boldsymbol{\alpha}'\mathbf{p} + (1 - \lambda)\gamma q - (1 - \lambda)f_{-1} + (1 - \lambda)w. \tag{6.12}$$

The reason for assuming independence of w and ε is now evident: w in part determines f, which has previously been assumed to be independent of ε. The latter assumption would be violated if w and ε were not independent. As a consequence of the assumption f may be treated as exogenous in the short-run factor-output equations when analyzing consistency.

6.2 Consistency of Least Squares When the Long-Run Equations Are Specified

In this section conditions under which unrestricted least squares estimation of the long-run variable input-output equations (6.10) yield consistent estimates of long-run parameters are considered.[14] Estimates will clearly be consistent if observed values of $\mathbf{y}^*$ and f are long-run equilibrium values or deviate from long-run equilibrium values by random errors that are independent of $\mathbf{p}$ and f. However, can less stringent conditions be considered, and are these likely to hold in cross-section data? Further are there conditions under which the estimated coefficients of $\mathbf{p}$ will be consistent for the short-run coefficients? Are these conditions likely to hold in time-series data? Throughout it is assumed that the data satisfy the short-run demand equations, that regressions of $\mathbf{y}$ on $\mathbf{p}$ and f would yield consistent estimates of $\mathbf{B}$ and $\boldsymbol{\alpha}$. The analysis generalizes and extends some results on consistency of cross-section estimates derived by Jan Kmenta in the context of a single-equation, single independent variable model.

First, rewrite the long- and short-run demand equations as

$$\mathbf{y}^* = (\mathbf{B} + \gamma\boldsymbol{\alpha}\boldsymbol{\alpha}' ; \gamma\boldsymbol{\alpha})\left(\frac{\mathbf{p}}{q}\right) + \varepsilon + \boldsymbol{\alpha}w = \Pi_L\tilde{\mathbf{p}} + \tilde{\varepsilon}, \tag{6.13}$$

$$\mathbf{y} = (\mathbf{B}; 0)\left(\frac{\mathbf{p}}{q}\right) + \boldsymbol{\alpha}f + \varepsilon = \Pi_S\mathbf{p} + \boldsymbol{\alpha}f + \varepsilon, \tag{6.14}$$

where $\Pi_L = (\mathbf{B} + \gamma\boldsymbol{\alpha}\boldsymbol{\alpha}' ; \gamma\boldsymbol{\alpha})$, $\tilde{\mathbf{p}}' = (\mathbf{p}'q)$, $\tilde{\varepsilon} = \varepsilon + \boldsymbol{\alpha}w$, and $\Pi_S = (\mathbf{B}; 0)$. Then Π_L and Π_S are the long- and short-run parameters.

Let Π be the probability limit of the matrix of coefficients from the regression of $\mathbf{y}$ on $\tilde{\mathbf{p}}$. Since the data satisfy the short-run equations, Π will always be given by

$$\Pi = \Pi_S + \boldsymbol{\alpha}\delta', \tag{6.15}$$

where $\boldsymbol{\delta}$ is the probability limit of the vector of coefficients obtained by regressing f on $\tilde{\mathbf{p}}$. This is obtained by noting that $\boldsymbol{\Pi}_S$ is the coefficient matrix of $\tilde{\mathbf{p}}$ in the short-run equations while $\boldsymbol{\alpha}$ is the coefficient vector of f and applying the usual omitted variable formula, where the omitted variable is f.[15]

A sufficient condition for consistency of both time-series and cross-section estimates for the long-run coefficients (as well as the short-run coefficients) is that the variable input-output ratios are independent of the fixed input-output ratios in the short run. That is, if $\boldsymbol{\alpha} = \mathbf{0}, \boldsymbol{\Pi} = \boldsymbol{\Pi}_L = \boldsymbol{\Pi}_S$. This also implies that the long-run cross-price elasticities between the fixed and variable inputs are zero, since the coefficient vector of the fixed input's price in the long-run equation is $\gamma \dot{\boldsymbol{\alpha}}$.

If $\boldsymbol{\alpha} \neq \mathbf{0}$, the question of consistency is reduced to evaluation of $\boldsymbol{\delta}$. Letting $\boldsymbol{\alpha}'$ denote $(\gamma \boldsymbol{\alpha}' ; \gamma)$, if $\boldsymbol{\delta} = \tilde{\boldsymbol{\alpha}}$, then $\boldsymbol{\Pi} = \boldsymbol{\Pi}_L$, while if $\boldsymbol{\delta} = \mathbf{0}, \boldsymbol{\Pi} = \boldsymbol{\Pi}_S$; that is, $\boldsymbol{\delta} = \tilde{\boldsymbol{\alpha}}$ implies consistency for long-run parameters, and $\boldsymbol{\delta} = \mathbf{0}$ implies consistency for short-run parameters.

To draw any conclusions, a relationship between f and $\tilde{\mathbf{p}}$ that always holds must be developed. One way to do this is to specify an adjustment process. Here it will be assumed that the Koyck adjustment equation (6.11) holds. Solve (6.11) for f, and substitute for f^* from (6.8) to obtain:

$$f = (1 - \lambda)\boldsymbol{\alpha}'\tilde{\mathbf{p}} + \lambda f_{-1} + (1 - \lambda)w. \tag{6.16}$$

Note that equation (6.16) implies that f is not entirely fixed in the short run; that is, current prices affect current f, although adjustment to long-run equilibrium is only partial. For this reason a second set of short-run coefficients are specified; these include the direct effects of current prices on $\mathbf{y}, \boldsymbol{\Pi}_S$, as well as the indirect effects due to their effect on current f. The indirect effects are given by the product of the coefficient vector of f in the short-run equations (6.14) and the coefficient vector of $\tilde{\mathbf{p}}$ in the adjustment equation (6.16). Let $\boldsymbol{\Pi}_S^\circ$ denote the second set of short-run parameters; then $\boldsymbol{\Pi}_S^\circ = \boldsymbol{\Pi}_S + (1 - \lambda)\boldsymbol{\alpha}\tilde{\boldsymbol{\alpha}}'$. If $\boldsymbol{\delta} = (1 - \lambda)$, $\boldsymbol{\Pi} = \boldsymbol{\Pi}_S^\circ$, so that estimates will be consistent for the second type of short-run coefficients,

$$f = (1 - \lambda) \sum_{t=0}^{\tau} \lambda^t \tilde{\boldsymbol{\alpha}}'\tilde{\mathbf{p}}_{-t} + (1 - \lambda) \sum_{t=0}^{\tau} \lambda^t w_{-t}. \tag{6.17}$$

where τ is sufficiently large so that for practical purposes $\lambda^\tau = 0$. The smaller is λ (the faster is the adjustment), the smaller is τ. The only difference between (6.17) and Kmenta's equation 30 is that he considers just one explanatory variable.

It is clear from (6.17) that $\boldsymbol{\delta}$ will depend upon the history of $\tilde{\mathbf{p}}$ at each observation for the previous τ periods. We now evaluate $\boldsymbol{\delta}$ under three different assumptions about the history of $\tilde{\mathbf{p}}$ at each observation.

First is an equal price change assumption: suppose that changes in $\tilde{\mathbf{p}}$ were equal across observations for the previous τ periods. Then

$$\tilde{\mathbf{p}}^i - \tilde{\mathbf{p}}^i_{-t} = \Delta \tilde{\mathbf{p}}_{-t} \tag{6.18}$$

for all $i, t = 1, \ldots, \tau$, where the superscript i indicates the ith observation. Substitution of (6.18) into (6.17), including for the moment the observational superscript, yields

$$f^i = \tilde{\boldsymbol{\alpha}}' \tilde{\mathbf{p}}^i - (1 - \lambda) \sum_{t=0}^{\tau} \lambda^t \tilde{\boldsymbol{\alpha}}' \Delta \tilde{\mathbf{p}}_{-t} + \tilde{w}^i, \tag{6.19}$$

where $\tilde{w}^i = (1 - \lambda) \sum_{t=0}^{\tau} \lambda^t w^i_{-t}.$

Since the term following the first sum sign is constant across observations, it will only affect the constant in the regression of f on $\tilde{\mathbf{p}}$. Hence $\boldsymbol{\delta} = \tilde{\boldsymbol{\alpha}}$ and $\boldsymbol{\Pi} = \boldsymbol{\Pi}_L$; in other words, consistency for long-run parameters is obtained. This is a generalization of the following result due to Kmenta: when there is no change in $\tilde{\mathbf{p}}$ for the previous τ periods for any observation, estimates will be consistent for long-run parameters.

If conditions (6.18) were to hold for time-series data, they would imply that the change in price was the same in every period, since periods and observations would then be synonymous. The observation matrix for prices would have only two independent rows, and any attempt at estimation would be foolish. If changes in prices deviated randomly from constant changes, estimation would be possible, but high collinearity in the prices would lead to very imprecise estimates.

In cross-section data the conditions might hold without ruling out substantial independent variation in price levels. This may be what Kuh had in mind—deviations from equilibrium are constant across observations. How plausible in general are conditions (6.18) for cross-section data? If data pertain to firms or geographical units within a country, they might sometimes be reasonable. Frequently prices vary geographically, but over time changes in prices in different regions may reflect changes in supply that affect prices in all regions equally. If the unit of observation is a country, the assumption might be less plausible since barriers to trade cause different changes in different countries (for instance, recent OPEC price hikes have had much less effect on oil prices in Canada than in the United States). Of course the plausibility of (6.18) in cross-section data will depend on the particular situation. However, time series of at least some prices for each or many observations are likely to be available, so that the conditions may be partially checked.

The second assumption to be made about the history of $\tilde{\mathbf{p}}$ will be referred to as the independent prices assumption. Specifically we assume that current prices at all observations are independent of lagged prices at all observations and also that lagged prices are independent across observations. According to (6.17), $\tilde{\mathbf{p}}_{-t}$ and w_{-t}, $t = 1 \cdots \tau + 1$ totally determine f_{-1}. Hence in (6.16) the term $(\lambda f_{-1} + (1 - \lambda)w)$ may be viewed as a random error, and a regression of f on $\tilde{\mathbf{p}}$ yields estimates that are consistent for $\boldsymbol{\delta} = (1 - \lambda)$. Consequently $\boldsymbol{\Pi} = \boldsymbol{\Pi}_S^\circ$, so that consistency for the second type of short-run parameters is obtained.

While price independence could hold in either time-series or cross-section data, most price data indicate that this is not the case. Correlations between current and lagged prices are frequently high in time-series data, while in cross-section data we expect prices across observations to move together over time (although imperfectly).

The third assumption to be made is that $\tilde{\mathbf{p}}$ is generated by a first-order multivariate autoregressive process with the same autoregressive parameter matrix, $\mathbf{R}$, for all observations:

$$\tilde{\mathbf{p}}^i = \mathbf{R}\tilde{\mathbf{p}}_{-1} + \boldsymbol{\xi}^i, \tag{6.20}$$

where the disturbances, $\boldsymbol{\xi}^i$, have zero expectation, may differ across observations, and also may have a different covariance matrix across observations but not over time. In general we shall denote $E(\mathbf{x}\mathbf{y}')$ by $\mathbf{C}_{xy}$, where $\mathbf{x}$ and $\mathbf{y}$ are any random vectors with zero means. Hence $\boldsymbol{\delta}$ may be written as

$$\boldsymbol{\delta} = \mathbf{C}_{\tilde{p}\tilde{p}}^{-1}\mathbf{C}_{\tilde{p}f}. \tag{6.21}$$

Further, using (6.17), $\mathbf{C}_{\tilde{p}f}$ can be written as

$$\mathbf{C}_{\tilde{p}f} = 1 - \lambda \sum_{t=0}^{\tau} \lambda^t \mathbf{C}_{\tilde{p}\tilde{p}_{-t}}\tilde{\boldsymbol{\alpha}}. \tag{6.22}$$

Substitution of (6.22) into (6.21) gives

$$\boldsymbol{\delta} = (1 - \lambda) \sum_{t=0}^{\tau} \lambda^t \mathbf{C}_{\tilde{p}\tilde{p}}^{-1}\mathbf{C}_{\tilde{p}\tilde{p}_{-t}}\tilde{\boldsymbol{\alpha}}. \tag{6.23}$$

Under the autoregressive assumptions described here $\mathbf{C}_{\tilde{p}\tilde{p}}^{-1}\mathbf{C}_{\tilde{p}\tilde{p}_{-t}} = \mathbf{R}^t$ for $t = 0 \cdots \tau$, where $\mathbf{R}^t$ denotes that $\mathbf{R}$ has been multiplied by itself t times and $\mathbf{R}^\circ = \mathbf{I}$.[16] Hence (6.23) becomes

$$\delta = (1 - \lambda) \sum_{t=0}^{\tau} (\lambda \mathbf{R})^t \tilde{\mathbf{a}} = (1 - \lambda)(\mathbf{I} - \lambda \mathbf{R})^{-1} \tilde{\mathbf{a}}. \tag{6.24}$$

Equation (6.24) specializes to Kmenta's equation 39 when $\mathbf{R}$ is a scalar. From (6.15) and (6.24)

$$\boldsymbol{\Pi} = \boldsymbol{\Pi}_S + (1 - \lambda)\mathbf{a}\tilde{\mathbf{a}}'(\mathbf{I} - \lambda \mathbf{R})^{-1}. \tag{6.25}$$

In general $\boldsymbol{\Pi}$ will not equal $\boldsymbol{\Pi}_S$, $\boldsymbol{\Pi}_S^{\circ}$, or $\boldsymbol{\Pi}_L$, and the direction of the difference is uncertain. However, the following special case is suggestive.

Suppose that $\mathbf{R} = \rho \mathbf{I}$; that is, the own price autoregressive parameters are all equal, and the other price parameters are zero. Then (6.24) becomes

$$\delta = \frac{(1 - \lambda)}{(1 - \rho \lambda)} \tilde{\mathbf{a}}. \tag{6.26}$$

As λ increases (adjustment becomes slower), the difference between δ and $\tilde{\mathbf{a}}$ increases; as ρ increases, the difference decreases. Substitute $\mathbf{R} = \rho \mathbf{I}$ into (6.25) to obtain

$$\boldsymbol{\Pi} = \boldsymbol{\Pi}_S + \frac{(1 - \lambda)}{(1 - \lambda \rho)} \mathbf{a}\mathbf{a}' \tag{6.27}$$

$$= \left(\mathbf{B} + \frac{(1 - \lambda)}{(1 - \lambda \rho)} \gamma \mathbf{a}\tilde{\mathbf{a}}'; \; \frac{(1 - \lambda)}{(1 - \lambda \rho)} \gamma \mathbf{a} \right).$$

For comparison purposes we reproduce the structure of $\boldsymbol{\Pi}_S$, $\boldsymbol{\Pi}_S^{\circ}$, and $\boldsymbol{\Pi}_L$:

$$\boldsymbol{\Pi}_S = (\mathbf{B}; \mathbf{0}), \tag{6.28}$$

$$\boldsymbol{\Pi}_S^{\circ} = \boldsymbol{\Pi}_S + (1 - \lambda)\mathbf{a}\tilde{\mathbf{a}}' = (\mathbf{B} + (1 - \lambda)\gamma \mathbf{a}\tilde{\mathbf{a}}'; (1 - \lambda)\gamma \mathbf{a}), \tag{6.29}$$

$$\boldsymbol{\Pi}_L = (\mathbf{B} + \gamma \mathbf{a}\tilde{\mathbf{a}}'; \gamma \mathbf{a}). \tag{6.30}$$

Consider the coefficients of $\mathbf{p}$, that is, all but the last column of $\boldsymbol{\Pi}$. Recall that the diagonal elements of both $\mathbf{B}$ and $\gamma \mathbf{a}\mathbf{a}'$ are nonpositive. For (6.27) through (6.29) the ith diagonal elements are

$$\pi_{ii} = \beta_{ii} + \frac{(1 - \lambda)}{(1 - \lambda \rho)} \gamma \alpha_i^2, \tag{6.31}$$

$$\pi_{ii}^S = \beta_{ii}, \tag{6.32}$$

$$\pi_{ii}^{S\circ} = \beta_{ii} + (1 - \lambda)\gamma \alpha_i^2, \tag{6.33}$$

$$\pi_{ii}^L = \beta_{ii} + \gamma \alpha_i^2. \tag{6.34}$$

Assuming $0 \le \rho \le 1$, we get

$$\pi_{ii}^L \le \pi_{ii} \le \pi_{ii}^{S^\circ} \le \pi_{ii}^S \le 0, \tag{6.35}$$

with $\pi_{ii} = \pi_{ii}^{S^\circ}$ when $\rho = 0$ and $\pi_{ii} = \pi_{ii}^L$ when $\rho = 1$. In words, the own price coefficients will be between the short- and long-run coefficients. In the case of no autocorrelation consistency for the second type of short-run coefficients is obtained. When autocorrelation is extreme ($\mathbf{R} = 1$), consistency for long-run parameters is obtained. This is a generalization of the no change in exogenous variables result of Kmenta.[17]

The inequalities of (6.35) will also hold if $\mathbf{R}$ is assumed to be diagonal with unequal diagonal elements, since equation (6.31) would not change except for the addition of the subscript i to ρ. This introduces the possibility that some parameters may be close to short-run values, while others are close to long-run values.

The typical element of the last column of $\mathbf{\Pi}$ will lie between the typical element of the last column of $\mathbf{\Pi}_L$ and the typical element of the last column of $\mathbf{\Pi}_S^\circ$. With no autocorrelation it will equal the corresponding element in $\mathbf{\Pi}_S^\circ$, and with $\mathbf{R} = \mathbf{I}$ it will equal the corresponding element in $\mathbf{\Pi}_L$. Again the result generalizes straightforwardly to the case of diagonal $\mathbf{R}$.

While the results cannot be generalized to the case of a full autocorrelation matrix, this analysis suggests that results will be closer to long-run coefficients the closer the eigenvalues of $\mathbf{R}$ are to unity; eigenvalues of unity correspond to the $\mathbf{R} = \mathbf{I}$ case, while eigenvalues of zero correspond to $\mathbf{R} = 0$.

As noted at the beginning of this chapter, sometimes the claim that time-series estimates are consistent for short-run parameters is made in the context of using data with trends removed. Suppose we want to include a time trend in the demand equations, say, to capture technological change. The results given here still apply once $\mathbf{y}$, $\mathbf{p}$, q, and d are redefined as deviations from their means. Detrended prices are probably less autocorrelated than original prices, so that time-series estimates will be closer to the second type of short-run parameter values when the trends are removed than when they are not. The same applies to using deviations of first differences of prices around their mean first differences; in fact the autocorrelation matrix for this transformation of prices will be identical to the autocorrelation matrix for detrended prices. Of course using detrended prices or deviations from mean first differences is not applicable to cross-section studies.

Consistency for the short-run coefficients, as originally defined, has not been found under any of the price history assumptions considered.

The reason for this is clear: the adjustment mechanism implies that f is not completely fixed in the short run, and it is inappropriate to treat f as a predetermined variable. If f really does partially adjust in the current period, probably the second type of short-run parameters will be of more interest to the policy maker than the first—if short run parameters are of interest at all. For the remainder of this section short-run parameters refer to the second type of short-run parameters.

In summary of the results of this section, we first found a special case in which both time-series and cross-section estimates of the long-run variable input-output equations are consistent for the long-run coefficients even if there are substantial adjustment lags: when the short-run variable input-output ratios are independent of the fixed input-output ratio, so that long-run cross-price elasticities between the fixed and variable inputs are zero. Otherwise consistency depends on the history of all input prices at all observations. For cross-section data an assumption of equal price changes across observations for a sufficient number of previous periods leads to consistency for the long-run coefficients. For time-series data estimates will be consistent for short-run coefficients if prices are independent over time. The set of short-run coefficients referred to includes the indirect effect of price changes on variable input demands through partial (one-period) adjustment of the fixed factor. For cross-section data, if prices are independent across observations as well as over time, the same result is obtained. However, it is not probable that such conditions will hold in either cross-section or time-series data. Finally, analysis of the model under the assumption that prices are generated by a first-order autoregressive process suggests that with both types of data, estimates of own price elasticities for the variable inputs and cross-price elasticities between the variable and fixed inputs will generally be between the long- and short-run elasticities.

We conclude that claims of consistency of time-series estimates for short-run parameters or of cross-section estimates for long-run parameters should be regarded with skepticism unless they are substantiated by an examination of price histories. Such an examination may be useful when the researcher is faced with the problem of interpreting previous work. Of course the best solution to estimating parameters of a model in which there is believed to be slow adjustment to long-run equilibrium is to model and estimate the adjustment process explicitly. Assumptions such as those in this section should be invoked to justify estimation of the unmodified long-run specification only as a last resort.

6.3 Estimation When the Fixed Factor Is Unobserved

We now investigate estimation of the model when the fixed factor, f, is unobserved. It is again assumed that the short-run equations hold at every observation.

Estimation procedures for linear models with unobserved variables are well known.[18] However, before they can be applied, it must be determined if the parameters of the model are identified in terms of the population covariance matrix of the observed variables. Estimation then proceeds by various methods of fitting the structure of the population covariance matrix to the sample covariance matrix. Hence all that we need to be concerned with here is the question of identification.

Identification is considered in three situations. In the first, only data on the variable factor-output ratios and variable factor prices are available. In the second, an unbiased, but error-contaminated, measure of the fixed factor is also used. In the third, the current change in the fixed factor (such as net investment) and the price of the fixed factor are observed. Throughout it is maintained that $\mathbf{B}$, the matrix of short-run variable input price coefficients, is symmetric and negative semidefinite.[19]

Variable Factors and Their Prices Observed

Suppose that $\mathbf{y}$ and $\mathbf{p}$ are observed. We ask, Are the model's parameters identified in terms of the population covariance matrices for $\mathbf{y}$ and $\mathbf{p}$, namely, $\mathbf{C}_{yy}$, $\mathbf{C}_{yp}$, and $\mathbf{C}_{pp}$?[20] Since equation (6.4) is assumed to hold at every observation, the structures of $\mathbf{C}_{yy}$ and $\mathbf{C}_{yp}$ are

$$\mathbf{C}_{yy} = \mathbf{B}\mathbf{C}_{pp}\mathbf{B} + \alpha\mathbf{C}_{fp}\mathbf{B} + \mathbf{B}\mathbf{C}_{pf}\alpha' + \alpha\mathbf{C}_{ff}\alpha' + \mathbf{C}_{\varepsilon\varepsilon}, \tag{6.36}$$

$$\mathbf{C}_{yp} = \mathbf{B}\mathbf{C}_{pp} + \alpha\mathbf{C}_{fp}. \tag{6.37}$$

(Note that $\mathbf{C}_{fp}$ is a row vector, $\mathbf{C}_{pf}$ is its transpose, and $\mathbf{C}_{ff}$ is a scalar). The short-run parameters will be identified if these equations can be solved for the unknown parameters: $\mathbf{B}$, α, $\mathbf{C}_{ff}$, $\mathbf{C}_{pf}$, and $\mathbf{C}_{\varepsilon\varepsilon}$. Recall that the covariance matrix for ε, here $\mathbf{C}_{\varepsilon\varepsilon}$, was originally assumed to be full. Hence at best equation (6.36) can only be used to identify $\mathbf{C}_{\varepsilon\varepsilon}$ if the remaining parameters can be identified using (6.37). However, since $\mathbf{C}_{ff}$ does not appear in (6.37), this is impossible. Nevertheless, it may be possible to identify $\mathbf{B}$, α, and $\mathbf{C}_{fp}$ from (6.37) since they involve $L(L + 1)/2 + 2L$ parameters compared to L^2 equations, where L is the number of variable inputs; for $L \geq 5$ the number of parameters is no greater than the number of equations. Unfortunately this is only a necessary condition. In fact without further restrictions on the parameters they will not be identified. This can be shown by looking at transformations of the parameters that will leave the structure of $\mathbf{C}_{yp}$ unchanged. There are three such transformations.

First, let $\boldsymbol{\alpha}^* = k\boldsymbol{\alpha}$ and $f^* = f/k$, where k is an arbitrary scalar. This transforms the model to

$$y = \mathbf{B}p + \boldsymbol{\alpha}^*f^* + \varepsilon, \tag{6.38}$$

and $\mathbf{C}_{yp}$ becomes

$$\mathbf{C}_{yp} = \mathbf{B}\mathbf{C}_{pp} + \boldsymbol{\alpha}^*\mathbf{C}_{fp}^*, \tag{6.39}$$

where $\mathbf{C}_{fp}^* = \mathbf{C}_{fp}^*/k$ which has the same structure as (6.37). This problem is well known in the unobserved variables literature and arises because the scale of the unobserved variable may be chosen arbitrarily.

Next let $\mathbf{B}^* = \mathbf{B} + k\boldsymbol{\alpha}\boldsymbol{\alpha}'$ and $f^* = f - k\boldsymbol{\alpha}'p$. Note that $\mathbf{B}^*$, like $\mathbf{B}$, will be symmetric and that for small enough k it will also be negative semidefinite. Now the model becomes

$$y = \mathbf{B}^*p + \boldsymbol{\alpha}f^* + \varepsilon, \tag{6.40}$$

and $\mathbf{C}_{yp}$ is given by

$$\mathbf{C}_{yp} = \mathbf{B}^*\mathbf{C}_{pp} + \boldsymbol{\alpha}\mathbf{C}_{fp}^*, \tag{6.41}$$

where $\mathbf{C}_{fp}^* = \mathbf{C}_{fp} - k\boldsymbol{\alpha}'\mathbf{C}_{pp}$ and the structure of (6.41) is identical to that of (6.37).

Finally, let $\boldsymbol{\theta}$ be the coefficients from the population regression of f on p; hence $\boldsymbol{\theta} = \mathbf{C}_{pp}^{-1}\mathbf{C}_{pf}$. Let ω be the disturbances in the population regression model; that is, $f = \boldsymbol{\theta}'p + \omega$, where ω is independent of p and has zero expectation. Let $\mathbf{B}^* = \mathbf{B} + k\boldsymbol{\theta}\boldsymbol{\theta}'$, $\boldsymbol{\alpha}^* = \boldsymbol{\alpha} - k\boldsymbol{\theta}$ and $\varepsilon^* = \varepsilon + k\boldsymbol{\theta}\omega$. Again $\mathbf{B}^*$ will be symmetric, and for small enough k, negative semidefinite. Then the model becomes

$$y = \mathbf{B}^*p + \boldsymbol{\alpha}^*f + \varepsilon^*, \tag{6.42}$$

and $\mathbf{C}_{yp}$ is given by

$$\mathbf{C}_{yp} = \mathbf{B}^*\mathbf{C}_{pp} + \boldsymbol{\alpha}^*\mathbf{C}_{fp} \tag{6.43}$$

and has the same structure as (6.37) Note that the disturbance of the transformed model is not independent of f, so that the assumptions of the transformed model are different from the original model. However, this only affects the structure of $\mathbf{C}_{yy}$, since $\mathbf{C}_{yy}$ provides no information with $\mathbf{C}_{\varepsilon\varepsilon}$ and $\mathbf{C}_{ff}$ unrestricted, the change in structure is irrelevant.

It is possible that economic theory or a priori information will suggest additional restrictions on **B**, **α**, and $\mathbf{C}_{fp}$ (besides the symmetry restrictions on **B**) that will remove these three sources of underidentification. However, in the absence of that, various arbitrary restrictions might be considered. Two such arbitrary restrictions, which will reduce the number of remaining restrictions necessary to one, will now be introduced.

First, solve (6.37) for $\mathbf{BC}_{pp}$ in terms of $\mathbf{C}_{yp}$, **α**, and $\mathbf{C}_{fp}$ and substitute into (6.36) to get

$$\mathbf{C}_{yy} = \mathbf{C}_{yp}\mathbf{C}_{pp}^{-1}\mathbf{C}_{py} + \mathbf{\alpha}(\mathbf{C}_{ff} - \mathbf{C}_{fp}\mathbf{C}_{pp}^{-1}\mathbf{C}_{pf})\mathbf{\alpha}' + \mathbf{C}_{\varepsilon\varepsilon}. \tag{6.44}$$

Now let the variance matrix of **y** after partialing out **p** be denoted by $\mathbf{C}_{yy\cdot p} = \mathbf{C}_{yy} - \mathbf{C}_{yp}\mathbf{C}_{pp}^{-1}\mathbf{C}_{py}$, and let the variance of f after partialing out **p** be denoted by $\mathbf{C}_{ff\cdot p} = \mathbf{C}_{ff} - \mathbf{C}_{fp}\mathbf{C}_{pp}^{-1}\mathbf{C}_{pf}$. Then (6.44) reduces to:

$$\mathbf{C}_{yy\cdot p} = \mathbf{\alpha}\mathbf{C}_{ff\cdot p}\mathbf{\alpha}' + \mathbf{C}_{\varepsilon\varepsilon}. \tag{6.45}$$

Now assume that $\mathbf{C}_{ff\cdot p} = 1$ and that $\mathbf{C}_{\varepsilon\varepsilon}$ is diagonal. Under these assumptions the reader familiar with factor analysis will recognize the right-handside of (6.45) as the usual structure of the variance matrix of the observed variables from and single-factor model, factor being the term used for the unobserved variable.[21] Here the factor is the fixed factor of production while the left-hand side differs from the variance matrix of the observed variables only in that **p** has been partialed out, and, since **p** is observed, this matrix is estimable. The first assumption, $\mathbf{C}_{ff\cdot p} = 1$, is a normalization, as is usually necessary in factor analysis to fix arbitrarily the scale of the unobserved variable, eliminating the first type of transformation considered here. The assumption that $\mathbf{C}_{\varepsilon\varepsilon}$ is diagonal in words is that the covariation remaining among the elements of **y** after controlling for **p** is entirely due to the unobserved factor. The single-factor model is just identified when there are three observed variables and is overidentified for more observed variables. Hence, if there are three or more variable inputs, **α** and the diagonal elements of $\mathbf{C}_{\varepsilon\varepsilon}$ can be identified from (6.45) once the restrictions are imposed.[22]

The restrictions on $\mathbf{C}_{\varepsilon\varepsilon}$ may be implausible for factor demand equations. If a disturbance in one equation is unusually large, the corresponding factor is overutilized for the given prices, and, if the firm is operating efficiently, some other factor or factors must be underutilized. Hence some negative covariance might be expected. A weaker assumption that will still allow **α** to be identified with four or more variable inputs is that the off-diagonal elements of $\mathbf{C}_{\varepsilon\varepsilon}$ are all equal.[23]

The normalization and the restrictions on $\mathbf{C}_{\varepsilon\varepsilon}$ rule out the first and third transformation types considered here since both involve transforming **α**, which is now determined. However, identification of **B** and $\mathbf{C}_{fp}$ from $\mathbf{C}_{yp}$, with **α** known, is still not possible since the second type of transformation preserves the structure of $\mathbf{C}_{yp}$ in equation (6.37) without transforming **α**. One more restriction on **B** or $\mathbf{C}_{fp}$ will eliminate this. For instance, we could restrict two diagonal elements of **B** to be equal or an off-diagonal element to be zero. Alternatively a single element of $\mathbf{C}_{fp}$ could be fixed at zero. Any of these will choose a particular transformation of f^* and eliminate the problem. The transformation chosen may be arbitrary, but perhaps theory will suggest one that is not, by providing restrictions on **B**.

It will be useful later on to put this result regarding the solution of equation (6.37) for **B** and $\mathbf{C}_{fp}$ with **α** known in a general form. Consider

$$\mathbf{A} = \mathbf{XC} + \mathbf{dy}', \tag{6.46}$$

where **A** is a known $n \times n$ matrix, **X** is an unknown $n \times n$ symmetric matrix, **C** is a known $n \times n$ matrix, **d** is a known vector of length **n**, and **y** is an unknown vector of length n. There will be a unique solution for **X** and **y** if there is at least one additional independent relation among the elements of **X** and **y**.

In summary the short-run parameters can be estimated when only **y** and **p** are observed provided that

1. an arbitrary scale for the unobserved variable is chosen (by fixing $\mathbf{C}_{ff \cdot p}$ or an element of **α**),
2. sufficient restrictions are put on $\mathbf{C}_{\varepsilon\varepsilon}$ to identify **α** (for $L = 3$, $\mathbf{C}_{\varepsilon\varepsilon}$ diagonal is sufficient, and for $L = 4$ equality of the off-diagonal elements is sufficient),
3. at least one additional independent relation among the elements of **B** and $\mathbf{C}_{fp}$ is specified.

While these conditions are sufficient for identification, they are not necessary; additional restrictions on **B**, **α**, and $\mathbf{C}_{fp}$ may permit identification without them.[24]

Fixed Factor Measured with Error
Suppose that, in addition to observing **y** and **p**, an unbiased measure of f, z, is available with the measurement error in z, v, being independent of **p** and **ε**:

$$z = f + v. \tag{6.47}$$

Then

$$\mathbf{C}_{zp} = \mathbf{C}_{fp}. \tag{6.48}$$

This rules out the first and second type of transformation considered here since both transformations involve transformations of $\mathbf{C}_{fp}$, which is now determined by $\mathbf{C}_{zp}$. The third transformation is also ruled out since

$$\mathbf{C}_{yz} = \mathbf{BC}_{pf} + \mathbf{C}_{ff}. \tag{6.49}$$

Under the third transformation the transformed disturbances, $\boldsymbol{\varepsilon}^*$, would have nonzero covariances with the transformed factor, and this covariance would appear in (6.49). If $\mathbf{C}_{fp}$ is known, and $L \geq 2$, equations (6.37) and (6.49) can be solved for $\boldsymbol{\alpha}$, $\mathbf{B}$, and $\mathbf{C}_{ff}$. To see this, first consider (6.37) alone. Postmultiply (6.37) by $\mathbf{C}_{pp}^{-1}$, transpose the result, and replace $\mathbf{C}_{pf}$ with $\mathbf{C}_{pz}$ to get

$$\mathbf{C}_{pp}^{-1}\mathbf{C}_{py} = \mathbf{B} + \mathbf{C}_{pp}^{-1}\mathbf{C}_{pz}\boldsymbol{\alpha}'. \tag{6.50}$$

Noting that $\mathbf{B}$ is implicitly postmultiplied by an identity matrix, the structure of equation (6.50) is the same as that of (6.46), with $\mathbf{B}$ and $\boldsymbol{\alpha}$ unknown. One additional independent relation among the elements of $\mathbf{B}$ and $\boldsymbol{\alpha}$ will permit solution. To obtain this, first substitute (6.48) into (6.49), and then postmultiply (6.49) by $\mathbf{C}_{zz}^{-1}$:

$$\mathbf{C}_{yz}\mathbf{C}_{zz}^{-1} = \mathbf{BC}_{pz}\mathbf{C}_{zz}^{-1} + \boldsymbol{\alpha}\mathbf{C}_{ff}\mathbf{C}_{zz}^{-1}. \tag{6.51}$$

Now solve (6.50) for $\mathbf{B}$ in terms of $\boldsymbol{\alpha}$, and substitute the result into (6.51):

$$\mathbf{C}_{yz}\mathbf{C}_{zz}^{-1} = (\mathbf{C}_{yp}\mathbf{C}_{pp}^{-1} - \boldsymbol{\alpha}\mathbf{C}_{zp}\mathbf{C}_{pp}^{-1})\mathbf{C}_{pz}\mathbf{C}_{zz}^{-1} + \boldsymbol{\alpha}\mathbf{C}_{ff}\mathbf{C}_{zz}^{-1}. \tag{6.52}$$

Rearranging (6.52) gives

$$\mathbf{C}_{yz}\mathbf{C}_{zz}^{-1} - \mathbf{C}_{yp}\mathbf{C}_{pp}^{-1}\mathbf{C}_{pz}\mathbf{C}_{zz}^{-1} = \boldsymbol{\alpha}(\mathbf{C}_{ff}\mathbf{C}_{zz}^{-1} - \mathbf{C}_{zp}\mathbf{C}_{pp}^{-1}\mathbf{C}_{pz}\mathbf{C}_{zz}^{-1}). \tag{6.53}$$

The only unknown parameters in (6.53) are $\boldsymbol{\alpha}$ and $\mathbf{C}_{ff}$. The term in parentheses on the right-hand side is a scalar; hence $\boldsymbol{\alpha}$ is determined apart from a scalar. Denoting the ith and jth elements on the left-hand side of (6.53) by c_i and c_j, respectively, we have

$$\alpha_i = \frac{c_i}{c_j}\alpha_j \tag{6.54}$$

for $i, j = 1, \ldots, L$. A single relation from (6.54) is sufficient to allow solution of (6.50) for $\boldsymbol{\alpha}$, and $\mathbf{B}$, provided that $L \geq 2$. If $L = 1$, there is no information in (6.54). The model will be overidentified if $L = 3$, since there will be two such relations available.

With $\mathbf{B}$, $\mathbf{C}_{pf}$, and $\boldsymbol{\alpha}$ known, $\mathbf{C}_{ff}$ is determined from (6.49), $\mathbf{C}_{\varepsilon\varepsilon}$ is determined from (6.36), and the variance of v, $\mathbf{C}_{vv}$, from $\mathbf{C}_{zz} = \mathbf{C}_{ff} + \mathbf{C}_{vv}$.

It is instructive to note that identification of $\boldsymbol{\alpha}$ and $\mathbf{B}$ is in terms of population regression coefficients for the observed variables. Let $\mathbf{\Pi}_{xy}$ in general denote the coefficients from the population regression of any random vector $\mathbf{x}$ on another random vector $\mathbf{y}$, with the ith row being the coefficients from the regression of x_i on $\mathbf{y}$. Then (6.50) and (6.53) can be rewritten as

$$\mathbf{\Pi}_{yp} = \mathbf{B} + \boldsymbol{\alpha}\mathbf{\Pi}_{zp} \tag{6.55}$$

$$\mathbf{\Pi}_{yz} - \mathbf{\Pi}_{yp}\mathbf{\Pi}_{pz} = \boldsymbol{\alpha}\,(\mathbf{\Pi}_{fz} - \mathbf{\Pi}_{zp}\mathbf{\Pi}_{pz}). \tag{6.56}$$

(To obtain 6.55, 6.50 was transposed; also note that $\mathbf{C}_{ff} = \mathbf{C}_{zf}$ so that $\mathbf{\Pi}_{fz} = \mathbf{C}_{ff}\mathbf{C}_{zz}^{-1}$.) Indirect least squares estimates of $\mathbf{B}$ and $\boldsymbol{\alpha}$ can be obtained by doing the corresponding sample regressions and solving the sample versions of (6.55) and (6.56) for $\boldsymbol{\alpha}$ and $\mathbf{B}$. To estimate the model efficiently, restrictions implied by the structure of the model should be imposed on the estimated least squares coefficients. The implied structure is clearly seen from (6.55) and rewriting (6.51) as

$$\mathbf{\Pi}_{yz} = \mathbf{B}\mathbf{\Pi}_{fz} + \boldsymbol{\alpha}\,\mathbf{\Pi}_{fz}. \tag{6.57}$$

As an extension of this case suppose that the price of the fixed input, q, is also available. The population regression of $\mathbf{y}$ on $\mathbf{p}$ and q will yield:

$$\mathbf{\Pi}_{yp \cdot q} = \mathbf{B} + \boldsymbol{\alpha}\mathbf{\Pi}_{fp \cdot q} \tag{6.58}$$

and

$$\mathbf{\Pi}_{yp \cdot p} = \boldsymbol{\alpha}\,\mathbf{\Pi}_{fq \cdot p}, \tag{6.59}$$

where in general $\mathbf{\Pi}_{yx \cdot z}$ denotes the coefficients of $\mathbf{x}$ from the population regression of $\mathbf{y}$ on $\mathbf{x}$ and $\mathbf{z}$. Equations (6.58) and (6.59) come directly from equation (6.15) (note that $\boldsymbol{\delta}' = (\mathbf{\Pi}_{fp \cdot q}\mathbf{\Pi}_{fq \cdot p})$).

The population regression of z on $\mathbf{p}$ and q yields

$$\mathbf{\Pi}_{zp \cdot q} = \mathbf{\Pi}_{fp \cdot q}, \tag{6.60}$$

$$\mathbf{\Pi}_{zq \cdot p} = \mathbf{\Pi}_{fq \cdot p}, \tag{6.61}$$

Equations (6.58) through (6.61) are easily solved for $\boldsymbol{\alpha}$ and $\mathbf{B}$:

$$\boldsymbol{\alpha} = \mathbf{\Pi}_{yq \cdot p}\mathbf{\Pi}_{zq \cdot p}^{-1}, \tag{6.62}$$

$$\mathbf{B} = \mathbf{\Pi}_{yq \cdot p}\mathbf{\Pi}_{yq \cdot p}^{-1}\mathbf{\Pi}_{zq \cdot p}^{-1}\mathbf{\Pi}_{zp \cdot q}. \tag{6.63}$$

Hence estimates of the long-run specification, even when the data are not long-run equilibrium points, can yield estimates of short-run parameters if properly used. In this case there is no minimum requirement for L other than the trivial one, $L = 1$.

Change in and Price of the Fixed Factor Observed

Suppose that the change in the fixed factor, $d = f - f_{-1}$, is observed as well as the fixed factor price, q, and that the Koyck adjustment mechanism of equation (6.10) holds. No unbiased measure of f is available. Then equations (6.11) and (6.16) also hold; these are reproduced here for convenience:

$$d = (1 - \lambda)\gamma \mathbf{ap} + (1 - \lambda)\gamma q - (1 - \lambda)f_{-1} + (1 - \lambda)w, \tag{6.64}$$

$$f = (1 - \lambda)\gamma \mathbf{a'p} + (1 - \lambda)\gamma q + \lambda f_{-1} + (1 - \lambda)w. \tag{6.65}$$

We will demonstrate that this model is identified in terms of the population coefficients from regressions of $\mathbf{y}$ and d on $\mathbf{p}$ and q if $L \geq 2$, and there is at least one more restriction on the elements of $\mathbf{B}$ and $\mathbf{a}$ (in addition to symmetry of $\mathbf{B}$). First, substitute (6.64) into the short-run equations (6.5) to get

$$\mathbf{y} = (\mathbf{B} + (1 - \lambda)\gamma \mathbf{aa'})\mathbf{p} + (1 - \lambda)\gamma \mathbf{a}q + \gamma \mathbf{a}f_{-1} + \boldsymbol{\varepsilon} + (1 - \lambda)\mathbf{a}w. \tag{6.66}$$

Now view (6.64) and (6.66) as a system of $L + 1$ equations, with f_{-1}, rather than f, being the unobserved variable. Application of the omitted variable formula yields the following expressions for population coefficients from regressions of $\mathbf{y}$ and d on $\mathbf{p}$ and q:

$$\boldsymbol{\Pi}_{yp \cdot q} = \mathbf{B} + (1 - \lambda)\gamma \mathbf{aa'} + \lambda \mathbf{a} \boldsymbol{\Pi}_{f_{-1} p \cdot q}, \tag{6.67}$$

$$\boldsymbol{\Pi}_{yq \cdot p} = (1 - \lambda)\gamma \mathbf{a} + \lambda \mathbf{a} \boldsymbol{\Pi}_{f_{-1} q \cdot p}, \tag{6.68}$$

$$\boldsymbol{\Pi}_{dp \cdot q} = (1 - \lambda)\gamma \mathbf{a'} - (1 - \lambda)\boldsymbol{\Pi}_{f_{-1} p \cdot q}, \tag{6.69}$$

$$\boldsymbol{\Pi}_{dq \cdot p} = (1 - \lambda)\gamma - (1 - \lambda)\boldsymbol{\Pi}_{f_{-1} q \cdot p}. \tag{6.70}$$

The unknown parameters include γ, λ, $\boldsymbol{\Pi}_{f_{-1} p \cdot q}$ as well as $\mathbf{a}$ and $\mathbf{B}$.

Solve (6.69) and (6.70) for $\boldsymbol{\Pi}_{f_{-1} p \cdot q}$ and $\boldsymbol{\Pi}_{f_{-1} q \cdot p}$, and substitute the results into (6.67) and (6.68) to get

$$\boldsymbol{\Pi}_{yp \cdot q} = \mathbf{B} + (1 - \lambda)\gamma \mathbf{aa'} + \lambda \mathbf{a}\left(\gamma \mathbf{a'} - \frac{1}{1 - \lambda}\boldsymbol{\Pi}_{dp \cdot q}\right), \tag{6.71}$$

$$\boldsymbol{\Pi}_{yq \cdot p} = (1 - \lambda)\gamma \mathbf{a} + \lambda \mathbf{a}\left(\gamma - \frac{1}{1 - \lambda}\boldsymbol{\Pi}_{dq \cdot p}\right), \tag{6.72}$$

which reduce to

$$\Pi_{yp \cdot q} = \mathbf{B} + \gamma \mathbf{a}\mathbf{a}' - \frac{\lambda}{1 - \lambda} \mathbf{a}\Pi_{dp \cdot q} \tag{6.73}$$

$$= \tilde{\mathbf{B}} + \tilde{\mathbf{a}} \Pi_{dp \cdot q},$$

$$\Pi_{yq \cdot p} = \gamma \mathbf{a} - \frac{\lambda}{1 - \lambda} \mathbf{a}\Pi_{dq \cdot p} \tag{6.74}$$

$$= (\tilde{\gamma} - \Pi_{dq \cdot p})\tilde{\mathbf{a}},$$

where

$$\tilde{\mathbf{a}} = \frac{\lambda}{1 - \lambda}\mathbf{a},$$

$$\tilde{\gamma} = \frac{(1 - \lambda)}{\lambda}\gamma,$$

$$\tilde{\mathbf{B}} = \mathbf{B} + \gamma \mathbf{a}\mathbf{a}' = \mathbf{B} + \tilde{\gamma}\tilde{\mathbf{a}}\tilde{\mathbf{a}}'.$$

After transposition (6.73) is of the same form as (6.46) and can be solved for $\tilde{\mathbf{B}}$ and $\tilde{\mathbf{a}}$ if one independent relation among their elements is found. Since the term in parentheses on the right-hand side of (6.74) is a scalar, (6.74) provides the needed relation if $L \geq 2$. Denoting the ith and jth elements of $\Pi_{yq \cdot p}$ by π_i and π_j, we have

$$\tilde{\alpha}_i = \frac{\pi_i}{\pi_j}\tilde{\alpha}_j, \tag{6.75}$$

for $i, j = 1, \ldots, L$. With $\tilde{\mathbf{a}}$ determined, $\tilde{\gamma}$ can be identified from (6.74) Now consider the expression for $\tilde{\mathbf{B}}$:

$$\tilde{\mathbf{B}} = \mathbf{B} + \tilde{\gamma}\mathbf{a}\tilde{\mathbf{a}}'. \tag{6.76}$$

With $\tilde{\gamma}$ and $\tilde{\mathbf{a}}$ known, this equation is also of the form of (6.46) and can be solved for $\mathbf{B}$ and $\mathbf{a}$ if there is one independent relation among the elements of $\mathbf{B}$ and $\tilde{\mathbf{a}}$. By the definition of $\tilde{\mathbf{a}}$, $\mathbf{a}$ differs from $\tilde{\mathbf{a}}$ by the factor $(1 - \lambda)/\lambda$. Unfortunately this does not provide the needed relation since the proportionality of $\mathbf{a}$ and $\tilde{\mathbf{a}}$ is embedded in (6.76) by construction. One additional restriction on the elements of $\mathbf{B}$ and $\mathbf{a}$ will identify the model.[25] Equation (6.76) together with the restriction will identify $\mathbf{a}$; with $\mathbf{a}$ and $\tilde{\mathbf{a}}$ known, λ and γ are easily found.

In sum we have demonstrated through several examples that the symmetry restrictions on $\mathbf{B}$ greatly aid in the identification of the model's important parameters when the fixed factor is measured with error or unobserved. When an error-contaminated measure of the fixed factor is available, no further information or restrictions are required, provided that there are at least two variable factors. When no measure is available, a few additional restrictions and/or arbitrary normalizations may serve to identify the model. Hence we conclude that the inability to measure fixed factors need not be a deterrent to estimating short-run demand systems.

6.4 Concluding Remarks

The factor-output functions considered in this chapter have all been linear in prices, and in short-run equations, linear in the fixed factor-output ratio. While this greatly simplified the analysis of bias in section 6.2 and the investigation of unobserved variable techniques in section 6.3, the linear functions do not have the desirable feature of homogeneity of degree zero in factor prices. Further it would be desirable to relax the assumption that the production function is homogeneous of degree one. To what extent can these assumptions be relaxed and still permit use of unobserved variable techniques?

The researcher content to estimate the short-run demand functions alone might consider using the transcendental logarithmic (translog) function. If used as a second-order loglinear approximation to the short-run cost function, the share of variable cost attributed to individual variable factors will be linear in the logarithms of factor prices, output and the fixed factor.[26] Homogeneity of degree zero in prices is imposed parametrically. The important features of the share system are the same as those of the linear input-output equations here.[27] We would also want to assume that any measure of the fixed factor was unbiased in the logarithms.

However, much important information is lost if only the short-run demand (or analogous) equations are estimated. It was noted in section 6.1 that one parameter in the long-run factor-output functions did not appear in the short-run function. Since full knowledge of the long-run demand equations is generally necessary to infer long-run elasticities of substitution, it is clear that estimation of more than the short-run factor-output equations alone is desirable. The problem is that the second derivative of the variable cost function with respect to the fixed factor appears in the long-run equations but not in the short-run variable input equations. This problem will arise for any short-run demand system from which it is not possible to infer this second derivative (for instance, the share equations from the translog function).

One way to resolve this problem is to estimate the variable cost function with the demand equations. In the linear model considered here, the function would be quadratic in prices and the fixed factor-output ratio. Since the latter is unobserved, this leads us to a nonlinearity in the unobserved variable which greatly complicates matters. A similar nonlinearity arises for the translog. Some progress might be made by assuming that the joint distribution of prices and the fixed factor is symmetric so that third-order moments around means would be zero.[28]

Another alternative considered here is to derive the long-run demand functions, specify an adjustment process, and estimate an equation for which the dependent variable is the (observed) change in the fixed factor. However, the long-run equations associated with the short-run translog cost function, as well as most other flexible functional forms, cannot be derived except in implicit form. Hence it appears we are left with the choice of dealing with the nonlinearity or accepting linear functions with their undesirable implication for price homogeneity. However, a third alternative is this: normalize prices and costs by dividing them by the price of a single, arbitrarily chosen factor; then specify a normalized variable unit cost function that is quadratic in prices, output, and the fixed-factor output ratio.[29] The variable factor-output ratios will be linear in the normalized prices, output, and the fixed-factor output ratio, except for the equation for the normalized factor. Moreover the long-run factor-output ratios will be linear in normalized prices and output, again with the exception of the ratio for the normalized factor. An adjustment mechanism can then be specified that will result in the change in the fixed factor-output ratio being a linear function of all normalized prices, output, and the level of the fixed factor-output ratio. Under constant returns to scale, estimation of the linear short-run equations and the adjustment equation will yield all of the necessary information. In fact the system under homogeneity is identical to the linear system here once prices are normalized and the factor-output ratio for the normalized factor is discarded. However, if constant returns to scale are not imposed, the discarded nonlinear equation must be used to obtain full information about the long-run equations. Another difficulty with this approach is that results will not be invariant to the choice of normalization.

Hence there are difficulties remaining in the application of unobserved variable techniques to demand systems. However, it appears that further work on these problems will be rewarded. That such research be pursued is especially important because many other difficulties in estimating such systems, besides slow adjustment to equilibrium, may be viewed as unobserved variable problems.[30]

The most obvious problem is simply poor measurement. Measurement of the services of capital is a prime example. Difficulties in measurement include nonconstant utilization rates, variable vintages and depreciation rates, and valuation in original rather than current prices. As Berndt (1976) has demonstrated, different methods of measurement may lead to strikingly different results. Differences in input qualities in general may not be reflected in usual input measures. For instance, the quality of labor may vary considerably depending on experience, education, and other factors. Age and years of schooling might be viewed as proxies for these two quality variables, but at best they are error-contaminated measures, which could be explicitly recognized.

When pooled cross-section time-series data are available one practice is to include dummy variables for each time period and each cross-section observation if the number of periods is sufficiently large.[31] The purpose of this is to allow for errors that are time specific or observation specific. Errors may be due to variation in economic conditions, managerial ability, technology, government intervention, or other institutional factors. A problem with the technique arises when there are limited observations; too many degrees of freedom are lost. The number of parameters could be reduced by limiting the number of unobserved variables and imposing the resulting structure on the disturbances in the model. Even with larger data sets such a structure should be considered; covariances among the disturbances must be explained by some finite number of factors.

Finally, what has been said here about factor demand systems carries over with little modification to consumer demand systems. In fact the problem of partial adjustment is as frequently cited in that literature as in the production literature, with the short-run fixed factor either being the consumer's stock of durables or habit.[32]

Notes

Research on this topic emerged from discussions with Ernst R. Berndt, and its content has benefited greatly from his assistance. Douglas Caves's comments at the Key Biscayne conference have also contributed to the revision.

1. See Marc Nerlove (1967a) for arguments supporting this approach over direct estimation of production functions.

2. A short-run disequilibrium is actually a temporary equilibrium that is optimal, given adjustment costs, price uncertainty, or other constraints. Here after, however, optimum refers to long-run equilibrium and disequilibrium to short-run equilibrium.

3. See, for instance, M. Ishaq Nadiri and Sherwin Rosen (1973, p. 1), James Griffin and Paul Gregory (p. 846), and Robert Pindyck (1979a, pp. 180–181).

4. Jan Tinbergen (pp. 231–245) discusses this claim in the context of import demand functions.

5. See, for example, Griffin and Gregory.

6. Let $b_{i0 \cdot k}$ and $b_{ik \cdot 0}$ be the coefficients from population regressions of X_{t-i} on X_t and K_{t-1}, $i = 1 \cdots n$. Then the probability limits of the coefficients of X_t and K_{t-1} in the investment regression with X_{t-i}, $i = 1 \cdots n$, omitted would be $b_0 + \sum_{i=1}^{n} b_i b_{i0 \cdot k}$ and $c + \sum_{i=1}^{n} b_i b_{ik \cdot 0}$ by applying the well-known omitted variable formula (see Henri Theil, 1971, pp. 549–553.) Little can be said regarding bias without assumptions on the magnitude and signs of the b_i, $b_{i0 \cdot k}$, and $b_{ik \cdot 0}$. The equal correlations concept tells us little if anything.

7. See Frank Brechling and Dale Mortensen and Ernst Berndt, Melvyn Fuss, and Leonard Waverman (1979b).

8. Examples are the work of Lawrence Lau and Pan Yotopolous (1971), Douglas Caves and Laurits Christensen, Randall Brown and Christensen (chapter 10), and Knut Mork (1978b). Perhaps one reason that such specifications are not more abundant in the literature is that the frequently used CES production function implies that the labor-output ratio is a loglinear function of the wage-output price ratio only; that is it is independent of capital whether or not the latter is presumed fixed in the short run. George Hildebrand and Ta-Chung Liu have criticized the CES on these grounds, and their modification of the equation to include the logarithm of the capital-labor ratio may be viewed as a second example of a short-run equilibrium model. (See also the discussion of this modification in Nerlove 1967b.)

9. Hereafter constant returns to scale will implicitly mean in the long run: in the short run returns to scale will depend on whether the fixed factor is greater or less than its long-run equilibrium value.

10. The cost function is a special case of the profit function. See Lau (1976) for discussion of restricted profit functions.

11. See Lau (1976).

12. Note that the inequality in property v is strict, which is usually not required. The reason for requiring it here is that γ would be undefined if equality were to hold. The reason for using the negative of the inverse of γ as the coefficient of f in the cost function will become evident.

13. Robert Pollak and Erwin Diewert (1974) provide proofs of this principle in models similar to that considered here.

14. In practice we would probably impose symmetry restrictions on the price coefficients in estimating the long-run specification. While it is sometimes hoped that imposing correct restrictions on an incorrectly specified model will improve results, this is unlikely here since both the short- and long-run coefficient matrices of $\mathbf{p}$ are symmetric; namely, change in bias with restrictions imposed could go either way. Analysis of a model with two variable inputs indicates this is the case.

15. See Theil (1971, pp. 549–553).

16. It is assumed that $(\gamma \mathbf{R})^\tau \simeq 0$, which will hold for large enough τ if the absolute values of the characteristic roots of $\mathbf{R}$ are all less than or equal to unity.

17. For the less likely case of $-1 < \rho < 0$, we get $\Pi_{ii}^L \leq \Pi_{ii}^{S^\circ} \leq \Pi_{ii} \leq \Pi_{ii}^S \leq 0$.

18. Maximum likelihood estimates are developed by Karl Joreskog; Vincent Geraci considers efficient alternatives.

19. All of the models considered here are special cases or slightly modified versions of models considered in Stapleton.

20. Recall our notational convention: $E(\mathbf{x}\mathbf{y}') = \mathbf{X}_{xy}$, where $\mathbf{x}$ and $\mathbf{y}$ are deviations of random variables from their means.

21. See Lawley and Maxwell.

22. Let c_{ij} be a typical element of $\mathbf{C}_{yy \cdot p}$ and α_i, α_j typical elements of α. Off-diagonal elements of $\mathbf{C}_{yy \cdot p}$ with the restrictions imposed are given by $c_{ij} = \alpha_i \alpha_j$, $i \neq j$. With $L = 3$ solutions for α_i, $i = 1, \ldots, 3$, in terms of the three off-diagonal elements are

$$\alpha_i = \left(\frac{c_{ij} c_{ik}}{c_{jk}} \right)^{1/2}, \quad i, j, k = 1, 2, 3, i \neq j \neq k.$$

23. Suppose every off-diagonal element of $\mathbf{C}_{\varepsilon\varepsilon}$ is equal to θ, say. Then the off-diagonal elements of $\mathbf{C}_{yy \cdot p}$ are $C_{ij} = \alpha_i \alpha_j + \theta$, $i \neq j$. With $L \geq 4$ this implies $(c_{hi} - \theta)(c_{jk} - \theta) = \alpha_h \alpha_i \alpha_j \alpha_k = (c_{hj} - \theta)(c_{ik} - \theta)$, $h \neq i \neq j \neq k$, which gives a quadratic equation to be solved for θ. Once θ is found, define $c_{ij}^* = c_{ij} - \theta$, and employ the solution described in note 22.

24. With regard to the first of these conditions, a less arbitrary scale might be chosen in the following way if a single observation for f is available: choose an arbitrary scale for estimation, and compute factor scores (predicted values) for f from the results; then rescale so that the factor score for the single observation is equal to the observed value. (See Lawley and Maxwell for construction of factor scores.)

25. Note that $\alpha_i = 0$ for any i is not an independent restriction since it implies that $\alpha_i = 0$ also. However, $\alpha_i = k$, where k is a nonzero constant will identify the model.

26. See Caves and Christensen.

27. As is well known, there is one linear dependency among the share equations in the translog system. As a result one equation must be omitted in estimating the model. Further, imposing homogeneity of degree zero in prices for variable factor demands can be done by dividing the prices of the $L - 1$ included factors by the price of the omitted factor. If constant returns to scale are imposed, the resulting share equations are identical in form to (6.4), with $\mathbf{y}$ representing the $L - 1$ included factor shares, $\mathbf{p}$ the logarithms of the $L - 1$ normalized input prices, and f the logarithm of the factor-output ratio.

28. Zvi Griliches and Vidar Ringstad (1970) make such an assumption in analyzing errors in variables bias when both the error-contaminated variable and its square are included in a regression.

29. This is a special case of the normalized quadratic profit function suggested by Lau (1976).

30. Excellent discussions of a number of problems appear in Hildebrand and Liu, Nerlove (1976b), and Lucas (1969).

31. Kuh provides an example.

32. See Kuh and Meyer and also Houthakker (1965).

7

On the Specification of Conditional Factor Demand Functions in Recent Studies of U.S. Manufacturing

Richard G. Anderson

Continuing increases in the price of energy have stimulated extensive research on energy demand and factor substitution. The U.S. manufacturing sector comprises approximately one-fourth of aggregate U.S. energy consumption if measured by purchased Btu's, and approximately 40 percent if measured by the Btu content of fuel used for electric power generation.[1] Hence this sector has been widely identified as a potential source of reductions in energy demand. The industrial sector of the economy was specifically targeted for conservation in the Energy Policy and Conservation Act of 1975, the Natural Gas Policy Act of 1978, and the Powerplant and Industrial Fuel Use Act of 1978.[2]

A large number of econometric studies of the possibilities of energy reductions in manufacturing have appeared in the past five years.[3] These recent empirical works have frequently employed aggregate cost function specifications defined over four aggregate categories of inputs: capital services, K, labor services, L, energy, E, and materials, M. In the theory of the firm, it is well known that the firm's conditional factor demand functions are easily obtained as the first partial derivatives of the cost function with respect to the prices of the factor inputs.[4] By analogy these studies have obtained the industry's conditional factor demand functions as the first partial derivatives of an industry aggregate cost function.

In industry-level studies, however, there exists more than a single measure of output. In past studies the aggregates output and materials have been specified as gross magnitudes, in the sense that they include, as output and as purchased materials of firms, the intraindustry shipments of intermediate products that move between firms. Thus output has been measured as total firms' value of shipments, and materials as the purchases by all industry firms of all materials, regardless of source.

This chapter presents an alternative specification of industry-level aggregate cost and factor demand functions. The alternative model presented utilizes cost and factor demand functions that are conditional upon the level of deliveries of the aggregate manufacturing sector to the balance of the economy, namely, upon the net output level of the manufacturing sector.

Conceptually, these alternative models may be viewed as describing movements along different isoquants. If our interest is in energy policy and conservation, should the Allen partial elasticities of factor substitution (and related conditional factor demand elasticities) be measured along an aggregate isoquant for total firms' value of shipments, or along an isoquant for the aggregate manufacturing sector's sales of product to the balance of the economy? If there are intermediate products moving between firms within the aggregate sector, and if the firms possess neoclassical technologies so that factor substitution is possible, then an increase in the external price of a primary input (such as energy) will induce factor substitution among the traded intermediate products and cause firms to move off of their initial isoquants, even while the quantity of each product delivered to demand outside of the manufacturing sector is held constant. Put differently, there exists factor and product substitution within the aggregate manufacturing sector.

This difficulty arises in all aggregate studies based upon complete data, for there exists no single unambiguous measure of output in such aggregate data.[5] We do not observe the individual firms and hence cannot estimate their separate factor demand responses along their isoquants. Rather we observe only the aggregate input and output choices of the firms and the industry. Each firm buys a portion of its inputs from firms outside of the aggregate industry sector of interest and the balance from firms within the same sector. Similarly each firm sells a portion of its output to firms within the same sector and a portion to firms, households, and governments outside of the aggregate sector. The latter portion constitutes our net output.

As an example of the difficulty, consider a case where we could in fact hold each firm upon its initial isoquant. An increase in the industry's price for a primary factor (such as energy) would induce each firm to alter its input mix away from energy toward labor, capital, and materials. Regardless, the unit cost and output price of the firm would rise. Since this occurs for all firms in the industry, there also will be attempts to substitute away from energy and the products produced by the other firms within the industry. Such actions will change the net supply of each firm's product delivered to the rest of the economy (since each firm was held upon its initial isoquant). Thus a consequence of the gross model formulation is that the industry's deliveries of product to the balance of the economy will fluctuate as primary factor prices change. Meaningful policy discussions regarding the energy intensity of the aggregate manufacturing sector become difficult when the level of available industry output fluctuates with the factor prices.

7.1 Factor Demand in a Simple Walrasian Model

The problem of finding the optimal, cost-minimizing factor demand functions for a competitive industry in which there are firms that trade intermediate goods is most easily treated as a special, albeit simple, topic in general equilibrium theory.

Consider a competitive industry composed of n firms, each producing a single product according to a concave, regular, first-degree homogeneous production function. Each firm is assumed to purchase r primary products —primary in the sense of being produced outside of the industry in question—and $(n - 1)$ products produced by the other firms that comprise the industry. It is assumed that no firm purchases product from itself in an observable market transaction. We further assume that the production function of each firm is strictly separable in the $(n + r - 1)$ factor inputs and that the industry purchases the r primary inputs at constant prices.

In perfect competition each firm is assumed to face the same set of factor prices and hence the dual unit cost functions of the n firms may be written in matrix notation as

$$\mathbf{C(P)} = \mathbf{WA}^\circ + \mathbf{PA}, \tag{7.1}$$

where

$\mathbf{C(P)} =$ an n-element row vector of unit cost functions,

$\quad\mathbf{W} =$ an r-element row vector of the prices of the primary inputs, defined as $\mathbf{W} = (p_{n+1}, \ldots, p_{n+r})$,

$\quad\mathbf{A}^\circ =$ an $r \times n$ matrix of unit output factor demand functions for the n firms and r primary inputs,

$\quad\mathbf{P} =$ an n-element row vector of output prices of the n firms, equal to the market prices of the n produced goods, $\mathbf{P} = (p_1, \ldots, p_n)$,

$\quad\mathbf{A} =$ an $n \times n$ matrix of unit output factor demand functions for the interfirm flow of traded intermediate products used as materials input.

The matrices $\mathbf{A}^\circ$ and $\mathbf{A}$ are not constant but will vary as the prices of the factor inputs facing the firms vary. These are often termed Walrasian input-output matrices, see Walras (pp. 382–392).

In the long-run equilibrium the market price of a commodity will be driven equal to its unit cost of production, such that equation (7.1) may be written as

$$\mathbf{P} = \mathbf{WA}^\circ + \mathbf{PA}, \tag{7.2}$$

and, if the Hawkins-Simons conditions hold locally for the equilibrium value of $\mathbf{A}$, the industry equilibrium price vector may be found as

$$\mathbf{P}^* = \mathbf{WA}^\circ(\mathbf{I} - \mathbf{A})^{-1}. \tag{7.3}$$

Equation (7.2) expresses the unit cost of each firm as a function of the prices and quantities of the $(n + r - 1)$ inputs purchased by the firm. If we consider each firm in isolation from the others, then we might regard the right-handside (RHS) vector $\mathbf{P}$ as a constant, independent of the values of the primary factor prices $\mathbf{W}$. In this case (7.2) is simply a matrix representation of the n unit cost functions of the firms of the industry. In contrast, (7.3) expresses the industry equilibrium price vector as a function of the prices of the r primary inputs. Each intermediate product has been decomposed into its primary factor content (direct + indirect), as represented by the familiar matrix $(\mathbf{I} - \mathbf{A})^{-1}$.

It is well known that the conditional factor demand functions for a competitive firm facing exogenous factor prices are easily obtained by application of Shephard's lemma. Differentiating the vector $\mathbf{C}(\mathbf{P})$ with respect to the vector $\mathbf{W}$, we find

$$\left[\frac{\partial \mathbf{C}(\mathbf{P})}{\partial \mathbf{W}}\right] = \mathbf{A}^\circ + [\mathbf{I}_r \otimes \mathbf{W}]\left[\frac{\partial \mathbf{A}^\circ}{\partial \mathbf{W}}\right] + [\mathbf{I}_r \otimes \mathbf{P}]\left[\frac{\partial \mathbf{A}}{\partial \mathbf{W}}\right] + \left[\frac{\partial \mathbf{P}}{\partial \mathbf{W}}\right]\mathbf{A}, \tag{7.4}$$

where $\mathbf{I}_r$ is the $r \times r$ identity matrix and

$$\frac{\partial C(P)}{\partial \mathbf{W}} = \begin{bmatrix} \dfrac{\partial c^1(\mathbf{P})}{\partial P_{n+1}} & \cdots & \dfrac{\partial c^n(\mathbf{P})}{\partial P_{n+1}} \\ \dfrac{\partial c^1(\mathbf{P})}{\partial P_{n+r}} & \cdots & \dfrac{\partial c^n(\mathbf{P})}{\partial P_{n+r}} \end{bmatrix}, \quad \frac{\partial \mathbf{P}}{\partial \mathbf{W}} = \begin{bmatrix} \dfrac{\partial P_1}{\partial P_{n+1}} & \cdots & \dfrac{\partial P_n}{\partial P_{n+1}} \\ \dfrac{\partial P_1}{\partial P_{n+r}} & \cdots & \dfrac{\partial P_n}{\partial P_{n+r}} \end{bmatrix},$$

$$\frac{\partial \mathbf{A}}{\partial \mathbf{W}} = \begin{bmatrix} \dfrac{\partial \mathbf{A}}{\partial P_{n+1}} \\ \vdots \\ \dfrac{\partial \mathbf{A}}{\partial P_{n+r}} \end{bmatrix}, \quad \frac{\partial \mathbf{A}^\circ}{\partial \mathbf{W}} = \begin{bmatrix} \dfrac{\partial \mathbf{A}^\circ}{\partial P_{n+1}} \\ \vdots \\ \dfrac{\partial \mathbf{A}^\circ}{\partial P_{n+r}} \end{bmatrix}.$$

Since each firm is a competitor in factor markets, for each firm in isolation

$$\left[\frac{\partial \mathbf{P}}{\partial \mathbf{W}}\right] = 0, \tag{7.5}$$

and Euler's theorem guarantees that

$$[\mathbf{I}_r \otimes \mathbf{W}]\left[\frac{\partial \mathbf{A}}{\partial \mathbf{W}}\right] + [\mathbf{I}_r \otimes \mathbf{P}]\left[\frac{\partial \mathbf{A}}{\partial \mathbf{W}}\right] = 0. \tag{7.6}$$

We conclude that, for the case of each firm considered in isolation,

$$\left[\frac{\partial \mathbf{C}(\mathbf{P})}{\partial \mathbf{W}}\right] = \mathbf{A}^\circ, \tag{7.7}$$

which is a multivariate version of Shephard's lemma.

The model presented in equations (7.4) through (7.7) is the basis of recent empirical specifications of factor demand in U.S. and Canadian manufacturing.[7] These studies consider four aggregate inputs: labor services, L, capital services, K, energy, E, and materials, M. The first three items are clearly primary to the nonenergy-producing manufacturing sector of the economy and are not at issue here.[8] Difficulty arises, however, with the treatment of the materials aggregate, since it is composed of both primary materials (such as transportation and financial services) and industry-produced internally traded intermediate products (such as steel, rubber, and machinery). While the price of primary materials may be properly taken as exogenous, the price of intermediate products must clearly be considered as an endogenous variable in an analysis of the industry's demand for primary inputs (namely, labor and energy). The materials aggregate should be separated explicitly into two disjoint subsets of products. In the notation of this chapter the vector $\mathbf{W}$ would contain four elements—the prices of labor, capital, energy, and primary materials—and the vector $\mathbf{P}$ would contain the prices of the n-traded intermediate products produced by the n firms that comprise the industry.

We entitle the case in which each competitive firm is considered as if it were isolated from the others as the gross output model of industry factor demand, since the factor demand functions of each firm were derived conditional upon the firm's output level being maintained constant. In the analysis of industry-level factor demand, however, the gross output level of each firm will vary as a direct result of the other firms' factor choices among traded intermediate products. This model we name the net model, since the firms' factor demand functions are derived conditional upon the level of industry deliveries of each product to the balance of the economy (net industry output).

The factor demand functions for the net model may be derived from (7.3). Differentiating $\mathbf{P^*}$ with respect to the vector of primary factor prices $\mathbf{W}$, we find

$$\left[\frac{\partial \mathbf{P^*}}{\partial \mathbf{W}}\right] = [\mathbf{A}^\circ(\mathbf{I} - \mathbf{A})^{-1}] + [\mathbf{I}_r \otimes \mathbf{W}]\left[\frac{\partial \mathbf{A}^\circ}{\partial \mathbf{W}}\right](\mathbf{I} - \mathbf{A})^{-1}$$

$$+ [\mathbf{I}_r \otimes (\mathbf{W}\mathbf{A}^\circ)]\left[\frac{\partial (\mathbf{I} - \mathbf{A})^{-1}}{\partial \mathbf{W}}\right]. \tag{7.8}$$

The last term on the right-hand side of (7.8) is equal to

$$[\mathbf{I}_r \otimes (\mathbf{W}\mathbf{A}^\circ(\mathbf{I} - \mathbf{A})^{-1})]\left[\frac{\partial \mathbf{A}}{\partial \mathbf{W}}\right](\mathbf{I} - \mathbf{A})^{-1}, \tag{7.9}$$

which equals

$$[\mathbf{I}_r \otimes \mathbf{P^*}]\left[\frac{\partial \mathbf{A}}{\partial \mathbf{W}}\right](\mathbf{I} - \mathbf{A})^{-1}. \tag{7.10}$$

The last two right-hand side terms of (7.8) may be written as

$$\left\{[\mathbf{I}_r \otimes \mathbf{W}]\left[\frac{\partial \mathbf{A}^\circ}{\partial \mathbf{W}}\right] + [\mathbf{I}_r \otimes \mathbf{P}]\left[\frac{\partial \mathbf{A}}{\partial \mathbf{W}}\right]\right\}(\mathbf{I} - \mathbf{A})^{-1}, \tag{7.11}$$

which is equal to zero by application of Euler's theorem. We conclude for our net model that

$$\left[\frac{\partial \mathbf{P^*}}{\partial \mathbf{W}}\right] = \mathbf{A}^\circ(\mathbf{I} - \mathbf{A})^{-1}, \tag{7.12}$$

which is the result stated by Samuelson (1953, p. 19) for conditional factor demand in Walrasian general equilibrium models.

For completeness we note that this result may also be obtained directly from (7.2), when the right-hand side vector $\mathbf{P}$ is treated as not being independent of changes in $\mathbf{W}$. From (7.2) we find that

$$\left[\frac{\partial \mathbf{P}}{\partial \mathbf{W}}\right] = \mathbf{A}^\circ + \left[\frac{\partial \mathbf{P}}{\partial \mathbf{W}}\right]\mathbf{A} + [\mathbf{I}_r \otimes \mathbf{P}]\left[\frac{\partial \mathbf{A}}{\partial \mathbf{W}}\right] + [\mathbf{I}_r \otimes \mathbf{W}]\left[\frac{\partial \mathbf{A}}{\partial \mathbf{W}}\right], \tag{7.13}$$

which is also

$$\left[\frac{\partial \mathbf{P}}{\partial \mathbf{W}}\right](\mathbf{I} - \mathbf{A}) = \mathbf{A}^\circ + [\mathbf{I}_r \otimes \mathbf{W}]\left[\frac{\partial \mathbf{A}^\circ}{\partial \mathbf{W}}\right] + [\mathbf{I}_r \otimes \mathbf{P}]\left[\frac{\partial \mathbf{A}}{\partial \mathbf{W}}\right], \tag{7.14}$$

or

$$\left[\frac{\partial \mathbf{P}}{\partial \mathbf{W}}\right] = \mathbf{A}^\circ (\mathbf{I} - \mathbf{A})^{-1} + \left\{ [\mathbf{I}_r \otimes \mathbf{W}] \left[\frac{\partial \mathbf{A}}{\partial \mathbf{W}}\right] \right.$$

$$\left. + [\mathbf{I}_r \otimes \mathbf{P}] \left[\frac{\partial \mathbf{A}}{\partial \mathbf{W}}\right] \right\} (\mathbf{I} - \mathbf{A})^{-1}. \tag{7.15}$$

The second right-hand side term is identical to (7.11), and hence we obtain

$$\left[\frac{\partial \mathbf{P}}{\partial \mathbf{W}}\right] = \mathbf{A}^\circ (\mathbf{I} - \mathbf{A})^{-1}, \tag{7.16}$$

which is identical to (7.12), when we assume that $\mathbf{P}$ is adjusted in the market to its optimal level $\mathbf{P}^*$. Thus the unit net output factor demand functions of the competitive industry are easily derived by application of Shephard's lemma to the system of unit cost functions of the firms that comprise the industry.

Consider next the factor demand elasticities implied by the gross output model and our alternative net output model. In the usual notation let $\mathbf{x}$ denote the n-element column vector of the gross outputs of the n firms, and let $\mathbf{X}$ denote the n-element column vector of deliveries of purchased product to final demand. Then gross and net quantities are related by the identity

$$\mathbf{x} = \mathbf{A}\mathbf{x} + \mathbf{X}, \tag{7.17}$$

or, assuming that the Hawkins-Simons conditions are locally satisfied in a neighborhood of the equilibrium price vector $\mathbf{P}^*$,

$$\mathbf{x} = (\mathbf{I} - \mathbf{A})^{-1}\mathbf{X}. \tag{7.18}$$

For the gross output model the unit gross output factor demand functions (equation 7.7) were

$$\left[\frac{\partial \mathbf{C}}{\partial \mathbf{W}}\right] = \mathbf{A}^\circ,$$

and hence the total gross output demands are

$$\mathbf{A}^\circ (\mathbf{I} - \mathbf{A})^{-1}\mathbf{X}. \tag{7.19}$$

These demand functions have slope (gross output constant)

$$\left[\frac{\partial \mathbf{A}^\circ}{\partial \mathbf{W}}\right] (\mathbf{I} - \mathbf{A})^{-1}\mathbf{X}. \tag{7.20}$$

In contrast, the unit net output factor demand functions (equation 7.13) were

$$\left[\frac{\partial \mathbf{P}^*}{\partial \mathbf{W}}\right] = \mathbf{A}^\circ(\mathbf{I} - \mathbf{A})^{-1},$$

and these functions have slope (net output held constant)

$$
\begin{aligned}
\left[\frac{\partial^2 \mathbf{P}^*}{\partial \mathbf{W}^2}\right] &= \left[\frac{\partial \mathbf{A}^\circ}{\partial \mathbf{W}}\right](\mathbf{I} - \mathbf{A})^{-1} + [\mathbf{I}_r \otimes \mathbf{A}^\circ]\left[\frac{\partial(\mathbf{I} - \mathbf{A})^{-1}}{\partial \mathbf{W}}\right] \\
&= \left[\frac{\partial \mathbf{A}^\circ}{\partial \mathbf{W}}\right](\mathbf{I} - \mathbf{A})^{-1} \\
&\quad + [\mathbf{I}_r \otimes (\mathbf{A}^\circ(\mathbf{I} - \mathbf{A})^{-1})]\left[\frac{\partial \mathbf{A}}{\partial \mathbf{W}}\right](\mathbf{I} - \mathbf{A})^{-1}.
\end{aligned}
$$

(7.21)

The total response of factor demand in the net model is then

$$\left\{\left[\frac{\partial \mathbf{A}^\circ}{\partial \mathbf{W}}\right](\mathbf{I} - \mathbf{A})^{-1} + [\mathbf{I}_r \otimes (\mathbf{A}^\circ(\mathbf{I} - \mathbf{A})^{-1})]\left[\frac{\partial \mathbf{A}}{\partial \mathbf{W}}\right](\mathbf{I} - \mathbf{A})^{-1}\right\}\mathbf{X}. \quad (7.22)$$

A direct comparison between the two models is provided by equations (7.20) and (7.22). Most energy policy discussions are concerned with the energy intensity of the product delivered by the sector to the balance of the economy, that is, energy consumption per unit of industry net output. Note that the first right-hand side term in (7.22) is identical to (7.20) and may be considered the direct effect due to the changes in primary factor prices. The second right-hand side term of (7.22) represents the effects due to substitution among intermediate products within the industry, a form of indirect substitution among primary factor inputs. Thus the gross model may be interpreted as a restricted version of the more general net model.[9]

If it were true that the n-produced, traded intermediate goods were all substitutes for the r primary inputs in the technology of each firm, then the matrix $[\partial \mathbf{A}/\partial \mathbf{W}]$ would be strictly negative, and the net factor demand elasticities would be strictly less than the gross estimates. Each firm would find that energy and all produced intermediate materials inputs have risen in cost, and hence substitution away from energy would be smaller than if only energy increased in price. In general, however, we cannot infer the direction of the change in the factor demand elasticities as we move from a gross output model to a net output model. Thus we present new estimates of these factor demand functions in the next section.

7.2 Empirical Specification and Estimates

We assume that the industry production technology is adequately represented by a first-degree homogeneous concave-regular aggregate production function, with image

$$Q = F(\mathbf{K, L, E, M}), \tag{7.23}$$

where $\mathbf{K, L, E, M}$ denote the input quantities of capital services, labor services, energy, and primary materials. We further assume that each input is available to the industry along an infinitely elastic supply curve, so that input prices do not vary with the quantity purchased.[10] The dual cost function has image[11]

$$C(\mathbf{Q, P}) = \mathbf{Q}c(\mathbf{P_K, P_L, P_E, P_M}). \tag{7.24}$$

We seek an estimable functional form for the unit cost function $c(\mathbf{P})$ which does not impose a priori constraints upon the set of assumable values for the Allen substitution elasticities. Uzawa (1962) has shown that there exists no functional form that admits both an arbitrary pattern of Allen substitution elasticities and constancy of the elasticities. Hence our functional form is necessarily of the variable elasticity of substitution family. We expand $\ln c(\mathbf{P})$ as a second-order Taylor series about a point $\mathbf{P^*}$:

$$\ln c(\mathbf{P}) = \ln c(\mathbf{P^*}) + \sum_i \left[\frac{\partial \ln c(\mathbf{P})}{\partial \mathbf{p}_i} \right]\Bigg|_{\mathbf{P^*}} (\mathbf{p}_i - \mathbf{p}_i^*)$$
$$+ (0.5) \sum_i \sum_j \left[\frac{\partial^2 \ln c(\mathbf{P})}{\partial \mathbf{p}_i \partial \mathbf{p}_j} \right]\Bigg|_{\mathbf{P^*}} (\mathbf{p}_i - \mathbf{p}_i^*)(\mathbf{p}_j - \mathbf{p}_j^*) + R, \tag{7.25}$$

where the prices are in log form and R denotes the remainder. The first-degree homogeneity of the cost function in $\mathbf{P}$ imposes restrictions upon (7.25), as demonstrated by Denny and Fuss. When evaluated at the point of expansion $\mathbf{P^*}$, (7.25) is the familiar translog function. Assuming cost-minimizing behavior and industry-level exogenous factor prices, application of Shephard's lemma yields a set of estimable factor share equations

$$\mathbf{M}_i = \alpha_i + \Sigma_j \gamma_{ij} \ln \mathbf{P}_j + \mu_i, \tag{7.26}$$

for $i, j = K, L, E, M$. Techniques for the estimation of such systems of demand equations are well known.[12]

We assume that each factor share equation in (7.26) contains an additive error and that there may exist serial correlation both within the disturbances of each equation and across equations. In matrix notation we write (7.26) as

$$M_t = \pi P_t + \mu_t, \tag{7.27}$$

where the stacked disturbance vector μ_t has covariance matrix Ω, which is not $(\Sigma \otimes I)$ due to the autocorrelation process in the disturbance, and μ_t follows

$$\mu_t = A(L)\mu_t + \varepsilon_t, \tag{7.28}$$

where $A(L)$ is a polynomial in the lag operator L, that is, $L^k\mu_t = \mu_{t-k}$.

In our estimation of (7.27) and (7.28) we have employed Box-Jenkins time-series techniques to investigate the order of the autoregressive process $A(L)$ and to suggest an appropriate parsimonious parameterization of the covariance matrix Ω (but not the parameter values). Examination of the autocorrelation and crosscorrelation functions confirmed that a first-order vector autoregressive error process was appropriate. We imposed the parameterization

$$\mu_t = R\mu_{t-1} + \varepsilon_t \tag{7.29}$$

upon Ω and estimated the nonlinear system

$$M_t = RM_{t-1} + \pi P_t - R\pi P_{t-1} + \varepsilon_t. \tag{7.30}$$

The autocorrelation and crosscorrelation functions also suggested several tests of the internal structure of the R matrix. The results of these tests are summarized in table 7.1; further details are contained in Anderson. The hypothesis that R is the null matrix ($R = 0$) is easily rejected, with the value of the LR test statistic exceeding twenty-three. The hypothesis that R is diagonal (with equal elements) is rejected at the 1 percent level but accepted at the 5 percent level. Finally, we test and fail to reject

Table 7.1
Tests regarding the structure of the autocorrelation process

Hypothesis	LR test statistic (degrees of freedom)		Chi-square critical value (one-tail test) 0.05	0.01
i. $R = 0$	23.1	(9)	16.9	21.7
ii. R diagonal	16.2	(8)	15.5	20.1
$[\rho_{KK} = \rho_{LL} = \rho_{EE}]$				
$[\rho_{KL} = \rho_{KE} = \rho_{LK} = \rho_{LE} = \rho_{EK} = \rho_{EL} = 0]$				
iii. R "sparse"	4.6	(5)	11.1	15.1
$[\rho_{KL} = \rho_{KE} = \rho_{LK} = \rho_{LE} = \rho_{EE} = 0]$				

Table 7.2
IZEF parameter estimates of *KLEM* translog cost function, net materials data,
first-order restricted vector autocorrelation for U.S. manufacturing, 1948 to 1971

α_K	0.1829 (0.0099)[a]	γ_{LE}	-0.0086 (0.0045)
α_L	0.3944 (0.0239)	γ_{LM}	-0.0306 (0.0045)
α_E	0.1400 (0.0072)	γ_{EE}	0.0475 (0.0044)
α_M	0.2827 (0.0242)	γ_{EM}	-0.0273 (0.0067)
γ_{KK}	0.0642 (0.0044)	γ_{MM}	0.0955 (0.0385)
γ_{KL}	-0.0150 (0.0069)	ρ_{KK}	0.2891 (0.1064)
γ_{KE}	-0.0116 (0.0031)	ρ_{LL}	0.6497 (0.1310)
γ_{KM}	-0.0376 (0.0076)	ρ_{EK}	0.1779 (0.0802)
γ_{LL}	0.0541 (0.0436)	ρ_{EL}	0.0654 (0.0226)

R^{2b}

K 0.8586

L 0.5393

E 0.9188

M 0.6603

[a] Standard error.
[b] Computed as one minus the ratio of the residual sum of squares to the total sum of squares.

Table 7.3
Maximum likelihood estimates of the Allen partial elasticity of substitution for
U.S. manufacturing, 1948 to 1971

	1948	1960	1971
σ_{KK}	-2.08	-2.32	-1.17
σ_{LL}	-1.10	-0.97	-0.93
σ_{EE}	-4.08	-3.84	-3.61
σ_{MM}	-0.85	-0.94	-0.89
σ_{KL}	0.59	0.64	0.53
σ_{KE}	-0.65	-0.69	-1.39
σ_{KM}	-0.02	-0.04	-0.35
σ_{LE}	0.74	0.74	0.73
σ_{LM}	0.82	0.82	0.83
σ_{EM}	0.18	0.05	0.04

Table 7.4
Maximum likelihood estimates of the conditional factor price elasticities of demand for U.S. manufacturing, 1948 to 1971

	1948	1960	1971
$\eta_{K,PK}$	-0.18	-0.22	-0.02
$\eta_{K,PL}$	0.24	0.28	0.24
$\eta_{K,PE}$	-0.05	-0.05	-0.10
$\eta_{K,PM}$	-0.01	-0.02	-0.14
$\eta_{L,PK}$	0.05	0.06	0.04
$\eta_{L,PL}$	-0.45	-0.43	-0.42
$\eta_{L,PE}$	0.06	0.05	0.05
$\eta_{L,PM}$	0.34	0.32	0.34
$\eta_{E,PK}$	-0.06	-0.06	-0.09
$\eta_{E,PL}$	0.31	0.33	0.34
$\eta_{E,PE}$	-0.33	-0.28	-0.25
$\eta_{E,PM}$	0.08	0.02	0.01
$\eta_{M,PK}$	-0.002	-0.004	-0.02
$\eta_{M,PL}$	0.34	0.37	0.38
$\eta_{M,PE}$	0.01	0.004	0.003
$\eta_{M,PM}$	-0.35	-0.37	-0.36

a set of five exclusion restrictions upon **R** suggested by the time-series analysis.[13]

Conditional upon the parameterization chosen by the Box-Jenkins methods and *LR* tests, we employ iterative Zellner-Aitken estimation (IZEF) to obtain the maximum likelihood parameter estimates.[14] Our final accepted estimates are reported in table 7.2 through 7.4.

Tables 7.5 and 7.6 present a summary and comparison of the methodology and results of recent studies of U.S. manufacturing. The Hudson-Jorgenson (1974, 1976, 1978a, 1978b) studies are omitted from table 7.6 because they present neither their estimated elasticities nor the data necessary to calculate them. Berndt and Wood (1975a) estimate the CRTS translog cost function model with Hicks neutral technical change and no autocorrelation correction. Berndt and Khaled generalize earlier functional forms by use of a Box-Cox transformation function. Berndt and Morrison extend the studies of Berndt and Wood (1975a) by relaxing the assumed aggregation of blue-collar and white-collar labor.

Table 7.6 summarizes the results of three CRTS translog studies of U.S. manufacturing. A comparison of the net and gross model results shows an estimated own price elasticity of energy demand of about -0.25 in the net model, approximately one-half of the value estimated in the gross output

Table 7.5
Major studies of energy demand for U.S. manufacturing, 1947 to 1971

Authors	Model	Data	Results
Hudson and Jorgenson (1974)	CRTS translog cost function; Hicks neutral linear technical change; no autocorrelation correction	Faucett Associates (1973); gross output and gross materials	$\eta_{E,PE} \sim -0.50$; no elasticities or data published in article
Berndt and Wood (1975a)	CRTS translog cost function; Hicks neutral linear technical change; no autocorrelation (but see Berndt & Savin)	E and M from Faucett Associates (1973); K and L from Berndt and Christensen (1973) gross data	$\eta_{E,PE} = -0.47$
Berndt and Khaled	Tests 12 models as derived from a Box-Cox ultraflexible form; variety of technical change models and functional forms; no autocorrelation correction	Cost data from Berndt and Wood (1975a); output data is cost data from Faucett Associates (1973) in constant 1947 dollar; gross output and materials	$\eta_{E,PE} = -0.451$ for CRTS, Hicks neutral technical change; other values from -0.551 to -0.712 as restrictions on Box-Cox form vary
Berndt and Morrison	CRTS translog cost function; estimates cost function and share equations; Hicks neutral quadratic technical change adopted on likelihood ratio test; no autocorrelation correction	Same as Berndt and Christensen (1973, 1974); separates blue-collar and white-collar workers; gross output and materials	See table 7.6
Anderson (this study)	CRTS translog cost function; Hicks neutral linear technical change; first-order vector autocorrelation	Berndt and Wood (1975a) for K, L, E; M data constructed from Faucett Associates (1973); estimates net output and gross output models	See table 7.6

Table 7.6
Comparison of results from studies of manufacturing energy demand for U.S. manufacturing, 1947 to 1971

	Berndt-Wood (1975a)[a]	Berndt-Morrison Blue	White	Anderson net data
1. Own price elasticity of energy demand	−0.49	−0.42	−0.42	−0.28
2. Capital-energy substitution				
Allen elasticity	−3.2	−3.66	−3.66	−0.7
$\eta_{K,PE}$	−0.16	−0.168	−0.168	−0.05
$\eta_{E,PK}$	−0.17	−0.177	−0.177	−0.06
3. Energy-labor substitution				
Allen elasticity:	0.68	6.101	−6.523	0.7
$\eta_{E,PL}$	0.20	1.063	−0.777	0.33
$\eta_{L,PE}$	0.03	0.280	−0.299	0.05
4. Capital-labor substitution				
Allen elasticity	1.01	0.911	1.094	0.6
$\eta_{K,PL}$	0.30	0.159	0.130	0.2
$\eta_{L,PK}$	0.05	0.044	0.053	0.06
5. Materials Allen elasticities				
MM	−0.39	−0.394	−0.394	−0.9
KM	0.49	0.263	0.263	−0.04
LM	0.61	0.818	0.523	0.8
EM	0.75	0.512	0.512	0.05
Price elasticities				
$\eta_{K,PM}$	0.35	0.161	0.161	−0.02
$\eta_{L,PM}$	0.37	0.501	0.320	0.3
$\eta_{E,PM}$	0.47	0.314	0.314	0.02
$\eta_{M,PK}$	0.03	0.013	0.013	−0.004
$\eta_{M,PL}$	0.17	0.143	0.062	0.37
$\eta_{M,PE}$	0.03	0.023	0.023	0.004
$\eta_{M,PM}$	−0.24	−0.241	−0.241	−0.37

[a] Representative values.

model.[15] The estimated price elasticities of labor are almost unchanged from those presented by Berndt and Wood (1975a) for the gross model. Capital and energy remain complements, but the Allen elasticity increases to about −1 from about −3, and the cross-price elasticity increases to about −0.10. Energy and labor are slight substitutes in both formulations, with Allen elasticities of about 0.70. Labor and capital remain weak substitutes, but the Allen elasticity is about 0.60, rather than unity. The estimated cross-price elasticity of capital and the price of labor is also substantially smaller, at 0.24 as opposed to previous estimates of about 0.30.

Changes also occur, as expected, in the net materials estimates. The own Allen elasticity falls from −0.39 to −0.90, while the own price elasticity falls from −0.24 to −0.37. The cross-price elasticity of energy with respect to the price of nonproduced primary materials falls from about 0.40 to zero. For policy purposes such an estimate suggests a smaller increase in manufacturing energy consumption whenever the costs of the outputs of nonmanufacturing firms rise. The elasticity of materials with respect to the price of energy is found to be approximately equal to zero.

In summary we note that there seems to be very little that is an adequate substitute for energy even when we allow for the possible intraindustry, inter firm product substitutions in the net model. With output held constant, an increase in the price of energy paid by manufacturers leads to small reductions in the quantity of energy and capital demanded and to very small increases in the quantities of labor and materials demanded.

7.3 A Test of the Exogeneity of Primary Input Prices

In the previous sections we proposed and estimated an alternative aggregate industry-level model for the estimation of conditional factor demand functions. While the model differed from past specifications by explicitly considering the effects of price-induced factor substitution by the industry component firms among industry internally produced products, a maintained hypothesis in that model was that the prices of the primary inputs purchased by the industry's firms were exogenous to the industry as a whole, in other words, that supply curves for primary inputs at the industry level were horizontal. The derivation of factor demand functions by the use of Shephard's lemma in both the gross and net models is dependent upon this assumed exogeneity of primary factor prices. In this section we examine the validity of this assumption.

Geweke has proposed statistical tests for the assumption (hypothesis) of econometric exogeneity of variables in simultaneous equation models,

SEM. An intuitive description of Geweke's tests is straightforward. In any econometric problem there exists a set of variables of interest; denote this set **Z**. In the model construction process we partition **Z** into two disjoint exhaustive subsets of variables. Let $\{x\}$ and $\{y\}$ denote the subsets of hypothesized exogenous and endogenous variables, respectively. At this stage an estimable algebraic econometric model need not be specified. A maintained hypothesis contained within the partitioning of $\mathbf{Z} = [\mathbf{y} : \mathbf{x}]$ is that there exists a set of models wherein the partition is correct: that there exists at least one model wherein **x** is properly taken to be exogenous. Let $\mathbf{M}^\circ$ denote that set of models. Then Geweke's tests may be interpreted as tests of the null hypothesis (denoted H°) that $\mathbf{M}^\circ$ is empty; that there does not exist any model wherein the subset $\{x\}$ is properly assumed to be exogenous. The tests are independent of the particular algebraic specification of the model, including discussions of structural versus reduced form models, since they contain the same partition of **Z**. The tests are also unrelated to classical specification error tests for omitted variables, since the tests assume that **Z** is complete, containing all of the relevant variables of the model.

Failure to reject H° indicates that the search for a model wherein the partition of $\mathbf{Z} = [\mathbf{y} : \mathbf{x}]$ is correct is in vain, for no such model exists. Rejection of H°, however, cannot be taken as an indication that a particular specific algebraic model specification lies within the set $\mathbf{M}^\circ$. Indeed Jacobs, Leamer, and Ward have demonstrated the difficulty of testing whether a specific model specification might lie within the set of models $\mathbf{M}^\circ$. The tests are also dependent upon the assumed autoregressive nature of the time series contained in $\{x\}$ and $\{y\}$ and cannot test for econometric exogeneity if these series are not autocorrelated.[16]

More rigorously, consider the complete dynamic simultaneous equation model, *CDSEM*,

$$\mathbf{B}(L)\mathbf{y}_t + \mathbf{\Gamma}(L)\mathbf{x}_t = \mathbf{\varepsilon}_t, \tag{7.31}$$

where $\mathbf{B}(L)$ and $\mathbf{\Gamma}(L)$ are matrices of polynomials of infinite order in nonnegative powers of the lag operator L (that is, $\mathbf{B}(L)$ and $\mathbf{\Gamma}(L)$ involve only current and past values of $\mathbf{y}_t$ and $\mathbf{x}_t$).[17] We assume that the model (7.31) has the properties

i. $E(\varepsilon_t) = 0$, for all t,
ii. $\mathrm{Cov}(\varepsilon_t, \varepsilon_{t-s}) = 0$, for all t and all $s \neq 0$,
iii. $\mathrm{Cov}(\varepsilon_t, y_{t-s}) = 0$, for all t and all $s > 0$,
iv. $\mathrm{Cov}(\varepsilon_t, x_{t-s}) = 0$, for all t and all $s \geq 0$,
v. $\mathbf{B}(z)$ has no roots in the interval $\{z : |z| \leq 1\}$.

Assumption i is trivial. Assumption ii is the absence of serial correlation in the error process. Assumptions iii through v are the exogeneity specification for the model, containing the distinction between the endogenous and exogenous variables. Assumption v asserts that the polynomial in the lag operator $\mathbf{B}(L)$ is stable, so that there exists $\mathbf{B}^{-1}(L) = [\mathbf{B}(L)]^{-1}$ and that (7.31) is equivalent to

$$\mathbf{y}_t = -\mathbf{B}^{-1}(L)\mathbf{\Gamma}(L)\mathbf{x}_t + \mathbf{B}^{-1}(L)\mathbf{\varepsilon}_t, \tag{7.32}$$

which may be interpreted as a dynamic time-series process that accepts as input the current and lagged values of the exogenous variables and the errors and yields as output the current values of the endogenous variables $\mathbf{y}_t$.

The static analog of (7.31) is useful, since factor demand models are often specified in static equilibrium form:

$$\mathbf{B}\mathbf{y}_t + \mathbf{\Gamma}\mathbf{x}_t = \mathbf{\varepsilon}_t, \tag{7.33}$$

where we assume

i'. $E(\mathbf{\varepsilon}_t) = 0$, for all t,
ii'. $\mathrm{Cov}(\mathbf{\varepsilon}_t, \mathbf{x}_t) = 0$, for all t,
iii'. $\mathbf{B}$ is nonsingular.

Assumptions ii' and iii' are the usual exogeneity specification, for then (7.33) may be written as

$$\mathbf{y}_t = -\mathbf{B}^{-1}\mathbf{\Gamma}\mathbf{x}_t + \mathbf{B}^{-1}\mathbf{\varepsilon}_t \tag{7.34}$$

and interpreted as a static *SEM* that accepts as input the current values of the exogenous variables and the errors and yields as output the current values of the endogenous variables $\mathbf{y}_t$.

Geweke has shown that the exogeneity specifications considered here imply (and are implied by) two sets of restrictions on the covariances of the time series $\mathbf{x}_t$ and $\mathbf{y}_t$. For the *CDSEM* these are concisely stated by Dent and Geweke:

First implication of exogeneity. Suppose that $\{y_t\}$ and $\{x_t\}$ are jointly [and hence singly] covariance stationary with autoregressive representation and that the linear regression of $\mathbf{y}_t$ on all current, lagged, and future values of $\mathbf{x}_t$ is

$$\mathbf{y}_t = \sum_{s=-\infty}^{\infty} \mathbf{K}_s \mathbf{x}_{t-s} + \mathbf{v}_t, \tag{7.35}$$

where $\mathrm{cov}(\mathbf{v}_t, \mathbf{x}_{t-s}) = 0$ for all s and t. There exists a *CDSEM* with exogenous $\mathbf{x}_t$ and endogenous $\mathbf{y}_t$ and no other variables iff $\mathbf{K}_s = 0$ for all $s < 0$.

Second implication of exogeneity. Suppose that $\mathbf{y}_t$ and $\mathbf{x}_t$ are jointly covariance stationary with autoregressive representation and that the linear regression of $\mathbf{x}_t$ on all past values of $\mathbf{x}_t$ and $\mathbf{y}_t$ is

$$\mathbf{x}_t = \sum_{s=1}^{\infty} \mathbf{F}_s \mathbf{x}_{t-s} + \sum_{s=1}^{\infty} \mathbf{G}_s \mathbf{y}_{t-s} + \boldsymbol{\varepsilon}_t, \qquad (7.36)$$

where $\text{cov}(\boldsymbol{\varepsilon}_t, \mathbf{x}_{t-s}) = 0$ and $\text{cov}(\boldsymbol{\varepsilon}_t, \mathbf{y}_{t-s}) = 0$ for all $s > 0$ and all t. There exists a *CDSEM* with exogenous $\mathbf{x}_t$ and endogenous $\mathbf{y}_t$ and no other variables iff $\mathbf{G}_s = 0$ for all $s > 0$.

These implications are stated for a dynamic *SEM*. For the case of a static *SEM*, the test of the first implication is modified to involve a regression of $\mathbf{y}_t$ solely on current and future values of $\mathbf{x}_t$:

$$\mathbf{y}_t = \sum_{s=0}^{-\infty} \mathbf{K}_s \mathbf{x}_{t-s} + \mathbf{v}_t, \qquad (7.37)$$

while the procedures for testing the second implication are unchanged: regardless of the process by which the series $\{x_t\}$ may evolve through time, we continue to assume that it is independent of the evolution of $\{y_t\}$.

We present in this section tests of the second implication of the exogeneity specification. Since some flexible functional forms are specified in share-log form (such as the generalized Cobb-Douglas, translog), while others are specified in levels (such as the generalized Leontief, quadratic, generalized concave), we present tests based on both models.

We do not consider tests based on the first implication for three reasons. First, the test of the first implication is sensitive to the presence of serial correlation in the error term. Under the null hypothesis of exogeneity, we should expect serial correlation in the error of the regression for the first implication. In contrast, the error process of the regression model for tests of the second implication is serially uncorrelated under the null hypothesis due to the presence of the lagged $\mathbf{x}_t$. Hence an efficient estimator must be employed in tests of the first implication. Since a priori knowledge regarding the parametric nature of the time-series process that generated the error is absent, a nonparametric frequency domain estimator is probably preferable.[18] Thus tests based upon the first implication are sensitive to the treatment of autocorrelation in the estimator, while tests of the second implication are not.

Second, the presence of singularity in models based upon factor shares requires a substantive change in the spectral estimator of the first implication but very little change in the specification of the multivariate regression model of the second implication. In translog models the system (7.31) or (7.33) defines a singular set of factor share equations. Singularity requires careful modification of the tests proposed here, for we may not simply disregard an equation and proceed with a test of the reduced nonsingular system. Geweke demonstrates that the first implication may be examined in the singular case by a procedure similar to the nonsingular case after a rotation is carried out to reduce the dimensionality of the original system. The procedure for testing the second implication is much simpler. We continue to assume that the evolution of the time series $\{x_t\}$ is independent of the path of $\{y_t\}$. Hence the right-hand side, the lagged x_t values are retained. The singularity constraint is seen to be equivalent to exact multicollinearity among the lagged y_t variables. After the omission of one lagged y_t (in the case of one constraint), the test procedure for the second implication may proceed as before. To maintain comparability between the test results for the two classes of flexible functional forms, it was felt that exogeneity in both classes should be tested through the same implication.

Third, tests of the first implication in the static model may be sensitive to misspecification of the dynamic process in the *SEM*. The hypothesis of exogeneity may be rejected even when valid if the future x_t are picking up the influence of lagged x_t that have incorrectly been omitted from the regression for the test of the first implication due to dynamic misspecification of the *SEM*.

The existence of these difficulties suggests that the test results of the second implication of exogeneity may be reasonably viewed with considerably more confidence than may those of the first implication. In practice tests of the first and second implications may yield conflicting results, with the researcher rejecting the hypothesis of exogeneity based upon the test of one implication and failing to reject the hypothesis based upon the test of the other. Since the exogeneity specification in the *SEM* implies (and is implied by) both implications, there are few defensible a priori criteria for choosing among the test results. We believe that these difficulties would be sufficient to dissuade us from accepting results of the test of the first implication if they were found to be in conflict with the test results from the second implication.[19] Hence we do not pursue tests of the first implication.

Regression estimates for the tests of the second implication are reported in tables 7.7 through 7.10. Tables 7.7 and 7.8 report the regressions corresponding to a translog four-factor $[K, L, E, M]$ model of the type estimated in section 7.2. The vector of proposed exogenous variables has

Table 7.7
Maximum likelihood estimates of constrained log price equations, Geweke exogeneity test, second implication, for U.S. manufacturing, 1949 to 1971

Independent variable	Dependent variable[a]			
	$\ln(PK)$	$\ln(PL)$	$\ln(PE)$	$\ln(PM)$
Constant	0.041	0.020	−0.031	0.018
	(0.024)	(0.008)	(0.010)	(0.021)
$\ln(PK)_{-1}$	0.356	−0.065	−0.074	0.020
	(0.166)	(0.051)	(0.071)	(0.141)
$\ln(PL)_{-1}$	−0.889	1.03	0.195	0.985
	(0.692)	(0.214)	(0.293)	(0.588)
$\ln(PE)_{-1}$	−0.666	−0.328	0.406	−0.973
	(0.398)	(0.123)	(0.169)	(0.338)
$\ln(PM)_{-1}$	−0.305	0.123	−0.045	0.645
	(0.243)	(0.075)	(0.103)	(0.206)
$\ln(PK)_{-2}$	−0.414	−0.045	−0.113	−0.067
	(0.126)	(0.039)	(0.053)	(0.107)
$\ln(PL)_{-2}$	2.22	0.091	−0.078	−0.527
	(0.746)	(0.230)	(0.316)	(0.634)
$\ln(PE)_{-2}$	−0.096	−0.002	0.118	0.078
	(0.461)	(0.143)	(0.196)	(0.392)
$\ln(PM)_{-2}$	−0.724	−0.069	0.339	−0.035
	(0.265)	(0.082)	(0.112)	(0.225)
R^{2}[b]	0.9471	0.9974	0.9375	0.9468

[a] Prices are explicit Divisia price indexes normalized to equal unity in 1959.
[b] R^2 is calculated as unity minus the ratio of the residual sum of squares to the total sum of squares.

been regressed as a multivariate Zellner system on one- and two-period lagged values of the exogenous variables and on one-period lagged values of the factor shares. In applications the infinite lags of (7.36) must be limited to finite length. In small samples the choice of lag length is critical. Too long a lag will unnecessarily reduce degrees of freedom and the power of the tests, while too parsimonious a lag structure will fail to adequately model the vector autoregressive process of the exogenous variables. In table 7.7 two lagged values of the logs of prices appear adequate to capture the autoregressive nature of the variables. The hypothesis of a second-order lag as a constraint on a third-order lag was not rejected in the data; the hypothesis of a first-order lag as a constraint on the second-order lag was rejected. The likelihood ratio test statistic for the second implication was 48.6, with twelve degrees of freedom, versus chi-square critical values of 21.0 (0.05) and 26.2 (0.01).

We next test the second implication in the context of models specified in the levels of the variables; the results are reported in tables 7.9 and 7.10.

Table 7.8
Maximum likelihood estimates of unconstrained log price equations, Geweke exogeneity test, second implication for U.S. manufacturing, 1949 to 1971

Independent variable	Dependent variable			
	$\ln(PK)$	$\ln(PL)$	$\ln(PE)$	$\ln(PM)$
Constant	0.331	0.688	−0.407	0.105
	(0.830)	(0.196)	(0.354)	(0.791)
$\ln(PK)_{-1}$	−0.136	−0.121	0.035	−0.459
	(0.408)	(0.096)	(0.174)	(0.389)
$\ln(PL)_{-1}$	−0.958	0.710	0.405	1.13
	(0.824)	(0.195)	(0.352)	(0.785)
$\ln(PE)_{-1}$	0.273	0.015	−0.077	−0.571
	(0.549)	(0.130)	(0.235)	(0.523)
$\ln(PM)_{-1}$	−0.742	−0.041	0.176	0.441
	(0.280)	(0.066)	(0.120)	(0.267)
$\ln(PK)_{-2}$	−0.570	−0.065	−0.046	−0.129
	(0.115)	(0.027)	(0.049)	(0.110)
$\ln(PL)_{-2}$	2.38	0.351	−0.251	−0.502
	(0.712)	(0.168)	(0.304)	(0.678)
$\ln(PE)_{-2}$	−0.027	−0.042	0.092	0.064
	(0.383)	(0.091)	(0.164)	(0.365)
$\ln(PM)_{-2}$	−0.823	0.055	0.326	−0.085
	(0.279)	(0.066)	(0.119)	(0.266)
MK^a_{-1}	2.26	0.094	0.309	4.27
	(4.68)	(1.11)	(2.00)	(4.46)
ML_{-1}	1.64	−0.669	−0.412	0.547
	(0.960)	(0.227)	(0.410)	(0.914)
ME_{-1}	−16.80	−4.87	7.16	−10.1
	(5.81)	(1.37)	(2.48)	(5.54)
R^2	0.9639	0.9989	0.9566	0.9543

[a] Singularity requires that one factor share be omitted from the regression.

As before, a two-period lag on the price variables was found to be the most parsimonious acceptable form. Our LR test statistic is 72.9 with sixteen degrees of freedom; critical values are 26.3 (0.05) and 32.0 (0.01). Hence we reject the second implication of exogeneity (and the hypothesis of exogeneity itself) for both classes of flexible functional form models.[20]

A natural next step would be to test the exogeneity of variables which have been employed in past studies as instrumental variables. Berndt and Wood, for example, employed ten variables as instruments. For the $[K, L, E, M]$ model that is of interest here, these tests are not feasible due to the short sample period. For the first implication, if we allow for the possibility of a dynamic model, we would face regressions with at least thirty RHS variables; the sample contains but twenty-five observations.

Table 7.9
Maximum likelihood estimates of constrained price equations, Geweke exogeneity test, second implication for U.S. manufacturing, 1949 to 1971

Independent variable	Dependent variable[a]			
	PK	PL	PE	PM
Constant	1.05	0.225	0.257	0.801
	(0.398)	(0.119)	(0.170)	(0.382)
PK_{-1}	0.473	−0.054	−0.092	0.160
	(0.178)	(0.053)	(0.076)	(0.171)
PL_{-1}	−1.36	1.07	0.141	1.55
	(0.748)	(0.224)	(0.319)	(0.718)
PE_{-1}	−0.350	−0.312	0.431	−1.03
	(0.374)	(0.112)	(0.160)	(0.359)
PM_{-1}	−0.287	0.097	−0.072	0.602
	(0.215)	(0.064)	(0.092)	(0.206)
PK_{-2}	−0.443	−0.043	−0.141	−0.140
	(0.164)	(0.049)	(0.030)	(0.157)
PL_{-2}	2.54	0.066	−0.005	−1.11
	(0.848)	(0.254)	(0.361)	(0.813)
PE_{-2}	0.007	−0.008	0.113	0.271
	(0.402)	(0.120)	(0.172)	(0.386)
PM_{-2}	−0.577	−0.019	0.337	−0.094
	(0.239)	(0.072)	(0.102)	(0.229)
R^2	0.9325	0.9979	0.9416	0.9535

[a] Prices are explicit Divisia price indexes normalized to unity in 1959.

A similar difficulty arises in tests of the second implication if we allow for a two-period lag on the hypothesized exogenous variables. Thus we cannot test the exogeneity of these instruments through these implications of exogeneity. Without a more complete specification of the underlying implicit *SEM*, the exogeneity of these variables must remain an untested assumption.

7.4 Conclusions

The estimation of factor demand functions conditional upon the level of value of shipments (industry gross output) is not interesting, since a change in the external price of a primary factor input will cause the prices of the firms' outputs to increase and will induce factor substitution among the intermediate products that flow between firms within the industry. These changes will cause firms to move off of their initial isoquants, even while the industry's value-of-shipments magnitude is held constant. Thus, unless we actually observe the reactions of individual firms, we cannot

Table 7.10
Maximum likelihood estimates of unconstrained price equations, Geweke exogeneity test, second implication for U.S. manufacturing, 1949 to 1971

Independent variable	Dependent variable[a]			
	PK	PL	PE	PM
Constant	1.21	0.152	0.248	1.18
	(0.491)	(0.101)	(0.206)	(1.463)
PK_{-1}	0.132	−0.061	0.063	−0.064
	(0.186)	(0.038)	(0.078)	(0.175)
PL_{-1}	−1.31	0.389	−0.334	0.977
	(1.05)	(0.216)	(0.441)	(0.989)
PE_{-1}	−0.362	−0.237	0.522	−1.15
	(0.409)	(0.084)	(0.171)	(0.384)
PM_{-1}	−0.568	0.197	0.061	0.378
	(0.275)	(0.056)	(0.115)	(0.259)
PK_{-2}	−0.593	−0.035	−0.062	−0.216
	(0.148)	(0.030)	(0.062)	(0.139)
PL_{-2}	3.01	0.368	−0.144	−0.585
	(0.762)	(0.156)	(0.319)	(0.716)
PE_{-2}	−0.175	−0.105	0.093	−0.049
	(0.363)	(0.074)	(0.152)	(0.341)
PM_{-2}	−0.659	0.013	0.269	−0.242
	(0.254)	(0.052)	(0.106)	(0.239)
QK^{b}_{-1}	0.148	0.171	−0.015	0.621
	(0.330)	(0.068)	(0.138)	(0.309)
QL_{-1}	0.706	−0.041	−0.287	0.444
	(0.234)	(0.048)	(0.098)	(0.220)
QE_{-1}	−0.627	−0.046	0.656	−0.408
	(0.556)	(0.114)	(0.233)	(0.523)
QM_{-1}	0.132	0.275	−0.091	0.147
	(0.333)	(0.068)	(0.139)	(0.313)
R^{2c}	0.9537	0.9993	0.9614	0.9693

[a] Prices are explicit Divisia price indexes normalized to equal unity in 1959.

[b] Quantities are explicit Divisia quantity indexes normalized to equal equity in 1959.

[c] Calculated as unity minus the ratio of the residual sum of squares to the total sum of squares.

equate the condition that industry's gross output is held constant to the condition that each firm remains upon its initial isoquant.[21]

In the alternative net model we derived factor demand functions conditional upon industry's net output equal to the level of deliveries by the aggregate manufacturing sector to the balance of the economy. Induced factor substitution among industry's internally produced intermediate products is seen to be an integral part of the aggregate factor substitution process, resulting in substantially different estimated aggregate conditional factor demand elasticities.

Policy discussions regarding the demand for energy and natural resources are usually conducted in terms of the intensity of usage of these inputs. The net model is concerned with energy and other input use per unit of industry output delivered to the balance of the economy, that is factor use along an aggregate isoquant for the industry's transformation function, and hence corresponds to the usual context of such policy discussions.[22]

We also tested the hypothesis that the prices of the primary nonindustry-produced factor inputs are exogenous at the industry level; this has been a maintained hypothesis in many recent studies of manufacturing energy demand, since it is a necessary condition in the application of Shephard's lemma to the derivation of the industry factor demand functions. Based upon time-series tests proposed by Geweke, we concluded that there exists no model wherein the prices of these primary factors are properly taken as exogenous variables at the industry level. An implication of this result is that the procedure of obtaining industry-level factor demand functions through the use of aggregate cost functions and Shephard's lemma should be reconsidered.[23]

Finally, we note two qualifications regarding the issues discussed in this chapter. First, data availability often limits the ability of researchers to construct the net output and materials series required for the net model. In the U.S. data recourse must be made to national input-output tables and related data on shipments of product among highly disaggregate sectors. In contrast, annual value-of-shipments data are readily available.

Second, the exclusion of materials data from these models, so as to evade the question of gross versus net formulations, does not resolve this dilemma and may cause incorrect policy conclusions to be drawn from the estimated factor demand elasticities (Berndt and Wood 1977a, 1979).

Notes

I wish to thank Ernst Berndt, Franklin Fisher, Dale Jorgenson, Robert Rasche, and V. Kerry Smith for helpful comments.

1. Calculations by the author from Hoch.

2. PL 94-163, PL 95-621, PL 95-620, respectively.

3. See, for example, Berndt and Wood (1975a, 1977b, 1979), Berndt and White, Berndt and Khaled, Berndt, Fuss, and Waverman (1977); Hudson and Jorgenson (1974, 1976, 1978a, 1978b).

4. The term conditional indicates Hicksian output-compensated changes.

5. A data set is said to be complete if it includes data on all purchased inputs and materials. For a discussion of the difficulties of using incomplete data, see Berndt and Wood (1977b, 1979).

6. A production function $f(\mathbf{x})$ is concave-regular iff for all $x \gg 0$, $f(\mathbf{x})$ is positive, finite, continuously twice differentiable, strictly monotone increasing, and strongly concave.

7. Fuss' (1977) study of Canadian manufacturing is typical. He derives gross materials as the residual remaining after labor, capital, and energy costs have been subtracted from total value of shipments. The materials aggregate includes internal shipments of intermediate products, and hence its price is not independent of the prices of the other primary inputs, such as energy.

8. We emphasize the role of materials in the net and gross models. We should, however, also distinguish between energy products that are primary to the manufacturing sector and those produced by manufacturing sector firms. The data necessary for such an adjustment were not available to the author at the time of this study.

9. The net and gross models will be equivalent if (1) firms have Leontief technologies, so that there is no induced factor substitution among intermediate products, or if (2) there are no traded intermediate products, that is, the intermediate products have been netted out in terms of their primary factor content. The second condition has been shown to be necessary for the consistent aggregation of the factor demand functions of firms with neoclassical technologies (Green, chapter 9) and is the usual practice in aggregation studies (Fisher, Solow, and Kearl).

10. If the primary factor prices are exogenous, and the firms are characterized by CRTS technologies, then the nonsubstitution theorem guarantees that the prices of the internally produced intermediate products are also independent of the quantities demanded.

11. A necessary and sufficient condition for the cost function to be defined over the aggregates (P_K, P_L, P_E, P_M) is that the aggregator functions for (K, L, E, M) be homothetic.

12. The system (7.26) is singular. Imposition of the parameter restrictions suggested by symmetry and first-degree homogeneity in $\mathbf{P}$ yields an estimable nonsingular three-equation system, see Berndt and Wood (1975a).

13. We believe that this procedure provides sufficient guidance in conducting likelihood ratio tests of the structure of **R** to avoid the small-sample difficulties discussed by Guilkey and also Guilkey and Schmidt.

14. This model is a simple member of the class of dynamic linear simultaneous equation models. Kohn has shown that parametric time-domain estimators of these models may be as efficient as frequency-domain spectral regression estimators if the correct finite parameterization of the error process is known. Magnus (1978) has extended the work of Oberhofer and Kmenta by showing that *IZEF* estimation yields *ML* estimates conditional upon any finite parameterization of the covariance matrix of the errors.

15. Similar results are obtained without the autocorrelation correction, see Anderson.

16. For a static model wherein the time series are not autocorrelated, the first and second implications fail to hold (in this case we cannot use these procedures to test for purely contemporaneous exogeneity). For a dynamic model the implications remain valid, but the statistical properties of the test statistics are unknown.

17. Note that L denotes the backshift operator throughout this section.

18. Geweke suggests a multivariate extension of Hannan's efficient estimator.

19. The second implication tests are also preferable on statistical grounds regarding the power of the tests, see Geweke, Meese, and Dent.

20. Similar tests have been conducted on the data for the gross model, with similar results.

21. The equivalence of these conditions has been argued by Jorgenson in his discussion remarks concerning this chapter.

22. It also corresponds to the treatment of such intermediate products in the theory of consistent aggregation, see note 9.

23. Some studies have employed three-stage, least squares estimation, while also assuming the exogeneity of the factor prices in the use of Shephard's lemma. Berndt and Wood (1977b) noted that their I3SLS and IZEF estimates were very similar. The results presented here suggest that this occurred because their instruments failed to purge the endogeneity of the factor prices rather than because endogeneity was unimportant, as they suggested.

8

**Measuring the Prospects for
Resource Substitution under
Input and Technology
Aggregations**

Raymond J. Kopp and
V. Kerry Smith

Concern over the implications of a narrowing in the supply of natural resources is at least as old as economic analysis itself. It is therefore not difficult to recount stories of Malthusian scares of all types from both the recent and the distant past. Indeed with the apparent grip of the OPEC cartel on short-run energy costs in the United States, it hardly seems necessary to motivate a study dealing with the measurement of the role of natural resources in production activities. Nonetheless, it is necessary to emphasize an important difference in the orientation of this chapter. We evaluate the practices used in measuring the prospects for resource substitution with neoclassical models rather than report new estimates of what these substitution possibilities might be.

Our research has been motivated by an apparent conflict between the interpretations given to (1) the conclusions of analytical work dealing with the implications of a narrowing in the resource base for sustaining material well-being and (2) the empirical evidence used to evaluate their importance. This disparity can be readily identified by comparing Solow's recent summaries (1974, 1978) of the natural resource problem, and its importance with Dasgupta and Heal's comments on the difficulties encountered in developing empirical evidence consistent with these same analytical models. Solow's arguments basically suggest that the importance of the resource exhaustion problem depends upon the extent to which resource-saving technological change is experienced in key sectors of the economy and on the ease with which reproducible factors in these sectors can substitute for the natural resources. While these conditions seem intuitively clear, there remains very little empirical basis for an unambiguous conclusion on them.

In their recent book on the economics of natural resources Dasgupta and Heal interpret the same types of analytical results quite differently. They note that the findings derived from these models are based on the extent to which substitution is possible between factors at extremely low levels of usage of one or more of them (near the corners of the conventional isoquant).[1] This question cannot be resolved with the existing estimates of substitution elasticities for natural resources and reproducible inputs, because it relates to relative input usage outside the range of our empirical evidence.

These differences in judgment serve to expose a fundamental problem. To date there has been no systematic attempt made to evaluate the neoclassical approach to representing production activities. Basically such an evaluation would inquire into the authenticity of these models' representation of the nature of input associations (substitution versus complementarity). In what follows, we report the findings of such an evaluation. Our approach is experimental and focuses on the ability of a neoclassical cost function (using a flexible functional specification) to describe accurately the nature of input associations in a complex set of engineering production activities. These activities have been represented with a set of large-scale process analysis models that incorporate both heat and materials balances in their descriptions.[2]

The use of the solutions from optimizing process analysis models in the estimation of neoclassical models (cost or profit functions) was first proposed by James Griffin (1977). His objectives were quite similar and focused on the statistical estimation of response surfaces for complex simulation models. That is, his estimated relations provided a compact summary of the models. When the estimated equations were formulated to be consistent with neoclassical theory, it was possible to derive parameter estimates with direct economic interpretations. Christened pseudodata analysis by Lawrence Klein, these practices have gained considerable attention and with it some controversy. Several authors, notably Maddala and Roberts, have questioned the merits of Griffin's approaches to model compaction on the grounds that they provide no more information than the underlying model.[3] While this argument is correct, it does not invalidate the convenience and potential value of model summaries for a wide variety of problems. In any case these arguments are not relevant to our application, since our objective calls for the use of pseudodata to evaluate the properties of neoclassical models in representing a true engineering technology (as given by the process analysis description).

Since most empirical studies of production activities are severely constrained by available data (and the measures of the role of natural resources are especially subject to this limitation), we have considered cases that resemble the difficulties encountered in practice, including (1) arbitrary aggregates of specific factor inputs, notably materials and fuels, and (2) high levels of aggregation across distinct technologies.

8.1 Experimental Evaluation of Neoclassical Models

After over a half a century of empirical work the neoclassical production function is now regarded by most economists as a fundamental concept to many aspects of micro analysis.[4] There has been a tendency in this work to assume that there exists a true production function that fully characterizes the transformations required to convert a given set of inputs into the desired outputs of the activity. Consequently evaluations of the performance of the various types of neoclassical models in depicting production technologies have uniformly assumed that the true technology is described by some smooth neoclassical relationship.[5] Even the recent analytical work (see Denny and Fuss, and Jorgenson and Lau) that modifies the interpretation of and tests with flexible functional forms, treating them as approximations, maintains these general assumptions.

We shall argue that this viewpoint has overlooked the original conception (and most reasonable interpretation) of the neoclassical production function. It is an approximation to the engineering activities that comprise any particular production technology.[6] When attention was directed exclusively on capital-labor substitution possibilities, it might have been argued that this distinction was more semantic than substantive. However, the current focus on attempts to measure the prospects for resource substitution are unlikely to be subject to these arguments.[7] In these cases, we can fully expect that physical realities, such as the first law of thermodynamics, will determine the feasible limits to substitution and as a consequence will play an important role in any resolution of the issues raised by Dasgupta and Heal (summarized at the outset of this chapter).

We propose to investigate the robustness of neoclassical approaches to measuring the patterns of association among inputs when these patterns are determined by engineering relationships. This evaluation will consider the effects of the form of available data in judging the performance of the neoclassical models. More specifically, attention will be directed to the effects of two distinct aggregation problems: (1) the aggregation of diverse inputs that should not (based on the features of the technology and patterns of factor price change) be combined and (2) the aggregation across diverse technologies whose patterns of association between inputs will differ.

This study is not the first time such aggregation practices have been evaluated. However, all the past research in this area has analyzed the processes involved by using largely neoclassical functions to represent the true micro technologies or the patterns of input association.[9] These approaches have the advantage of analytical tractability but suffer from the weakness of relevance to actual production processes.

The approach selected for our evaluation is experimental and involves assuming that the process-analysis models represent the true technology. Neoclassical models are then used to attempt to identify selected features of these technologies from alternative sets of data that have been derived from them. In this study we have utilized the Russell-Vaughan models of three distinct iron- and steel-making production activities to represent each of three true micro technologies. Since these models are based on the assumption of cost minimization, we have used a cost function as our neoclassical model for describing the technologies involved. It is important to note that the use of these engineering models assures control over the inputs' definition, the inputs' prices, the outputs' levels and mix, the behavioral objectives (cost minimization), and all other exogenous influences.

The Russell-Vaughan Process Analysis Models
The models used in our experiments were developed as part of Resources for the Future's industry studies program. Their objective was to estimate the response patterns of specific technologies to constraints on the discharges of residuals from the production activities. Therefore each unit process in the various iron and steel technologies is modeled with heat and materials balances explicitly recognized to permit the estimation of the residual by-products resulting from that step. The models are quite detailed and identify between 480 to 541 structural activities (or columns). The three technologies considered are distinguished by the steel-making furnace, including the basic oxygen, *BOF*, the open hearth, *OH*, and the electric arc, *ARC*, furnaces. Each technology is treated as a separate cost-minimizing plant with the same fixed capacity (2,000 short tons of finished shapes per day) and a constant product mix in terms of ingots, semi-finished shapes, plate, and strip. Therefore these models minimize the variable costs of production and maintain a constant rate of utilization of the fixed plant and equipment which is held at the same size across plants.

Figure 8.1 provides a simple schematic diagram of the production activities for all three technologies. The primary distinguishing feature for the individual technologies is the source and degree of control over heat. Each technology's ability to use alternative sources of iron depends on the control that can be exercised over the refining temperatures in the process

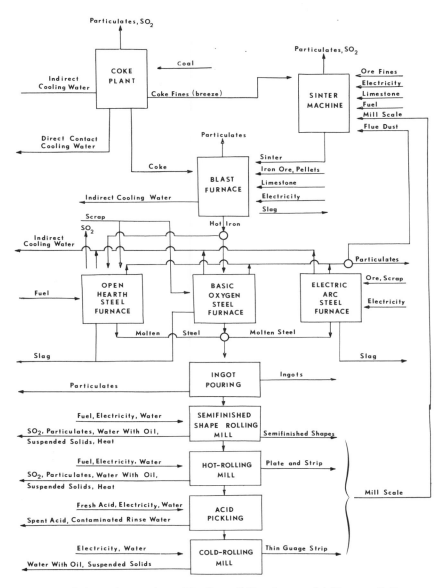

Figure 8.1 Schematic overview of the Russell-Vaughan model (Source: C. S. Russell and W. J. Vaughan, *Steel Production: Processes, Products, and Residuals*, Baltimore, 1976, p. 22)

of reducing a given metal practice (combination of molten iron and scrap) to molten steel. The *BOF* and *OH* furnaces are usually designated hot metal technologies because they rely upon a substantial proportion of hot metal to scrap in the process of oxidizing the unnecessary silicon, manganese, phosphorus, and carbon from the combination to produce molten steel. The molten iron in these cases provides a source of both the essential ferrous material to production and the heat. As a result the *BOF* technology has very limited ability to vary refining temperatures and cannot accommodate a large proportion of scrap in its metal practices. By contrast the *OH* furnace has the ability to utilize auxiliary heat sources. This permits more control over refining temperatures and, correspondingly, greater variety in the mixes of hot and cold metal to be used. The *ARC* technology differs substantially from these other furnaces. It is quite inflexible in its usage of materials inputs (except those associated with auxiliary electric power generation) and is primarily designed for direct reduction of scrap to molten steel. Therefore the furnace does not utilize to any great extent the coking, sintering, and blast furnace activities identified in figure 8.1.

While our description might be greatly expanded, these summary remarks provide sufficient background to appreciate that the patterns of input association (complementarity versus substitutability) are likely to be quite different across these three technologies.

The Implementation of the Experiments

At a conceptual level the objective of our analysis is straightforward. It calls for evaluation of the performance of neoclassical cost functions in estimating the nature of input associations when the true production technology is represented by a large-scale, cost-minimizing, process analysis model. However, in developing an operational procedure for that evaluation, a number of substantive issues arise.

The first of these relates to the criteria used to evaluate the performance of the neoclassical models. Most economic analyses of input association rely upon a measure of the elasticity of substitution, generally the Allen partial elasticity for models involving more than two inputs, to gauge the nature of relationships between pairs of inputs.[10] This elasticity is defined for a conventional cost function in equation (8.1):

$$\sigma_{ij} = \frac{C \cdot C_{ij}}{C_i \cdot C_j},$$

(8.1)

where

C = total variable costs of production,

$C_i = \partial C/\partial P_i$,

$C_{ij} = \partial^2 C/\partial P_j \partial P_i$,

P_i = price of the ith factor input,

σ_{ij} = Allen partial elasticity of substitution.

Once the production technology is assumed to be represented by an engineering model whose cost surface is not a smooth function, it becomes clear that there are no true values for these elasticities to compare with the estimates from the neoclassical cost function. Therefore it is necessary to use what is known of the technology, together with indexes of input substitution based on the process analysis model's solutions, to evaluate the authenticity of the neoclassical model's representation.

We have used the engineering information available in Russell and Vaughan together with a derived arc elasticity of substitution to meet this need. The latter is defined as the product of the arc crosselasticity of input demand with the inverse of the cost share of the factor whose price is changing.[11] This index has the advantage (over other definitions of the *ARC* elasticity, see Bever et al.) of assuring that the direction of all input associations is correctly identified.[12]

The second issue in developing an operational scheme lies in formally describing the ways in which neoclassical estimates are used to depict a given production technology. Simply stated, this issue requires that we postulate the conditions under which a practitioner is likely to believe an association between two inputs based on the estimated elasticity of substitution. Following conventional practice, we assume that estimates are screened with a significance test.[13] That is, an elasticity is only regarded as informative if the ratio of the estimate to its asymptotic standard error exceeds two in absolute magnitude.[14]

The cost function is genuinely an approximation to the cost structure implied by the process analysis models. Thus our evaluation of the neoclassical approach will be conditional to both the specification of the cost function and the process model assumed to depict the true technology. We have adopted a translog specification (see Christensen, Jorgenson, and Lau 1971) because it offers a flexible representation and is the most popular of the new flexible specifications for neoclassical production and cost functions. With this background it is now possible to turn to the technical details of our evaluation.

Experimental Design and Estimation

The data for our experiments correspond to the cost-minimizing solutions for each of the three plants (*BOF*, *OH*, and *ARC*). Each model is confronted with twenty-one different sets of factor prices, and the solutions comprise our samples. Large-scale process analysis models, such as those developed by Russell and Vaughan, introduce variations in the methods available for producing a given output mix by distinguishing the inputs to the production activities according to their attributes and the processing steps by their technical features. For example, coal might be identified by its sulfur, ash, carbon, and moisture content. Each variety of coal can be treated as a separate input to the model. However, when all varieties are aggregated into a single input, the aggregation can give the impression of flexibility in input combinations used in production, and a neoclassical model would likely perceive these variations as indications of substitution relationships with other inputs. Of course the extent to which we can correctly identify these input associations in terms of broad aggregates is affected by how we measure the aggregate and its price.

Our analysis identifies nine factor inputs: maintenance, M, pollution abatement and by-product recovery capital equipment, K, coal, C, natural gas, G, fuel oil F, iron ore, O, scrap, S, labor, L, and all other operating inputs, A.[15] While each category may have a diverse array of constituents, we assure consistent aggregation by varying the price of the components within each class in exactly the same proportion. They are therefore akin to Hicksian composite commodities (see Katzner for details). The specific solutions are derived by allowing each price to vary individually from a base level (the 1973 values) to a low and a high value.[16] Since these limits were different multiples of the base for several of the inputs, solutions were also derived for all inputs at their low and at their high prices simultaneously. This provides the twenty-one observations (the base solution, eighteen solutions for individual price variations for each of nine factors and two solutions for all nine at their low and high values).

These solutions were derived for each furnace technology and form the basis of our evaluations of the performance of the neoclassical methods at the micro level. Following conventional practice, the parameters of our translog cost functions are estimated using the input cost share equations as represented in equation (8.2):

$$\frac{P_i X_i}{C} = \alpha_i + \sum_{j=1}^{n} \beta_{ij} \ln P_j + \varepsilon_i, \tag{8.2}$$

where

X_i = optimal level of usage of ith factor,

n = number of factor inputs in each model,

ε_i = stochastic error assumed present in each equation,

α_i, β_{ij} = parameters.

The stochastic errors arise because these equations approximate the underlying cost structure. There are no stochastic elements inherent in the data derived from out process analysis models.

The sets of cost equations corresponding to each cost model were each jointly estimated with a restricted variant of Zellner's seemingly unrelated regressions estimator.[17] The restrictions involved reflect the properties of the cost function—homogeneity of degree one in factor prices and symmetry in cross-price effects. Of course there is no reason to form an opinion a priori as to whether conventional estimation and inference (our representation of practitioners' judgments) will have particularly desirable properties. While the approximation errors are unlikely to conform to full ideal conditions, this does not in itself imply that they will lead to serious distortions.[18] In any case our interest is in the conclusions that would be drawn from conventional practices.

With these estimates of the parameters of the neoclassical models we organize their performance in qualitative terms. The first step in this process requires an evaluation of the estimates at the disaggregated level (for each type of plant, namely, *BOF*, *OH*, and *ARC*). Based on the comparisons between the informative estimates and our indexes of input associations, it is possible to judge the degree of error a formulation introduces under the best conditions. Following this assessment, we proceed to gauge the impact of the two types of aggregations (over inputs and across technologies) on the performance of the neoclassical cost functions. To facilitate our description of these findings, we have identified three types of errors:

1. False association: an error that arises when the estimated σ_{ij} leads to a conclusion on an input association directly opposite to the actual relationship.

2. Nonassociation: an error that arises when either the estimated σ_{ij} does not pass the significance test, and the underlying association between the inputs is clearly that of substitution or complementarity, or when an estimate indicates some form of association, and there is none.

3. False magnitude: an error that arises when the estimated σ_{ij} grossly overstates the degree of association or when the estimate is judged in-

formative, and the pattern of association is mixed and dependent on the levels of factor prices.

To examine the robustness of these methods in the presence of departures from ideal conditions, we considered two classes of aggregations to these data: across materials inputs and across technologies. Four aggregations were considered with each furnace type for the materials inputs, and these are described in table 8.1. In each of these cases two different aggregate price indexes were used: (1) share-weighted or Paasche price index and (2) price index derived from using a translog unit cost function (see Fuss 1977, Pindyck 1979, and Kopp and Smith 1981 for further details). The parameters of the latter were estimated up to a factor of proportionality, using the appropriate cost share equations and the same restricted systems estimator.

The second set of aggregations maintained inputs in their disaggregated form but aggregated across the three technologies. Eleven different weighting schemes were defined to reflect the effects of diverse combinations of the micro technologies. They are reported in table 8.2. In these cases the estimated elasticities (those derived from the cost share equations estimated using aggregated expenditure data) were compared with the micro estimates for each plant type.[19]

8.2 Aggregations of Materials Inputs and Substitution Elasticities

Prior to developing our evaluation of the performance of the neoclassical cost functions in estimating the nature of input associations with progres-

Table 8.1
The outline of factor aggregations

Aggregation Number	Number of distinct factors	Number of aggregates	Composition of aggregates[a]
1	7	2	$AF11$ = coal and iron ore $AF21$ = fuel oil and natural gas
2	6	2	$AF12$ = coal, iron ore and scrap $AF22$ = fuel oil and natural gas
3	5	2	$AF13$ = maintenance, coal, iron ore and scrap $AF23$ = fuel oil and natural gas
4	4	1	$AF14$ = maintenance, coal, iron ore, scrap, fuel oil and natural gas

[a] $AFij$ designates the ith aggregated factor for the jth aggregation scheme.

Table 8.2
Weighting functions for aggregating *BOF*, *ARC*, and *OH* technologies

Weighting type	Furnace type		
	BOF	*ARC*	*OH*
I	0.333	0.333	0.333
II	0.250	0.500	0.250
III	0.250	0.250	0.500
IV	0.750	0.125	0.125
V	0.125	0.125	0.750
VI	0.530	0.170	0.300
VII	0.400	0.200	0.400
VIII	0.200	0.400	0.400
IX	0.400	0.400	0.200
X	0.500	0.250	0.250
XI	0.125	0.750	0.125

sive increases in the levels of aggregation of the materials inputs, it is important to consider how well these models perform in the disaggregated case. Indeed, it is of considerable interest to judge whether these micro estimates can be used as a standard for comparison with those derived from models with one or more materials aggregates. Overall our results suggest that their use in this context is reasonably safe. While there are some differences in the agreement between the derived arc and estimated Allen elasticities across furnace types, the neoclassical cost functions seem to perform quite well when the evaluation is confined to the informative estimates.[20] When the association between inputs is not clear for all levels of factor prices, the neoclassical cost model generally leads to noninformative estimates. The translog model seems to err on the conservative side of a given association. The greatest errors in applying it arise in measuring the associations between inputs required by processes that involve a complex intermediate output relationship. For example, in the measured association between either one of the fuels and pollution abatement capital for the open hearth furnace, the use of this capital for both residual treatment and by-product recovery (with the by-products involved functioning as substitutes for purchased fuels) introduces some tendency for confusion as to the exact nature of what is the correct association.

Table 8.3 summarizes the types of errors arising from each of the four types of materials aggregations by furnace. It also identifies the input pair involved in each error. Overall it seems that progressive aggregation of the materials inputs tends to reduce the neoclassical model's ability to

Table 8.3
Errors in estimated input association with input aggregation

Aggregation/errors	ARC technology Share aggregate	ARC technology Translog aggregate	BOF technology Share aggregate	BOF technology Translog aggregate	OH technology Share aggregate	OH technology Translog aggregate
1. False association	None	None	None	None	None	None
Nonassociation	Scrap-(oil-gas)[a]	Scrap-(coal-ore)[a] Scrap-(oil-gas)[a] Capital-scrap[a]	Capital-scrap Capital-(oil-gas) Capital-labor	Capital-scrap Capital-(oil-gas) Labor-maintenance Capital-labor	Capital-maintenance[a] Labor-scrap	Capital-maintenance[a] Labor scrap Labor-maintenance Capital-labor
False magnitude	None	None	None	None	None	None
2. False association	None	None	None	None	None	None
Nonassociation	(Coal-ore-scrap)	None	Capital-(Oil-gas) (Coal-ore-scrap)-(oil-gas) Capital-labor	Capital-(oil-gas) Capital-labor	Capital-labor	Capital-labor
False magnitude	None	None	None	None	None	None
3. False association	None	None	None	None	None	None
Nonassociation	Capital-(maintenance-coal-ore-scrap) Labor-(maintenance-coal-ore-scrap) (maintenance-coal-ore-scrap)-(oil-gas)	Capital-(maintenance-coal-ore-scrap) Labor-(oil-gas)	Capital-(maintenance-coal-ore-scrap) Labor-(maintenance-coal-ore-scrap) Capital-labor	Capital-(maintenance-coal-ore-scrap) Labor-(maintenance-coal-ore-scrap)	Labor-(maintenance-coal-ore-scrap) Capital-labor	Labor-(maintenance-coal-ore-scrap) Labor-(oil-gas) (maintenance-coal-ore-scrap)-(oil-gas)
False magnitude	None	None	None	None	None	Capital-(maintenance-coal-ore-scrap)
4. False association	None	None	None	None	None	None
Nonassociation	Capital-(maintenance-coal-ore-scrap-oil-gas) Labor-(maintenance-coal-ore-scrap-oil-gas)	Labor-(maintenance-coal-ore-scrap-oil-gas)	Capital-labor	Capital-labor Capital-(maintenance-coal-ore-scrap-oil-gas)	Capital-labor Labor-(maintenance-coal-ore-scrap-oil-gas)	Capital-labor
False magnitude	None	None	None	None	None	None

[a]Indicates that the perceived aggregate relationship was consistent with the noninformative benchmark estimate. Thus, under a weaker criterion for judging informative estimates, these errors of nonassociation would vanish.

identify input relationships by leading to a greater number of noninformative estimates. In some cases these noninformative estimates arise because
of conflicting associations between each of several constituents in the
aggregate and the other input involved in the elasticity estimate. This
pattern is clearest for the technologies with the largest number of informative estimates at the disaggregated level (*BOF* and *OH*). This factor
explains why there appears to be less errors due to aggregation with the
ARC furnace. At the most disaggregate level there are few informative
elasticity estimates with this technology.

Table 8.3 also summarizes the results for each of the two-price aggre-
gators—Paasche, or share aggregation, and translog aggregation. Neither
index seems superior to the other when the aggregation of inputs is inconsistent with the features of the technology. Indeed, if one used the likelihood ratio tests for the linear separability implied in aggregation four, the
test calls for rejection of these parameter restrictions with all furnaces.[21]

The factors most often involved in errors (primarily errors of nonassociation) are pollution abatement capital, coal, fuel oil, and natural
gas. One explanation of these errors is in the relatively poor job the
neoclassical model does in accounting for the role of by-product intermediate inputs produced by some of these technologies. These intermediate products seem to have an important effect on the nature of input
associations for the purchased inputs.

Several general conclusions seem to emerge from these experiments
(more detail is available in Kopp and Smith 1981):

1. As a rule neoclassical cost functions with these models did not lead to
errors of false association (confuse the nature of input associations).
2. Aggregation across inputs generally reduces the ability of these cost
functions to provide information on the nature of input associations.
When the neoclassical functions are combined with a significance test of
the type described here, they tend to be conservative. In the absence of
such tests there can be no assurance that the estimates offer reliable information on the characteristics of the technology that is being approximated.
3. On the basis of the models and aggregations considered here, there is
no advantage to the more complex price aggregations, such as the translog
price function (or equivalently the Törnqvist approximation to the Divisia
index). When the aggregation is incorrect, a detailed price aggregator
does not mitigate the errors that can result.
4. Our results suggest that the existence of by-product recovery activities
that lead to valuable intermediate outputs confuses the neoclassical model.

Table 8.4
Estimated Allen elasticities of substitution by furnace type and composition of aggregate[a]

	Micro estimates			Aggregate estimates for alternative weights										
σ_{ij}	ARC	BOF	OH	I	II	III	IV	V	VI	VII	VIII	IX	X	XI
M/M	-0.426	-0.303	-0.268	—	—	—	—	—	—	0.024	—	—	—	—
M/K	—	—	—	—	—	—	-16.20	—	—	—	—	—	-10.17	—
M/C	—	—	—	—	—	—	—	—	—	—	—	—	—	—
M/G	—	—	—	—	—	—	—	—	—	—	—	—	—	—
M/F	—	—	—	—	—	—	—	—	—	—	—	—	—	—
M/O	0.053	0.215	0.217	0.224	0.235	0.193	—	—	0.203	—	0.217	0.365	0.228	0.233
M/S	—	—	—	—	—	—	—	—	—	—	—	-0.226	—	—
M/L	—	—	—	—	—	—	—	—	—	—	—	—	—	—
M/A	—	—	—	-0.312	-0.326	-0.414	—	-0.513	—	-0.281	-0.427	-0.377	—	-0.318
K/K	-1,134.0	-205.7	-379.3	-1,175.0	-2,483.0	-1,855.0	495.0	-2,478.0	—	-489.9	-3,397.0	-694.0	—	-7,469.0
K/C	—	-2.315	-3.980	-6.965	—	-7.401	-4.351	-8.349	-5.373	-6.270	—	-4.218	-5.724	—
K/G	—	306.0	-82.86	—	—	—	—	—	—	—	—	—	—	—
K/F	—	—	-34.48	—	—	—	—	-37.28	—	—	—	-16.66	—	—
K/O	—	4.935	7.649	11.09	10.75	9.98	9.70	9.09	10.51	10.74	—	5.445	11.00	—
K/S	—	6.735	—	—	—	—	—	—	—	—	—	2.193	—	—
K/L	—	-3.297	-4.800	—	—	—	-3.785	—	-4.049	—	—	—	-4.104	—
K/A	11.918	6.609	14.73	23.52	28.26	31.21	11.43	46.96	15.77	20.82	35.63	20.03	16.17	42.15
C/C	-14.40	-2.263	-3.321	-3.946	-4.808	-3.822	-2.812	-3.598	-3.199	-3.453	-4.473	-3.391	-3.436	-7.313
C/G	—	—	6.786	—	—	5.269	—	7.611	—	—	—	4.428	—	—
C/F	—	19.14	7.917	4.480	3.126	5.022	10.11	5.774	7.250	6.119	3.726	6.503	5.889	—
C/O	—	0.760	0.443	0.548	—	0.506	0.736	0.473	0.657	0.595	—	—	0.640	—
C/S	—	1.138	1.892	1.202	1.265	1.283	1.089	1.482	1.163	1.215	1.290	1.395	1.125	—
C/L	—	-0.287	-0.189	-0.273	-0.285	-0.258	-0.241	-0.225	-0.258	-0.262	-0.268	-0.554	-0.265	—
C/A	—	0.262	—	—	—	—	0.268	—	—	—	—	—	—	—
G/G	-39.61	-31,173.0	-259.9	-185.1	-119.7	-232.6	-456.0	-368.5	-330.5	-286.3	-149.3	-123.0	-246.5	-71.80
G/F	28.93	—	—	52.74	43.92	59.05	108.9	75.24	78.39	67.98	48.07	32.81	63.06	36.53
G/O	—	—	—	—	—	—	—	—	—	—	—	—	—	—

Table 8.4 (continued)

σ_{ij}	Micro estimates			Aggregate estimates for alternative weights										
	ARC	BOF	OH	I	II	III	IV	V	VI	VII	VIII	IX	X	XI
G/S	—	—	—	—	—	—	—	—	—	—	—	—	—	—
G/L	—	—	—	—	—	—	—	—	—	—	—	—	—	—
G/A	—	—	—	—	—	—	—	—	—	—	—	—	—	—
F/F	−22.28	−415.8	−85.59	8.717	−34.19	−50.59	−143.1	−57.76	−83.50	−65.30	−38.05	−56.13	−64.90	−24.56
F/O	—	—	—	—	—	—	—	—	—	—	—	—	—	—
F/S	—	—	—	—	—	—	—	—	—	—	—	—	—	—
F/L	—	—	—	—	—	—	—	—	—	—	—	—	—	—
F/A	—	—	—	—	—	—	—	—	—	—	—	—	—	—
O/O	−10.03	−1.110	−2.038	−2.135	−2.678	−2.127	−1.382	−2.083	−1.633	−1.827	−2.536	−2.176	−1.759	−4.273
O/S	—	0.911	2.836	1.171	1.129	1.414	0.922	1.920	1.177	1.301	1.282	1.742	1.062	1.251
O/L	—	0.335	0.240	—	—	—	0.258	—	0.211	—	—	—	—	—
O/A	—	—	—	—	—	—	—	—	0.031	—	—	—	—	—
S/S	—	−17.25	−12.56	−3.539	−2.413	−4.443	−7.312	−6.743	−5.953	−5.280	−2.994	−4.817	−4.511	−1.536
S/L	0.285	—	0.443	0.371	0.347	0.386	0.404	0.417	0.400	0.395	0.361	0.567	0.384	0.315
S/A	0.624	—	—	0.682	0.700	0.627	0.634	0.465	0.623	0.620	0.679	0.675	0.678	0.682
L/L	−0.674	−0.376	−0.351	−0.435	−0.475	−0.381	−0.463	−0.332	−0.435	−0.411	−0.404	−0.163	−0.457	−0.553
L/A	—	—	0.312	0.318	0.290	0.388	—	0.461	0.293	0.334	0.364	0.493	0.277	—

[a]The elasticity estimates reported in this table satisfy the criteria that $|\hat{\sigma}_{ij}/\sqrt{\text{Var}(\hat{\sigma}_{ij})}| \geq 2.0$. The symbols designate each factor input as follows: M = maintenance, K = capital, C = coal, G = natural gas, F = fuel oil, O = iron ore, S = scrap, L = labor, and A = all other operating inputs.

The latter has been designed to analyze primary inputs and seems to perform less adequately in the presence of production activities involving intermediate outputs.

8.3 Aggregation of Technologies and Substitution Elasticities

Table 8.4 reports the estimated Allen partial elasticities of substitution for each of the three micro technologies and the eleven different aggregates of them. Following the conventions discussed in section 8.1, we report only the informative estimates. As with our analysis of input aggregation these elasticities are calculated for the sample mean cost shares (see note 17).

With a few notable exceptions the majority of the errors arising from aggregation are nonassociation and false magnitude.[22] In our attempt to decipher the performance pattern of neoclassical methods in these cases, we have focused on the special features of each estimated elasticity (across the three technologies) and the share of the aggregate costs accounted for by each. As a result several observations can be offered:

1. The estimated elasticity at the aggregate level was informative for six of the eight elasticities, with informative estimates in all three micro technologies. Moreover the magnitude of the aggregate estimate was reasonably close to the weighted average of the micro elasticities. However, in seven of these cases the elasticities involved measured own substitution effects (σ_{ii}). Therefore there was no theoretical rationale for a conflicting association across the three technologies.
2. In cases where two of the three micro elasticities were judged informative and the nature of their mutual association was consistent (substitutes or complements), the weighted averages of the micro elasticities (with the weights corresponding to the share of the total costs accounted for by each) were approximate estimates of the elasticities estimated with the aggregated data. If the nature of the input associations was not consistent across the three technologies, it was much more difficult (if not impossible) to predict the direction of the effect in estimates at an aggregate level.
3. Our findings on the effects of compositional changes seem consistent with Fisher et al.'s (1977) experimental evaluation of the effects of aggregation of neoclassical production functions. That is, in both cases (ours and theirs) compositional changes (the weighting functions) did not have clear-cut effects. In some experiments where a single micro technology exhibited informative elasticity estimates, we found that the character of

the weights did not seem to affect the significance of the same elasticities estimated at the aggregate level, while in others the weights seem quite important to whether the aggregate estimates were judged informative. One important consideration is the relative magnitude of the micro elasticities. In those cases involving somewhat large (in absolute magnitude) elasticities, the aggregate estimates were more likely to resemble their micro counterparts.

Overall these results suggest that, if the neoclassical cost function is not effective as an approach to modeling production at the most micro level of both input measurement and technological description, there is little reason to expect improvement with aggregation. Equally important, it is not reasonable to expect that aggregate elasticity estimates (over distinct technologies), interpreted after some significance test, will provide useful information on the features of the micro technology. There is no alternative to understanding the technologies (and their disparities) in judging the impacts of aggregation.

8.4 Implications

The findings of these experiments suggest that the physical properties of materials and the technical features of the technologies using them have direct implications for what are the appropriate methods of measuring the prospects for materials substitution. Neoclassical models of production activities are best viewed as approximations of the underlying technologies. They can offer a convenient means for summarizing the features of these processes. However, as with any other approximation scheme one must be aware of their limitations. Our results suggest that a rudimentary understanding of the production activities is an essential ingredient for any attempts to judge whether a particular form of input or technology aggregation will distort the Allen elasticity of input substitution.

At the most disaggregated level (in terms of both input measurement and technology) estimation using translog cost functions together with an approximate significance test provided a remarkably good description of the features of each of the three iron- and steel-making technologies we studied. Estimates of cost functions using material aggregates tended to yield noninformative estimates. There did not appear to be a tendency for informative estimates that lead to incorrect judgments on input associations. Of course in the absence of some type of screening of the estimates based on a significance test, there can be no assurance that the neoclassical estimates will tend to be conservative in judging an input association.

Aggregation across technologies raises much greater difficulties. Even with some form of significance test, one cannot be assured estimates of input associations with aggregated data (over the three technologies but disaggregated with respect to inputs) will yield credible information on the patterns of input associations in these cases. They are (1) the degree to which the neoclassical approach can reasonably approximate a given association between two inputs at the micro level, (2) the consistency in the nature of these associations (substitution or complementarity) across the technologies being aggregated, and (3) the distribution of capacities assumed present in each of the technologies. Without information on each of these issues it would be difficult to utilize the elasticity estimates based on aggregated data.

As with any set of experimental work it is important to recognize that our findings may well be quite sensitive to the specific features of the technologies we have used. Indeed, because of this potential limitation, it may be necessary to consider comparable evaluations with each of a variety of classes of physical transformations before a reliable set of general guidelines on the use of neoclassical models for estimating the nature of input associations can be derived. Such efforts are likely to be limited by the availability of engineering models comparable in quality to those of Russell and Vaughan. Many of these models have not attempted to reflect heat and materials balances completely. As a consequence they are not likely to be useful vehicles for experimental evaluations of the neoclassical approach.

Therefore it is desirable to propose some preliminary guidelines for using neoclassical models to estimate the features of production technologies, recognizing that further evidence may lead to modifications. First, an understanding of the process technology is essential to informed judgment concerning the definition of inputs to that technology and whether that particular input aggregation may distort the features of that technology.

In our case knowledge of the importance of the source of heat and the resulting control over refining temperatures was important to understanding the nature of the input associations in the three steel-making technologies.

Lau (1981) has recently argued that disaggregation to the end-use level seems essential to measuring the roles of materials in production processes. Our analysis reveals, and the second guideline suggests, that this may not be far enough. More careful and comprehensive identification of the types of production processes (in terms of engineering features) may well be necessary for neoclassical methods to offer reasonable estimates of the features of the technology.

Third, materials should be measured, as nearly as possible, in disaggregated formats. Fourth, and perhaps most important, the evaluation of neoclassical estimates should be combined with some type of significance test (even if its properties are not well known in small samples). This practice tended, for our experiments, to lead the neoclassical models to conservative outcomes rather than distortions in the perceived nature of input associations.

The first three of these suggestions might have been offered without the benefit of these experiments. However, our findings serve to highlight how important departures from these guidelines can be to the perceptions formed on the nature of the roles materials play in production activities.

Notes

Thanks are due Ernst Berndt, Barry Field, and David Wood for their most constructive comments on an earlier draft of this chapter. This research was partially supported by National Science Foundation contract no. NSF-C-ERS77-15083 and grant no. DAR-7921805.

1. More specifically Dasgupta and Heal (chapter 7, pp. 17–18) observed:

The main analytical novelty that exhaustible resources present in the analysis of growth possibilities open to an economy is that one has to be particularly conscious about the properties of production functions at the "corners." The banality of this observation is matched only by the problems this poses in obtaining empirical estimates. . . . The assumption that the elasticity of substitution is independent of the capital/resource ratio may be a treacherous one to make. Past experience may not be a good guide for judging substitution possibilities for large values of K/R [capital for natural resources].

2. This argument directly follows the suggestions recently made by Marsden, Pingry, and Whinston (1974). They argued that the form of the production function should be derived from an analysis of physical transformations taking place in production processes. More specially, they write (p. 127):

Our basic disagreement with these formulations and developments of production function forms is that they are based on varying combinations of desirable economic properties and assumed market parameter relationships. . . . What we wish to do is to break from this approach and, viewing the production function as a technical relationship representing the "maximal output achievable from a given set of inputs," proffer an alternative derivation method based on the general reaction principles of many processes. *The primitives are thus shifted from the economic properties to the engineering relationships used. The validity of the final production functional form rests on the accuracy of the engineering relationships used rather than on the preciseness of the economic properties assumed* [emphasis added].

We amend this argument to recognize that in practice most production activities are so complex as to defy convenient analytical representation, and so we are always approximating the actual relationship between outputs and inputs.

3. Maddala's arguments also include the questioning of (1) the use of a translog function to approximate a piecewise linear surface, (2) the appropriateness of the stochastic specification used in estimating a translog model, and (3) the value of estimates of economic parameters (such as elasticities of factor substitution or factor demand) in contrast to those from actual data.

4. For an interesting and informative overview of the origins of the Cobb-Douglas function, see Douglas.

5. Examples of such studies include Gapinski, Gapinski and Kumar, Guilkey and Lovell, and Hazilla.

6. See note 2 for a further description of the Marsden, Pingry, and Whinston (1974) arguments.

7. There is compelling evidence that the conventional studies are limited by this exclusive focus on capital and labor. Berndt's attempt (1976) to reconcile the diverse estimates of the elasticity of substitution between capital and labor makes this conclusion quite clearly.

8. The first law of thermodynamics states that matter is neither created nor destroyed by any physical process. In applying it to production processes, RFF's industry modeling used these principles to develop accounting schemes to estimate the residuals from different production processes (see Bower for more details). This law also suggests that in resource substitution there is a lower limit to the mass of raw materials inputs in a production process given by the mass of the outputs. Actually the feasible lower limit is probably higher than this as a result of the energy-bearing materials that may not be directly related to the manufactured products. See Ayres, pp. 38–53, for further discussion of first and second law implications for production.

9. These studies fall into three categories: (1) Analytical investigations of the effects of aggregation across technologies, following the approach developed by Houthakker (1955–1956), that seek to evaluate the aggregate technology which would be implied by a given set of micro technologies and distribution of capital intensities. Additional examples include Levhari, Johansen, and Sato. (2) Analytical studies of the effects of input aggregation with the early example given in Leontief and more current work by Diewert (1976). (3) Experimental evidence with neoclassical functional forms in aggregation exercises across different technologies, see Fisher and Fisher, Solow, and Kearl as examples.

10. There are at least two other concepts of elasticities of substitutions: (1) the direct elasticity of substitution defined as

$$d_{ij} = \frac{\partial \ln (X_i/X_j)}{\partial \ln (P_j/P_i)}$$

(for more detail, see Sato and Koizumi) and (2) the shadow elasticities of substitution (McFadden 1963) which measure the percentage change in the ratio of input prices in response to an exogenous percentage change in input quantity ratio.

11. The specific form of the elasticity is given as:

$$\sigma_{ij}^A = \frac{1}{c_{j2}} \cdot \frac{\left[\dfrac{Q_{2i} - Q_{1i}}{Q_{2i} + Q_{1i}}\right]}{\left[\dfrac{P_{2j} - P_{1j}}{P_{2j} + P_{1j}}\right]},$$

where

c_{j2} = cost share of the jth factor input at P_{2j} prices,

Q_{2i} = quantity of the ith factor demanded at a price P_{2j} for the jth factor and all other prices and output held constant,

Q_{1i} = quantity of ith factor demanded at a price P_{ij} for the jth factor and all other prices and output held constant.

12. For more detail on these comparisons, see Kopp and Smith (1981).

13. The specific details of such tests are complicated because the elasticity estimates from a translog cost function are nonlinear functions of the parameter estimates and the cost shares of the factors involved. Conventional practice calls for the use of the asymptotic variance in these tests. The assumptions underlying the derivation of the variance of $\hat{\sigma}_{ij}$ require that the cost shares (the m_i and m_j) are nonstochastic. However, in the estimation of the model using the cost share equations, we assume they are stochastic. It is generally argued that the relationship is an approximation. Unfortunately little is known of the properties of this approximation in small samples (see Hazilla for sampling results with three-factor input cost models). The Allen elasticity for a translog model is given as

$$\hat{\sigma}_{ij} = \frac{(\hat{\beta}_{ij} + m_i m_j)}{m_i m_j},$$

$$\text{asy. var}(\hat{\sigma}_{ij}) = \frac{\text{var}(\hat{\beta}_{ij})}{(m_i m_j)^2},$$

where m_i = ith factor's cost share. Occasionally it is argued that one should replace asy. var $(\hat{\sigma}_{ij})$ with the variance calculated by replacing $\hat{\sigma}_{ij}$ with a linear Taylor series expansion. Here again, however, there is no clear-cut case for an advantage. Indeed, the literature on the exact variance of products of random variables would lead to doubts over the reliability of this procedure as well (see Goodman). One possible resolution of this issue can be derived from extensive sampling experiments.

14. Conventional practice in most applications has been to use some form of significance test (usually the 95 percent significance level) in interpreting statistical estimates of economic parameters. However, in recent work with the flexible functional forms for production and cost functions, this practice has not been entirely uniform. In the case of translog production function estimates, derivation of an estimated covariance structure becomes subject to considerable question. With the translog cost function, asymptotic estimates have been used. However, often the significance tests are not used because of the lack of information on their properties (see Berndt and Wood 1975a, 1979; Pindyck 1979; Griffin and Gregory 1977).

15. All remaining plant and equipment are fixed inputs at levels designed to produce 2,000 short tons of finished steel products per day. Since the output level and mix is

held constant for all solutions of all three models, the amount of this capital and its rate of utilization can be assumed to be fixed.

16. The input prices were set as multipliers of the 1973 levels. These multipliers are given as follows:

	Low	High
Maintenance, M	0.59	1.41
Pollution abatement capital, K	0.50	1.50
Coal, C	0.27	1.73
Natural gas, G	0.27	1.73
Fuel oil, F	0.27	1.73
Iron ore, O	0.67	1.33
Scrap, S	0.22	1.78
Labor, L	0.59	1.41
All other operating inputs, A	0.50	1.50

17. The majority of applications using systems of cost share equations to estimate a translog model have relied upon an iterative version of the restricted Zellner seemingly unrelated regressions estimator (see Berndt et al. 1974 for further discussion). This preference is based on the finding that iterative application of the Zellner estimator yields estimates numerically equivalent to the maximum likelihood results.

For systems of the size used in our applications the computational costs prevented its use. Theory suggests that selection of the one-step version of the Zellner estimator may yield results sensitive to the cost share equation that was omitted.

We have explored the effects of using the one-step versus the iterative estimator with some of the smaller models estimated. Our findings indicate very slight differences in the coefficient estimates. None of these changes would be sufficient to change our conclusions with respect to any of the elasticity estimates. For further details, see Kopp and Smith (1981).

18. Griffin's (1978b) recent experiments with data generated from the Russell-Vaughan model (formulated in a different manner) indicate that the translog form seems superior to other flexible specifications in approximating the features of the underlying technology. He has noted (p. 9):

For the widest price range $0.5p_i$ to $2.0P_i$ [where P_i = base price for the ith input][i], the translog dominates both the generalized Leontief and the generalized square root quadratic. The mean absolute error of 0.32 indicates that the translog's approximation error is 72 percent of that of the rival generalized Leontief function and 34 percent lower than the generalized square root quadratic.

19. The Allen partial elasticities are evaluated at the sample mean cost shares. This procedure corresponds to the most common practice and conforms to Moroney and Toevs's (1977) suggestions for using the asymptotic variance for these estimated elasticities.

20. Tables 8.A.1 through 8.A.3 in the appendix report the sequence of results by plant type, level of aggregation, and price index.

21. The calculated likelihood ratio statistics to test the null hypothesis of linear separability corresponding to aggregation IV for each furnace are given as:

Restriction	BOF	OH	ARC
Aggregation IV	224.31	251.45	222.40

While the distribution assumptions required to use these tests for inference are not likely to be satisfied in these cases, they can show what judgments might be made when these data are used in ways that resemble conventional practice. Comparing them with the critical values implied by a chi-square distribution suggests that the restrictions implied by linear separability corresponding to aggregation IV would be rejected at the 99 percent significance level.

22. There are only two cases of errors of false association: $\hat{\sigma}_{MM}$ under aggregation VII and $\hat{\sigma}_{FF}$ under aggregation I.

Appendix

Table 8.A.1
Overview of informative Allen elasticities of substitution across aggregations for the electric arc furnace

Inputs	σ_{ij}	Aggregation 1		Aggregation 2		Aggregation 3		Aggregation 4	
		Share aggregation[a]	Translog aggregation[b]	Share aggregation[a]	Translog aggregation[b]	Share aggregation[a]	Translog aggregation[b]	Share aggregation[a]	Translog aggregation[b]
Coal-ore	—								
Oil-gas	28.92								
Scrap-coal	—		2.030						
Scrap-ore	—								
Scrap-oil	—	0.511	0.515						
Scrap-gas	—								
Maintenance-coal	—	—	—						
Maintenance-ore	—	—		0.174	0.185				
Maintenance-scrap	0.0527								
Maintenance-oil	—	—	—	—	—				
Maintenance-gas	—	—							
Capital-coal	—	—		—					
Capital-ore	—					1.105	5.919		
Capital-scrap	—							1.102	
Capital-maintenance	—	—		—		—	—		
Capital-oil	—	—	—	—	—	—	—		
Capital-gas	—	—		—		—			

Table 8.A.1 (continued)

Inputs	σ_{ij}	Aggregation 1		Aggregation 2		Aggregation 3		Aggregation 4	
		Share aggregation[a]	Translog aggregation[b]	Share aggregation[a]	Translog aggregation[b]	Share aggregation[a]	Translog aggregation[b]	Share aggregation[a]	Translog aggregation[b]
Labor-coal	—	—	—	0.165	0.231				
Labor-ore	—					0.493.	—		
Labor-scrap	0.2851		—					0.522	0.139
Labor-maintenance	—								
Labor-oil	—	—	—	—	—	—	21.363		
Labor-gas	—	—							
Coal-oil	—								
Coal-gas	—		—						
Ore-oil	—	—		0.265	—				
Ore-gas	—	—				0.522	—		
Scrap-oil	—								
Scrap-gas	—								
Maintenance-oil	—								
Maintenance-gas	—								

[a] Share-weighted aggregate price index.
[b] Translog aggregate price index.

Table 8.A.2
Overview of informative Allen elasticities of substitution across aggregation for the basic oxygen furnace

Inputs	σ_{ij}	Aggregation 1 Share aggregation[a]	Aggregation 1 Translog aggregation[b]	Aggregation 2 Share aggregation[a]	Aggregation 2 Translog aggregation[b]	Aggregation 3 Share aggregation[a]	Aggregation 3 Translog aggregation[b]	Aggregation 4 Share aggregation[a]	Aggregation 4 Translog aggregation[b]
Coal-ore	0.768								
Oil-gas	—		—						
Scrap-coal	1.139	1.234	—						
Scrap-ore	0.911	—	—						
Scrap-oil	—				—				
Scrap-gas	—								
Maintenance-coal	—	—							
Maintenance-ore	0.215		—	—	—				
Maintenance-scrap	—								
Maintenance-oil	—		—	—	—				
Maintenance-gas	—								
Capital-coal	−2.315	—	—	—	—				
Capital-ore	4.935			—		1.751	386.942		
Capital-scrap	6.735							1.585	—
Capital-maintenance	—								
Capital-oil	—		—	—	—	—	—		
Capital-gas	305.5	—							

Table 8.A.2 (continued)

Inputs	σ_{ij}	Aggregation 1 Share aggregation[a]	Aggregation 1 Translog aggregation[b]	Aggregation 2 Share aggregation[a]	Aggregation 2 Translog aggregation[b]	Aggregation 3 Share aggregation[a]	Aggregation 3 Translog aggregation[b]	Aggregation 4 Share aggregation[a]	Aggregation 4 Translog aggregation[b]
Labor-coal	−0.287	—	—						
Labor-ore	0.335			—	—	—	−144.4	—	—
Labor-scrap	—							—	—
Labor-maintenance	—								
Labor-oil	—	—	—	—	—	—	1.245		
Labor-gas	—								
Coal-oil	19.137	10.502							
Coal-gas	—		14.029						
Ore-oil	—			—	16.483	—			
Ore-gas	—								
Scrap-oil	—								
Scrap-gas	—								
Maintenance-oil	—								
Maintenance-gas	—								

[a] Share-weighted aggregate price index.
[b] Translog aggregate price index.

Table 8.A.3
Overview of informative Allen elasticities of substitution across aggregations for the open hearth furnace

Inputs	σ_{ij}	Aggregation 1 Share aggregation[a]	Aggregation 1 Translog aggregation[b]	Aggregation 2 Share aggregation[a]	Aggregation 2 Translog aggregation[b]	Aggregation 3 Share aggregation[a]	Aggregation 3 Translog aggregation[b]	Aggregation 4 Share aggregation[a]	Aggregation 4 Translog aggregation[b]
Coal-ore	0.443								
Oil-gas	—								
Scrap-coal	1.892	2.808	2.555						
Scrap-ore	2.836								
Scrap-oil	—	—	—						
Scrap-gas	—	—							
Maintenance-coal	—	—							
Maintenance-ore	0.217	—		—	—				
Maintenance-scrap	—								
Maintenance-oil	—	—	—	—	—				
Maintenance-gas	—	—							
Capital-coal	−3.980	—	—	—	—	—			
Capital-ore	7.649						273.6		
Capital-scrap	—							—	—
Capital-maintenance	—								
Capital-oil	−34.3	−38.9	−78.8	−37.3	−88.2	−37.7			
Capital-gas	−82.8								

Table 8.A.3 (continued)

Inputs	σ_{ij}	Aggregation 1 Share aggregation[a]	Aggregation 1 Translog aggregation[b]	Aggregation 2 Share aggregation[a]	Aggregation 2 Translog aggregation[b]	Aggregation 3 Share aggregation[a]	Aggregation 3 Translog aggregation[b]	Aggregation 4 Share aggregation[a]	Aggregation 4 Translog aggregation[b]
Labor-coal	−0.189	—	—						
Labor-ore	0.240			—	—	0.273	−18.9		
Labor-scrap	0.443							0.264	—
Labor-maintenance	—								
Labor-oil	—	—	—	—	—	—	1.075		
Labor-gas	—								
Coal-oil	7.917	3.802							
Coal-gas	61,786.0		3.033						
Ore-oil	—			2.093		1.428			
Ore-gas	—				2.508				
Scrap-oil	—								
Scrap-gas	—								
Maintenance-oil	—								
Maintenance-gas	—								

[a] Share-weighted aggregate price index.
[b] Translog aggregate price index.

III
Dynamic Models

Introduction to Part III

The chapters of the preceding two sections of this book have reported results and have raised important issues regarding the interpretation of measured resource substitutability. In almost all cases the analytical framework used has been based on static optimization. The four chapters in the final section of this book consider various forms of dynamic models, models that recognize that in the short run all inputs may not be at their full or long-run equilibrium levels.

In chapter 9 R. S. Brown and L. R. Christensen present a model that recognizes explicitly that in the short run certain inputs are fixed and that this affects demands for variable inputs. Although this model still utilizes the static optimization framework, it is firmly rooted in the theory of cost and production and has convenient applicability. Brown-Christensen are able to obtain long-run estimates of elasticities, even though their model is essentially short run; this is accomplished by use of the envelope theorem. The empirical application to U.S. agriculture is of interest in its own right, for it has long been assumed that the agriculture sector has had an excess supply of labor input.

In chapter 10 J. R. Norsworthy and M. S. Harper extend dynamic model applications considerably by carefully specifying cost functions in such a way that consistent partial adjustment share or demand equations can be derived. They compare a number of such models and obtain the important result that energy-capital complementarity is not just a short-run phenomenon in U.S. manufacturing: the extent of complementarity is significant even in the long run.

In chapter 11 M. Denny, M. A. Fuss, and L. Waverman outline a model of factor demands based on explicit dynamic cost minimization, with increasing marginal internal costs of adjustment. This innovative model is applied to a number of two-digit manufacturing industries in the United States and Canada, and comparisons are then made.

In chapter 12 E. R. Berndt, C. J. Morrison, and G. C. Watkins survey and critically assess what they call three generations of dynamic models of demand for energy. The various approaches are examined in terms of the role of economic theory and potential empirical applicability, and empirical results are presented from the different models based on a common body of data. The chapter concludes with suggestions for future research on dynamic models of demand for natural resources.

9

Dynamic Models of Energy Substitution in U.S. Manufacturing

J. R. Norsworthy and Michael J. Harper

The impact of energy price increases on output, productivity, and prices depends critically upon the extent to which other factors of production —labor, capital, and intermediate products—can be substituted for energy inputs. Similarly the quantitative effect of tax and depreciation incentives to capital formation on output, productivity, and prices depends on the relationship between capital and energy in production and specifically on whether the relationship is one of substitutability or complementarity. If capital and energy are complements in production, then increases in energy prices would result in a decline in the rate of capital formation. This is likely to result in a decrease in labor productivity growth. Further any particular tax or depreciation incentive to capital formation will have a smaller impact than in the 1960s when energy prices were rising more slowly. Alternatively, if capital and energy are substitutes, then the increase in energy prices would tend to encourage more rapid capital formation, and the impact of the incentive would be quantitatively greater than if energy prices were rising more slowly. The issue is thus important not only to understanding the recent slowdown in labor productivity growth, but also to anticipating the likely results of remedies to the recent slowdown in capital formation.

The substitution-complementarity issue has been addressed by Berndt and Wood (1975a, 1979) and Griffin and Gregory, with uncertain results to date. Although the weight of time-series evidence seems to favor the complementarity argument, inclusion of cross-section data appears to favor substitutability.[1]

Berndt and Wood (1979) have correctly pointed out that findings of substitutability between capital and energy in cross-section data may be compatible with a time-series relationship of complementarity. However, Griffin and Gregory have speculated that short-term complementarity between capital and energy may mask long-term substitutability. The

Griffin-Gregory position could be correct if in fact the conventional equilibrium assumptions underlying the measurement of factor inputs and the estimation of production models are substantially violated.

In this chapter we examine a variety of approaches to the disequilibrium adjustment problem to explore capital/energy substitutability. In an earlier study we estimated disequilibrium and equilibrium cost function models for manufacturing with four input factors: capital, labor, energy, and materials.[2] The parameters characterizing the dynamic adjustment process were found to be significant. Complementarity between capital and energy was found to characterize both models. However, the disequilibrium nature of the model was reflected only in that a lagged adjustment of factor shares to changes in factor prices and (implicitly) the level of output was permitted. The equilibrium assumptions embodied in measuring capital input were retained. Further, while the long-term cost function consistent with the estimated model could be explicitly written, as well as the substitution and demand elasticities, the short-term substitution relationships could not be explicitly derived.

We will extend and generalize our earlier disequilibrium model in the following manner:
1. Both short- and long-term substitution representations in the production process are explicit in the disequilibrium specification of the share equations.
2. Estimates of both short- and long-run elasticities of factor substitution and factor demand can be derived. This feature we believe to be especially pertinent to the substitution-complementarity issue, and in particular to the Griffin-Gregory speculation.
3. The equilibrium assumptions embodied in the service price of capital are relaxed, albeit in an ad hoc manner.

A disequilibrium model is next used to simulate the 1973 to 1977 period, first, to assess the impact of increases in energy prices on capital formation and, then, the effects of tax and depreciation incentives to encourage capital formation.

9.1 Disequilibrium Modeling of the Production Process

Most satisfactory models of the production process are based on the assumption that each observation of input quantities represents an equilibrium production technique fully adjusted to current prices and—if it is explicitly considered—current output.[3] Perhaps the most complete and currently conventional representative of this class of models is the translog production or cost function, which allows variable elasticities of substitution among input factors and through time. Especially when estimated on annual data, the cost and production function variants have shown themselves to be quite robust and have led to plausible inferences about factor substitution. However, not even the most fervent apostles of the equilibrium doctrine would maintain that, for example, quantities of factor inputs show the same variability as their prices. There may have been some others who estimated cost and production functions from the same data and observed disquieting differences that clearly would lead to rejection of the duality hypothesis. The point is that quantities clearly adjust to price changes with a lag. However, there have been trends in the relative prices of major input factors that have persisted throughout most of the postwar period, so that relative price changes from year to year contained few surprises.

Certainly the most serious challenge to the equilibrium assumption arises from the fact that the quantity of physical capital cannot be rapidly adjusted without incurring significant economic adjustment costs. It is reasonable to suppose that with one major input factor out of equilibrium, other more rapidly adjustable factors will be adjusted to achieve lower production costs, and, as the sluggish factor is brought toward equilibrium, the other factors will accommodate by further adjustment.

This appealing relationship underlies the Nadiri-Rosen (1969, 1973) work.[4] Their model implies a richly interdependent structure of production, in which the disequilibrium in a single production factor influences every other factor. The implementation was somewhat ad hoc, however. The factor demand equations were not simultaneously estimated (they used *OLS* techniques), and the loss of estimation efficiency was probably serious. Mohr extended the Nadiri-Rosen method to a number of input factors, including the cost of adjustment of capital, and simultaneously estimated the factor shares for two capital and two labor inputs. The approach was still ad hoc, in the sense that only the long-run cost function could be described; the short-run cost function that would yield the estimated dynamic share equations was not discovered.

The Nadiri-Rosen and Mohr papers are extremely useful in that they imply two different kinds of factor substitution taking place: long-run substitution motivated by changes in relative prices and short-run substitution in response to sluggish adjustment to long-run desired factor proportions. It is likely that the latter process will contaminate estimates that ignore the fact that both processes are going on. Clearly it is this kind of effect which Griffin-Gregory speculate may bias the Berndt-Wood conclusions noted earlier.

Another major problem resides in the equilibrium assumptions that underlie the neoclassical measurement of capital input: the service prices of capital assets and the quantity of capital services are computed based on equilibrium assumptions. The service prices so computed vary considerably from year to year. Sometimes the variation is not quite what we would expect. Inclusion of inventories in the capital stock can have unusual effects—the physical quantity of capital may rise just when output falls. Treatment of involuntary inventory investment in the same manner as investment in equipment and structures inputs is not appealing.

The events since 1973 have greatly enriched the data base for studies of factor substitution: relative prices have changed dramatically from their former patterns. Recent events have also rendered suspect some of our conventional approaches to studying factor substitution, as well as their results. The silver lining is that the issues of factor substitution are much more important than before 1973.

Of course this brief critique implies an enormous agenda. In this chapter we overcome some of the ad hoc problems that characterize our own earlier work (Norsworthy and Harper 1979) as well as that by Nadiri-Rosen and Mohr. In particular we are able to specify and estimate share equations that incorporate long- and short-term effects and measure the associated elasticities of substitution. In one specification we allow for a longer-term perspective on the price of capital services within the estimation. The other problems associated with disequilibrium measurement of capital input, and the inventory problem in particular, we defer for future investigations.

A major qualification to our approach must be acknowledged. Only annual data are used, and it is likely that major dimensions of the short-run versus long-run substitution issue cannot be captured in such low frequency data[5]. The sluggishness in capital adjustment will play a dominant role. Since adjustment of energy input frequently requires adaptation of capital equipment, the capital-energy issue may be reasonably well assessed in annual models.

9.2 Disequilibrium Models

Equilibrium Model
The manufacturing production process is represented by the transcendental logarithmic—or translog—cost function with constant returns to scale:

$$\ln C = a_0 + \Sigma_i a_i \ln P_i + \tfrac{1}{2}\Sigma_i\Sigma_j b_{ij} \ln P_i \ln P_j,$$

for $i, j = K, L, E, M$, where C is nominal unit cost and the P_i the input prices of K (capital), L (labor), E (energy), and M (intermediate input), each normalized to 1.0 in 1972.

The associated equations for the share of each factor input i in total cost are derived by differentiation of the total cost function with respect to $\ln P_i$ as follows:

$$s_i = \frac{\partial \ln C}{\partial \ln P_i} = a_i + \Sigma_j b_{ij} \ln P_j,$$

for $i, j = K, L, E, M$.

Underlying this formulation is the assumption that each observation represents fully adjusted cost-minimizing equilibrium.

This model is estimated by Berndt-Wood and Griffin-Gregory (the latter omit materials) subject to the restrictions

$b_{ij} = b_{ji}$ (symmetry),

$\Sigma a_i = 1$ (homogeneity),

$\Sigma_j b_{ij} = \Sigma_i b_{ij} = \Sigma_i \Sigma_j b_{ij} = 0$ (homogeneity).

For n input factors only $n - 1$ of these factor share equations are independent, so that $n - 1$ equations are estimated in the form:

$$s_i = a_i + \Sigma_j b_{ij} \ln P_j + e_i$$

The Ad Hoc Disequilibrium Model
Suppose now that factor inputs are adjusted to changes in factor prices and output only with a lag. Then, if we denote the fully adjusted factor share in total cost for the ith input by s_i^* and the current year share by s_i, any particular observation on factor shares, prices, and quantities may be characterized by inequality between the fully adjusted and current—or desired and actual—factor shares. Estimation of the equilibrium share equations under such circumstances may lead to bias in estimates of the elasticities of substitution between pairs of factors, if the desired factor shares are taken to represent the cost-minimizing production technology. If only one input factor did not adjust instantaneously, then in general all factor shares will diverge from their long-run desired values.[6] This form does not impose the assumption that adjustment cost for any particular factor, say, capital, is infinite in the short run and zero in a longer period. Rather it permits relative adjustment costs to determine the rates of

adjustment of all factors. Consequently we specify the first disequilibrium model as

$$ds_i = \Sigma_j c_{ij}(s_j^* - s(-1)_j),$$

for $i, j = K, L, E, M$, where $s(-1)_i$ represents the share of input i in the prior period and

$$ds_i = s_i - s(-1)_i.$$

The coefficents c_{ij} represent the effect of disequilibrium in the share of factor j on the adjustment of the share of factor i. Clearly in static equilibrium

$$s_i^* = s_i = s(-1)_i,$$

and

$$ds_i = 0.$$

Imposing symmetry and homogeneity of degree one in the logs of factor prices, we arbitrarily chose to normalize with respect to labor and obtain the estimating form:

$$ds_i = \Sigma_j(c_{ij} - c_{iL})(a_j + \Sigma_k b_{jk}(\ln P_k - \ln P_L) - s(-1)_j) + e_i,$$

for $i, j, k = K, E, M$. It can be shown that only the differences in adjustment coefficients $c_{ij} - c_{i1}$ can be determined because only three of the share equations are independent. In consequence there is no prior restriction on the size or sign of the coefficients. It can further be shown that for the eliminated equation, using $\Sigma_i ds_i = 0$, for $i = K, L, E, M$:

$$ds_L = -\Sigma_j(c_{LL} - c_L)(s_j^* - s(-1)_j).$$

The differences in adjustment coefficients are determined by

$$(c_{Lj} - c_{LL}) = \Sigma_k[-(c_{kj} - c_{kL})],$$

for $j = K, E, M$.

Thus for n input factors, there are n^2 adjustment coefficients. Only $(n - 1)^2$ differences in these coefficients are independent, and $n - 1$ additional differences may be determined from the independent differences. The model in this form may be given two interpretations. Interpreted strictly as a dynamic model determining ds_i, the underlying assumption is that the disequilibrium effects will be captured in the adjustment coefficients and that the long-run substitution properties of the cost function will be captured in the parameters of s_i^*. As we have shown in earlier work, this approach leads to reasonable results: in general the long-term elasticities of substitution and demand were larger in magnitude than those estimated in an equilibrium model. Elasticities of substitution measured from the long-term structure were computed in the usual manner from the translog parameters in the s_i^*.

In such an approach, however, the plaguing question arises: What kind of cost function is consistent with this specification?[7] There is in the model, as described, no analytic expression for the observed or current period share in total cost; there is no cost function from which these share equations can be derived based on the usual cost minimization assumptions.

The pure Ad Hoc Model

A purer form of the ad hoc model is not subject to the objection that the disequilibrium measure spans two periods. This form describes the change in shares in the current period in terms of the disequilibrium in the prior period; no current period price information enters the model at all. This form is estimated as

$$ds_i = \Sigma_i(c_{ij} - c_{iL})(s(-1)_j^* - s(-1)_j),$$

for $i, j = K, E, M$. This model has the advantage that the adjustment coefficients may be unambiguously interpreted as speed-of-adjustment measures. Again only the differences between the coefficients can be identified.

The Improved Disequilibrium Model

The cost function specification

$$\ln C = a_0 + \Sigma_i a_i \ln P_i + \tfrac{1}{2}\Sigma_i\Sigma_j b_{ij} \ln P_i \ln P_j + \Sigma_i\Sigma_j c_{ij} \ln P_i D_j,$$

where $D_j = S_j^* - S_j(-1)$ has the property that the disequilibrium portion of the model disappears when $s_i^* = s(-1)_i$. Thus the cost function itself represents both equilibrium and disequilibrium situations.
The share equations for this function are given by

$$\frac{\partial \ln C}{\partial \ln P} = s_i + \Sigma_j c_{ij} D_j + \Sigma_j c_{ij} \ln P_i + \Sigma_k c_{kj} \ln P_k,$$

for $i, j = K, L, E, M, k \neq i$.

The estimating form of the model is then derived by imposing homogeneity constraints on the c_{ij}:

$$\Sigma_i c_{ij} = \Sigma_j c_{ij} = \Sigma_i \Sigma_j c_{ij} = 0.$$

Because $\Sigma_i s_i = 1$, $\Sigma_i ds_i = 0$, and the coefficients c_{ij} cannot be directly identified in the estimation. Thus when one share equation (materials) is eliminated from the estimating form, we may observe only the differences

$$g_{ij} = \bar{c}_{ij} - c_{iM},$$

for $i, j = K, L, E$. Thus the estimating form of the share equation is

$$s_i = s_i^* + \Sigma_j g_{ij} D_j + \Sigma_j g_{ij} \ln P_i + \Sigma_k g_{kj} \ln P_k + e_i,$$

for $i, j, = K, L, E, k \neq i$. The share elasticities are then

$$\frac{\partial^2 \ln C}{\partial \ln P_i \, \partial \ln P_j} = b_{ii} + \Sigma_j c_{ij} b_{ij} = se_{ii}, \, i = j,$$

$$= b_{ij} + \Sigma_k c_{kj} b_{jk} = se_{ij}, \, i \neq j,$$

from whence the elasticities of substitution are derived.[8] The short-run elasticities of substitution are computed, using the estimated share equations:

$$e_{ii} = 1 - \frac{1}{s_i} + \frac{se_{ii}}{s_i},$$

$$e_{ij} = 1 + \frac{se_{ii}}{s_i s_j}.$$

The long-run elasticities are similarly computed except that $D_j = 0$, so that the disequilibrium portion of each share expression vanishes. In this way the short-term disequilibrium effects are removed from the elasticity of substitution measures. The resulting measure is termed the equilibrium or long-run elasticity of substitution.

A major advantage of this model is that the long-run elasticities are well defined in terms of the cost function. If one eschews the naive interpretation of the ad hoc model, and hence the elasticities of substitution computed from its application, this specification is more appealing.

9.3 The Price of Capital Services

As noted in section 9.2 a major problem in disequilibrium modeling is that the underlying neoclassical theory of capital depends heavily on equilibrium assumptions. In principle it is recognized that real capital input is not instantaneously adjustable to changes in factor prices or the quantity of output and that planning horizons for capital investment are not limited to the current year. It is only the latter proposition that we modify, and that in an ad hoc manner. The motivation is simply that long-run variations in the capital stock almost certainly take into account recent and expected future investment prices and rates of return, precisely because the physical capital stock cannot be instantaneously adjusted.

Three approaches were adopted. The first substituted for the current price of capital services a five-year moving average of that price centered on the current year. This method took account of rising nominal prices in a simple way. The price thus computed was then used to modify total cost and factor cost shares, and the model was estimated on that basis.

The second approach is more parametric but hardly more defensible in principle. The prices of capital services for each of the five years were entered in the estimating equations for the cost shares as follows:

$$\ln P_{kt} = \Sigma_r z_{t+r} \ln P_{kt+r},$$

for $r = -2, -1, 0, 1, 2$, subject to the restriction

$$\Sigma_r z_{t+r} = 1.$$

In this form an a priori assignment of weights is avoided. The final approach consisted in using the service prices, as calculated based on equilibrium assumptions.

9.4 *KLEM* Data for Manufacturing, 1958–1977

For the estimation, historical time-series data on the prices and gross output shares of capital, labor, energy, and intermediate input were assembled for total manufacturing for the period 1958 to 1977.

Following is a description of the sources and methodology used to create the data.

Output

The goal of the estimation is to represent adjustments in input shares to relative prices in the previous period. The output data appear in table 9.1, and the input data in table 9.2. To observe the effect of materials prices on substitution elasticities, it is necessary to base shares on a gross output measure. To create the output measure, we selected census value of shipments and an implicit deflator for it computed by the BLS Division of Industry Productivity Studies. Since the shares must be shares in actual output, it was necessary to measure output as production rather than shipments, so that shipments were adjusted for changes in inventories of finished goods. Preliminary data for current dollar changes in real

Table 9.1
Output data production for shipments with an inventory change

	Quantity	Cost	Price
1958	0.552440	326.871	0.782000
1959	0.607100	362.874	0.789960
1960	0.614730	368.827	0.792960
1961	0.616470	370.351	0.794000
1962	0.661360	398.324	0.796000
1963	0.697840	420.294	0.796000
1964	0.738690	447.131	0.800000
1965	0.798880	491.421	0.813000
1966	0.849580	537.408	0.836020
1967	0.865490	555.319	0.848000
1968	0.914750	602.154	0.870010
1969	0.940250	640.997	0.901010
1970	0.892400	632.018	0.936020
1971	0.917640	672.095	0.968000
1972	1.00000	756.631	1.00000
1973	1.07884	876.708	1.07402
1974	1.05893	1015.89	1.26793
1975	0.972080	1039.99	1.41398
1976	1.06058	1184.37	1.47591
1977	1.12401	1331.98	1.56619

inventories by stage of processing are from BEA. The change in inventories of finished goods was added to current period shipments to produce a measure of current period production, the denominator for the factor share measures. Finished inventory changes were deflated, using the implicit deflator for all inventories published in the *Survey of Current Business*. Constant dollar finished inventory changes were then added to deflated shipments to obtain real production.

Capital

The measure of capital price is the derived price implicit in a translog index of equipment, structures, inventories, and land. Capital service prices for each asset are derived as explained in Norsworthy and Harper (1979). This approach to measuring the service price of capital assets follows Christensen and Jorgenson (1970). (Note that for this study we include inventories in the capital measure. In our earlier study they were excluded. The biases that resulted from exclusion of inventories from the service prices of other assets were judged to be more unfavorable than the

Table 9.2
Input factors

	Quantity	Price	Cost	Share
Capital				
1958	0.647030	0.662460	35.4070	0.108320
1959	0.654700	0.794410	42.9623	0.118390
1960	0.662340	0.772930	42.2884	0.114660
1961	0.669070	0.759480	41.9757	0.113340
1962	0.685770	0.837440	47.4396	0.119100
1963	0.699700	0.896440	51.8127	0.123280
1964	0.725620	0.947230	56.7773	0.126980
1965	0.763860	1.02450	64.6446	0.131550
1966	0.829620	1.01102	69.2858	0.128930
1967	0.884310	0.925940	67.6378	0.121800
1968	0.923380	0.973130	74.2256	0.123270
1969	0.963540	0.917790	73.0497	0.113960
1970	0.983970	0.820860	66.7200	0.105570
1971	0.985100	0.907290	73.8297	0.109850
1972	1.00000	1.00000	82.6048	0.109170
1973	1.03776	1.03404	88.6415	0.101110
1974	1.07873	0.921000	82.0688	0.807800E-01
1975	1.06327	1.07827	94.7056	0.910600E-01
1976	1.09054	1.25273	112.851	0.952800E-01
1977	1.11531	1.38748	127.828	0.959700E-01
Labor				
1958	0.813840	0.526730	88.4029	0.270450
1959	0.868370	0.546300	97.8307	0.269600
1960	0.871760	0.564970	101.570	0.275390
1961	0.844070	0.584790	101.792	0.274850
1962	0.882770	0.604450	110.039	0.276260
1963	0.888290	0.625120	114.515	0.272460
1964	0.906310	0.651830	121.829	0.272470
1965	0.957170	0.667010	131.663	0.267920
1966	1.02408	0.694080	146.582	0.272760
1967	1.02361	0.727800	153.635	0.276660
1968	1.04224	0.779740	167.593	0.278320
1969	1.05876	0.831380	181.525	0.283190
1970	1.00158	0.888880	183.600	0.290500
1971	0.962880	0.945990	187.845	0.279490
1972	1.00000	1.00000	206.225	0.272560
1973	1.05712	1.06967	233.193	0.265990

Table 9.2 (continued)

	Quantity	Price	Cost	Share
Labor				
1974	1.03899	1.17862	252.539	0.248590
1975	0.944670	1.31118	255.438	0.245620
1976	0.988400	1.42454	290.369	0.245170
1977	1.02858	1.54735	328.221	0.246410
Energy				
1958	0.545300	0.789370	5.06700	0.155000E-01
1959	0.600370	0.784540	5.54460	0.152800E-01
1960	0.624880	0.783740	5.76510	0.156300E-01
1961	0.636250	0.777770	5.82530	0.157300E-01
1962	0.680840	0.771590	6.18400	0.155300E-01
1963	0.696030	0.777410	6.36970	0.151600E-01
1964	0.740270	0.769620	6.70660	0.150000E-01
1965	0.761800	0.777610	6.97340	0.141900E-01
1966	0.791740	0.790330	7.36590	0.137100E-01
1967	0.812120	0.804570	7.69170	0.138500E-01
1968	0.889910	0.789640	8.27210	0.137400E-01
1969	0.938720	0.791960	8.75140	0.136500E-01
1970	0.931960	0.859090	9.42490	0.149100E-01
1971	0.963560	0.920460	10.4405	0.155300E-01
1972	1.00000	1.00000	11.7717	0.155600E-01
1973	1.02786	1.12537	13.6166	0.155300E-01
1974	1.06613	1.54845	19.4333	0.191300E-01
1975	1.00784	1.95865	23.2374	0.223400E-01
1976	1.08361	2.16268	27.5870	0.232900E-01
1977	1.10566	2.51709	32.7612	0.246000E-01
Intermediate input (materials)				
1958	0.566530	0.766360	197.994	0.605720
1959	0.619630	0.766310	216.536	0.596730
1960	0.631340	0.761370	219.204	0.594330
1961	0.631970	0.766000	220.758	0.596080
1962	0.674990	0.762350	234.661	0.589120
1963	0.701020	0.774500	247.596	0.589100
1964	0.735990	0.780070	261.819	0.585550
1965	0.791890	0.797890	288.139	0.586340
1966	0.837760	0.822350	314.174	0.584610
1967	0.863440	0.828830	326.355	0.587690
1968	0.909130	0.849180	352.063	0.584670
1969	0.934330	0.886380	377.670	0.589190

Table 9.2 (continued)

	Quantity	Price	Cost	Share
1970	0.890640	0.916570	372.273	0.589020
1971	0.917930	0.955500	399.979	0.595120
1972	1.00000	1.00000	456.030	0.602710
1973	1.07487	1.10422	541.257	0.617370
1974	1.09270	1.32821	661.851	0.651500
1975	0.979390	1.49253	666.608	0.640980
1976	1.06768	1.54770	753.566	0.636260
1977	1.12206	1.64782	843.174	0.633020

instability in the aggregate capital stock induced by involuntary inventory investment.) Capital's share of total factor cost in each year is the ratio of current period nonlabor payments (gross product originating in manufacturing less labor compensation) to current period production. Capital payments are divided among the four asset types taking account of depreciation, tax regulations, capital gains, and a real internal after tax rate of return assumed equal for all assets.

Labor
Hours and compensation for labor are published BLS series. The hours series was multiplied by an adjustment for changes in effective labor input based on changes in labor force composition.[10] This series was computed from the Gollop-Jorgenson labor force composition data base for 1958 to 1976. Within manufacturing annual hours and compensation are simultaneously partitioned by twenty two-digit industries, two sexes, two classes of workers (employees and self-employed), eight age groups, five educational attainment groups, and ten occupations. Divisia indexes of hours were computed from this breakdown of 32,000 time series and compared to an index of aggregate hours. The ratio of the two indexes is the adjustment series used. Labor force composition was assumed unchanged between 1976 and 1977.

Energy
The primary sources for the quantity and price data on energy were the census of manufactures, *CM*, and the annual survey of manufactures, *ASM*. A secondary source was the BLS wholesale price indexes, *WPI*. Historical quantities and total cost for purchased electricity and total cost for purchased fuels are available annually in the *CM* for total manufacturing. In census years and more frequently in recent years purchased fuel

Table 9.3
Estimation results

	A	B	C	D
	Equilibrium model	Ad hoc model	Pure ad hoc model (real price of capital)	Pure ad hoc model (average price of capital)
AK	0.1195 (193.86)	0.1192 (143.79)	0.1237 (19.13)	0.1140 (34.10)
BKK	0.0728 (20.67)	0.0615 (11.10)	0.0756 (2.02)	0.0540 (4.00)
BKM	−0.0599 (−7.56)	−0.0459 (−5.28)	−0.0681 (−1.28)	−0.0272 (−1.12)
BKE	−0.0022 (−3.77)	−0.0033 (−4.08)	−0.0162 (−0.99)	−0.0142 (1.72)
AM	0.5999 (158.15)	0.5978 (73.21)	0.5953 (53.92)	0.6080 (27.06)
BMM	0.0674 (1.58)	0.0887 (1.16)	0.0443 (0.47)	−0.0448 (−0.36)
BME	−0.0190 (−13.76)	−0.0168 (−9.43)	0.0018 (0.81)	−0.0142 (1.72)
AE	0.0139 (149.90)	0.0139 (107.64)	0.0130 (4.22)	0.0179 (10.88)
BEE	0.0181 (42.03)	0.0174 (18.38)	0.0146 (1.73)	0.0105 (3.16)
GKK	—	1.1128 (9.01)	−0.8195 (−0.73)	1.6150 (3.59)
GKM	—	0.0486 (0.88)	0.0332 (0.11)	0.3366 (2.23)
GKE	—	−1.4000 (−1.92)	1.0024 (0.31)	−5.0636 (−2.12)
GMM	—	0.1275 (0.30)	0.1104 (0.36)	−0.2013 (−0.84)
GMK	—	−0.7961 (−2.21)	1.2342 (1.12)	−0.8597 (−0.99)
GME	—	4.0959 (2.32)	0.1332 (0.42)	6.1819 (1.52)
GEE	—	0.8567 (8.76)	0.3752 (0.72)	0.8669 (2.01)
GEK	—	−0.0025 (−0.15)	0.1856 (2.00)	−0.0364 (−0.49)
GEM	—	−0.0121 (−1.22)	−0.0426 (−1.84)	−0.0641 (−2.31)

Table 9.3 (continued)

	A Equilibrium model		B Ad hoc model	C Pure ad hoc model (real price of capital)	D Pure ad hoc model (average price of capital)
Z1					
Z2					
Z3					
Z4					
Dependent variable R^2 (unadjusted)					
SK	0.9755	DSK	0.9329	0.3059	0.6115
SM	0.4777	DSM	0.6450	0.2806	0.4418
SE	0.9912	DSE	0.9516	0.8560	0.7835
LLF	282.17		323.23	280.15	281.54

Table 9.3 (continued)

	E Disequilibrium model (real price of capital)	F Disequilibrium model (estimated price of capital)	G Equilibrium model (average price of capital)
AK	0.1196 (126.14)	0.1201 (29.5)	0.1131 (91.62)
BKK	0.0789 (4.60)	0.0879 (1.5)	0.0792 (14.40)
BKE	−0.0183 (−0.52)	0.0008 (0.0)	−0.0735 (−2.66)
BKL	−0.0866 (−0.59)	−0.0166 (−0.2)	−0.0020 (−2.66)
AL	0.2734 (36.73)	0.2742 (120.0)	0.6041 (97.41)
BLE	−0.0322 (−0.11)	0.0196 (1.4)	0.0905 (2.04)
BLL	−0.3207 (−0.36)	0.2020 (4.0)	−0.0198 (−11.38)
AE	0.0142 (23.45)	0.0139 (67.8)	0.0160 (115.24)
BEE	0.0282 (0.37)	0.0159 (6.0)	0.0181 (30.44)
GKK	−0.0204 (−0.22)	−0.1409 (−0.2)	—
GKL	−0.0178 (−0.20)	−0.0009 (−0.0)	—
GKE	0.0918 (0.18)	−0.2406 (−0.3)	—
GLK	−0.4587 (−2.47)	0.0143 (0.0)	—
GLL	−0.6657 (−2.88)	−0.2403 (−2.4)	—
GLE	0.3395 (0.27)	−0.9457 (−1.4)	—
GEK	0.0325 (2.18)	0.0271 (1.4)	—
GEL	0.0531 (3.87)	0.0231 (1.4)	—
GEE	−0.2696 (−2.85)	−0.0822 (−0.7)	—

Table 9.3 (continued)

	E Disequilibrium model (real price of capital)	F Disequilibrium model (estimated price of capital)		G Equilibrium model (average price of capital)
Z1		0.1598 (0.8)		
Z2		1.0071 (2.4)		
Z3		−0.2936 (−0.4)		
Z4		0.2120 (1.1)		
		Dependent variable R^2 (unadjusted)		
DSK	0.9142	0.9149	SK	0.9496
DSL	0.2334	0.3797	SM	0.5380
DSE	0.9353	0.7621	SE	0.9910
LLF	352.59	319.32	LLF	273.14

Note: The t-statistic is given in parentheses after the estimated value.

Table 9.4
Selected Allen own and partial elasticities of substitution

	A Equilibrium model	B Ad hoc model	C Pure ad hoc (real price of capital)	D Pure ad hoc (average price of capital)	E Long-run (real price of capital)	F Short-run disquilibrium	G Equilibrium (average price of capital)
KK							
1959	−2.2228	−3.0549	−1.9752	−3.5713	−2.4877	−2.4730	−1.7219
1972	−2.0976	−2.9476	−1.8301	−3.6157	−2.3794	−2.3654	−1.6456
1977	−1.6246	−2.6815	−0.7034	−3.6215	−1.9348	−1.8760	−1.1044
LL							
1959	−2.7803	−2.0327	−3.1893	−3.4359	−2.6478	−2.4684	−2.7717
1972	−2.7972	−2.0970	−3.2433	−3.9811	−2.6396	−3.1342	−2.7851
1977	−2.7471	−2.6069	−3.1212	−3.7006	−2.9877	−3.4483	−2.7508
EE							
1959	13.8263	14.2844	−3.7214	−18.1352	−28.5686	−28.7641	13.7572
1972	9.6388	4.2781	−7.7656	−22.1251	−28.7391	−28.5926	7.5762
1977	−9.6383	−11.2604	−16.0066	−22.6031	−25.8103	−23.9713	−9.5581
MM							
1959	−0.4801	−0.4629	−0.5354	−0.8646	−0.4376	−0.4692	−0.4125
1972	−0.4670	−0.4279	−0.5194	−0.7662	−0.6423	−0.5630	−0.4072
1977	−0.4655	−0.3363	−0.5104	−0.7908	−0.4986	−0.4477	−0.4041
KL							
1959	0.6610	0.6365	1.2862	0.4252	0.6444	0.6592	0.8795
1972	0.6418	0.5837	1.3024	0.3262	0.6247	0.5700	0.8764
1977	0.6002	0.4419	1.3632	0.2953	0.5289	0.4665	0.8621

Table 9.4 (continued)

	A Equilibrium model	B Ad hoc model	C Pure ad hoc (real price of capital)	D Pure ad hoc (average price of capital)	E Long-run (real price of capital)	F Short-run disequilibrium	G Equilibrium (average price of capital)
KE							
1959	−0.2613	−0.9182	−7.9837	−2.8872	−0.4692	−0.3149	−0.1438
1972	−0.2634	−0.8926	−7.6407	−2.3599	−0.4931	−0.3170	−0.1141
1977	0.0722	−0.3860	−5.8575	−1.8493	−0.1159	0.0177	0.1824
KM							
1959	0.1423	0.3263	0.0166	0.6133	0.2973	0.2736	−0.0569
1972	0.1070	0.2691	−0.0188	0.6082	0.1373	0.1791	−0.0472
1977	−0.0087	0.2454	−0.2442	0.5647	0.1098	0.1322	−0.2074
LE							
1959	1.7659	1.6299	0.9583	3.5325	1.3992	1.3363	1.8960
1972	1.7325	1.5700	0.9612	3.2585	1.3825	1.3820	1.8922
1977	1.4695	1.4478	0.9756	2.6658	1.2745	1.2684	1.5535
LM							
1959	1.0720	0.8443	1.1367	1.5217	1.0342	1.0333	1.0171
1972	1.0716	0.8451	1.1367	1.5453	1.0396	1.0427	1.0172
1977	1.0706	0.8284	1.1323	1.5269	1.0392	1.0422	1.0169
EM							
1959	−1.0901	−0.9873	1.1925	−0.6843	0.2441	0.3133	−1.1643
1972	−0.9701	−0.7035	1.1747	−0.2984	0.1575	0.3013	−1.1458
1977	−0.2779	−0.0308	1.1121	−0.0171	0.5030	0.5818	−0.3346

cost and quantities are available in some detail. Data were collected for coal, coke, fuel oil, and natural gas for 1958, 1962, 1967, 1971, 1974, 1976, and 1977. (Data for 1977 are from a preliminary bulletin based on the 1977 *CM*.) From this a benchmark index was then interpolated for intermediate years using the corresponding component of the *WPI*. Intermediate year quantity indexes for each energy type were then adjusted, so that total cost was exhausted. Since there are extra degrees of freedom in this adjustment, relative fuel cost proportions were first interpolated between benchmarks, and then these proportions were assumed fixed for a given intermediate year. A single quantity scalar could then be found to exhaust cost for the given prices and input factor cost proportions. After annual price and quantity data were estimated, a translog quantity index was computed across electricity, coal, coke, fuel oil, and natural gas. A price index was computed as the ratio of total cost of purchased fuels and electricity to quantity.

Materials
Materials quantity was defined as constant dollar production less constant dollar gross product originating less deflated energy costs. The same computation was performed in current dollars and the ratio of current to constant dollar input was used to estimate the materials deflator.

9.5 Model Estimation Results

The models were estimated using 1959 to 1977 data with the iterative Zellner generalized least squares technique. Data are listed in tables 9.1 and 9.2. The dynamic models were sensitive to initial values. However, once convergence in one dynamic model was achieved, its estimated parameters used as initial values in subsequent estimations brought rapid convergence. Table 9.3, columns A through G, shows the model estimation results, and table 9.4, columns A through G, shows the Allen partial elasticities of substitution, *APES*, computed from the estimated models.

Equilibrium Model
The equilibrium model estimation results are shown in table 9.3, columns A and G, for actual and average prices of capital services. Although the data are somewhat different and more recent than those in the Hudson-Jorgenson (1974) work, the same positive own *APES* for energy characterizes most of the estimation period. Both models show capital-energy complementarity. Although the unadjusted *R*-squared statistics have little clear meaning, they are nevertheless shown to indicate the relative

success of the models in explaining variation in the dependent variables. On this criterion the model with actual capital prices seems to perform slightly better in describing movements in capital's share and somewhat worse in the case of materials. The log of the likelihood function, LLF, indicates that the standard equilibrium model gives a better description of the manufacturing production process. Our subsequent discussion will therefore use the standard equilibrium model as the norm for comparison.

The Ad Hoc Model
The ad hoc model (column B in tables 9.3 and 9.4) shows a substantial improvement over the equilibrium model in terms of the LLF. With nine additional parameters to describe the adjustment process, this result is not surprising. However, as noted earlier, the $APES$ are biased. They are nevertheless rather well behaved, and all own $APES$ are negative. Capital and energy are complements. The a_i and b_{ij} coefficients characterizing the long-run cost function are not greatly different from those in the equilibrium model. Some of the difference may be attributable to bias.

Five of the nine g_{ij} coefficients characterizing the adjustment process are significant. Because the coefficients represent differences between adjustment coefficients, it is difficult to assign specific meanings to them.[11] In any event the bias in the long-term substitution parameters will be reflected in the short-term adjustment parameters as well. Perhaps the best position is an agnostic one—the lagged adjustment structure is clearly significant, but the parameters of the structure represent throw-away information from the perspective of long-run substitution. It is nevertheless noteworthy that g_{ME} is large and positive for this model and for most other dynamic models estimated. The strong relationship between energy and materials may be an artifact of the data used to estimate the model, in that energy prices substantially influence the prices of raw materials through extraction and transport costs. A far more elaborate model, such as the Hudson-Jorgenson (1974) model and its progeny, that accounts for interindustry flows would be required to isolate this effect. In general there is also a strong b_{ME} coefficient in the various models.

From the perspective of simulation the ad hoc model would be expected to perform quite well, in particular to outperform the equilibrium model if the biases in long- and short-term coefficients are compensating.

The Pure Ad Hoc Model
The pure ad hoc model was estimated in two variants: with real and average prices of capital services. Estimation results are shown in columns C and D of table 9.3, and $APES$ in columns C and D of table 9.4. The

comparatively low explanatory power of the two models probably results from the fact that the decision horizon for factor input adjustment is for most input factors considerably shorter than one year. Furthermore, since shares rather than quantities are specified as dependent on lagged prices only, stocks in current period prices that affect shares while quantities cannot respond are better explained in the ad hoc model. The variant of the model with average prices describes movements in capital's share much better, and all parameter estimates are more significant. However, the large g_{KE} and g_{ME} parameters suggest that something is amiss. Indeed simulation with this model was performed with difficulty. We attribute the difficulty to these coefficients in particular and to the specification in general.

The own *APES* are negative and stable for the variant with average prices, and capital and energy are complements in both models.

The Disequilibrium Cost Function Model

As noted in section 9.2, this specification is preferred on theoretical grounds because it is derived from a variant of the translog cost function that has the long-term substitution properties of that specification and allows for short-term disequilibrium in each factor. The specification could be estimated in only one variant, with real and estimated capital prices. The complexity of the model led to considerable difficulties in estimation, seemingly by due to loss of precision. Convergence was obtained by dropping the M equation rather than the L equation as in other models. Results are shown in columns E and F of table 9.3. This model is superior to the equilibrium model in terms of fit judged by t-statistics, and *LLF*. Its substitution characteristics, as revealed in the *APES*, are similar to those of the other variants. The adjustment coefficients are much better behaved in this model variant—none exceeds one in absolute value. This result undoubtedly improves the simulation properties of the model.

It is only in the comparison of this model with the equilibrium model that the difference between the equilibrium and disequilibrium estimates of the *APES* can be seen because, as noted earlier, the *APES* in the ad hoc model are biased. The second-order translog parameters, b_{ij}, differ substantially from the equilibrium model, which leads to the expectation that the *APES* will be altered substantially.

The *APES* are in fact substantially different when estimated in the disequilibrium model. Capital and energy are more strongly complementary, though less than in the ad hoc model variants. The complementarity is also stronger than in either variant of the equilibrium model.

The Price of Capital Services
The attempts to reflect a longer-term perspective in the capital decision process are somewhat interesting. Introducing a five-year average price of capital services (centered on the current year) in the equilibrium model has very little impact on the estimation results. The fit is marginally worse, but the *APES* are largely unchanged.[12] The disequilibrium cost function model (model F) with estimated weights determining a price of capital services proved extraordinarily hard to estimate, presumably because of the large number of parameters and the complexity of the share equations.[13] Loss of precision in the iterative Zellner estimation process appears to have been a problem. In any event these nonlinear specifications are difficult to estimate, because they are quite sensitive to starting values.

The estimation results for model F show a generally poorer fit in both the translog parameters and the adjustment coefficients compared with the disequilibrium cost function model (model E). The only significant parameter in the price of capital estimation is $Z2$, the coefficient on the current year price of which the estimated value is quite near 1. We therefore concluded that this specification does not improve on model E—in fact it is worse—and therefore rejected it from further consideration.

Attempts to estimate the disequilibrium cost function model based on an average price of capital services were even less successful.

Thus our efforts to improve on the method of incorporating the price of capital in the cost function failed. In some measure disequilibrium information is eliminated in the capital price smoothing process and the equilibrium model. We were disappointed, however, that we made no progress in this direction.

Summary of Estimation Results
In general the various disequilibrium models represent improvement over the basic translog cost function, in terms of fit and in the plausibility of elasticity estimates. Only the disequilibrium cost function model yields soundly based elasticity extimates; however, all the disequilibrium variants appear to have better properties for short-term simulation. The difficulty of estimating the disequilibrium cost function model is a problem, but its a priori properties make it the best of the lot.

In general the disequilibrium forms describe the changes in capital's and energy's shares very well (as measured by the admittedly imperfect R-squared criterion). This fact probably accounts for the stability of capital-energy complementarity across the range of models. In contrast, the materials and labor shares are not well explained. Presumably there are other factors involved that must be included to improve the disequilibrium model's explanatory power for these inputs.

9.6 Energy-Capital Substitution or Complementarity

The estimation results strongly favor the dynamic over the equilibrium models. On a priori grounds the disequilibrium cost function model is the only acceptable variant for studying interfactor substitution in aggregate manufacturing.

This model shows a relatively large own *APES* for energy; this corresponds to an own price elasticity of demand for energy that is near 0.2. As table 9.2 shows, the energy price increase began substantially before 1973, although not as dramatically as in the following years. This earlier increase arose primarily from increasing coal prices that followed the mining regulations of 1969. In consequence there is longer-term experience with rising energy prices in manufacturing than the conventional wisdom might suppose, and the estimates may be considered fairly reliable.

The relationship of complementarity between energy and capital is stronger than in the equilibrium model and perhaps more consistent with the large observed decline in capital formation than is indicated in this model.

A difficulty in interpreting the short- and long-term elasticities is of course that it is unclear just how long the long term really is. This question is one that would best be addressed through detailed simulations more complex than those undertaken here.

The measured complementarity between capital and energy may reside in two phenomena. First, changing the level of required energy input in a particular manufacturing process, or substituting among energy input types, typically requires a change in equipment and thus entails a relatively long adjustment period. Second, the production technology in U.S. manufacturing was developed in a period when energy was the factor input with the least rapidly rising price. The technology embodied in equipment design endeavored to save labor through the introduction of capital, often increasingly energy-using capital. This pattern, which led to lower total costs in the past, may so permeate current technology that measured complementarity between capital and energy is built into the record of the past and much of the technology of the present. The price signals are different now—the price of energy since 1973 has risen most rapidly of all factor prices. As these new price signals affect the technology, we may very well see an economizing of energy—consistent with the high measured own *APES*—still accompanied by equipment investment in accordance with capital-energy complementarity.

Thus strong capital-energy complementarity, especially in the light of a high price elasticity of demand for energy, need not be interpreted as indicating that economizing energy inputs in manufacturing is very difficult, nor that rising energy prices over the long term will lead to declining capital investment or a permanently lower rate of productivity growth. The lag in shifting from a pattern of energy-using to energy-saving technical progress would cause deferral of equipment spending in itself. It is noteworthy that capital-energy complementarity is not necessarily inconsistent with adoption of more energy-efficient equipment.

The perceived capital-energy relationship may be further biased by technical progress associated with scale effects. The rate of output growth in manufacturing was much slower in 1973 to 1977 than in 1959 to 1973. If there are scale effects at work that are capital using and energy neutral, then the slower output growth in the recent period could bias the capital-energy *APES* toward complementarity.

9.7 Simulation

To explore the policy implications of our estimation results, we simulated the historical period with one of our models. We wished to explore two questions. First, what effect would an investment tax credit on structures have on productivity? Second, how much of the productivity slowdown could reasonably be attributed to the sharp energy price increases?

A simulation was developed for the years 1973 to 1977 using the coefficients from model *E*, the disequilibrium model with an equilibrium aggregator function for capital assets. The basic simulation used actual prices to generate shares to which "add factors" were then applied to yield the actual shares. Keeping the add factors in place, we then compared this simulation, first, to one in which the investment tax credit was applied to structures at the same rate as it was to equipment and, second, to one in which energy prices from 1973 to 1977 were allowed to rise at only their average rate from 1959 to 1971. In a third setting all prices from 1973 to 1977 were allowed to rise at only their average 1959 to 1971 rates. Reported quantities and productivities assume that output grew as it actually did. However, we recognize that, since output prices were lower in the comparison cases, demand could have been greater, expanding the quantities and biasing the productivities.

The simulation program performed the following major steps:

1. simulated the capital aggregator function to determine capital asset shares,
2. computed the overall capital price,
3. altered the capital price,
4. simulated the *KLEM*-lagged adjustment model to determine input shares,
5. obtained add factoring of the shares,
6. computed the price of output,
7. imputed the input quantities,
8. computed the productivity growth rates.

Simulation Structure

The inputs to the simulation included total output (constant dollar production), prices and multiplicative levers for labor, energy, and materials. The equations for the prices of equipment, structures, inventories, and land, together with the actual data that entered them, were required inputs. This permitted alteration of the components of the asset prices in test cases. Additional inputs were actual capital payments, a multiplicative lever for total capital's price, and add factors for the final shares of capital, energy, and materials. The levers and add factors were used to adjust simulation results to actual historical experience before case comparisons.

The four capital asset prices were functions of depreciation, capital gains, a common internal rate of return, and income and property taxes. (See Norsworthy and Harper 1980). Instead of solving four price equations and a product exhaustion constraint for four prices and an internal rate of return, the actual rate of return was used. Thus when the investment tax credit was applied to the tax rate on structures in a comparison case, we implicitly assumed that the internal rate of return was unaffected.

Two alternative base simulations that were tried involved solving for a new internal rate of return based on (1) the simulated tax assumption alone and (2) the simulated tax assumption, the simulated payments to capital from the *KLEM* function, and the simulated capital asset quantities.

The second simulation was unstable because capital payments, asset deflators, and asset quantities were not determined simultaneously with capital's price. The first was stable but turned out to be inappropriate for analyzing the effect of the structure tax credit for the following reason. Given that capital payments are the same in both simulations, a tax cut on one asset raises the internal rate of return, which in turn slightly raises the prices of all assets. The overall affect is little or no change on the final price of capital. Therefore we decided to use the rate of return imputed from actual data in both the basic and comparison simulations. These asset prices were then passed to a capital aggregator function. The aggregator function was an equilibrium translog cost function of the prices of equipment, inventories, and a translog index of structures and land (land constitutes only about 3 percent of capital payments in manufacturing). Two of the three share equations were fitted, using the iterative Zellner method and historical data for 1959 to 1977. The resulting parameters were then used with the asset prices to produce annual asset shares, thus allowing for substitution of capital assets before computing the overall capital price. The fitted share equations for the aggregate function were:

$$SS = 0.272 + 0.106 (\ln PS - \ln PI) - 0.036 (\ln PE - \ln PI),$$

$$SE = 0.404 - 0.036 (\ln PS - \ln PI) + 0.160 (\ln PE - \ln PI),$$

where SS and SE are the shares of structures plus land and equipment, respectively, and PS, PE, and PI are the prices of structures plus land, equipment, and inventories, respectively, normalized to 1.0 in 1972.

Once the asset shares were determined by the aggregator function, a translog price index of the asset prices was computed, using the shares as weights. Before the $KLEM$ model was simulated in the base case, the capital price was multiplied by a lever that made it equal the actual capital price. In the comparison cases this lever was carried forward. Thus in the basic case the $KLEM$ model was simulated, using the same price series as those of the estimation, while in the comparison cases dissimilarities in input prices were scaled, so that only the relative effects of the price changes being studied were simulated. In the simulation of the $KLEM$ disequilibrium model, current period changes in shares were computed from simulated lagged shares, lagged prices, first- and second-order translog parameters, and disequilibrium adjustment parameters. The model, as described in section 9.2, produces the change in each share from last period to the current period as the sum of the disequilibriums in three of the four shares multiplied by their respective estimated adjustment coefficients. Each current simulated share was then computed as its simulated lagged share plus its simulated change in share. Hence the model was simulated one year at a time, and any drift from actual historical lagged shares was allowed to persist and build on itself.

Following the basic $KLEM$ simulation, add factors were applied to the shares to make them equal to the true shares. The same add factors were then applied to the comparison versions.

Simulation Results

For the purposes of reporting, several measures were computed based on the simulated shares. First an output price index was computed as a translog index of input prices, using the simulated shares as weights. The output quantity is exogenous to our model. We chose to use the actual output quantity to produce the reported factor quantities demanded and productivity levels in all the variations. Since the shares are by definition $s_i = p_i q_i / \Sigma_j p_j q_j$, we can substitute output quantity, QP, times output price, PP, for $\Sigma_j p_j q_j$ to obtain an approximation to the input quantities as $q_i = s_i QP \cdot PP / P_i$. This substitution necessarily assumes zero growth in total factor productivity in the base case since actual output cost has been substituted for factor cost. To the extent that different input shares occurred in alternate simulations, total factor productivity growth greater or less than zero resulted from an index of factor input that grew less or more than the assumed output level. For computation of productivity rates the input quantities were scaled down by the rate of total factor productivity growth measured in the actual data, 0.14.

We report results for five simulations. Simulation B is the base simulation. Simulation A is the same as B, without levering the price of capital or incorporating add factors. C is the same as B, but with the investment tax credit on equipment carried over to structures. D is the same as B, but with energy prices from 1973 to 1977 growing at 1.34 percent annually (their average rate from 1959 to 1971). Finally, E is similar to D, except that all input prices grow at only their 1959 to 1971 average rates during the simulation period.

In table 9.5 the 1977 shares and the 1973 to 1977 percent changes of several other variables are presented. In the table PK, PL, PE, and PM are the average rates of change of the input prices used in the $KLEM$ simulation, PP is the growth rate of the price of output computed as a translog index of the factor prices; and SK, SL, SE, and SM are the simulated shares in 1977. In case B they are also the actual shares. QK, QL, QE, and QM are the imputed input quantity rates of change from 1973 to 1977.

The section on percent changes includes the growth of output, QP, which is exogenous and held equal to its actual 1973 to 1977 annual rate of 1.10 percent. The factor input is the growth rate of a translog index of the input quantities, and total factor productivity growth is the difference between QP and factor input. Total factor productivity has been forced by definition to its actual rate in simulation B. We have also included the growth rates of value-added labor productivity, the capital labor ratio, KLR, and the capital labor ratio times capital's share in value added ($W_k \cdot KLR$). Finally, we include the growth rate of the Hicks-neutral

Table 9.5
Results of simulating the true cost function model for the period 1973 to 1977

Model/measure	A No add factors	B Base simulation and actual historical measures	C ITC on structures	D Cheap energy	E All factor prices at 1959–1971 rates
1977 shares
SK	0.0948	0.0960	0.0938	0.0988	0.1041
SL	0.2521	0.2464	0.2455	0.2496	0.2570
SE	0.0235	0.0246	0.0248	0.0159	0.0186
SM	0.6296	0.6330	0.6359	0.6358	0.6203
Average annual rates of change, 1973–1977
PK	5.61	8.27	7.85	8.27	4.66
PL	9.67	9.67	9.67	9.67	4.68
PE	24.04	24.04	24.04	1.38	1.38
PM	10.81	10.81	10.81	10.81	1.79
PP	10.05	10.39	10.36	9.99	2.70
QK	1.83	2.32	2.35	2.69	2.26
QL	−0.29	−0.02	−0.17	−0.04	−1.30
QE	−0.55	1.39	1.51	10.41	6.99
QM	2.01	1.79	1.84	1.53	2.23
QP	1.34	1.34	1.34	1.34	1.34
Factor Input	1.18	1.20	1.24	1.18	1.20
Total factor productivity	1.16	0.14	0.10	0.16	0.14
QP/QK	−0.56	−1.05	−1.09	−1.41	−0.99
QP/QL	1.71	1.35	1.49	1.40	3.06
QP/QE	2.21	−0.13	−0.25	−8.09	−5.23
QP/QM	−0.55	−0.37	−0.41	−0.12	−0.85
Value-added labor productivity	0.76	0.69	0.70	0.79	1.05
Capital labor ratio	2.27	2.65	2.83	3.10	4.22
$Wk \cdot KLR$	0.62	0.74	0.78	0.87	1.19
Hick's neutral term	0.14	−0.05	−0.08	−0.08	−0.14

rate of technical change, defined as value-added labor productivity less $W_k \cdot KLR$.

Examination of simulation A yields some insights about predicted versus actual behavior (simulation B). In the face of rapidly increasing energy prices, the model predicts even more conservation of energy, capital, and labor and more use of materials than actually occurred.

The investment tax credit on structures (case C) makes the price of capital grow about 0.5 percent slower from 1973 to 1977. As a result more capital is purchased. Capital growth is lessened about 0.03 percent per year, and labor productivity growth improved about 0.14 percent per year.

In simulation D, where energy prices only were kept low, the major effect was much more use of energy, with energy usage growing over 9 percent per year faster than in the base simulation. Since much of the growth in the other factor prices has often been blamed on feedback from the energy price change, we chose a final scenario, E, in which all factor prices grew during the simulated 1973 to 1977 period at only their 1959 to 1971 average rates. Comparing these historical conditions to actual conditions, we got an improvement at 0.36 and 0.45, respectively, in labor productivity and the share weighted capital-labor ratio.

9.8 Conclusions

Both the model estimation and simulation results of this investigation confirm the general finding of energy-capital complementarity. While a conservative appraisal of the results is in order, it is probably reasonable to claim the following:

1. The disequilibrium model derived from an explicit dynamic cost function represents an improvement in principle over the ad hoc model, whose elasticity of substitution estimates are demonstrably biased.
2. The disequilibrium model represents a suggestive alternative to the instantaneous adjustment equilibrium model.
3. The finding of capital-energy complementarity is robust—a wide variety of dynamic models, good and bad, lead to findings that are similar although different in magnitude.
4. The simulation results point to a significant impact of energy prices on labor productivity growth and confirm the superiority of the disequilibrium cost function model.

Certain further investigations seem to be implied:

1. Other functional forms should be considered in the dynamic adjustment setting. The generalized Box-Cox function used by Berndt and Khaled (1979) is attractive, as is the idea of a generalized dynamic cost function approximation.

2. The properties of the dynamic model and explicit hypothesis tests contrasting it with the equilibrium model should be examined further. For example, cost minimizing with respect to the disequilibrium factors, D_i, seems to imply nonlinear restrictions on the adjustment coefficients.

3. Further attention should be given to the measurement of factor inputs. The weak separability assumptions on which the capital, labor, and energy aggregates depend should be studied further.

4. Simulation experiments should be conducted with the preferred model to aid in assessing its properties.

Notes

The views expressed in this chapter do not necessarily represent those of the Bureau of Labor Statistics or its staff. We thank Ernst Berndt, Kent Kunze, and Leonard Waverman for helpful comments.

1. See also Berndt and Jorgenson, who find complementarity, and Humphrey and Moroney, who in a cross-section study of manufacturing industries find substitutability.

2. Norsworthy and Harper (1979).

3. A "satisfactory" model is in our view one that at a minimum simultaneously determines the demands for several input factors.

4. Nadiri-Rosen focused on the cost of adjustment, which is certainly better economics than the time required to adjust factor inputs.

5. Since our major objective is to study the capital-energy relationship with data showing as much of the recent energy price increase as possible, we chose capital, labor, energy, and intermediate inputs through 1977 as inputs. Of these only labor hours are available quickly, and even for the hours data no labor force composition factor could be obtained.

6. See Nadiri and Rosen (1969, 1973).

7. This point was missed by Nadiri and Rosen.

8. See Binswanger (1974b).

9. Measures of gross product originating, compensation, and hours are identical to those used in *BLS* productivity and cost computations for the manufacturing sector.

10. Capital is adjusted for changes in asset type only. Labor is adjusted for age, sex, education, occupation, class of worker and (two-digit) interindustry shifts following Gollop and Jorgenson. See Norsworthy, Harper, and Kunze.

11. In particular the conclusion that factors i and j are short-term substitutes or

short-term complements based on the sign of g_{ij} seems hard to defend. However, see Mohr.

12. The estimated average price was substituted in computation of the *APES* for this model variant.

13. In retrospect it would be informative to have estimated the equilibrium model in the same fashion.

10

Estimating Elasticities of Substitution in a Model of Partial Static Equilibrium: An Application to U.S. Agriculture, 1947 to 1974

Randall S. Brown and Laurits R. Christensen

During the 1970s the neoclassical cost function gained substantial popularity as a tool for estimating the structure of production—especially substitution possibilities. This surge of popularity can be attributed to the widespread application of duality theory to economic analysis and the concomitant development of flexible functional forms.[1] An important assumption that underlies most cost function applications is that all inputs are in static equilibrium. In many instances, however, the assumption of full static equilibrium is suspect and hence so are the empirical results.[2]

Two basic approaches can be followed to relax the assumption of full static equilibrium. First, costs of adjustment can be recognized explicitly, and the firm can be assumed to be continuously in dynamic equilibrium rather than static equilibrium. The theoretical foundations for models of dynamic equilibrium with explicit costs of adjustment were provided by Eisner and Strotz, Lucas (1967a), and others. Berndt, Morrison, and Watkins (chapter 12) provide a brief review of empirical applications based on this approach, which they refer to as third-generation dynamic models. Second, the firm can be assumed to be in static equilibrium with respect to a subset of inputs (rather than all inputs) conditional on the observed levels of the remaining inputs. It is convenient to refer to this framework as one of partial static equilibrium. The inputs that are in partial static equilibrium are referred to as variable inputs and the remaining inputs are designated as fixed or quasi-fixed inputs.

The specification of dynamic equilibrium is theoretically attractive and leads to elegant models. However, these models are difficult to implement empirically. Furthermore departures from full static equilibrium may result from factors other than internal costs of adjustment. For example, regulatory restrictions may hinder capital mobility. In such cases dynamic equilibrium will be an inappropriate specification.

The specification of partial static equilibrium covers the case of dynamic equilibrium as well as other departures from full static equilibrium. Even if dynamic equilibrium is an appropriate specification, the partial static equilibrium specification may be preferred since explicit modeling of the adjustment process can be avoided. The theoretical basis for the partial static equilibrium cost function (hereafter referred to as the variable cost function) can be found in discussion of the variable profit function, of which it is a special case. Diewert (1974) attributes the notion of a variable profit function to Samuelson (1953) and early discussion of its properties to Gorman and a 1970 unpublished version of McFadden (1978). The first empirical application of a variable profit function appears to be Lau and Yotopoulos (1971).

Lau (1976) provides a general theoretical treatment of variable profit functions. Both static equilibrium cost functions and variable cost functions can be treated as special cases of the variable profit function. Lau makes clear that, under quite general regularity conditions, estimates of the structure of production can be obtained from either cost function specification. Furthermore knowledge of the production structure allows one to infer measures such as elasticities of substitution conditional on the levels of any subset of inputs.

Our objectives in this chapter are to derive specific procedures for estimating elasticities of substitution when the partial static equilibrium formulation is appropriate and then to apply the procedures to U.S. agriculture using the translog variable cost function.[3]

We chose to examine the production structure of U.S. agriculture because the U.S. farm sector is widely thought to have been in disequilibrium throughout the postwar period.[4] The principal source of alleged disequilibrium is the lack of mobility of self-employed farm labor. Although the number of self-employed farmers has declined throughout the postwar period, the exodus is thought not to have been rapid enough to achieve the cost-minimizing mix of farm inputs. For this reason we treat self-employed farm labor as a quasi-fixed factor in the cost function for the farm sector. We regard land as a fixed factor for the farm sector, since there is little latitude in the amount of land held by the entire sector. A case could be made for including agricultural structures and equipment in the quasi-fixed category. However, since the stocks of structures and equipment have grown steadily for most of the postwar period, they seem to be better characterized as variable rather than quasi-fixed factors.

All of the data are taken from Brown who constructed new estimates of the entire range of inputs for the farm sector. While the data permit specification of a large number of variable factors, we limit our application to three aggregates: services from hired labor, services from structures and equipment, and all other purchased inputs such as fertilizer, feed, seed, and energy referred to as materials.

10.1 Methodology

We begin by specifying a general production function for the case of a single output and multiple inputs:[5]

$$Y = F(X_1, \ldots, X_n, t), \tag{10.1}$$

where the inclusion of time, t, allows the structure of production to vary over time. If the production function has convex isoquants, and if for any level of output the cost-minimizing input mix is employed, then there exists a total cost function that is dual to (10.1):

$$CT = G(Y, P_1, \ldots, P_n, t), \tag{10.2}$$

where the P_i are the prices of the X_i and $CT = \sum_{i=1}^{n} P_i X_i$ is total cost. If the cost-minimizing output mix is not employed, (10.2) is not valid. However, if cost is minimized with respect to a subset of the factor inputs conditional on the level of output and the remaining inputs, then there exists a variable cost function that is dual to (10.1):

$$CV = H(Y, P_1, \ldots, P_l, Z_1, \ldots, Z_m, t), \tag{10.3}$$

where the Z_i represent the subset of the X_i not necessarily in static equilibrium, $l + m = n$ and $CV = \sum_{i=1}^{l} P_i X_i$.

Uzawa (1962) has shown that the elasticities of substitution defined by Allen can be computed from the partial derivatives of the cost function. The static equilibrium elasticities of substitution can be computed from the total cost function:

$$\sigma_{ij} = \frac{CT \cdot CT_{ij}}{CT_i \cdot CT_j}, \tag{10.4}$$

where $CT_i = \partial CT / \partial P_i$, and so on. The partial static equilibrium elasticities of substitution can be computed from the variable cost function:

$$\sigma_{ij}^P = \frac{CV \cdot CV_{ij}}{CV_i \cdot CV_j}, \tag{10.5}$$

where $CV_i = \partial CV / \partial P_i$, and so on.

The partial static equilibrium elasticities of substitution are valid only for the levels of the fixed factors at which they are evaluated. Furthermore they do not provide any information as to the substitution possibilities among the fixed factors or between the fixed and variable factors. However, this information can be obtained from the variable cost function, as we demonstrate explicitly next.

If all factors are at their static equilibrium levels, total cost can be written as the sum of the variable cost function and expenditure for the Z_i:

$$CT = H(Y, P, Z^*) + \sum P_i Z_i^* = I(Y, P, Z^*), \tag{10.6}$$

where Z_i^* indicates the equilibrium level of Z_i. Our task is to compute the σ_{ij} from (10.6). In doing so, we make use of the full static equilibrium condition for a quasi-fixed factor:

$$\frac{\partial CV}{\partial Z_i^*} = -P_i. \tag{10.7}$$

Let us define b_i as a binary variable that is unity if i is a fixed factor and zero if i is a variable factor. The first partial derivatives of CT are

$$\frac{\partial CT}{\partial P_i} = \frac{\partial CV}{\partial P_i} + \left\{ \sum_k \frac{\partial CV}{\partial Z_k^*} \frac{\partial Z_k^*}{\partial P_i} + \sum_k P_k \frac{\partial Z_k^*}{\partial P_i} \right\} + b_i Z_i^*, \quad \forall_i, \tag{10.8}$$

but the terms in braces sum to zero by (10.7). The second partial derivatives of CT are

$$\frac{\partial^2 CT}{\partial P_i \partial P_j} = \frac{\partial^2 CV}{\partial P_i \partial P_j} + \sum_k \frac{\partial^2 CV}{\partial P_i \partial Z_k^*} \frac{\partial Z_k^*}{\partial P_j}$$

$$+ \sum_k \frac{\partial Z_k^*}{\partial P_i} \left(\frac{\partial^2 CV}{\partial Z_k^* \partial P_j} + \sum_l \frac{\partial^2 CV}{\partial Z_k^* \partial Z_l^*} \frac{\partial Z_l^*}{\partial P_j} \right) + b_i \frac{\partial Z_i^*}{\partial P_j} \tag{10.9}$$

$$+ b_j \frac{\partial Z_j^*}{\partial P_i} + \left\{ \sum_k \frac{\partial CV}{\partial Z_k^*} \frac{\partial^2 Z_k^*}{\partial P_i \partial P_j} + \sum_k P_k \frac{\partial^2 Z_k^*}{\partial P_i \partial P_j} \right\}, \quad \forall_{i,j},$$

where again the terms in braces sum to zero by (10.7).

Equations (10.8) and (10.9) contain partial derivatives of CV that can be evaluated from an estimated variable cost function. Evaluation of (10.8) and (10.9) also requires estimates of the $\partial Z_i^*/\partial P_j$. For many of the functional forms commonly used for cost functions in empirical work, including the translog, no closed form expression for the Z_i^* are available. Thus one must compute these derivatives indirectly.

The first-order condition that defines the optimal levels of the fixed factors given in equation (10.6) can be rewritten as the implicit functions:

$$\frac{\partial CT}{\partial Z_i^*} = \frac{\partial I(Y, P, Z^*)}{\partial Z_i^*} = I_i = 0, \quad \forall_i. \tag{10.10}$$

These functions can be solved for the Z_i^* as functions of Y and P, and hence for the $\partial Z_i^*/\partial P_j$.

Define

$$
\mathbf{B} = \begin{bmatrix}
\dfrac{\partial I_1}{\partial Z_1^*} & \dfrac{\partial I_1}{\partial Z_2^*} & \cdots & \dfrac{\partial I_1}{\partial Z_m^*} \\
\vdots & & & \\
\dfrac{\partial I_m}{\partial Z_1^*} & \dfrac{\partial I_m}{\partial Z_2^*} & \cdots & \dfrac{\partial I_m}{\partial Z_m^*}
\end{bmatrix},
\tag{10.11}
$$

$$
\mathbf{a}_i' = \left(\dfrac{\partial I_1}{\partial P_i} \quad \dfrac{\partial I_2}{\partial P_i} \quad \cdots \quad \dfrac{\partial I_m}{\partial P_i} \right).
\tag{10.12}
$$

The total differential of I_i can be written

$$
dI_i = 0 = \frac{\partial I_i}{\partial Y} dY + \sum_k \frac{\partial I_i}{\partial P_k} dP_k + \sum_j \frac{\partial I_i}{\partial Z_j^*} dZ_j^*.
\tag{10.13}
$$

Setting $dY = dP_j = 0$, $\forall_j \neq i$, and dividing both sides by dP_i, we have

$$
0 = \mathbf{a}_i + \mathbf{B}
\begin{bmatrix}
\dfrac{\partial Z_1^*}{\partial P_i} \\
\vdots \\
\dfrac{\partial Z_m^*}{\partial P_i}
\end{bmatrix}, \quad \forall_i.
\tag{10.14}
$$

It follows that

$$
\begin{bmatrix}
\dfrac{\partial Z_1^*}{\partial P_i} \\
\vdots \\
\dfrac{\partial Z_m^*}{\partial P_i}
\end{bmatrix}
= -\mathbf{B}^{-1}\mathbf{a}_i,
\tag{10.15}
$$

which can be evaluated for each i. We note that for a single fixed factor (10.15) simplifies to:

$$
\frac{\partial Z^*}{\partial P_i} = -\frac{\partial I_{Z^*}/\partial P_i}{\partial I_{Z^*}/\partial Z^*}.
\tag{10.16}
$$

With these results evaluation of equation (10.9) is straightforward, for any functional form selected for the variable cost function CV. Before proceeding to the application of these results to a specific example, however, note the following simplified forms of equations (10.8) and (10.9):[6]

$$\frac{\partial CT}{\partial P_i} = \begin{cases} \dfrac{\partial CV}{\partial P_i}, & i \in VF \\[2ex] Z_i^*, & i \in FF \end{cases} \tag{10.17}$$

$$\frac{\partial^2 CT}{\partial P_i \partial P_j} = \begin{cases} \dfrac{\partial^2 CV}{\partial P_i \partial P_j} + \sum\limits_k \dfrac{\partial Z_k^*}{\partial P_j} \dfrac{\partial^2 CV}{\partial Z_k^* \partial P_i}, & i, j \in VF, \\[3ex] \sum\limits_k \dfrac{\partial Z_k^*}{\partial P_i} \dfrac{\partial^2 CV}{\partial Z_k^* \partial P_j}, & i \in FF, j \in VF, \\[3ex] \dfrac{\partial Z_i^*}{\partial P_j}, & i, j \in FF, \end{cases} \tag{10.18}$$

where VF is the set of variable factors and FF is the set of fixed factors. Note also that if i is a fixed factor the xth element of $\mathbf{a}_i$ is

$$a_{ik} = \frac{\partial I_k}{\partial P_i} = \begin{cases} 1, & \text{if } k = i \\ 0, & \text{if } k \neq i. \end{cases} \tag{10.19}$$

Hence from equation (10.15)

$$\frac{\partial Z_k^*}{\partial P_i} = \begin{cases} [-B^{-1}]_{ik}, & \text{for } i \in FF, \\[2ex] [-B^{-1}\mathbf{a}_i]_k, & \text{for } i \in VF. \end{cases} \tag{10.20}$$

As before, all derivatives in (10.17), (10.18), (10.19) and (10.20) are evaluated at the point $Z = Z^*$.

The results in (10.18) and (10.20) can also be used to show that the Le Chatelier principle holds if the variable cost function is convex in the fixed factors, at $Z = Z^*$, or equivalently, if the second-order conditions necessary for Z^* to minimize CT are met. The Le Chatelier principle requires that the own price response of variable factors decrease in absolute value with the number of factors that are quasi-fixed; hence

$$\frac{\partial^2 CV}{\partial P_i^2} \geq \frac{\partial^2 CT}{\partial P_i^2}, \quad i \in VF.$$

From equation (10.18) we see that for variable factors

$$\frac{\partial^2 CT}{\partial P_i^2} = \frac{\partial^2 CV}{\partial P_i^2} + \sum_k \frac{\partial Z_k^*}{\partial P_i} \frac{\partial^2 CV}{\partial Z_k^* \partial P_i}, \quad i \in VF.$$

However, from equations (10.12) and (10.20),

$$\sum_k \frac{\partial Z_k^*}{\partial P_i} \frac{\partial^2 CV}{\partial Z_k^* \partial P_i} = a_i'[\mathbf{B}^{-1}]a_i,$$

which is negative semidefinite provided that **B** is positive semidefinite. Hence, if **B** is positive semidefinite, the Le Chatelier principle holds.[7]

The requirement that CV be convex everywhere in Z, including at $Z = Z^*$, guarantees that $\mathbf{B}(\equiv \partial^2 CT/\partial \mathbf{Z}^{*2} = \partial^2 CV/\partial \mathbf{Z}^{*2})$ is positive semidefinite, and thus that the Le Chatelier principle holds. It might also be noted that the second-order conditions for Z^* to yield a proper minimum of CT require that $\partial^2 CT/\partial \mathbf{Z}^{*2}$ be positive definite. Thus operationally, in solving for the value(s) of Z that minimize CT, verification that the second-order conditions hold will ensure that CV is convex in Z^* and that the Le Chatelier principle holds.

To implement the method just described, we specify a translog form for the variable cost function with additive error term ε_c:

$$\ln CV = \alpha_0 + \alpha_Y \ln Y + \sum_i^l \alpha_i \ln P_i + \sum_i^m \beta_i \ln Z_i + \frac{1}{2}\gamma_{YY}(\ln Y)^2$$

$$+ \frac{1}{2}\sum_i^l \sum_j^l \gamma_{ij} \ln P_i \ln P_j + \frac{1}{2}\sum_j^m \sum_j^m \delta_{ij} \ln Z_i \ln Z_j$$

$$+ \sum_i^l \rho_{Y_i} \ln Y \ln P_i + \sum_i^l \sum_j^m \rho_{ij} \ln P_i \ln Z_j \qquad (10.21)$$

$$+ \sum_i^m \Pi_i \ln Y \ln Z_i + \phi_t t + \frac{1}{2}\phi_{tt} t^2$$

$$+ \phi_{tY} t \ln Y + \sum_i \phi_{tP_i} t \ln P_i$$

$$+ \sum_i^m \phi_{tZ_i} t \ln Z_i + \varepsilon_c.$$

From Shephard's lemma (1953) we know that at the levels of the variable factors that minimize variable cost, the derivatives $\partial \ln CV/\partial \ln P_i$ are equal to the shares of these factors in variable cost, $S_i = P_i X_i/\sum_{i=1}^l P_i X_i$. Adding disturbance terms ε_i to reflect errors in optimization yields:

$$S_i = \alpha_i + \rho_{Y_i} \ln Y + \sum_j^l \gamma_{ij} \ln P_j$$

$$+ \sum_j^m \rho_{ij} \ln Z_j + \phi_{tP_i} t + \varepsilon_i, \quad \forall_i. \qquad (10.22)$$

The set of equations (10.21) and (10.22) will be used to estimate the parameters of CV, from which the elasticities of substitution will be derived.

10.2 Data

Estimation of the variable cost function for the U.S. farm sector requires time-series data on the levels of output and the fixed inputs, the prices of the variable factors, and the level of variable cost. The data in this section are taken from Brown.

The three variable inputs that we distinguish are hired labor services, capital services, and materials. A translog index of hired labor was constructed from data provided by Gollop and Jorgenson.[8] The implicit wage rate for this index was then used as the price index for hired labor services. The capital services index was based on estimated capital stocks of farm equipment, structures, and inventories. A price index for farm capital services was then estimated, using the assumption that on average over the postwar period the rate of return in farming has been the same as in the U.S. corporate sector. Translog quantity and price indexes were derived for materials from detailed data on fertilizer and liming materials, feed, seed, livestock, electricity, petroleum products, and fourteen miscellaneous categories. The level of variable cost was then calculated as the sum of compensation for hired labor, annualized capital costs, and expenditures on other purchased inputs.

The two fixed inputs that we distinguish are self-employed labor services and land. A translog index of self-employed labor was developed from data on hours worked provided by Gollop and Jorgenson. The weights used are based on the assumption that relative wage rates for self-employed workers are the same as for hired workers with the same personal characteristics. An index of land in the farm sector was created from farm acreage by states, obtained from various USDA publications. The weights for the index are based on estimates of the value of land per acre from the USDA publications *Farm Real Estate Historical Series* (for years prior to 1963) and *Farm Real Estate Market* (for 1965 to 1974).

Finally, a measure of farm output was constructed from basic data published annually by the USDA in *Agricultural Statistics*. A translog index was used to aggregate twelve distinct classes of livestock and nine major classifications of crops into a single measure.

For comparison purposes we also estimate the translog variable cost function with self-employed labor treated as a variable rather than quasi-fixed factor. This requires a price index and cost estimate for self-employed labor as total farm income minus all other input costs. This figure is then divided by the quantity index to obtain the appropriate price index.

10.3 Estimates of Partial Static Equilibrium Substitution Possibilities from the Translog Variable Cost Function

The parameters of the variable cost function were estimated by performing multivariate regression on equations (10.21) and (10.22). Efficient estimates were obtained using a modification of Zellner's method. Since the cost shares in (10.22) sum to unity, the estimated covariance matrix is singular, and one of the share equations must be deleted at the second stage of the estimation procedure. The estimates obtained are independent of which equation is deleted, and the estimates are asymptotically equivalent to maximum likelihood estimates.

Without loss of generality, symmetry was imposed on the γ_{ij} and δ_{ij}. We also required the theoretical restriction of homogeneity of degree one in input prices to hold, using the following linear restrictions:

$$\sum_i^l \alpha_i = 1,$$

$$\sum_i^l \gamma_{ij} = \sum_i^l \gamma_{ji} = \sum_i^l \rho_{Yi} = \sum_i^l \rho_{ij} = \sum_i^l \phi_{tP_i} = 0, \quad \forall_j.$$

(10.23)

Finally, constant returns to scale was imposed on the underlying structure of production by requiring (see Lau 1978):

$$\alpha_Y + \sum_i^m \beta_i = 1,$$

$$\rho_{Yi} + \sum_j^m \rho_{ij} = 0, \quad \forall_i;$$

$$\gamma_{YY} + \sum_i^m \Pi_i = 0,$$

(10.24)

$$\Pi_j + \sum_i^m \delta_{ij} = 0, \quad \forall_i;$$

$$\phi_{tY} + \sum_i^m \phi_{tZ_i} = 0.$$

The variable cost function (10.21) has thirty-six parameters; with the imposition of symmetry, linear homogeneity in factor prices, and constant returns to scale, there are twenty-one independent parameters to be estimated. The full set of parameter estimates is presented in table 10.1. The fitted variable cost function satisfies at every sample point the regularity conditions that it be nondecreasing and concave in prices of

Table 10.1
Parameter estimates for translog variable cost function (standard errors in parentheses)

Parameters	Estimates	Parameters	Estimates	Parameters	Estimates
α_0	10.1827 (0.0069)	γ_{HM}	0.0165 (0.0110)	ρ_{HF}	0.0001 (0.0304)
α_Y	−0.3224 (0.2255)	γ_{MM}	0.1600 (0.0138)	ρ_{MF}	−0.0812 (0.0151)
α_K	0.4233 (0.0023)	δ_{AA}	−26.1954 (8.692)	Π_A	31.4549 (8.795)
α_H	0.1421 (0.0026)	δ_{AF}	−5.2595 (2.863)	Π_F	4.8143 (2.683)
α_M	0.4345 (0.0013)	δ_{FF}	0.4452 (1.780)	ϕ_T	4.0973 (0.6505)
β_A	1.1109 (0.2148)	ρ_{YK}	−0.1833 (0.0808)	ϕ_{TT}	−250.211 (75.48)
β_F	0.2115 (0.0853)	ρ_{YH}	0.1572 (0.0861)	ϕ_{TY}	96.8287 (25.96)
γ_{YY}	−36.2692 (9.429)	ρ_{YM}	0.0261 (0.0442)	ϕ_{TPK}	0.7175 (0.2502)
γ_{KK}	0.2207 (0.0209)	ρ_{KA}	0.1022 (0.0790)	ϕ_{TPH}	−0.6997 (0.2698)
γ_{KH}	−0.0440 (0.0202)	ρ_{HA}	−0.1573 (0.0860)	ϕ_{TPM}	−0.0178 (0.1270)
γ_{KM}	−0.1766 (0.0123)	ρ_{MA}	0.0551 (0.0407)	ϕ_{TZA}	−86.4174 (24.06)
γ_{HH}	0.0275 (0.0239)	ρ_{KF}	0.0811 (0.0279)	ϕ_{TZF}	−10.4113 (9.460)

Note: K = capital (structures and equipment), H = hired labor, M = materials, and A = land (acreage), F = self-employed (family) labor, Y = aggregate output index.

variable factors and nonincreasing and convex in the levels of the fixed factors. The R^2 statistics are 0.997, 0.770, 0.809, and 0.947 for the cost function and shares of capital, hired labor, and materials, respectively.[9]

The estimated partial static equilibrium elasticities of substitution among the variable factors are presented in the first three columns of table 10.2. These estimates indicate that hired labor is highly substitutable for materials and moderately substitutable for capital. Capital and materials are estimated to be poor substitutes. The only significant trend in the estimated elasticities of substitution is the decline for capital and labor. Table 10.2 also contains the own price elasticities for the three variable inputs. These elasticities are computed as the product of the cost share and the Allen own elasticity of substitution. Demand for all three variable

Table 10.2
Substitution and own price elasticities estimated under the assumption of partial
static equilibrium

Year	σ_{KH}	σ_{KM}	σ_{HM}	η_{KK}	η_{HH}	η_{MM}
1947	0.424	−0.108	1.197	−0.040	−0.662	−0.199
1948	0.471	−0.094	1.224	−0.056	−0.664	−0.198
1949	0.422	−0.094	1.203	−0.043	−0.664	−0.199
1950	0.398	−0.075	1.207	−0.043	−0.666	−0.198
1951	0.414	−0.054	1.226	−0.053	−0.667	−0.200
1952	0.394	−0.063	1.213	−0.046	−0.667	−0.199
1953	0.372	−0.063	1.208	−0.041	−0.667	−0.197
1954	0.356	−0.046	1.215	−0.043	−0.668	−0.197
1955	0.355	−0.044	1.215	−0.043	−0.668	−0.197
1956	0.329	−0.048	1.209	−0.036	−0.668	−0.194
1957	0.332	−0.023	1.224	−0.045	−0.668	−0.196
1958	0.353	−0.021	1.231	−0.050	−0.668	−0.198
1959	0.324	−0.024	1.223	−0.044	−0.668	−0.195
1960	0.324	−0.022	1.224	−0.044	−0.668	−0.196
1961	0.318	0.003	1.242	−0.051	−0.668	−0.197
1962	0.305	0.011	1.246	−0.052	−0.668	−0.197
1963	0.296	0.016	1.248	−0.052	−0.667	−0.197
1964	0.270	0.025	1.252	−0.051	−0.666	−0.195
1965	0.286	0.034	1.266	−0.056	−0.665	−0.198
1966	0.250	0.051	1.278	−0.056	−0.662	−0.197
1967	0.268	0.040	1.268	−0.055	−0.665	−0.197
1968	0.268	0.039	1.267	−0.055	−0.665	−0.197
1969	0.271	0.056	1.297	−0.060	−0.661	−0.199
1970	0.220	0.062	1.285	−0.056	−0.660	−0.196
1971	0.232	0.044	1.264	−0.052	−0.664	−0.194
1972	0.219	0.054	1.274	−0.054	−0.661	−0.195
1973	0.224	0.073	1.307	−0.059	−0.656	−0.198
1974	0.087	0.084	1.292	−0.050	−0.650	−0.188

factors is estimated to be price-inelastic, but the elasticity for hired labor is substantially higher than for capital or materials.

10.4 Estimates of Static Equilibrium Substitution Possibilities from the Translog Variable Cost Function

Let us denote the elasticity of variable cost with respect to the ith variable input price (the predicted value of S_i in equation 10.22) by θ_i. Making use of this notation, we can express the derivatives that we need to evaluate (10.17) and (10.18) in terms of the derivatives of $\ln CV$ as follows:

$$\frac{\partial CV}{\partial P_i} = \begin{cases} \dfrac{\widehat{CV}\theta_i}{P_i}, & i \in VF, \\[2ex] 0, & i \in FF, \end{cases} \tag{10.25}$$

$$\frac{\partial CV}{\partial Z_k^*} = \frac{\widehat{CV}}{Z_k^*}\frac{\partial \ln CV}{\partial \ln Z_k^*}, \tag{10.26}$$

$$\frac{\partial^2 CV}{\partial P_i \partial P_j} = \begin{cases} \dfrac{\widehat{CV}}{P_i P_j}\left(\theta_i\theta_j + \dfrac{\partial^2 \ln CV}{\partial \ln P_i \partial \ln P_j} - \omega_{ij}\theta_i\right), \\[2ex] 0 & i \text{ or } j \in FF \end{cases} \tag{10.27}$$

$$\omega_{ij} = \begin{cases} 1, & \text{if } i = j, \\ 0, & \text{if } i \neq j, \ i, j \in VF, \end{cases}$$

$$\frac{\partial^2 CV}{\partial P_i \partial Z_k^*} = \begin{cases} \dfrac{\widehat{CV}}{P_i Z_k^*}\left(\theta_i\dfrac{\partial \ln CV}{\partial \ln Z_k} + \dfrac{\partial^2 \ln CV}{\partial \ln P_i \partial \ln Z_k^*}\right), & i \in VF, \\[2ex] 0, & i \in FF, \end{cases} \tag{10.28}$$

where VF is the set of variable factors, FF is the set of fixed factors, and $\widehat{CV}$ is the fitted value of $\ln CV$ exponentiated.

The steps required to obtain the estimated static equilibrium elasticities are
(1) Numerically solve (10.10) for the optimal levels of the quasi-fixed factors in each year, (2) evaluate the variable cost function at the optimal levels of the quasi-fixed factors for each year, (3) evaluate the derivatives (10.20), (10.25), (10.26), (10.27), and (10.28), (4) evaluate the derivatives (10.17) and (10.18), and finally (5) compute the elasticities of substitution from (10.4). The own price elasticities are then computed by multiplying the long-run Allen own elasticities of substitution by the shares of total cost estimated at the optimal levels of the quasi-fixed factors.

This operational procedure suggests the following intuitive explanation of how inferences about the long run are being drawn from estimates of the variable cost function. The estimated variable cost function enables us to plot out a number of partial static equilibrium average total cost functions. Using equation (10.7), we obtain the points of tangency between these curves and the full static equilibrium average total cost curve. These points enable us to construct the full static equilibrium cost function.

In our application family labor is considered to be a quasi-fixed factor, while land is a fixed factor.[10] Thus we first solve for the optimal level of family labor in each year.[11] These estimates are presented in table 10.3 along with the actual values for family labor. The estimates indicate that there was a very large surplus of family farm labor in the early postwar years. In subsequent years both actual and optimal levels of family labor declined, but the ratio of optimal to actual increased.

The estimated optimal levels of farm family labor from table 10.3 are then used to obtain the estimated static equilibrium elasticities of substitution presented in table 10.4. Comparing the estimates in tables 10.2 and 10.4, we find little difference between the estimated substitution possibilities among K, H, and M in partial and full static equilibrium. The estimated elasticities of substitution between family labor and the variable factors indicate that family labor is substitutable with hired labor and materials but complementary with capital.

Table 10.5 contains the estimated price elasticities of demand for the inputs in static equilibrium. As in table 10.2 we find a very price-inelastic demand for capital. The demand for hired labor is the most elastic of all the inputs, and the estimated elasticities are virtually the same in partial and full static equilibrium. The demand for materials is found to be somewhat more price elastic in full static equilibrium than in partial static equilibrium. The own price elasticity for family labor is estimated to be fairly small and declining over time.

The large discrepancies between actual and optimal levels of family labor in table 10.3 tends to confirm the specifications of family labor as a quasi-fixed factor rather than a variable factor. It would be of interest to know, however, how much different our estimates of substitution possibilities in the farm sector would be if family labor were specified as a variable factor. It is straightforward to investigate this question by estimating a translog variable cost function with family labor moved from the quasi-fixed to the variable category. We estimate such a cost function, with land still treated as a fixed factor, and present the estimated elasticities of substitution in table 10.6.

The estimated elasticities of substitution in table 10.6 are quite different

Table 10.3
Actual (Z_F) and cost-minimizing (Z_F^*) levels of the quasi-fixed factor family labor

Year	Z_F	Z_F^*
1947	2.224	0.765
1948	2.070	0.408
1949	2.014	0.591
1950	1.969	0.788
1951	1.864	0.675
1952	1.840	0.600
1953	1.807	0.666
1954	1.779	0.809
1955	1.728	0.710
1956	1.607	0.776
1957	1.477	0.821
1958	1.361	0.543
1959	1.361	0.554
1960	1.308	0.505
1961	1.191	0.560
1962	1.159	0.588
1963	1.066	0.497
1964	1.014	0.637
1965	0.998	0.506
1966	0.934	0.649
1967	1.000	0.508
1968	0.995	0.457
1969	0.970	0.458
1970	0.935	0.578
1971	0.886	0.324
1972	0.893	0.328
1973	0.897	0.277
1974	0.856	0.668

Table 10.4
Full static equilibrium elasticities of substitution estimated from the translog variable cost function

Year	σ_{KH}	σ_{KM}	σ_{HM}	σ_{KF}	σ_{HF}	σ_{MF}
1947	0.331	−0.189	1.275	−0.106	0.368	0.646
1948	0.301	−0.121	1.251	−0.256	0.262	0.563
1949	0.294	−0.155	1.263	−0.193	0.313	0.600
1950	0.327	−0.122	1.286	−0.097	0.353	0.639
1951	0.336	−0.059	1.284	−0.147	0.298	0.605
1952	0.276	−0.091	1.268	−0.208	0.285	0.580
1953	0.267	−0.102	1.275	−0.174	0.311	0.598
1954	0.292	−0.078	1.298	−0.090	0.378	0.634
1955	0.268	−0.073	1.289	−0.139	0.322	0.610
1956	0.262	−0.093	1.301	−0.077	0.366	0.642
1957	0.296	−0.059	1.326	−0.067	0.388	0.671
1958	0.265	−0.024	1.293	−0.161	0.289	0.590
1959	0.223	−0.038	1.288	−0.182	0.290	0.581
1960	0.210	−0.031	1.280	−0.224	0.263	0.559
1961	0.249	0.026	1.299	−0.188	0.263	0.567
1962	0.247	0.040	1.305	−0.186	0.248	0.566
1963	0.215	0.050	1.292	−0.248	0.208	0.529
1964	0.242	0.061	1.319	−0.168	0.248	0.571
1965	0.220	0.081	1.306	−0.238	0.195	0.529
1966	0.236	0.100	1.342	−0.166	0.226	0.567
1967	0.196	0.089	1.304	−0.262	0.178	0.513
1968	0.975	0.084	1.297	−0.281	0.173	0.503
1969	0.189	0.117	1.321	−0.257	0.163	0.511
1970	0.177	0.115	1.337	−0.209	0.201	0.538
1971	0.068	0.070	1.278	−0.362	0.143	0.459
1972	0.056	0.086	1.285	−0.358	0.137	0.457
1973	0.033	0.118	1.296	−0.369	0.112	0.441
1974	0.064	0.140	1.357	−0.218	0.197	0.523

Table 10.5
Full static equilibrium own price elasticities estimated from the translog variable
cost function

Year	η_{KK}	η_{HH}	η_{MM}	η_{FF}
1947	0.043	−0.676	−0.279	−0.304
1948	0.034	−0.670	−0.251	−0.231
1949	0.048	−0.673	−0.261	−0.268
1950	0.016	−0.677	−0.277	−0.294
1951	−0.007	−0.675	−0.268	−0.258
1952	0.025	−0.674	−0.256	−0.248
1953	0.029	−0.675	−0.261	−0.266
1954	0.004	−0.678	−0.275	−0.291
1955	0.013	−0.677	−0.266	−0.274
1956	0.015	−0.680	−0.277	−0.303
1957	−0.016	−0.681	−0.290	−0.316
1958	−0.006	−0.675	−0.261	−0.251
1959	0.010	−0.675	−0.255	−0.251
1960	0.011	−0.674	−0.248	−0.232
1961	−0.024	−0.673	−0.255	−0.224
1962	−0.029	−0.672	−0.256	−0.220
1963	−0.028	−0.670	−0.244	−0.189
1964	−0.038	−0.671	−0.259	−0.221
1965	−0.043	−0.668	−0.247	−0.179
1966	−0.053	−0.666	−0.260	−0.204
1967	−0.044	−0.667	−0.242	−0.165
1968	−0.039	−0.667	−0.238	−0.161
1969	−0.056	−0.662	−0.244	−0.153
1970	−0.052	−0.662	−0.250	−0.184
1971	−0.020	−0.665	−0.218	−0.135
1972	−0.027	−0.663	−0.219	−0.130
1973	−0.043	−0.657	−0.218	−0.108
1974	−0.050	−0.652	−0.244	−0.181

Table 10.6
Full static equilibrium elasticities of substitution estimated from the translog
variable cost function with family labour treated as a variable factor

Year	σ_{KH}	σ_{KM}	σ_{HM}	σ_{KF}	σ_{HF}	σ_{MF}
1947	0.377	−0.464	1.424	0.342	0.200	0.589
1948	0.472	−0.311	1.465	0.407	0.119	0.522
1949	0.406	−0.350	1.426	0.351	0.142	0.574
1950	0.397	−0.287	1.420	0.337	0.094	0.578
1951	0.445	−0.181	1.438	0.364	0.011	0.541
1952	0.425	−0.177	1.413	0.329	0.014	0.559
1953	0.398	−0.181	1.403	0.306	0.009	0.575
1954	0.391	−0.140	1.405	0.300	−0.042	0.574
1955	0.393	−0.119	1.403	0.295	−0.064	0.571
1956	0.361	−0.141	1.399	0.279	−0.056	0.588
1957	0.378	−0.091	1.419	0.304	−0.120	0.571
1958	0.415	−0.046	1.430	0.322	−0.167	0.544
1959	0.394	−0.027	1.408	0.282	−0.196	0.557
1960	0.425	0.015	1.392	0.259	−0.236	0.537
1961	0.463	0.091	1.397	0.250	−0.375	0.492
1962	0.476	0.129	1.386	0.216	−0.458	0.471
1963	0.498	0.172	1.376	0.175	−0.572	0.434
1964	0.491	0.185	1.372	0.153	−0.622	0.433
1965	0.525	0.231	1.370	0.111	−0.794	0.366
1966	0.519	0.259	1.374	0.074	−0.959	0.342
1967	0.548	0.280	1.340	−0.038	−1.052	0.286
1968	0.544	0.283	1.336	−0.056	−1.077	0.286
1969	0.560	0.318	1.353	−0.095	−1.374	0.196
1970	0.533	0.320	1.342	−0.140	−1.401	0.237
1971	0.537	0.320	1.327	−0.192	−1.406	0.229
1972	0.538	0.343	1.328	−0.273	−1.662	0.173
1973	0.560	0.387	1.340	−0.454	−2.375	0.027
1974	0.514	0.395	1.317	−0.662	−2.650	0.007

from those in table 10.4. Treating family labor as a variable input causes the following changes in the estimated elasticities of substitution: (1) family labor and hired labor are found to be highly complementary (in recent years) rather than substitutable; (2) family labor and materials are found to be much less substitutable in recent years; (3) family labor and capital are found to be complementary only in recent years, rather than in all years; (4) capital and materials are found to be more complementary in early years and more substitutable in recent years; (5) substitution possibilities between capital and hired labor are estimated to have increased over time rather than decreased. The only estimated elasticity of substitution that did not change much was that between hired labor and materials.

The estimated elasticities of substitution in table 10.6 do not appear to be as plausible as those in table 10.4. Much of the implausibility can be attributed to the fact that the curvature conditions are violated for the last eight years of the sample. Even for the earlier years, however, the results based on family labor as a quasi-fixed factor appear more plausible. For example, substitutability between family labor and hired labor with complementarity between family labor and capital seems much more plausible than the converse.

The estimated own price elasticities in table 10.7 are quite similar to those in table 10.5. For the three inputs treated as variable in both cost functions, the difference between the two sets of estimates are quite small. The family labor estimates are similar until the early 1960s, after which they differ substantially.

10.5 Concluding Remarks

We have presented an empirical framework for estimating substitution possibilities in situations where full static equilibrium is not a tenable assumption. Economists have long questioned whether it is appropriate to assume that capital stocks are in full static equilibrium. Our framework can be used to investigate such cases. Furthermore this formulation is not limited to treating one or more capital stocks as quasi-fixed inputs. Any inputs thought to be in disequilibrium can be treated as quasi fixed, as we have shown by treating family labor as a quasi-fixed input in the U.S. farm sector.

Although our example dealt with only one quasi-fixed factor, application of the method developed to models with more fixed factors introduces no methodological complications. The principal practical complication is

Table 10.7
Full static equilibrium own price elasticities estimated from the translog variable
cost function with family labor treated as a variable factor

Year	η_{KK}	η_{HH}	η_{MM}	η_{FF}
1947	−0.047	−0.546	−0.290	−0.268
1948	−0.118	−0.543	−0.275	−0.264
1949	−0.076	−0.543	−0.292	−0.266
1950	−0.080	−0.538	−0.298	−0.264
1951	−0.117	−0.533	−0.295	−0.257
1952	−0.102	−0.535	−0.301	−0.256
1953	−0.089	−0.533	−0.305	−0.257
1954	−0.095	−0.528	−0.306	−0.253
1955	−0.098	−0.526	−0.307	−0.251
1956	−0.082	−0.524	−0.308	−0.254
1957	−0.105	−0.516	−0.308	−0.250
1958	−0.125	−0.515	−0.306	−0.243
1959	−0.115	−0.515	−0.309	−0.238
1960	−0.123	−0.521	−0.310	−0.224
1961	−0.143	−0.518	−0.310	−0.197
1962	−0.148	−0.519	−0.310	−0.174
1963	−0.154	−0.521	−0.310	−0.139
1964	−0.153	−0.519	−0.310	−0.129
1965	−0.163	−0.521	−0.310	−0.072
1966	−0.165	−0.514	−0.310	−0.037
1967	−0.164	−0.529	−0.309	−0.039
1968	−0.164	−0.529	−0.309	−0.047
1969	−0.170	−0.522	−0.309	−0.129
1970	−0.166	−0.518	−0.307	−0.125
1971	−0.164	−0.524	−0.305	−0.150
1972	−0.166	−0.520	−0.304	−0.229
1973	−0.172	−0.513	−0.305	−0.464
1974	−0.166	−0.508	−0.294	−0.539

that the cost function must be minimized with respect to all quasi-fixed factors simultaneously.

In our empirical application three sets of elasticities of substitution were presented for the farm sector over the 1947 to 1974 period. The first two sets were estimated under the assumption that family labor is a quasi-fixed factor. The first set portrays substitution possibilities among the variable inputs conditional on the observed level of family labor. The second set portrays substitution possibilities that would prevail among family labor and the variable inputs if family labor were at its optimal level. These two sets of elasticities of substitution are quite similar. The third set of elasticities of substitution is based on the assumption that the observed levels of family labor were in fact optimal. These elasticities differ substantially from the other two sets. We conclude that the specification of particular inputs as variable or quasi fixed may have important consequences in the estimation of substitution possibilities.

Notes

This research was supported in part by the Electric Power Research Institute. The authors wish to thank Douglas Caves and Ernst Berndt for helpful comments on a draft of this chapter and Philip Schoech, Michael Tretheway, and Mario Miranda for assistance in obtaining our empirical results.

1. Diewert (1974) and Fuss and McFadden (1978a, vol. 1) provide extensive discussions of these topics.

2. Full static equilibrium and partial static equilibrium are often referred to as long-run and short-run equilibrium. We avoid the short-run terminology because movement from partial to full static equilibrium requires input adjustments that may not take place with the passage of time.

3. Caves, Christensen, and Swanson have recently demonstrated how to estimate shifts in the production structure (productivity growth) when the partial static equilibrium approach is appropriate.

4. Tweeten provides discussion and further references.

5. We do not develop the theory for the multiproduct case since our emphasis is on substitution possibilities among factor inputs. Generalization of our methodology to the multiproduct case is straightforward.

6. These simplifications result from applying (10.14) and from the fact that derivatives of CV with respect to prices of fixed factors are equal to zero. These results were first derived by Lau (1976, p. 150).

7. Note that this result (also presented in Lau 1976) is necessarily true only in the neighborhood of the long-run equilibrium. That is, the relationship given in (10.18) holds only when all derivatives are evaluated at $Z = Z^*$. Thus, while $\partial^2 CT/\partial Z^{*2}$

≥ 0 guarantees that $\partial^2 CV/\partial P_i^2|_{z=z^*} \geq \partial^2 CT/\partial P_i^2$, it may not be true that $\partial^2 CV/\partial P_i^2|_{z=z_0} \geq \partial^2 CT/\partial P_i^2$.

8. The translog index number formula can be written:

$$\ln(Y_t/Y_{t-1}) = \sum \overline{W}_i \ln(Y_{t,i-1}),$$

where $\overline{W}_i = (W_{it} + W_{i,t-1})/2$, and $W_i = P_i Y_i/\sum P_i Y_i$. This formula was suggested by Fisher, advocated by Tornqvist, Theil (1965), and Kloek, and has been used extensively by Christensen and Jorgenson (1973) and others. Diewert (1976) showed that this index is exact for a translog function.

9. The R^2 statistic for each equation is defined as $R^2 = 1 - \sum e_t^2/\sum (y_t - \bar{y})^2$, where e_t is the residual and y_t the value of the dependent variable in period t. Of course for estimation procedures other than ordinary least squares R^2 cannot in general be interpreted as the proportion of variance explained, since the residuals are no longer orthogonal to the regressors. However, it still provides a useful indicator of goodness-of-fit.

10. In the development up to this point it has been assumed that CT refers to total costs. Treating land as fixed in the long run simply implies that CT includes only nonland costs and that land is left at its actual value in performing the calculations necessary to construct the long-run elasticities. The quasi-fixed factors (family labor in this application) are set at those values which minimize CT.

11. Due to the nonlinear way in which Z enters the translog variable cost function, no closed form solution for Z^* results from the first-order conditions given in equation (10.7). However, a variety of computer algorithms are available for minimizing a function such as CT. We found the algorithm given in Berndt et al. (1979), which we modified to use the actual second derivatives $\partial^2 CT/\partial Z^2$ rather than the approximation they suggest, to be easy to use and reliable. This algorithm also performed well in experiments with two fixed factors. However, a numerical zero-finding routine, used to solve for those Z values which satisfied the first-order conditions for the two-fixed factor case, produced results that seemed very reasonable but corresponded to a saddle point rather than a minimum. This highlights the importance of selecting a reliable optimization algorithm and of course checking the second-order condition.

11

Substitution Possibilities for Energy: Evidence from U.S. and Canadian Manufacturing Industries

M. Denny, M. Fuss, and L. Waverman

The rapidly escalating energy prices of the 1970s have focused attention on the ability of consumers and firms to lower energy consumption. How manufacturing firms react to increases in energy prices depends on the manner in which energy combines with other inputs in the production process and the ability of firms to change production techniques quickly.

We provide evidence on the substitution possibilities for energy in eighteen U.S. and eighteen Canadian manufacturing industries. We also investigate the interaction among energy types in the Canadian manufacturing sector. The evidence is based on the econometric estimation of a dynamic partial adjustment model of input choice. The firm is assumed to minimize the present value of future costs, subject to internal rising marginal costs of adjusting its capital input.

In both countries we find that the input demand functions are primarily inelastic. There is very little difference between the short-run and long-run demand for energy because energy demand is only weakly dependent on the path of capital accumulation. The results on input substitution for the two countries are very different. Energy and labor are long-run complements in twelve of the eighteen U.S. industries and long-run substitutes in ten of the eighteen Canadian industries. Capital and energy are long-run complements in fourteen of the eighteen U.S. industries and substitutes in twelve of the eighteen Canadian industries. In Canada fuel oil is a long-run substitute for natural gas and coal and a complement with electricity.

The dynamic properties of many industries show that the short-run responses often overshoot the long-run responses and sometimes the sign changes. The adjustment of the capital stock is modest, since about 30 to 40 percent of the adjustment is complete in one year.

11.1 The Theoretical Model

Static or long-run equilibrium models of factor demands cannot deal satisfactorily with situations where very large changes in relative prices occur over a short period of time, since firms generally are unable to adjust quickly to new desired production techniques without incurring substantial additional costs.[1] Estimates of factor demands utilizing static translog models, for example, are highly unstable when the data for 1972 to 1974, years of rapid price changes, are included.[2] A dynamic model of factor demands was therefore constructed to incorporate four major considerations: (1) the lagged adjustment process should be endogenous to the firm's decision-making process and should also be based on optimizing behavior, (2) the lagged adjustment specification should incorporate general disequilibrium in factor demands, (3) the specification should be consistent with the basic Le Chatelier principle, that is, the longer the time period allowed for adjustment, the greater the amount of adjustment occurring, and (4) the observed output must be producible by the predicted inputs (output feasibility).

We postulate that any observed lags in adjustment in response to substantial increases in energy prices are due to the increasing marginal costs that will be incurred during rapid adjustment of the energy-using capital stock. There are two basic ways of dealing with this increasing marginal cost of adjustment. One can assume that the costs are external to the firm due to delivery lags or rising supply functions of factors. The second approach, the one we take, is to assume that increasing marginal costs of adjustment result from internal disruptions within the firm. The greater the amount of adjustment required in any quasi-fixed factor in any single period, the greater are the marginal costs of disruption factors taken away from producing sellable output. We rely on Treadway's (1974) analysis for our basic model.

Assume factor markets for variable inputs $\mathbf{v} = \{V_j\}, i = 1, \ldots, m$, are perfectly competitive with prices $\mathbf{w} = \{\hat{w}_j\}, j = 1, \ldots, m$, that are assumed to be known with certainty and expected to remain stationary over time.[4]

The production function can be written in the implicit form

$$F(\mathbf{v}, \mathbf{x}, \dot{\mathbf{x}}, Q, t) = 0, \tag{11.1}$$

where Q is the level of output and $\mathbf{x} = \{x_i\}, i = 1, \ldots, n$, is a set of quasi-fixed inputs. The term $\partial Q/\partial \dot{x}_i < 0$ represents the internal cost of foregone output of a change in the stock of the quasi-fixed factor.[5] Current production is affected by the accumulation or decumulation of the quasi-fixed factor; the greater the rate of accumulation (or decumulation), the greater is the marginal loss of productive ability.

Assuming that the firm minimizes the present value of the future stream of costs, the objective functional can be written as

$$L(0) = \int_0^\infty e^{-rt}\left(\sum_{j=1}^m \hat{w}_j v_j + \sum_{i=1}^n \hat{q}_i z_i\right),\tag{11.2}$$

where

$r =$ the firm's discount rate,

$z_i =$ the gross addition to the stock of the ith quasi-fixed factor ($z_i = \dot{x}_i + \delta_i x_i$, where δ_i is the depreciation rate),

$\hat{q}_i =$ the asset purchase price of the ith quasi-fixed factor.

The problem of the firm is to minimize $L(0)$ with respect to the production function (11.1). The output level and the technology are known and are expected to remain constant. This minimization is accomplished by choosing the time paths of the control variables $\mathbf{v}(t)$, $\dot{\mathbf{x}}(t)$, and the state variables $\mathbf{x}(t)$, so as to minimize $L(0)$, given any initial $\mathbf{x}(0)$, and $\mathbf{v}(t)$, $\mathbf{x}(t) > 0$.

We can obtain a factor requirements function for $v_1(t)$ by solving the implicit production function (11.1) for

$$v_1(t) = f[v_2(t), \ldots, v_m(t), \mathbf{x}(t), \dot{\mathbf{x}}(t), Q(t), t].\tag{11.3}$$

Substituting (11.3) into the objective functional (11.2), and solving the optimization problem for the $v_j(t)$, yields the cost-minimizing variable factor demands conditional on the level of the quasi-fixed factors and output. The optimization problem is now characterized by

$$L(0) = \int_0^\infty e^{-rt}[\hat{w}_1 f(v_2(t), \ldots, v_m(t), \mathbf{x}(t), \dot{\mathbf{x}}(t), Q(t), t)$$

$$+ \sum_{j=2}^m \hat{w}_j v_j + \sum_{i=1}^n \hat{q}_i z_i]\,dt.$$

The necessary conditions for minimization with respect to the variable factor control variables ($j = 2, \ldots, m$) are

$$\frac{\partial L(0)}{\partial v_j} = \hat{w}_1 f_{v_j} + \hat{w}_j = 0,\tag{11.4}$$

or

$$f_{v_j} = -w_j,\tag{11.5}$$

where $w_j = \hat{w}_j/\hat{w}_1$. It should be noted that $f_{v_j} < 0$, since an increase in the availability of the jth factor reduces the amount of the first factor required to produce a given level of output.

Given strict quasi convexity of the implicit production function in the variable factors, equations (11.5) can be solved for the cost-minimizing, short-run variable factor demand functions

$$\bar{\mathbf{v}}(t) = v(\mathbf{w}(t), \mathbf{x}(t), \dot{\mathbf{x}}(t), Q(t), t), \tag{11.6}$$

where $\mathbf{w}(t) = (w_2(t), \ldots, w_j(t), \ldots, w_m(t))$. Suppose we now form the function

$$G(t) = \sum_{j=1}^{m} w_j \bar{v}_j(t) = G(\mathbf{w}(t), \mathbf{x}(t)\, \dot{\mathbf{x}}(t), Q(t), t). \tag{11.7}$$

The term $\hat{w}_1 G(t)$ is the minimum variable cost attainable at time t, conditional on the level of the quasi-fixed factors or state variable $\mathbf{x}(t)$, the control variable $\dot{\mathbf{x}}(t)$, and output $Q(t)$. Therefore $G(t)$ is a restricted cost function, normalized by $\hat{w}_1$, in other words, it is a normalized restricted cost function, $NRCF$, conceptually similar to the normalized restricted profit function discussed by Lau (1976). It can be shown that the $NRCF$ has the following properties:

i. G is decreasing in $\mathbf{x}$ and $\dot{\mathbf{x}}$ and increasing in $\mathbf{w}$ and Q:

$$G_{x_i} < 0, \quad G_{\dot{x}_i} < 0, \quad G_{w_i} > 0, \quad G_Q > 0.$$

ii. G is concave in $\mathbf{w}$.
iii. G is convex in $\mathbf{x}$ and $\dot{\mathbf{x}}$.
iv. $\partial G/\partial w_j = \bar{v}_j$, the conditional cost-minimizing input level.

Substituting (11.7) into the objective functional yields

$$L(0) = \int_0^\infty \hat{w}_1 e^{-rt} \left[G(\mathbf{w}, \mathbf{x}, \dot{\mathbf{x}}, Q, t) + \sum_{i=1}^{n} q_i z_i \right] dt. \tag{11.8}$$

Substituting for $z_i = \dot{x}_i + \delta x_i$, we obtain

$$\bar{\bar{L}}(0) = \frac{\bar{L}(0)}{\hat{w}_1} = \int_0^\infty e^{-rt} \left[G(\mathbf{w}, \mathbf{x}, \dot{\mathbf{x}}, Q, t) + \sum_{i=1}^{n} q_i \delta_i x_i \right] dt$$

$$+ \int_0^\infty e^{-rt} \sum_{i=1}^{n} q_i \dot{x}_i dt. \tag{11.9}$$

The last term in (11.9) can be integrated by parts to yield

$$\int_0^\infty e^{-rt} \sum_i q_i \dot{x}_i dt = \int_0^\infty e^{-rt} \sum_i r q_i x_i dt - \sum_i q_i x_i(0), \tag{11.10}$$

where the transversality condition $\lim_{t\to\infty} e^{-rt} x_i(t) = 0$ is obtained by assuming the existence of a locally (near the steady state $\mathbf{x}^*$) optimal stable path (Treadway 1974). Combining (11.9) and (11.10), we obtain

$$\overline{\overline{L}}(0) - \sum_{i=1}^n q_i x_i(0) = \int_0^\infty e^{-rt} \left[G(\mathbf{w}, \mathbf{x}, \dot{\mathbf{x}}, Q, t) + \sum_{i=1}^n u_i x_i \right] dt, \tag{11.11}$$

where $u_i = q_i(r + \delta_i)$, the normalized user cost of the ith quasi-fixed factor. Minimizing (11.11) with respect to $x(t)$ is equivalent to minimizing (11.2) with respect to $\mathbf{x}(t)$, $\mathbf{v}(t)$, since (11.11) incorporates the optimal $\mathbf{v}(t)$, conditional on $\mathbf{x}(t)$.

The problem of minimizing (11.11) with respect to the state variables $\mathbf{x}(t)$ and the control variables $\dot{\mathbf{x}}(t)$ (subject to the initial conditions $\mathbf{x}(0)$ and the transversality conditions $\lim_{t\to\infty} e^{-rt}\mathbf{x}(t) = 0$) is a standard problem in control theory. A solution can be obtained using Pontryagin's maximum principle. Construct the Hamiltonian

$$H(\mathbf{x}, \dot{\mathbf{x}}, \lambda, t) = e^{-rt} \cdot [G(\mathbf{x}, \dot{\mathbf{x}}, Q, t) + \mathbf{u} \cdot \mathbf{x}] + \lambda \dot{\mathbf{x}}, \tag{11.12}$$

where λ is a vector of costate variables and $\mathbf{u} \cdot \mathbf{x} = \sum_{i=1}^n u_i x_i$. The necessary conditions for a minimum are

$$\frac{\partial H}{\partial \dot{\mathbf{x}}} = 0 \quad \text{and} \quad \dot{\lambda} = -\frac{\partial H}{\partial \mathbf{x}}. \tag{11.13}$$

The conditions (11.13) are also sufficient since H is convex in $\mathbf{x}$ (Mangasarian) by virtue of the fact that G is convex in $\mathbf{x}$.

$$\frac{\partial H}{\partial \mathbf{x}} = e^{-rt} G_x + \lambda = 0, \tag{11.14}$$

$$\dot{\lambda} = -\frac{\partial H}{\partial \mathbf{x}} = -e^{-rt} G_x - e^{-rt} \mathbf{u}. \tag{11.15}$$

Differentiating (11.14) with respect to time yields

$$-re^{-rt} G_{\dot{x}} + e^{-rt}[G_{x\dot{x}} \dot{\mathbf{x}} + G_{xx} \dot{\mathbf{x}}] + \dot{\lambda} = 0. \tag{11.16}$$

Combining (11.15) and (11.16) to eliminate λ, we obtain the necessary conditions

$$-G_x - rG_{\dot{x}} - \mathbf{u} - B\ddot{\mathbf{x}} = C\dot{\mathbf{x}} = 0, \tag{11.17}$$

where

$$\mathbf{B} = [-G_{\dot{x}\dot{x}}] \quad \text{and} \quad \mathbf{C} = [-G_{x\dot{x}}] \tag{11.18}$$

A steady state solution $\mathbf{x}^*$ is given by

$$-G_x(\mathbf{w}, \mathbf{x}^*) - rG_{\dot{x}}(\mathbf{w}, \mathbf{x}^*) - \mathbf{u} = \mathbf{0}, \tag{11.19}$$

and $\mathbf{x}^*$ is unique as long as

$$|\mathbf{A}^* + r\mathbf{C}^*| \neq \mathbf{0}, \tag{11.20}$$

where $\mathbf{A} = [G_{xx}]$ and * indicates evaluation at $\mathbf{x} = \mathbf{x}^*$, and $\dot{\mathbf{x}} = 0$. Rewrite (11.19) as $-G_x(\mathbf{x}, \mathbf{x}^*) = \mathbf{u} + rG_{\dot{x}}(\mathbf{w}, \mathbf{x}^*)$. The left-hand side is the marginal benefit to the firm of changing capital, while the right-hand side represents the marginal cost (the user cost plus the marginal adjustment cost of a change in the flow of capital services at $\dot{\mathbf{x}} = 0$).[6] In equilibrium marginal benefits equal marginal costs. The steady state demand for variable factors can be obtained as $\mathbf{v}^*(t)$ by substituting $\mathbf{x}(t) = \mathbf{x}^*(t)$, $\dot{\mathbf{x}}(t) = 0$ in equation (11.6).

Treadway (1971, 1974) links this model to the ad hoc partial adjustment or flexible accelerator literature by showing that the demands for the quasi-fixed factors can be generated from (11.17) and (11.19) as an approximate solution (in the neighborhood of $\mathbf{x}^*(t)$) to the multivariate linear differential equation system

$$\dot{\mathbf{x}} = \mathbf{M}^*(\mathbf{x}^* - \mathbf{x}), \tag{11.21}$$

where $\mathbf{M}^*$ satisfies the condition

$$\mathbf{B}^*\mathbf{M}^{*2} - (\mathbf{C}^* - \mathbf{C}^{*\prime} - r\mathbf{B}^*)\mathbf{M}^* - (\mathbf{A}^* + r\mathbf{C}^*) = \mathbf{0}. \tag{11.22}$$

In the following analysis we will assume that $\mathbf{C}^*$ is symmetric, so that $\mathbf{C}^* - \mathbf{C}^{*\prime} = 0$. We do so for two reasons. First, Mortensen has shown that $\mathbf{C}^*$ symmetric is necessary and sufficient for $\mathbf{x}^*$ to have the properties of long-run demand functions generated by static profit maximization (such as symmetry, negative own price effect). This allows the model development to remain within the Marshallian long-run/short-run framework. Second, we will approximate $G(t)$ by a quadratic expansion that automatically constrains $\mathbf{C}^*$ to be symmetric.[7] Imposing symmetry, (11.22) becomes

$$\mathbf{B}^*\mathbf{M}^{*2} + r\mathbf{B}^*\mathbf{M}^* - (\mathbf{A} + r\mathbf{C}^*) = \mathbf{0}. \tag{11.23}$$

In the case of a single quasi-fixed factor (11.21) becomes

$$\dot{x}_1 = \beta^*(x_1^* - x_1), \tag{11.24}$$

and (11.23) becomes

$$-G^*_{\dot{x}_1\dot{x}_1} \beta^{*2} - rG^*_{\dot{x}_1\dot{x}_1} \beta^* + (G^*_{\dot{x}_1\dot{x}_1} + rG^*_{\dot{x}_1\dot{x}_1}) = 0. \tag{11.25}$$

Solving (11.25) for the stable root yields

$$\beta^* = -\frac{1}{2}\left[r - \left(\frac{r^2 + 4(G_{x_1 x_1} + rG_{x_1 \dot{x}_1})}{G_{\dot{x}_1 \dot{x}_1}}\right)^{1/2}\right] \tag{11.26}$$

Dynamic Demand for Energy with Capital as a Quasi-Fixed Factor
Assume there exists a production function

$$F(E, L, M, K, \dot{K}, Q, t) = 0, \tag{11.27}$$

where

Q = gross output,

E = aggregate energy input,

L = labor input,

M = materials input,

K = capital input,

t = time.

E, L, M, and $\dot{K}$ are control variables, and K is the state variable. Suppose factor prices and output are exogenously determined and capital is fixed in the short run (that is, quasi fixed). The theory of duality between cost and production implies that, given short-run cost-minimizing behavior, the characteristics of production implied by (11.27) can be uniquely represented by a normalized restricted variable cost function, $G(p_E, p_M, K, \dot{K}, Q, t) = L + p_E E + p_M M$, where p_E and p_M are normalized (by the price of labor) input prices. Before proceeding we make two further assumptions:

i. continuous changes in capital $\dot{K}$ can be represented by discrete changes $K_t - K_{t-1}$, or ΔK.
ii. The output in period t is a function of the capital in place at the beginning of the period, K_{t-1}. Capital introduced in period t is not used to produce output in period t.

For empirical analysis we have chosen as our approximation to the *NRCF* one of the family of flexible functional forms, the quadratic function.[8] This approximation was chosen for three reasons. First, it constrains **C***
to be symmetric. Second, the Hessian of second-order partial derivatives is a matrix of constants, thus facilitating the linking of short- and long-run responses (Lau 1976). Third, the characterization of the optimal path for the quasi-fixed factor is globally as well as locally valid, since for the

quadratic approximation the underlying differential equations are linear (Treadway 1974). Two special cases of a quadratic cost function will be introduced.

The quadratic normalized restricted cost function takes the form:

$$G = L + p_E E + p_M M = \alpha_0 + \alpha_{0t} t + \sum_j \alpha_j p_j + \sum_j \alpha_{jt} p_j t + \alpha_Q Q$$

$$+ \alpha_K K_{-1} + \frac{1}{2} \sum_j \sum_l \gamma_{jl} p_j p_l$$

$$+ \frac{1}{2} (\gamma_{QQ} Q^2 + \gamma_{KK} K^2_{-1} + \gamma_{\dot{K}\dot{K}} (\Delta K)^2)$$

$$+ \sum_j \gamma_{jK} p_j K_{-1} + \sum_j \gamma_{jQ} p_j Q + \gamma_{QK} K_{-1} Q$$

$$+ \sum_j \gamma_{j\dot{K}} p_j \Delta K + \gamma_{Q\dot{K}} Q \Delta K + \gamma_{K\dot{K}} \Delta K K_{-1}$$

$$+ \alpha_{\dot{K}} \Delta K + \alpha_{t\dot{K}} t \Delta K, \tag{11.28}$$

where

$$j = E, M,$$

$$t = 1, \ldots, T,$$

$$\gamma_{jl} = \gamma_{lj}, l \neq j.$$

Within G, internal costs of adjustment are represented by

$$C(\Delta K) = \alpha_{\dot{K}} \Delta K + \frac{1}{2} \gamma_{\dot{K}\dot{K}} (\Delta K)^2 + \gamma_{E\dot{K}} p_E \Delta K + \gamma_{M\dot{K}} p_M \Delta K$$

$$+ \gamma_{Q\dot{K}} \Delta K Q + \gamma_{K\dot{K}} \Delta K K_{-1} + \alpha_{t\dot{K}} \Delta K t. \tag{11.29}$$

At a steady state $\Delta K = 0$ implies $C(\Delta K) = 0$. We assume that marginal adjustment costs are also zero at $\Delta K = 0$ (that is, $\lim_{\Delta K \to 0} C'(\Delta K) = 0$), which implies that

$$\frac{\partial G}{\partial \Delta K} = C'(\Delta K)$$

$$= \alpha_{\dot{K}} + \gamma_{\dot{K}\dot{K}} \Delta K + \gamma_{E\dot{K}} p_E + \gamma_{M\dot{K}} p_M + \gamma_{Q\dot{K}} Q + \gamma_{K\dot{K}} K_{-1} + \alpha_{t\dot{K}} t = 0. \tag{11.30}$$

But at any stationary point, when net capital accumulation $\Delta K = 0$, $C'(0) = 0$ will occur for all values of the exogenous variables if and only if the following restrictions are imposed in (11.30):

$$\alpha_{\dot{K}} = \gamma_{E\dot{K}} \; \gamma_{M\dot{K}} = \gamma_{Q\dot{K}} = \gamma_{K\dot{K}} = \alpha_{t\dot{K}} = 0. \tag{11.31}$$

Hereafter we impose the restrictions (11.31), thereby ensuring that at a stationary point marginal costs of adjustment will be zero. Finally, we note that the requirement that marginal costs be increasing implies $\gamma_{KK} > 0$ since $C''(\Delta K) = \gamma_{KK}$.

Short-run conditional demand functions for variable inputs are obtained using the *NRCF* property iv. This yields

$$\frac{\partial G}{\partial P_E} = E = \alpha_E + \alpha_{Et}t + \gamma_{EE}P_E + \gamma_{EM}P_M + \gamma_{EQ}Q + \gamma_{EK}K_{-1}, \quad (11.32)$$

$$\frac{\partial G}{\partial P_M} = M = \alpha_M + \alpha_{Mt}t + \gamma_{EM}P_E + \gamma_{MM}P_M + \gamma_{MQ}Q$$

$$+ \gamma_{MK}K_{-1}, \quad (11.33)$$

where, for *NRCF* conditions i and ii to hold, it should be true that γ_{EE}, $\gamma_{MM} \leq 0$ and that $\gamma_{EQ}, \gamma_{MQ} > 0$ The short-run conditional demand for the normalized variable input labor is obtained by noting that the function G embodies optimizing behavior assumptions. Since $G = L + p_E E + p_M M$, we substitute (11.32) and (11.33) into (11.28) and obtain the labor demand function

$$L = G - p_E E - p_M M = \alpha_0 + \alpha_{0t}t - \frac{1}{2}(\gamma_{EE}p_E^2 + 2\gamma_{EM}p_E p_M$$

$$+ \gamma_{MM}p_M^2) + \gamma_{QK}K_{-1}Q + \alpha_Q Q + \frac{1}{2}\gamma_{QQ}Q^2 + \alpha_K K_{-1}$$

$$+ \alpha_{Kt}K_{-1}t + \frac{1}{2}\gamma_{KK}K_{-1}^2 + \frac{1}{2}\gamma_{\dot{K}\dot{K}}(\Delta K)^2. \quad (11.34)$$

Recall from (11.24) that $\Delta K \equiv K - K_{-1} = \beta^*(K^* - K_{-1})$ where, using (11.26) the partial adjustment coefficient β^* (with restrictions (11.31) imposed) becomes

$$\beta^* = -\frac{1}{2}\left[r - \left\{r^2 + \frac{4\gamma_{KK}}{\gamma_{\dot{K}\dot{K}}}\right\}^{1/2}\right]. \quad (11.35)$$

Two features of (11.35) are worth noting. First, in order for $0 < \beta^* \leq 1$ for any r, it is necessary and sufficient that $\gamma_{KK}/\gamma_{\dot{K}\dot{K}} \leq 1 + r$. Hence a global sufficient condition for $0 < \beta^* \leq 1$ for any nonnegative r is that $\gamma_{KK}/\gamma_{\dot{K}\dot{K}} < 1$. Second, it is clear from (11.35) that β^* depends on r. It can easily be shown that $\partial\beta^*/\partial r < 0$, that is increases in r reduce the rate at which the gap between desired and actual capital is closed.

To obtain an expression for the steady state capital stock K^* we use (11.19), impose the restrictions (11.31), and solve for K^*, obtaining

$$K^* = \left[\left(\frac{-1}{\gamma_{KK}} \right) \cdot \left(\alpha_K + \gamma_{EK} p_E + \gamma_{MK} p_M + \gamma_{QK} Q + \alpha_{Kt} t + p_K \right) \right].$$

$$(11.36)$$

where p_K is the normalized user cost of capital services. In order for $\partial K^*/\partial p_K < 0$ and $\partial K^*/\partial Q > 0$, it is necessary that $\gamma_{KK} > 0$ and $\gamma_{QK} < 0$. Since we showed above that $\gamma_{KK}/\gamma_{\dot{K}\dot{K}} < 1$, it follows that the parameters must satisfy the inequality $0 < \gamma_{KK} < \gamma_{\dot{K}\dot{K}}$.

Using (11.35) and (11.36), we now can write the equation characterizing the optimal path of the quasi-fixed factor K as the flexible accelerator formula:

$$\Delta K = \beta^*(K^* - K_{-1}) = -\frac{1}{2} \left[r - \left\{ r^2 + \frac{4\gamma_{KK}}{\gamma_{\dot{K}\dot{K}}} \right\}^{1/2} \right] \cdot \left[\left(\frac{-1}{\gamma_{KK}} \right) \right.$$

$$\left. \cdot (\alpha_K + \gamma_{EK} p_E + \gamma_{MK} p_M + \gamma_{QK} Q + \alpha_{Kt} t + p_K) - K_{-1} \right].$$

$$(11.37)$$

In summary four equations are to be estimated as a system of equations: short-run demand equation (11.34) for L, (11.32) for E, and (11.33) for M; and a net capital accumulation equation (11.37). Note that the endogenous variable ΔK appears as a right-hand side variable in the short-run demand equation (11.34) for L. A nonlinear iterative 3SLS procedure was employed to account for possible simultaneous equations bias. This was accomplished by forming, in the first stage, predicted values of ΔK, using as instrumental variables the exogenous variables in the system.

The Input-Output Model

We applied the theoretical model developed in the last section to U.S. and Canadian two-digit industry data. The Canadian data are available by region and include rich information on fuel subtypes. In contrast, the American data base has no regional breakdown and contains information only on the electricity and nonelectricity divisions of energy data. The model, as given by equations (11.32), (11.33), (11.34), and (11.37), was estimated with U.S. data. However, the quadratic approximation used in deriving (11.28) has several weaknesses when applied to a pooled cross-section time-series data base, as was available for the Canada industries. This is due to the heterogeneous nature of regional data. Industries in Canada are characterized by considerable disparities with respect to both the composition and magnitude of manufacturing activities within any two-digit industry. This required adjustments in the basic quadratic model. To account for the possibility of different regional mixes of underlying production processes, some of the parameters of the quadratic function were allowed to vary across regions. The zero-order and the first-order terms associated with p_E, p_M, Q, and K were permitted to be region-specific through the use of the dummy variable technique. Account must also be taken of the different production levels in each region. If two regions produced exactly the same composition of output, used identical production techniques, and faced the same set of prices, price elasticities would be the same. This would not be the case for the quadratic approximation (11.28) if there happened to be more firms in one region than another, that is, if the levels of inputs and output were higher in a region. But the anomaly could be corrected by specifying the basic theoretical model in terms of input choices per unit of output.

A firm in any region is assumed to minimize the variable costs per unit of output, conditional on the capital stock available per unit of output in determining short-run demand for variable factors. Costs of adjustment are caused by variations in the capital-output ratio rather than variations in the capital stock alone. Attention is now focused on the belief that a change in the technique of production is the major factor leading to increasing marginal adjustment costs, rather than a change in the level of production (a change in K).

A normalized restricted cost function that satisfies the requirements just stated is the average normalized restricted cost function, $ANRCF$,

$$
\frac{G}{Q} = \frac{L}{Q} + p_E \frac{E}{Q} + p_M \frac{M}{Q}
$$

$$
= \sum_{i=1}^{4} \alpha_{0i} D_i + \alpha_{0t} \cdot t + \left(\sum_{1}^{4} \alpha_{Ei} D_i \right) p_E + \left(\sum_{1}^{4} \alpha_{Mi} D_i \right) p_M
$$

$$
+ \left(\sum_{1}^{4} \alpha_{Qi} D_i \right) Q + \left(\sum \alpha_{Ki} D_i \right) \left(\frac{K_{-1}}{Q} \right) + \alpha_{\dot{K}} \left(\frac{\Delta K}{Q} \right)
$$

$$
+ \frac{1}{2} \left[\gamma_{EE} p_E^2 + \gamma_{MM} p_M^2 + \gamma_{QQ} Q^2 + \gamma_{KK} \left(\frac{K_{-1}}{Q} \right)^2 + \gamma_{\dot{K}\dot{K}} \left(\frac{\Delta K}{Q} \right)^2 \right]
$$

$$
+ \gamma_{EM} p_E p_M + \gamma_{EQ} p_E Q + \gamma_{MQ} p_M Q - \gamma_{EK} p_E \left(\frac{K_{-1}}{Q} \right)
$$

$$+ \gamma_{MK} p_M \left(\frac{K_{-1}}{Q}\right) + \gamma_{QK} Q \left(\frac{K_{-1}}{Q}\right) + \gamma_{E\dot{K}} p_E \left(\frac{\varDelta K}{Q}\right) + \gamma_{M\dot{K}} p_M \left(\frac{\varDelta K}{Q}\right)$$

$$+ \gamma_{Q\dot{K}} Q \left(\frac{\varDelta K}{Q}\right) + \gamma_{K\dot{K}} K_{-1} \left(\frac{\varDelta K}{Q}\right) + \alpha_{Et} p_E t + \alpha_{Mt} p_M t$$

$$+ \alpha_{Kt} t \left(\frac{K_{-1}}{Q}\right) + \alpha_{\dot{t}\dot{K}} t \left(\frac{\varDelta K}{Q}\right), \tag{11.38}$$

where $D_i = 1$ if the observation is in region i and is zero otherwise.[9]

We again assume that, when there is no adjustment in the capital stock, marginal adjustment costs are zero. Marginal adjustment costs for the *ANRCF* are given by

$$\frac{\partial G/Q}{\partial (\varDelta K/Q)} = \alpha_{\dot{K}} + \gamma_{\dot{K}\dot{K}} \left(\frac{\varDelta K}{Q}\right) + \gamma_{E\dot{K}} p_E + \gamma_{M\dot{K}} p_M + \gamma_{Q\dot{K}} Q$$

$$+ \gamma_{K\dot{K}} \left(\frac{K_{-1}}{Q}\right) + \alpha_{t\dot{K}} t. \tag{11.39}$$

We require

$$\frac{\partial G/Q}{\partial \varDelta K/Q}\Bigg|_{\varDelta K=0} = 0$$

for all p_E, p_M, Q, $K_{-1} \neq 0$, which implies the following parameter restrictions:[10]

$$\alpha_{\dot{K}} = \gamma_{E\dot{K}} = \gamma_{M\dot{K}} = \gamma_{Q\dot{K}} = \gamma_{K\dot{K}} = \alpha_{t\dot{K}} = 0. \tag{11.40}$$

We can now specify the equations to be estimated. Utilizing the property that $(\partial G/Q)/\partial p_i = v_i/Q$, we obtain

$$\frac{E}{Q} = \sum \alpha_{Ei} D_i + \gamma_{EE} p_E + \gamma_{EM} p_M + \gamma_{EQ} Q + \gamma_{EK} \left(\frac{K_{-1}}{Q}\right) + \alpha_{Et} t, \tag{11.41}$$

$$\frac{M}{Q} = \sum \alpha_{Mi} D_i + \gamma_{EM} p_E + \gamma_{MM} p_M + \gamma_{MQ} Q + \gamma_{MK} \left(\frac{K_{-1}}{Q}\right) + \alpha_{Mt} t. \tag{11.42}$$

The capital accumulation equation for the *ANRCF* can be written as

$$\frac{K}{Q} - \frac{K_{-1}}{Q} = -\frac{1}{2} \left[r - \left(r^2 + \frac{4\gamma_{KK}}{\gamma_{\dot{K}\dot{K}}}\right)^{1/2} \right]$$

$$\cdot \left[\frac{1}{\gamma_{KK}} \{ -\sum \alpha_{Ki} D_i - \gamma_{EK} p_E - \gamma_{MK} p_M - \alpha_{Kt} t - p_K \} - \frac{K_{-1}}{Q} \right]. \tag{11.43}$$

The remaining input-output function is derived as

$$\frac{L}{Q} = \frac{G}{Q} - p_E \frac{E}{Q} - p_M \frac{M}{Q}$$

$$= \sum \alpha_{0i} D_i + \alpha_{0t} t - \frac{1}{2}\gamma_{EE} p_E^2 - \frac{1}{2}\gamma_{MM} p_M^2 - \gamma_{EM} p_E p_M$$

$$+ \alpha_Q Q + \alpha_K \left(\frac{K_{-1}}{Q}\right) + \alpha_{Kt} \left(\frac{K_{-1}}{Q}\right) t + \frac{1}{2}\gamma_{QQ} Q^2 + \gamma_{KK} \left(\frac{K_{-1}}{Q}\right)^2$$

$$+ \gamma_{\dot{K}\dot{K}} \left(\frac{\Delta K}{Q}\right)^2 + \gamma_{QK} Q \left(\frac{K_{-1}}{Q}\right). \tag{11.44}$$

Four equations are to be estimated: the input-output equations (11.41), (11.42), and (11.44) and the capital formation equation (11.43).

The model represented by the two sets of estimating equations (11.32), (11.33), (11.34), (11.37) and (11.41), (11.42), (11.43), (11.44) meets the four criteria specified earler for dynamic models:

1. The adjustment process is endogenous and results from direct application of economic theory.
2. The potential for general disequilibrium exists. An increase in the amount of capital, for example, affects the short-run demands for all inputs. These effects depend on the complementarity or substitutability of these variable factors in both production and investment.
3. The Le Chatelier principle is met—long-run own price elasticities exceed (in absolute terms) short-run own price elasticities when evaluated at the initial short-run equilibrium point.
4. Since the production function is explicitly incorporated through the cost function, output feasibility is guaranteed.

The Energy Submodel

Implicit in our analysis of aggregate inputs for the Canadian case is the assumption that the production function is weakly separable in the variable factors. In particular we assume that the production function can be written in the form

$$F[E(E_1, \ldots, E_n, Q, K, t), K, \Delta K, L, M, Q, t] = 0. \tag{11.45}$$

so that the level of the quasi-fixed factor affects substitutability among energy subtypes.

Weak separability allows a consistent two-stage, short-run optimization procedure (conditional on K_{-1}) to be developed for application of the model to Canadian data where explicit disaggregated energy information is available. In the first stage the mix of energy subtypes is chosen to minimize the short-run cost of a unit of energy. In the second stage aggregate L, E, and M are chosen to minimize overall variable costs (conditional on K_{-1}). Given this two-stage procedure, it can then be shown that the average normalized restricted cost function G/Q takes the form:

$$\frac{G}{Q} = G\left(\frac{\hat{p}_E(\hat{p}_{E_1}, \ldots, \hat{p}_{E_n}, K_{-1}, Q, t)}{\hat{p}_L}, \frac{\hat{p}_M}{\hat{p}_L}, \frac{K_{-1}}{Q}, \frac{\Delta K}{Q}, Q, t\right) \tag{11.46}$$

The function $\hat{p}_E(\cdot)$ is called a restricted price aggregator function. Note that $\hat{p}_E(\cdot)$ is an unnormalized restricted price aggregator function.

We approximate the unnormalized restricted price aggregator function $\hat{p}_E$ by a variant of the translog approximation to a unit cost function:

$$\ln \hat{p}_E = \sum_h \sum_k \beta_h^k D_k \ln \hat{p}_{E_h} + \sum_h \sum_f \beta_{hf} \ln \hat{p}_{E_h} \ln \hat{p}_{E_f}$$

$$+ \sum_h \beta_{hk} \ln \hat{p}_{E_h} \ln\left(\frac{K_{-1}}{Q}\right) + \sum_h \beta_{ht} \ln \hat{p}_{E_h} t, \tag{11.47}$$

where $D_k = 1$ if the observation is in region k and 0 otherwise. The indices h and f index the fuel types (six in number).

The energy submodel consists of the unnormalized restricted price aggregator function (11.47) and the restricted (short-run) demand functions for the energy components, in terms of cost shares, obtained from Shephard's lemma:

$$\frac{\partial \ln \hat{p}_E}{\partial \ln \hat{p}_{E_h}} = S_{E_h} = \sum_k \beta_h^k D_k + \sum_f \beta_{hf} \ln \hat{p}_{E_h} + \beta_{hK} \ln\left(\frac{K_{-1}}{Q}\right) + \beta_{ht} t, \tag{11.48}$$

where S_{E_h} is the ith energy subtype's cost share of total energy costs. Estimation of equations (11.48) (the first stage) yields estimates of the parameters of (11.47) The resulting estimate of $\ln \hat{p}_E$ (say $\ln \bar{p}_E$) is used as an instrumental variable in place of $\ln \hat{p}_E$ in the estimation of the dynamic model for aggregate inputs.[11]

11.2 Data

U.S. Data
We gathered national data from various sources on twenty two-digit U.S. manufacturing industries for the 1949 to 1971 period. The sources may not be of comparable quality, but they are the best that could be easily

gathered. We obtained from the Department of Commerce worksheets value of production data, Q, in both current and constant dollars and the cost of materials, including energy, $(E + M)$, also in current and constant dollars. The value of production is the value of shipments corrected for changes in the value of finished goods inventories.[12] Data on labor manhours, L, and the wage rate, P_L, and as well as data on capital stock series and the user cost of capital were obtained from Wharton EFA.[13] Information on the constant dollar energy expenditures were taken from Gollop and Jorgenson (1976).[14] Using the Gollop-Jorgenson data on energy in conjuction with the Department of Commerce data on energy and materials allows us to isolate materials data in real and current dollars for each two-digit SIC industry.

Canadian Data

Information on output, labor, and materials for the years 1961 to 1975 was obtained from the public tape of the *Census of Manufacturers*. Unlike the annual U.S. *Survey of Manufactures*, the Canadian data base contains a regional breakdown of the annual information.[15] Consistent fuels data were taken from Statistics Canada, *Consumption of Purchased Fuel and Electricity, by the Manufacturing, Mining, and Electric Power Industries*. In these publications energy data are provided in natural units, British thermal units (Btu), and cost for six fuel types: coal and coke, gasoline, fuel oil, liquefied petroleum gases (lpg), natural gas, and electricity. Energy used as feedstock is reported as material purchases. The fuel purchased data were corrected for the own generation of electricity to arrive at consumption data. Data on capital stocks and the user cost of capital were constructed from investment, investment price indexes, and average lifetime data for the 1871 to 1977 period.[16]

11.3 Results

In most industries the rate of increase of labor services did not match the rate of increase of physical outputs. As a result labor-output ratios fell in every two-digit manufacturing industry in the United States over the 1949 to 1971 period. In a third of the sample, labor use fell absolutely over the period. However, the share of labor service costs in total costs did not decline to the same extent as labor use per unit of output. Energy represented for most industries a very small proportion of total costs. For the United States over the entire 1948 to 1971 period, energy costs were under 1 percent of total costs for ten industries; in only two industries were energy costs over 3 percent of total costs at some point between 1949 and

1971 (stone, clay, and glass, primary metals). The energy share of total costs was relatively constant for most industries over the period, since the price of energy was falling in these years and energy use was increasing. Nor were energy costs an important component of total costs in the Canadian manufacturing sector. In 1975 four industries—paper, primary metals, nonmetallic minerals, and chemicals—had energy costs over 3 percent of total costs. The share of capital costs, however, in total costs rose appreciably for most of these two-digit industries over the period covered. In very few two-digit industries did the capital-output ratio fall over the period as compared to the fall in the labor-output ratio. This implies that the capital-labor ratio rose. Our analysis of energy demand characteristics (estimated from dynamic models of overall input demand) covers a period where for the most part output growth was rapid, capital growth was more rapid than output growth, and labor-output ratios remained fairly constant or fell.

U.S. Data

Parameter estimates for U.S. manufacturing can be found in Berndt, Fuss, and Waverman (1979) and for Canada in Denny, Fuss, and Waverman (1979). The estimated cost function for each of the eighteen industries exhibited the correct curvature for cost minimization. In addition most parameters whose signs were determinate a priori were of the correct sign. On several occasions, where a parameter was of the wrong sign, it was insignificant and set to zero. In all eighteen industries the own price elasticities of demand are negative, as implied by economic theory. These own price elasticities of demand are presented in table 11.1. Two important points stand out. First, of the 72 long-run own price elasticities of demand, 63 are less than unity. Input demand is primarily inelastic, even in the long run. In 11 of the 18 industries long-run energy own price elasticities are less than 0.5 in absolute value. Industries 21 (tobacco) and 35 (nonelectrical machinery) have the lowest long-run price elasticities of demand for energy; industries 24 (lumber) and 26 (paper) exhibit the most elastic demand for energy. Second, there is little difference between short- and long-run price elasticities of demand for energy but greater differences between short- and long-run price elasticities for labor and materials. This result is somewhat surprising for it implies that firms were able to adjust quickly energy usage to the desired level, but not labor or materials usage.

To cast light on these results, it is useful to consider the expressions for the two elasticities (v_i is a variable input):

Table 11.1
Price elasticities of demand of U.S. industries, 1948 to 1971

(1)	(2) Energy		(3) Capital, long run	(4) Labor		(5) Materials		(6) Labor-energy		(7) Capital-energy, long run	(8) β*
SIC	Short run	Long run		Short run	Long run	Short run	Long run	Short run	Long run		
20 Food	−0.57	−0.57	−0.21	−0.13	−0.16	−0.03	−0.13	0.01	0.01	0.03	0.44
21 Tobacco	0	−0.01	−0.58	−0.39	−0.44	−0.07	−0.14	−0.02	−0.02	−0.01	0.30
22 Textiles	−0.18	−0.19	−1.10	−0.22	−0.47	−0.11	−0.33	−0.01	0.02	−0.01	0.21
23 Apparel	−0.01	−0.36	−0.84	−0.22	−0.22	−0.12	−0.23	−0.01	−0.01	−0.13	0.20
24 Wood	−1.09	−1.10	−2.18	−0.53	−1.41	−0.34	−0.85	−0.01	0.02	−0.03	0.12
25 Furniture	−0.08	−0.16	−1.27	−0.35	−0.57	−0.27	−0.35	−0.01	0.01	−0.07	0.21
26 Paper	−0.61	−0.73	−0.50	−0.02	−0.69	−0.02	−0.07	0.02	0.12	−0.06	0.49
27 Printing	−0.48	−0.69	−0.42	−0.38	−0.40	−0.46	−0.65	−0.03	−0.02	−0.04	0.36
28 Chemicals	−0.15	−0.15	−0.48	−0.12	−0.21	−0.04	−0.35	0.03	0.03	0	0.51
30 Rubber	−0.50	−0.51	−0.29	−0.11	−0.17	−0.04	−0.14	0.04	0.04	−0.01	0.61
32 Stone, Clay, and glass	0	−0.38	−0.60	−0.33	−1.80	−0.51	−0.52	−0.15	−0.05	−0.04	0.19
33 Primary metals	−0.55	−0.65	−0.52	−0.61	−1.06	−0.30	−0.32	0.04	−0.04	0.06	0.40
34 Metal fabricating	0	−0.25	−1.00	0	−1.18	0	0	0	0.10	−0.09	0.11
35 Machinery electrical	0	−0.01	−2.15	0	−2.56	0	0	0	0.03	−0.02	0.13
36 Machinery	−0.11	−0.16	−2.25	−0.08	−0.30	−0.06	−0.99	0.01	0.02	−0.05	0.06
371 Motor vehicles	−0.13	−0.13	−0.55	−0.54	−0.97	−0.17	−0.19	−0.03	−0.03	0	0.63
372 Other Transportation equipment	−0.30	−0.35	−1.64	−0.01	−0.75	−0	−0.01	0.01	0.03	−0.05	0.09
38 Instruments	−0.50	−0.59	−0.45	−0.51	−0.55	−0.57	−0.82	0	0	−0.01	0.31

Note: Short run represents one year; the long run, time to steady state, dependent on β* in each industry; β*, the percentage of the gap between the desired capital stock and the actual capital stock closed within one year.

$$\varepsilon_{iP}^{L} = \left(\frac{P_i}{v_i}\right)\left(\gamma_{ii} - \frac{\gamma_{iK}^2}{\gamma_{KK}}\right),$$

$$\varepsilon_{iP_i}^{S} = \left(\frac{P_i}{v_i}\right)(\gamma_{ii}).$$

The difference between long- and short-run elasticities is

$$\varepsilon_{iP_i}^{L} - \varepsilon_{iP_i}^{S} = \left(-\frac{\gamma_{iK}^2}{\gamma_{KK}}\right)\left(\frac{P_i}{v_i}\right).$$

When γ_{iK} is relatively small in value, that is when a variable input is neither highly substitutable for nor highly complementary with capital, the fact that capital may adjust slowly to its equilibrium value has little impact on the demand for the variable factor at any specific point in time. The observations on own price elasticities of demand therefore indicate that energy is relatively independent of capital, while labor and materials are more highly related to capital use. We now turn to a fuller examination of the relationships among factors—of the elasticities of substitution and the cross-price elasticities of demand.

A number of economists have attempted to measure the relationships between energy and capital and energy and labor in the manufacturing sector to determine the impact that higher energy prices have on the growth path of the economy and on employment levels. If energy is a substitute for both capital and labor, then higher energy prices will tend to accelerate investment and increase employment. Some research with international data has indicated that these substitution relationships exist.[17] Examination of American aggregate manufacturing data has shown a complementary relationship between capital and energy, leading to conclusions that higher energy prices will retard investment and hence growth.[18] An analysis of the substitution possibilites for energy in the manufacturing sector is therefore important for public policy decision making.

In table 11.1 the cross-price elasticities of demand for the U.S. two-digit manufacturing industries represent input demand responses to price changes when the output level is held constant. The cross-price elasticities of demand between labor and energy and capital and energy are given in columns 6 and 7. These cross-price elasticities denote the percentage change in capital or labor use given a 1 percent change in the price of energy. The absolute values of these cross-price elasticities are low for two reasons. First, as we have already indicated, a comparison of the estimates of the short- and long-run own price elasticities of energy demand indicate that long-run changes in capital and energy uses are largely independent.

Second, energy is in most cases a far smaller percentage of total costs then are labor or capital costs. Therefore a 1 percent change in the price of energy may induce a small relative change in labor use, but this induced change in labor may be a large absolute amount. The Allen-Uzawa elasticities of substitution given in tables 11.2 and 11.3 show the proportionate change in the input ratio divided by the proportionate change in the ratio of factor prices. The substitution elasticities, G_{ij}, are easily derived from the cross-price elasticities by the relationship

$$G_{ij} = \frac{\varepsilon_{ij}}{S_j},$$

where S_j is the cost share of the jth input.

In many cases these elasticities of substitution are large while the corresponding cross-price elasticities are small, indicative of the relatively small magnitude of energy costs in relation to total costs.

As can be seen from either table 11.1 or table 11.2, in 14 of the 18 U.S.

Table 11.2
Elasticities of substitution of U.S. industries

Industry		Capital-energy	Labor-energy Short run	Labor-energy Long run	Share of energy in total costs[a]
20	Food	8.05	2.90	3.24	0.0041
21	Tobacco	−2.59	−6.28	−5.38	0.0039
22	Textiles	−1.06	−0.43	0.13	0.0135
23	Apparel	−22.40	−1.05	−0.90	0.0058
24	Wood	−2.07	−0.45	1.22	0.013
25	Furniture	−9.29	−1.21	1.35	0.008
26	Paper	−2.74	0.95	5.48	0.021
27	Printing	−6.61	−4.09	−2.82	0.0066
28	Chemicals	0	1.25	1.36	0.024
30	Rubber	−1.21	3.54	4.24	0.01
32	Stone, clay, and glass	−1.47	−5.62	−2.01	0.026
33	Primary metals	2.43	1.54	−1.58	0.026
34	Metal fabricating	−9.70	0	10.93	0.0089
35	Machinery electrical	−4.09	0.02	5.02	0.0054
36	Machinery	−8.11	1.02	3.52	0.0061
371	Motor vehicles	0.67	−5.64	−6.40	0.0045
372	Other transportation Equipment	−9.39	1.18	6.10	0.0049
38	Instruments	−1.42	−0.67	−0.25	0.0052

[a] Energy share calculated for 1971.

Table 11.3
Price elasticities of demand of Canadian industries, 1962 to 1975

(1) SIC	(2) Energy		(3) Capital, long run	(4) Labor		(5) Materials		(6) Labor-energy		(7) Capital-energy, long run	(8) β^*
	Short run	Long run		Short run	Long run	Short run	Long run	Short run	Long run		
1 Food	−0.44	−0.51	−0.86	−0.07	−0.25	−0.07	−0.29	0.008	−0.02	0.08	0.21
2 Tobacco	−0.49	−0.49	−0.54	−0.29	−0.46	−0.03	−0.12	0.01	0.02	−0.004	0.14
3 Rubber	−0.72	−0.73	−0.80	−0.21	−0.27	−0.10	−0.36	0.01	0.007	0.03	0.83
4 Leather	−0.46	−0.46	−0.49	−0.20	−0.41	−0.10	−0.12	0.01	0.004	0.02	0.67
5 Textiles	−0.07	−0.07	−0.68	−0.41	−0.77	−0.16	−0.49	0.009	−0.03	0.009	0.47
6 Knitting mills	−0.07	−0.77	−4.92	−0.13	−0.89	−0.08	−1.08	0.003	−0.04	0.19	0.08
8 Wood	−0.41	−0.43	−1.37	−0.09	−0.59	−0.08	−0.49	−0.02	−0.007	0.07	0.38
9 Furniture	−0.67	−0.67	−0.85	−0.08	−0.37	−0.05	−0.11	0.007	0.008	−0.003	0.32
10 Paper	−0.45	−0.51	−0.81	−0.26	−1.70	−0.14	−0.18	0.017	−0.11	0.08	0.33
11 Printing	−0.57	−0.57	−0.15	−0.11	−0.26	−0.14	−0.14	−0.005	−0.004	−0.001	0.19
12 Primary metals	−1.04	−1.96	−1.59	−0.11	−0.36	−0.04	−1.62	0.09	−0.10	0.36	0.28
13 Metal fabricating	−0.09	−0.09	−0.27	−0	−0.47	−0	−0	0.030	0.033	0.003	0.38
14 Machinery	−1.46	−1.47	−0.62	−0.03	−0.06	−0.02	−0.25	0.015	0.018	−0.02	0.33
15 Transportation equipment	−0.69	−0.69	−1.66	−0.10	−0.94	−0.03	−0.03	−0.011	−0.024	−0.05	0.19
16 Electrical	−0.52	−0.52	−0.42	−0.10	−0.20	−0.04	−0.09	0.009	0.008	0.002	0.75
17 Nonmetallic minerals	−0	−0	−0.86	−0.27	−1.00	−0.19	−0.43	−0.03	0.06	−0.07	0.45
19 Chemicals	−1.01	−2.83	−1.11	−0.19	−0.27	−0	−0.60	0.19	0.03	0.46	0.50
20 Miscellaneous	−0.87	−0.87	−0.33	−0.04	0.17	−0	−0.06	0.03	0.1	−0.002	0.43

Note: Short run represents one year; the long run, time to steady state, dependent on β^* in each industry; β^*, the percentage of the gap between the desired capital stock and the actual capital stock closed within one year.

two-digit SIC manufacturing industries, the capital-energy cross-price elasticity is negative, indicating that an increase in the price of energy leads to a reduction in the amount of capital used. The weight of this evidence then is that higher energy prices tend to reduce investment and as a result the growth rate of capital accumulation. These results are consistent with the U.S. studies of aggregate manufacturing. Of the 4 most energy-intensive industries, however, 2 industries—chemicals and primary metals—exhibit capital-energy substitutability while 2 industries—paper, stone, clay and glass—show capital-energy complementarity. *

In 6 of the 18 U.S. manufacturing industries labor and energy are long-run complements, that is, an increase in the price of energy tends to reduce employment. In 11 industries, however, labor and energy are long-run substitutes. Of the 5 most energy-intensive industries 2 industries—paper and chemicals—show long-run substitutability between labor and energy while 2 industries—primary metals, stone, clay, and glass—show long-run complementarity. Because of these divergences in the sign of the labor-energy cross-price elasticities (and the corresponding elasticities of substitution) across these 18 industries, any summary statement of the degree of complementarity or substitutability between energy and labor in manufacturing is quite inappropriate. In the short run 9 industries exhibit complementarity between energy and labor (as compared to 6 in the long run). Five industries exhibit sign reversals between the short and long runs in the relationship between labor and energy. In 4 industries—textiles, wood, furniture, paper—labor and energy change from being short-run complements to long-run substitutes. In the primary metals industry labor and energy change from being short-run substitutes to long-run complements. This evidence on the switching of relationships between the short- and long-runs is a most interesting property of the dynamic model. These results suggest that in the short run in 4 industries, when the price of energy increases, the volume of energy consumed as well as the quantity of labor services used decreases.[19] However, in the long run, when the firm is fully able to adjust its capital stock, the firm substitutes the relatively cheaper labor for energy.[20] In 4 other industries—metal fabricating, electrical machinery, other machinery, and other transportation equipment—labor and energy are more substitutable in the long run than they are in the short run. The results for 8 industries indicate that the short-run effects of increases in energy prices on labor could either decrease labor use or slightly increase it. The long-run effects for these 8 industries, however, are increased use of labor at the expense of energy. Policy makers should be made aware that the evidence in labor markets shortly following increases in energy prices are not indicative of the long-run response of firms to energy prices.

An important parameter of the dynamic model is β^*, the variable representing the degree to which the firm closes the gap in one year between its desired capital stock and the actual beginning period capital stock. A β^* close to zero indicates a very slow response to exogenous shocks, a slow adjustment of the capital stock, while a β^* close to unity denotes a very quick adjustment. The average adjustment coefficient for all 18 industries is 0.3. In the first year, following an exogenous change such as an increase in energy prices, 30 percent of the difference is closed between the capital stock actually held by the firm at the beginning of the year and its new desired optimal stock of capital. Ninety-five percent of the change to the desired level is accomplished over an eight-year period. On average the time period represented between the short- and long-run results given in tables 11.1 and 11.2 is substantial. Rapid adjustment (β^* greater than 0.5) occurs in 4 industries—paper, chemicals, motor vehicles, rubber; very slow adjustment (β^* less than 0.2) occurs in 9 industries—textiles, apparel, wood, furniture, stone, clay, and glass, metal fabricating, electrical machinery, other machinery, other transportation equipment.

Canadian Industries

Table 11.3 and 11.4 present some of the major results of applying the dynamic model to the Canadian two-digit SIC industrial manufacturing data. We see that in only 6 of the 18 industries is there a negative sign in the long-run relationship between capital and energy cross-price elasticity. In the majority of cases capital and energy are long-run substitutes, a conclusion at variance with our results for the United States.[21] The 5 most energy-intensive industries—primary metals, nonmetallic minerals, chemicals, paper, wood—show long-run capital-energy substitutability. The overall relationship between labor and energy is complex because of the differences in short-run and long-run effects. Of the 18 Canadian industries, 8 exhibit long-run labor-energy complementarity and 10 labor-energy substitutability; in the short run only 4 industries exhibit labor-energy complementarity. For 6 industries the sign of the energy-labor elasticity changes between the short and long runs; five of these elasticity changes indicate a switch from short-run substitutability to long-run complementarity; for the sixth, a switch from short-run complementarity to long-run substitutability. Four Canadian industries exhibit both short- and long-run labor-energy substitutability but in the long-run less substitutability—rubber, textiles, electrical equipment,

Table 11.4
Elasticities of substitution of Canadian industries

	Industry	Capital-energy	Labor-energy Short run	Long run	Share of energy in total costs
1	Food and beverage[a]	6.83	0.70	−1.62	0.001
2	Tobacco	−1.13	−3.59	4.79	0.004
3	Rubber	2.50	1.08	0.56	0.012
4	Leather	2.45	1.26	0.47	0.009
5	Textiles	0.61	0.61	−2.24	0.015
6	Knitting mills	18.6	0.31	−4.01	0.010
8	Wood	3.97	−1.15	−0.41	0.017
9	Furniture	−.035	0.85	0.94	0.008
10	Paper	1.93	0.39	−2.61	0.042
11	Printing	−0.16	−0.90	−0.65	0.006
12	Primary	9.60	2.48	−2.52	0.038
13	Metal fabricating	0.29	3.59	3.23	0.010
14	Machinery	−4.29	2.54	3.20	0.006
15	Transporation equipment	−9.00	−2.16	−4.71	0.005
16	Electrical products	0.32	1.50	1.29	0.006
17	Non metallic minerals	−1.30	−0.57	1.15	0.054
19	Chemicals	13.82	5.86	0.88	0.033
20	Miscellaneous	−0.31	5.27	5.08	0.006

[a] Industries 1 and 10 are calculated at 1973 values. All other industries are calculated at sample means.

chemicals. These results are also at variance with those for the United States where labor and energy become more substitutable in the long run.

The average adjustment parameter, β^*, for the Canadian industries is 0.38, a value very close to that estimated for the 18 U.S. industries. The slowest adjustments occur in food, tobacco, knitting mills, printing and transportation equipment. Very quick adjustments occur in rubber, leather, electrical equipment, and chemicals.

The estimates of the own price elasticities of demand for the Canadian industries given in the first four columns of table 11.3 show that overall input demand is inelastic, again a result consistent with our U.S. findings. There is very little difference between short- and long-run elasticities for energy but somewhat more than that experienced in the United States. The lack of divergence between short- and long-run energy own price elasticities is indicative of an independent relationship between capital and energy in the long run. again verifying our U.S. results. Industries 24

Table 11.5
Cross price elasticities of demand showing substitutions among energy subtypes in Canadian industries

Industry	Natural gas-fuel oil Short run	Long run	Electricity-fuel oil Short run	Long run	Coal-fuel oil Short run	Long run
1 Food and beverage	0.349	0.327	0.020	0.049	0.005	−0.002
2 Tobacco	0.445	0.445	−0.114	−0.114	0.300	0.300
3 Rubber	0.511	0.511	−0.119	−0.207	0.302	0.300
4 Leather	0.682	0.680	0.157	0.154	0.445	0.443
5 Textiles	0.528	0.528	−0.127	−0.130	1.95	1.95
6 Knitting mills	−0.056	−0.095	−0.009	−0.048	1.19	1.18
8 Wood	−0.694	−0.691	0.042	0.048	0.463	0.472
9 Furniture	−0.169	−0.169	−0.150	−0.150	0.131	0.131
10 Paper	0.113	0.124	−0.294	−0.299	0.656	0.672
11 Printing	−0.035	−0.035	−0.185	−0.185	0.784	0.784
12 Primary metals	−0.066	−0.222	−0.149	−0.394	−0.190	−0.019
13 Metal fabricating	0.181	0.181	−0.082	−0.082	0.396	0.396
14 Machinery	0.060	0.060	−0.142	−0.144	0.332	0.329
15 Transportation equipment	0.034	0.034	−0.050	−0.050	0.057	0.053
16 Electrical products	0.011	0.011	−0.079	−0.079	0.213	0.213
17 Nonmetallic minerals	0.736	0.716	−0.408	−0.404	0.532	0.519
19 Chemicals	0.155	−0.151	−0.179	−0.537	0.074	−0.241
20 Miscellaneous	−0.072	−0.072	−0.112	−0.112	0.431	0.431

(lumber) and 26 (paper) exhibit the most elastic long-run demand for energy.

Substitution among Canadian Energy Types

The Canadian data included observations on fuel types, data not readily available in the United States. A fuel choice submodel was estimated for Canadian industries, as given by equations (11.47) and (11.48). From the submodel some interesting substitution possibilities could be seen among energy types.[22] In table 11.5 we present three specific cross-price elasticities of demand for natural gas, electricity, and coal, following a 1 percent increase in the price of fuel oil. Both short- and long-run (steady state equilibrium with a new desired capital stock) elasticities are given. The short-run elasticity at the mean is calculated as

$$\varepsilon^S_{E_h, P_E} = \frac{\beta_{hf} + S_{E_h} \cdot S_{E_f}}{S_{E_h}} + \varepsilon^Q_{EE} \cdot S_{E_h}.$$

The corresponding long-run elasticity is

$$\varepsilon^L_{E_h, P_{E_f}} = \varepsilon^S_{E_h, P_{E_f}} + [\varepsilon_{K, P_E}][\beta_{hK} + \gamma_{EK} \frac{K}{E} S_{E_f}],$$

where

S_{E_f} = the share of the fth energy type cost in total energy costs,

ε^Q_{EE} = the elasticity of aggregate energy with respect to its price (output held constant),

ε_{K, P_E} = the elasticity of capital with respect to the price of aggregate energy,

K = the mean capital stock,

E = the mean aggregate energy input.[23]

Five major observations follow from the results. First, with two exceptions the cross-elasticities of demand are inelastic and in most cases quite inelastic (less than 0.5 in absolute terms); on average the electricity-fuel oil relationship is the least elastic while the coal-fuel oil relationship is the most elastic. This general result makes good intuitive sense: most of us feel that fuel oil and electricity are used for different purposes and therefore expect the cross-elasticity of demand between these two fuels to be low. If coal were replaced as a boiler fuel by fuel oil in this period, the cross-elasticity would be substantial.

Second, with seven exceptions there are little differences between short- and long-run cross-price elasticities. In the primary metals and chemical industries all three relationships show substantial differences between the short and long runs as does the electricity-fuel oil cross-price elasticity in the rubber industry. The differences between long- and short-run elasticities can be written as

$$\varepsilon^L_{E, P_{E_f}} - \varepsilon^S_{E_h, P_{E_f}} = [\varepsilon_{K, P_E}][\beta_{hK} + \gamma_{EK} \frac{K}{E} S_{E_f}].$$

If the elasticity of capital with respect to the price of energy is close to zero, as most of our results suggest, then γ_{EK} will be small, and there will be little difference between short-and long-run cross-price elasticities of demand for fuel subtypes.

The remaining three major conclusions revolve around the nature of the relationships between fuel oil and the other three inputs. In 16 of the 18 industries, electricity and fuel oil are complements in both the short and long runs, a result consistent with our previous view that electricity and fuel oil are not substitutes in manufacturing. Coal and fuel oil are, however, seen to be substitutes in all industries in the short run and in 15 of the 18 industries in the long run. Between natural gas and fuel oil substitution relationships predominate in 12 of the 18 industries in the short run and in 11 in the long run.[24]

Only four sign reversals occur between the short and long runs, suggesting that changing the capital stock does not alter the basic ways in which fuel types interact.[25]

In table 11.6 we present the own price elasticities of demand for the fuel subtypes (as well as the total energy own price elasticity for comparison). All own price elasticities are negative, as economic theory suggests. Electricity demand, on average, is the least elastic while coal demand is the most elastic.

Table 11.6
Long-run own price elasticity for energy and energy components in Canadian industries

	Industry	Energy	Coal	Fuel oil	Natural gas	Electricity
1	Food and beverage	−0.510	−0.641	−0.597	−1.292	−0.383
2	Tobacco	−0.487	−1.226	−0.508	−1.594	−0.411
3	Rubber	−0.731	−1.667	−0.726	−1.159	−0.384
4	Leather	−0.463	−0.724	−1.143	−1.454	−0.800
5	Textiles	−0.071	−1.039	−0.643	−0.808	−0.192
6	Knitting mills	−0.774	−2.184	−1.263	−0.929	−0.703
8	Wood	−0.432	−0.855	−0.074	−0.855	−0.664
9	Furniture	−0.670	−1.234	−0.191	−0.577	−0.531
10	Paper	−0.514	−1.474	−0.057	−0.901	−0.545
11	Printing	−0.568	−0.382	−0.282	−0.835	−0.349
12	Primary metals	−1.964	−1.444	−0.743	−1.175	−1.423
13	Metal fabricating	−0.091	−0.877	−0.578	−0.751	−0.426
14	Machinery	−1.456	−1.012	−0.966	−1.146	−1.128
15	Transportation equipment	−0.693	−0.905	−0.411	−0.839	−0.891
16	Electrical products	−0.515	−1.471	−0.431	−1.146	−0.413
17	Nonmetallic minerals	−0.030	−0.817	−0.753	−1.967	−0.009
19	Chemicals	−2.825	−1.599	−0.984	−1.210	−1.770
20	Miscellaneous	−0.872	−1.678	−0.714	−1.505	−1.076

11.4 Summary

It would be impossible to cover here all the implications of this large body of results. A wide variety of responses remains to be examined across industries within each country and of course across countries.

The distinct difference in the patterns of input substitution between the countries is disconcerting. We cannot at this time speculate on the exact reason. The Canadian estimates are for a cross section of regions over time. We do not have lengthy time series in many Canadian industries. We intend to estimate our models from national Canadian time-series data. If these results are substantially different, more attention to both cross-section and time-series specification will be required.

The data for the two countries show surprisingly different input share levels and movements over identical time periods. There are serious problems in both countries with some of the data, and there has been no attempt to establish data comparability across countries. At present the divergence in the Canadian and U.S. results is not explained.

The model used here for dynamic factor demands is only the beginning of what promises to be a fruitful line of research. Epstein, and Epstein and Denny have developed and estimated a model that permits the number of quasi stocks to be larger than one, without restricting the interaction of the adjustment paths. The usefulness of these models in a wider variety of empirical contexts needs to be tested.

The continuing rapid rates of change in the relative price of energy offers an excellent opportunity for studying the sensitivity of the estimates of dynamic models to data periods. Much of the adjustment to a higher relative energy price is still incomplete. Adding observations will permit us to test the response pattern to higher energy prices over a longer period of time.

There were extensive debates about the value of the elasticity of substitution when the *CES* function was introduced. These debates continue with the more flexible functional forms of the last decade. We suspect that many of these problems will remain as alternative dynamic models become commonplace. The results presented here are only the beginning.

Notes

Financial support for the research reported in this chapter was provided by the Electric Power Research Institute and the Ontario Ministry of Industry and Tourism and is gratefully acknowledged.

1. The development in this section draws heavily from Berndt, Fuss, and Waverman (1979).

2. In Berndt, Fuss, and Waverman (1979) the translog model yielded positive price elasticities for energy when estimated with data for aggregate U.S. manufacturing over the 1947 to 1974 period.

3. See Nadiri and Rosen (1973) for an example of such a model.

4. We actually require only stationary expectations with respect to relative prices. Suppose all factor prices (including those of quasi-fixed factors) are expected to increase at a rate λ. Then the development in the text that follows carries through as long as the discount rate r is interpreted as the real rate (the nominal rate minus the rate of inflation λ).

5. If $\partial^2 F/\partial \mathbf{v} \partial \dot{\mathbf{x}} = 0$, the model represented by (11.1) reduces to Lucas' (1967b) separable internal adjustment cost model. If in addition, $\partial^2 F/\partial \mathbf{x} \partial \dot{\mathbf{x}} = 0$, (11.1) reduces to Treadway's (1969) separable internal cost of adjustment model.

6. We show below that it is reasonable to assume $G_{\dot{x}}(\mathbf{w}, \mathbf{x}^*) = 0$, so that (11.19) is identical to the steady-state marginal condition obtained when adjustment costs are not explicitly considered. This is due to the fact that the adjustment costs result from net rather than gross changes in the quasi-fixed factors. For an elaboration of this point see Nickell.

7. Mortensen has also shown that $\mathbf{C}^*$ symmetric implies $(\mathbf{A}^* + r\mathbf{C}^*)^{-1}$ and $\mathbf{M}^*(\mathbf{A}^* + r\mathbf{C}^*)^{-1}$ are negative definite. Therefore the corresponding expressions obtained from the quadratic cost function used in the econometric analysis are $(\gamma_{KK} + r\gamma_{K\dot{K}})^{-1}$ and $(\beta^*/\gamma_{KK} + \gamma_{\dot{K}K}) < 0$ and the Marshallian short-run, long-run dichotomy (short-run elasticities being less than long-run) holds.

8. The quadratic has certain advantages. Other functional forms could, however, be used.

9. The dummy variable technique was not applied to $\alpha_{\dot{K}}$ since $\alpha_{\dot{K}} = 0$ is a reasonable restriction. The technique was not applied to α_{0t} since the resulting additional parameters led to an estimation problem that exceeded the capacity of our existing computer software.

10. Recall that the adjustment cost is the cost incurred in excess of the service price of capital p_K. Hence (11.40) is a reasonable restriction. Note, however, that one effect of this assumption, when the restricted cost function takes the form (11.38), is to impose a separable adjustment costs specification on the technology.

11. For a detailed analysis of the two-stage procedure and the instrumental variable technique in the context of a static model of energy demand, see Fuss (1977).

12. The value of production (as distinct from the value of shipments) is normally available only in census years due to the absence of detailed information on finished goods inventories in non census years. The changes in the value of finished goods inventories have been estimated for non census years for each industry by the Bureau of Economic Analysis (BEA) of the Department of Commerce. These worksheets are released by the BEA under the following proviso: "None of the data have been published by the Bureau of Economic Analysis since some of the statistics do not meet BEA standards of reliability."

13. We are grateful to Wharton EFA for making a data tape available to us.

14. The regrouping of four-digit industries made by Gollop-Jorgenson for some two-digit industries has not been done for nonenergy data.

15. We constructed a consistent data set for five regions: Atlantic, Quebec, Ontario, Prairies, and British Columbia (also containing the northern region). Several minor adjustments were made to census data (see Denny, Fuss, and Waverman 1979).

16. Details are in Denny, Fuss, and Waverman (1979), section 4.4.

17. See Pindyck (1979).

18. For example, see Hudson and Jorgenson (1974).

19. A corresponding increase in the purchase of materials allows the given level of output to be produced.

20. This substitution effect further reduces the demand for energy. A substitution effect between labor and materials implies that the firm also reduces its demand for materials from the level attained during the short-run response.

21. This result also conflicts with Fuss's (1977) results for aggregate manufacturing, where, using a static translog model, he found capital and energy to be weak complements. The discrepancy could be due either to the different levels of aggregation or the different models employed. Estimates contained in Denny, Fuss, and Waverman (1979) shed light on this issue. They estimated static translog cost functions for the 18 industries using Fuss's two-stage model. In 16 of these industries capital and energy were substitutes, suggesting that the discrepancy is due to aggregation effects.

22. There are several ways to compute substitution relationships among fuel types. One natural interpretation would be to consider the movement along the energy isoquant, holding all aggregate inputs constant, including total energy. The results we report here are the substitution relationships among fuel types, allowing total energy and all other aggregate inputs to change but holding output constant.

23. The long-run price elasticity depends on the optimal capital stock; we have used the mean of the actual capital stock in our calculations.

24. From estimates of static translog cost functions referred to in note 21, Denny, Fuss, and Waverman (1979) found electricity-fuel oil complementarity in 11 of the 18 industries; coal-fuel oil substitutability in 14 of the 18 industries; and natural gas-fuel oil substitutability in 12 of the 18 industries.

25. Of the four sign reversals three are for coal-fuel oil in food and beverages (where the cross-price elasticity is tiny), primary metals, and chemicals. The fourth reversal occurs in the natural gas-fuel oil relationship in the chemicals industry.

12

**Dynamic Models of
Energy Demand:
An Assessment and
Comparison**

Ernst R. Berndt,
Catherine J. Morrison, and
G. Campbell Watkins

For short periods people take the stock of appliances for production as practically fixed; and they are governed by their expectations of demand in considering how actively they shall set themselves to work those appliances. In long periods they set themselves to adjust the flow of these appliances to their expectations of demand for the goods which the appliances help to produce.—Marshall (p. 374).

Instructors of principles of economics courses have traditionally stressed the Marshallian distinction between short and long run, and have noted that own price responses in the short run are likely to be smaller than in the long run. Applied researchers have also attempted to incorporate this Marshallian framework into econometric models, typically through the use of partial adjustment and other distributed lag specifications. Such attempts to introduce dynamic analyses into applied econometrics have not been particularly convincing. Marc Nerlove (1972, p. 223), for example, has summarized this practice as follows: "The extent and variety of topics to which distributed lag analysis has been applied in empirical economics is astounding, but, what is more remarkable, is the virtual lack of theoretical justification for the lag structures superimposed on basically static models."

The analysis of short- and long-run energy substitution possibilities provides a useful illustration of how applied econometricians in the last few decades have approached problems in modeling dynamic demand for an important factor of production: energy.

In this chapter we shall review and assess three generations of dynamic energy demand models.[1] First generation models are essentially single-equation models using the Koyck partial adjustment or Balestra-Nerlove captive and flexible demand framework. The role of economic theory in these first generation models is limited, and interactions with other inputs are neglected. The second generation models are more general in that they explicitly incorporate interrelated factor demands into the firm's short-run demand responses, but the role of economic theory is still limited in that economic factors affecting the time path of adjustment from short to long run are not formally introduced. The third generation models explicitly incorporated dynamic optimization and thereby provide well-defined measures of short, intermediate, and long-run price elasticities within the traditional Marshallian framework. A significant property of certain second and all third generation models is that a measure of capacity utilization can be defined and constructed, as can a measure of endogenous capital utilization.

12.1 First Generation Dynamics

For a variety of reasons firms are generally unable to adjust factor demands instantaneously to long-run equilibrium levels. In the context of energy demand, for example, a great deal of energy use is tied to the particular technical characteristics of capital equipment in place, and thus price-induced changes in energy demand are constrained by the rate at which the capital-using equipment is retrofitted or replaced.

In the simplest dynamic partial adjustment models, energy demand is viewed largely in isolation from other inputs, although lagged adjustment is permitted.[2] Typically a variant of the Koyck partial adjustment model is specified:

$$E_t - E_{t-1} = \lambda(E_t^* - E_{t-1}),$$ (12.1)

for $0 < \lambda \leq 1$, where E_t is the actual amount of energy demanded at time t, E_t^* is the long-run equilibrium level of energy demand, and λ is the proportional adjustment parameter. According to (12.1) the actual change in the quantity of energy demanded between time periods t and $t - 1$ is equal to a proportion λ of the long-run change. Static economic theory is usually called upon to provide guidance in the specification of variables affecting E_t^*. For example, let us specify that

$$\ln E_t^* = \ln \alpha_0 + \sum_{j=1}^{N} \gamma_{Ej} \ln P_j + \gamma_{EY} \ln Y,$$ (12.2)

where P_j is the price of the jth factor, and let us impose the restriction of factor demand theory that input demand functions are homogeneous of degree zero in factor prices,

$$\sum_{j=1}^{N} \gamma_{Ej} = 0.$$ (12.3)

This enables us to write

$$\gamma_{EN} = -\sum_{j=1}^{N-1} \gamma_{Ej}. \tag{12.4}$$

Substituting (12.4) into (12.2) and collecting terms, we obtain

$$\ln E_t^* = \ln \alpha_0 + \sum_{j=1}^{N-1} \gamma_{Ej} \ln\left(\frac{P_{jt}}{P_{Nt}}\right) + \gamma_{EY} \ln Y_t. \tag{12.5}$$

Now we specify a log-linear lagged adjustment mechanism:

$$\ln E_t - \ln E_{t-1} = \lambda(\ln E_t^* - \ln E_{t-1}). \tag{12.6}$$

Substituting (12.6) into (12.5) and rearranging, we obtain the estimable equation

$$\ln E_t = \lambda \ln \alpha_0 + \lambda \sum_{j=1}^{N-1} \gamma_{Ej} \ln\left(\frac{P_{jt}}{P_{Nt}}\right) + \lambda \gamma_{EY} \ln Y_t + (1 - \lambda)\ln E_{t-1}. \tag{12.7}$$

As noted by H. S. Houthakker and L. D. Taylor and others, short-run price elasticities are constant and are computed easily as

$$\varepsilon_{EP}^S = \frac{\partial \ln E}{\partial \ln P_j} = \lambda \gamma_{Ej}, \tag{12.8}$$

for $j = 1, \ldots, N$, while long-run price elasticities simply become

$$\varepsilon_{EP}^L = \gamma_{Ej}, \tag{12.9}$$

for $j = 1, \ldots, N$. The corresponding energy demand elasticities with respect to output in this simple model are of course

$$\varepsilon_{EY}^S = \lambda \gamma_{EY},$$
$$\varepsilon_{EY}^L = \gamma_{EY}. \tag{12.10}$$

The most important advantage of such a specification of the short- and long-run demand elasticities is its simplicity, although this itself creates several major difficulties. Some of these problems are as follows:

1. The ratio of all long- to short-run elasticities depends only on the speed of adjustment λ,

$$\frac{\varepsilon_{EP_j}^L}{\varepsilon_{EP}^S} = \frac{\varepsilon_{EY}^L}{\varepsilon_{EY}^S} = \frac{1}{\lambda}, \tag{12.11}$$

for $0 < \lambda \leq 1$. Hence if $\lambda = 0.25$, all long-run elasticities are four times larger than the corresponding short-run elasticities.[3] Moreover, if constant returns to scale holds in the long run, so that $\gamma_{EY} = 1$, then the short-run elasticity of demand for energy with respect to output equals λ, 0.25.

2. Although it may appear reasonable to specify a simple partial adjustment mechanism like (12.6) for energy, such a specification is largely ad hoc and does not explicitly incorporate the optimizing behavior of economic theory. In (12.6) the speed of adjustment is exogenous and fixed; a preferable approach would treat adjustment costs explicitly and then derive λ_t as an endogenous choice variable based on dynamic cost minimization.

3. Because the specification (12.6) of partial adjustment involves no explicit economic optimizing behavior, it is not at all clear precisely what is changing and what remains fixed, as E_t adjusts to E_t^*. It is therefore difficult to interpret the short- and long-run elasticities (12.8) to (12.10) unambiguously. This is reminiscent of the oft-quoted confession of Saint Augustine, "For so it is, O Lord my God, I measure it; but what it is I measure, I do not know."

4. Another problem with specification (12.6), and one related to the previous two drawbacks, is that the rate at which E_t adjusts to E_t^* does not depend explicitly on the extent of disequilibrium in other factor markets. For example, the extent to which demand for electricity at time t has adjusted to its long-run equilibrium level should depend on the extent to which the stock of electricity using capital has also adjusted to its long-run equilibrium level by replacing, for example, the stock of oil-using equipment. If this general disequilibrium were incorporated into (12.6), the ratio of long-run to short-run energy elasticities would depend not only on λ but also on the adjustment parameter in a demand for capital equation.

More generally, since it is not possible for only one factor market to differ from its long-run equilibrium state, lagged adjustment specifications for energy demand should not be isolated but rather should take into account this general disequilibrium. Failure to do so may create, for example, an output feasibility problem: given an increase in demand for output, not all factors can adjust partially to their new long-run equilibrium level; for the production of the greater output to be feasible, there must be some temporary overshooting of at least one factor during the adjustment process. This is not captured in the specification (12.6).

In summary, although the partial adjustment mechanism (12.6) is simple and easily implemented empirically, it is not based on economic optimization. It yields elasticity estimates whose interpretation is nebulous and fails to account for interrelated aspects of the adjustment process, especially the extent of disequilibrium in the capital factor demand equation.

An alternative single-equation approach to dynamic modeling of energy demand is that presented by Pietro Balestra, and Pietro Balestra and Marc Nerlove. Balestra-Nerlove attempted to model the demand for a particular fuel—natural gas—in the residential and commercial sector. A distinctive feature of their approach is an explicit recognition that much energy demand is captive, in that it is tied to the existing stock of energy-using equipment.[4]

Balestra-Nerlove define the energy demand of fuel i, denoted E_{it}, as the product of a utilization rate u_{it} and the full capacity energy use associated with the fixed capital stock using fuel i:

$$E_{it} = u_{it}K_{it}. \tag{12.12}$$

The term K_{it} could be measured as the Btu capacity of a furnace, water heater, and the like, in the case of natural gas or, following F. M. Fisher and Carl Kaysen, as the horsepower or kilowatt-hour rating of electricity-consuming equipment. Using the perpetual inventory identity of capital accumulation,

$$K_{it} = I_{it} + (1 - \delta_{it})K_{i,t-1}, \tag{12.13}$$

where I_{it} is gross investment in fuel type i-using capital and δ_{it} is the rate of economic depreciation. We can substitute (12.13) into (12.12) to obtain

$$E_{it} = u_{it}I_{it} + u_{it}(1 - \delta_{it})K_{i,t-1}. \tag{12.14}$$

If depreciation were constant and geometric, then $\delta_{it} = \delta_i$, $t = 1, \ldots, T$. According to Balestra for residential-commercial natural gas demand variations in utilization rates are due primarily to climatic differences, given the predominance of space-heating end use. Thus Balestra notes that, since he uses degree day adjusted gas consumption data, it is not unreasonable to assume constant utilization rates.[5] Moreover a high technical efficiency of combustion is easily obtained in space-heating equipment. This constrains the scope for technical change over time, again implying that the assumption of constant utilization-efficiency rates is plausible.[6]

Assuming then that u_{it} is constant and equal to $\bar{u}_i$, Balestra rewrites (12.14) as

$$E_{it} = \bar{u}_iI_{it} + \bar{u}_i(1 - \delta_i)K_{i,t-1} \tag{12.15}$$

and defines flexible demand as the first term of (12.15),

$$E_{it}^f = \bar{u}_i I_{it}.$$ (12.16)

The gross investment in fuel i-using equipment is specified as a function of relative prices, income or commercial sector activity, households, and perhaps technical change as represented by time,

$$E_{it}^f = f_i(P_j, Y, H, t),$$ (12.17)

where P_j are relative prices of fuels and other commodities and H represents a household variable. The second term in (12.14) is called captive demand,

$$E_{it}^c = \bar{u}_i(1 - \delta_i)K_{i,t-1}.$$ (12.18)

Thus total demand for fuel i (12.15) can be rewritten as the sum of flexible and captive demand,

$$E_{it} = E_{it}^f + E_{it}^c.$$ (12.19)

In the Balestra formulation the short-run effects of price changes are confined to flexible demand associated with variations in gross investment. The short-run response is smaller than the long-run effect, since only in the long run can new fuel i-using capital stock fully substitute for the fuel j-using equipment.[7]

To implement this model empirically, it is necessary to specify a functional form for flexible demand (12.17) and also to incorporate captive demand (12.18). Since data on K_{it} are often unavailable, the assumption of a constant utilization rate is important, for it permits Balestra to substitute $E_{i,t-1} = \bar{u}_i K_{i,t-1}$ from (12.12), as well as (12.17) into (12.15), thereby obtaining

$$E_{it} = f_i(P_j, Y, H, t) + (1 - \delta_i)E_{i,t-1}.$$ (12.20)

Hence, once we specify a functional form for f_i in (12.20), empirical implementation is straightforward.

Short-run price elasticity estimates for this model can be computed simply as

$$\frac{\partial \ln E_{it}}{\partial \ln P_{jt}} = \frac{\partial E_{it}^f}{\partial P_{jt}} \cdot \frac{P_{jt}}{E_{it}} = \frac{\partial f_i(P_j, Y, H, t)}{\partial P_{jt}} \cdot \frac{P_{jt}}{E_{it}} = f_{ijt} \cdot \frac{P_{jt}}{E_{it}}.$$ (12.21)

The effect of a price change in the short run is the sum of its effects on net investment and replacement investment.

The calculation of long-run price elasticities is a bit more complicated, for in the long run all the capital stock is allowed to be replaced. Precisely what should be held constant is not clear, since the estimating equation

(12.20) has not been derived as the outcome of a dynamic economic optimization problem subject to cònstraints. Intuitively the long-run elasticity would be the elasticity of flexible demand with respect to price, since in the long run all demand is flexıble. More formally from (12.19) and (12.20) we can write

$$E_{it} = E_{it}^f + E_{it}^c = f_i(P_j, Y, H, t) + E_{it}^c. \tag{12.22}$$

At time t the ratio of the long-run to short-run price elasticity is given by the ratio of total to flexible demand at that point in time,

$$\frac{\varepsilon_{P_j}^L}{\varepsilon_{P_j}^S} = \frac{E_{it}}{E_{it}^f}. \tag{12.23}$$

Thus the divergence between long- and short-run elasticities depends on the relative magnitude of flexible demand in year t: the greater the flexible demand, the smaller the ratio of long-run to short-run elasticities.

In long-run equilibrium net investment in fuel equipment can be treated as zero, and thus gross investment in fuel i-using equipment would be equal to replacement investment as governed by the average depreciation rate for all fuel equipment (say, δ). Here the long-run elasticity would approach $1/\delta$ times the short-run price elasticity. Hence the divergence between short- and long-run elasticities in long-run equilibrium would depend only on δ, the average rate of depreciation.

One attactive feature of the Balestra-Nerlove formulation is that data on energy-using equipment are not necessary, as long as we assume constant utilization and efficiency parameters and an average time invariant depreciation rate. This is convenient in terms of empirical implementation but also very restrictive a priori. If we relax the constant efficiency assumption, we might be able to construct an aggregate capital stock as the weighted sum of efficiencies of various vintages, where the weights were the proportions of each vintage composing the total capital stock. Unfortunately the necessary data on efficiency characteristics of energy-using equipment are seldomly available. Even if such data were available, we would be faced with the problem of modeling endogenous utilization of equipment with differing energy efficiencies. Thus the principal drawback of the Balestra model in its pristine form is its assumption of constant utilization.

Several other drawbacks of this model should also be noted here. First, we could use the Balestra-Nerlove approach for residential-commercial markets in modeling demand for industrial energy. For example, we could specify that relative input prices and output quantity affect flexible demand for a specific energy type or for total energy. Again coefficients on these parameters would be interpreted as representing the effects of price or output changes on gross investment in energy-using equipment, which is utilized at a constant rate. What is not permitted by this specification is increased (decreased) utilization of capital in the short run as output increases (decreases), or substitution of, for example, maintenance labor for utilized capital when the relative price of energy increases. Neither retrofitting nor changes in technical efficiency can be modeled by the conventional Balestra specification. Second, it should be recognized that the Balestra-Nerlove single equation model is essentially based on two identities, (12.12) and (12.13); the estimating equations are not based on any explicit dynamic economic optimization process. Thus it is not at all clear how other inputs interact with energy and with each other as gross investment in energy-using equipment takes place. In short, even though the Balestra-Nerlove approach is convenient in terms of empirical implementation, it is not based on explicit economic optimization, and thus empirical results are somewhat difficult to interpret.

12.2 Second Generation Dynamics

The distinguishing feature of what we have called the first generation dynamic models is that they are essentially single-equation models whose form is not based explicitly on economic optimization simultaneously involving several inputs. In this section we review two types of second generation models, both of which recognize the interrelatedness of factor demands; one is basically an extension of the single-equation partial adjustment model, while the other obtains short-run demand equations for variable inputs based on static minimization of a restricted variable cost function.

A major development of the late 1960s was the introduction of inter-related disequilibrium by M. I. Nadiri and Sherwin Rosen (1969, 1973), whereby disequilibrium in one factor market (say, energy) was formally related to the extent of disequilibrium in other factor markets.

Define the vector of n inputs at time t as $\mathbf{q}_t = (q_{1t}, q_{2t}, \ldots, q_{nt})$ and the long-run equilibrium level of these inputs as $\mathbf{q}_t^*$. In the Nadiri-Rosen approach the Koyck single-equation adjustment mechanism is generalized, so that

$$\mathbf{q}_t - \mathbf{q}_{t-1} = \mathbf{B}(\mathbf{q}_t^* - \mathbf{q}_{t-1}), \tag{12.24}$$

where B is an $n \times n$ (not necessarily symmetric) partial adjustment matrix. A typical equation in (12.24) is of the form

$$q_{it} = \sum_{\substack{j=1 \\ j \neq i}}^{n} b_{ij}(q_{jt}^* - q_{j,t-1}) + (1 - b_{ii})q_{i,t-1} + b_{ii}q_{it}^*. \tag{12.25}$$

This representation incorporates some important features. First, the generalized adjustment scheme (12.24) permits disequilibrium in one factor market ($q_{jt}^* - q_{j,t-1} \neq 0$) to affect the demand for another factor, say, the ith input, whereas this generalized adjustment is not permitted in the single-equation first generation dynamic models. Second, the difference between short- and long-run elasticities for the ith input no longer depends only on b_{ii} but on all b_{ij}; this accommodates short-run overshooting for, say, output elasticities.

For short-run own price elasticities to be smaller in absolute value than the corresponding long-run own price elasticities, it is necessary that the characteristic roots of the **B** matrix lie within the unit circle. This condition, unfortunately, is not sufficient. Berndt, Fuss, and Waverman (1977, ch. 3) have presented examples in which the **q*** equation derived from a translog or generalized Leontief cost function yields results inconsistent with this short-run, long-run relationship. Essentially, as Berndt, Fuss, and Waverman point out, the problem is that these inequalities are not guaranteed unless the adjustment equations (12.24) can be derived explicitly as the solution to a dynamic economic optimization problem subject to constraints. When such an economic framework is not provided, it is difficult, if not impossible rigorously, to characterize the short, intermediate, and long run consistently, to specify how constraints are modified as adjustments take place, and thus to define short, intermediate, and long-run elasticities in such a way that elasticities satisfy the Le Chatelier principle.

It should be pointed out here that Nadiri-Rosen did not propose their representation (12.24) as a mere generalized ad hoc adjustment mechanism but rather viewed it as an "approximation" (1969, p. 159) to underlying differential equations which in fact were the solution to a dynamic optimization problem. In particular Nadiri-Rosen noted the result of Robert E. Lucas (1967a) that, when the set of all inputs **q** was decomposed into variable inputs **v** and quasi-fixed inputs **x** (quasi-fixed inputs defined as inputs whose purchase involved increasing marginal costs of adjustment), the flexible accelerator equation,

$$\mathbf{x}_t - \mathbf{x}_{t-1} = \mathbf{M}_t^*(\mathbf{x}_t^* - \mathbf{x}_{t-1}), \tag{12.26}$$

could be viewed as an approximate solution (in the vicinity of **x***) to the differential equation system derived explicitly from a dynamic economic optimization problem. However, the Nadiri-Rosen representation (12.24) differs from its Lucas parentage (12.26) in two important ways. First, in the Lucas framework the endogenous partial adjustment matrix $\mathbf{M}_t^*$ depends on at least the discount rate r_t and the parameters of technology and thus is not necessarily constant over time. In the Nadiri-Rosen framework, by contrast, the adjustment matrix $\mathbf{B}$ is a matrix of constant parameters. Second, in the Lucas framework (12.26) there is an adjustment matrix only for the quasi-fixed inputs $\mathbf{x}$; in the Nadiri-Rosen specification the adjustment matrix is extended to all $\mathbf{q}$ inputs, both variable and quasi fixed.

Problems inherent in an approximation of this type, where dynamic optimization is not explicitly taken into account and thus consistency with theory is not assured, are evident in the Nadiri-Rosen empirical implementation and results. Nadiri-Rosen derive equations for $\mathbf{q}^*$ using a Cobb-Douglas production function. This production function implies cross-equation constraints on their estimating equations and on the b_{ij}. However, these overidentifying restrictions are not taken into account in the Nadiri-Rosen empirical implementations.[8] Perhaps this explains some of their implausible empirical results; in Nadiri-Rosen (1969), for example, estimated quarterly returns to scale are about 1.24, which implies annual returns to scale of approximately $(1.26)^4 = 2.54$.[9] Although the overidentifying restrictions have been properly taken into account in an unpublished paper by Frank Brechling and Dale Mortenson, Brechling-Mortenson find that, while there are strong and significant dynamic cross effects, they "are unable to obtain plausible estimates of some of the parameters of the Cobb-Douglas function" (1971, p. 38). They conclude that their results "cast some doubts on the appropriateness of single-equation approaches to the study of factor demand and on the appropriateness of the Cobb-Douglas assumption in studies of factor demand generally" (1971, p. 3).[10]

In summary, the distinguishing feature of the Nadiri-Rosen second generation dynamic models of factor demands is that they involve systems of interrelated disequilibrium equations, rather than a single demand equation. As a result short-run overshooting is possible, and the difference between short- and long-run price elasticities for a particular input i depends not only on the partial adjustment parameter b_{ii} but also on all b_{ij} $(i \neq j)$. Hence it is possible that, even when b_{ii} is small, the difference between short- and long-run elasticities could be small. However, the typical implementation of second generation models does not specify explicitly what function is being optimized or to what constraints the dynamic optimization problem is subject but instead presents first-order difference equations (12.24) as approximations to the solution factor

demand equations. Moreover, functional forms used have been restrictive—typically Cobb-Douglas technologies have been assumed, and
partial adjustment coefficients have been constrained to be constant
parameters, often yielding implausible empirical results.[11]

An alternative second generation approach is based on the notion of a
restricted variable cost, or restricted variable profit function, a concept
first introduced by Paul A. Samuelson (1953) and developed further by
L. J. Lau (1976) and Daniel McFadden (1978). The restricted variable
cost function reflects production or technological constraints facing the
firm when output Y and certain input quantities $\mathbf{x}$ are fixed in the short
run, and when the firm's optimization problem is to minimize variable
costs of production given these short-run constraints. Demand equations
for the variable inputs $\mathbf{v}$ are obtained using the Shephard-Uzawa-Mc-
Fadden lemma, which states simply that the variable cost-minimizing
demands $\mathbf{v}$ are equal to the partial derivative of the restricted variable
cost function, $G = G(Y, \mathbf{P_v}, \mathbf{x})$, with respect to the prices of the variable
inputs $\mathbf{P_v}$,

$$\bar{\mathbf{v}} = \frac{\partial G}{\partial \mathbf{P_v}} = G\left(Y, \mathbf{P_v}, \mathbf{x}\right). \tag{12.27}$$

Notice that these demand functions for variable inputs reflect the interrelatedness of the disequilibrium process; for example, the demand for a
variable input like energy depends not only on the prices of variable inputs
and the quantity of output but also on the quantities of the inputs fixed
in the short run, such as the stocks of energy-using capital equipment.

Once we specify a functional form for the restricted variable cost function G and derive estimating equations for the variable inputs using
(12.27), we can obtain estimates of the short-run own and cross-price
elasticities of demand among variable inputs using standard econometric
techniques.[12] However, what is not so obvious is that long-run elasticity
estimates among both variable and fixed inputs can also be retrieved from
the short-run restricted variable cost function. Hence estimation of a
restricted short-run variable cost function can provide a complete characterization of short- and long-run elasticities.

To see this, consider the simple case of a single quasi-fixed input, say
capital, K. Given factor prices for the variable inputs, the short-run
variable costs and the fixed costs can be summed and divided by output,
Y, to yield a family of short-run average total cost curves, $SRAC$, each
$SRAC$ curve depending on a particular combination of Y and K. The five
$SRAC$ curves depicted in figure 12.1 correspond to five different levels
of K; each $SRAC$ curve first falls with increases in Y and then rises with

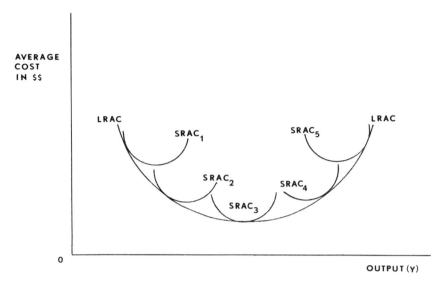

Figure 12.1 Short- and long-run average cost curves

Y, so that each $SRAC$ curve is U-shaped. It is of course a well-known result that the long-run average total cost curve, $LRAC$, is simply the envelope of the $SRAC$ curves, each point on the $LRAC$ curve being a point of tangency with a particular $SRAC$ curve. Hence, once we specify a common functional form for the $SRAC$ curves, we implicitly obtain a representation of the $LRAC$ curve.

The important link between $SRAC$ and $LRAC$ curves is based on the tangency condition. Paul A. Samuelson (1953, pp. 19, 20) has shown that the derivative of the restricted variable cost function with respect to the quantity of the fixed input $\mathbf{x}$ in long-run equilibrium must equal the negative of the rental price of the fixed input $\mathbf{P}_x$; intuitively this rental price is simply the negative of the shadow cost of the short-run fixed input constraints,

$$-\mathbf{P}_x = \frac{\partial G}{\partial_x} = G_x(Y, \mathbf{P}_v, \mathbf{x}). \tag{12.28}$$

Optimal (long-run) cost-minimizing levels of demand for the fixed inputs $\mathbf{x}^*$, given Y, $\mathbf{P}_v$, and $\mathbf{P}_x$, can then be obtained by solving (12.28) for $\mathbf{x}^*$,

$$\mathbf{x}^* = G^*(Y, \mathbf{P}_v, \mathbf{P}_x). \tag{12.29}$$

Long-run own and cross-price demand responses among variable inputs are obtained by substituting $\mathbf{x}^*$ of (12.29) into (12.27) and differentiating appropriately, while long-run price responses for fixed inputs are easily derived by directly differentiating (12.29). Notice also that the difference between short- and long-run elasticities does not depend on adjustment parameters (none are estimated in this approach) but rather only on technological constraints.

In summary, the second generation short-run restricted variable cost function approach to dynamic modeling consists of specifying a restricted short-run variable cost function and then using estimates of variable input demand equations (12.27) plus the shadow cost relationships (12.28) and (12.29) to obtain a complete characterization of short- and long-run price elasticities.

One additional attractive feature of the restricted short-run cost function approach is that it permits estimation of capital and capacity utilization. Define the optimal capacity level Y^* as that level of output in the short run for which the $SRAC$ curve in figure 12.1 is tangent to the $LRAC$ curve. Obviously, if in the long run there were constant returns to scale, the $LRAC$ curve would be perfectly horizontal, and Y^* would then simply be defined as that level of Y for which $SRAC$ is minimized. Once Y^* is computed, we can define and calculate the rate of capacity utilization as the ratio Y/Y^*.[13]

Empirical applications based on the second generation restricted variable cost function approach are somewhat limited, since the approach is not yet widely known. To the best of our knowledge, the first short-run, long-run empirical applications based on a restricted short-run function are the Cobb-Douglas studies of Indian agriculture by L. J. Lau and Pan A. Yotopoulos (1971, 1972, 1973). Pichit Lerttamrab estimated a quadratic restricted profit function with four variable and four fixed inputs using data on Thailand; the choice of a quadratic form is of interest, since it places no a priori restrictions on substitution elasticities yet permits analytic derivation of the $\mathbf{x}^*$ equation (12.28). Short- and long-run price elasticities for energy and other inputs in the United States, 1947 to 1975, based on another flexible functional form—a variant of the generalized Leontief restricted variable cost function—have been obtained by Knut Anton Mork (1978a, 1978b). However, Mork is unable to solve (12.28) analytically for $\mathbf{x}^*$.

Randall S. Brown and Laurits R. Christensen estimate in chapter 10 a translog restricted variable cost function using U.S. agriculture data and are also unable to obtain a closed form analytic solution for $\mathbf{x}^*$ using (12.28). Rather they turn to numerical procedures to obtain a solution for $\mathbf{x}^*$ and then perturb $\mathbf{P}_v$ and $\mathbf{P}_x$ to obtain approximate derivatives of

x^* with respect to P_v and P_x. Hence, even though analytic solutions for x^* do not appear to be possible based on the translog form, Brown-Christensen are able to obtain both short- and long-run elasticity estimates. Incidentially, to the best of our knowledge no empirical estimates of capacity utilization based on the procedure outlined here have yet been published, even though such a calculation was suggested years ago by L. R. Klein (1962, pp. 54, 58).[14]

In summary the short-run demand equation approach of second generation models has several very attractive properties:

1. It generates short-run demand equations for variable inputs (like energy) that depend not only on the prices of variable inputs but also on the quantities of inputs fixed in the short-run; hence this approach explicitly recognizes the interrelatedness of the disequilibrium process.
2. It generates long-run demand equations for both variable and fixed inputs.
3. The short-run restricted variable cost function permits calculation of an economically meaningful measure of capacity utilization.

The short-run demand equation approach also has several important shortcomings, however:

1. At the present time there does not appear to be any procedure by which we can decide which inputs are fixed and which are variable.[15]
2. Even though the second generation models yield estimates of short- and long-run price responses, there is no way of measuring the time interval between short and long run: no information is given on the time path of the adjustment from short to long run. This simply reflects the static optimization behavioral assumption employed. In the energy demand context the question of the time path or dynamics of energy conservation is extremely important for policy purposes, and on this issue the short-run demand equation approach provides less information than the Nadiri-Rosen procedure.
3. More fundamentally the short-run demand equation approach is incomplete in that it does not indicate why certain inputs are fixed; to address that issue it is necessary to incorporate dynamic optimization considerations explicitly.

12.3 Third Generation Dynamics

The distinguishing feature of third generation dynamic models is that they are based explicitly on dynamic economic optimization incorporating costs of adjustment for the quasi-fixed factors. This property of third generation dynamic models has several important implications. First, speeds of adjustment of quasi-fixed factors to their long-run equilibrium levels are endogenous and time varying, rather than exogenous and fixed. Second, short-run demand equations for variable inputs depend on, among other things, prices of variable inputs, output, and stocks of the quasi-fixed inputs. These short-run equations can be interpreted as utilization equations. For example, the short-run demand equation for energy, E, depends explicitly on Y, P_E, and the beginning-of-year capital stock, K. Thus the ratio E/K is endogenous and can be interpreted as a short-run input utilization equation.[16] Third, the dynamic path of adjustment to long-run equilibrium is based on economic optimization at each point in time; thus short, intermediate, and long run are clearly defined and follow the short-run, long-run framework discussed by Alfred Marshall. Fourth, and finally, the transition from short to long run for the variable inputs involves not only adjustments in the quasi-fixed factors but also incorporates economically optimal variations in their rates of utilization.

The theoretical foundations of third generation dynamic models are drawn primarily from the works of Robert E. Lucas (1967a, b), L. J. Lau (1976), and Daniel McFadden (1978). Define the production function of a firm as

$$Y = F(\mathbf{v}, \mathbf{x}, \dot{\mathbf{x}}, t), \tag{12.30}$$

which represents various efficient combinations of variable inputs $\mathbf{v}$ and quasi-fixed inputs $\mathbf{x}$ that can be used to produce output Y at time t. If levels of the quasi-fixed inputs vary ($\dot{\mathbf{x}} \neq 0$), output falls for any given amount of $\mathbf{x}$ and $\mathbf{v}$, because of the necessity to devote resources to changing the stock rather than producing output. This diminution in output brought about by $\dot{\mathbf{x}} \neq 0$ constitutes internal costs of adjustment.[17]

In the short run firms can be viewed as maximizing restricted variable profits (revenue minus variable costs) conditional on variable input prices $\hat{w}_j (j = 1, \ldots, M)$, output price P, levels of the quasi-fixed inputs x_i, and changes in these quasi-fixed input levels $\dot{x}_i$. Alternatively we can view firms as minimizing normalized variable costs $G = \sum_{j=1}^{M} w_j v_j$, $w_j = \hat{w}_j / \hat{w}_1$, conditional on w_j, Y, x_i, $\dot{x}_i$. The normalized restricted cost function

$$G = G(\mathbf{w}, \mathbf{x}, \dot{\mathbf{x}}, Y, t), \tag{12.31}$$

where t is intended to represent technology, can be shown under reasonable regularity conditions on F to be increasing and concave in $\mathbf{w}$, increasing and convex in $\dot{\mathbf{x}}$, and decreasing and convex in $\mathbf{x}$.

Two properties of G are especially important for empirical implementation. First, the partial derivative of G with respect to the normalized price of any variable input w_j equals the short-run cost-minimizing demand for v_j,

$$\frac{\partial G}{\partial w_j} = v_j, \tag{12.32}$$

for $j = 2, \ldots, M$. In section 12.2 we called this the Shephard-Uzawa-McFadden lemma. Second, as noted earlier, the partial derivative of G with respect to the quantity of any quasi-fixed input equals the negative of the normalized shadow cost or normalized rental price of the quasi-fixed input,

$$\frac{\partial G}{\partial x_i} = -u_i, \tag{12.33}$$

for $i = 1, \ldots, N$, where $u_i = a_i(r + \delta_i)$ and a_i is the normalized asset or acquisition price of the ith quasi-fixed input, r is the rate of return, and δ_i is the rate of depreciation.

The long-run or dynamic economic problem facing the firm is to minimize the present value of the future stream of costs,

$$L(0) = e^{-rt}\left(\sum_{j=1}^{M} \hat{w}_j v_j + \sum_{i=1}^{N} \hat{a}_i z_i\right) dt, \tag{12.34}$$

where $z_i = \dot{x}_i + \delta_i x_i$ is the gross addition to the stock of the ith quasi-fixed factor. This minimization problem is solved by choosing the time paths of the control variables $\mathbf{v}(t)$, $\dot{\mathbf{x}}(t)$ and the state variable $\mathbf{x}(t)$ that minimize $L(0)$, given initial conditions $\mathbf{x}(0)$ and $\mathbf{v}(t)$, $x(t) > 0$.

Since the normalized, restricted variable cost function G incorporates the solution to the short-run cost minimization problem, that is, it yields the optimal demand for the variable factors conditional on the values of the quasi-fixed factors, we can substitute (12.31) into (12.34). When the resulting function is integrated by parts, we obtain

$$L(0) + \sum_{i=1}^{N} a_i x_i(0) = \int_0^\infty e^{-rt}\left\{G(w, x, \dot{x}, Y, t) + \sum_{i=1}^{N} u_i x_i\right\} dt. \tag{12.35}$$

This can be interpreted as follows: since G assumes short-run optimization behavior conditional on $Y(t)$, $\mathbf{w}(t)$, $\mathbf{x}(t)$, and $\dot{\mathbf{x}}(t)$, the optimization problem (12.34) facing the firm is to find among all the possible $G(\mathbf{w}(t)$,

$\mathbf{x}(t)$, $\dot{\mathbf{x}}(t)$, $Y(t)$) combinations that time path of $\mathbf{x}(t)$, $\dot{\mathbf{x}}(t)$ that minimizes the present value of costs.

A solution to (12.34) can be obtained using either the Euler first-order conditions or Pontryagin's maximum principle. Assuming static expectations with respect to normalized factor prices and output, we can write the Hamiltonian as

$$H(\mathbf{x}, \dot{\mathbf{x}}, \boldsymbol{\mu}, t) = e^{-rt}\left[G(\mathbf{w}, \mathbf{x}, \dot{\mathbf{x}}, Y, t) + \sum_{i=1}^{N} u_i x_i \right] + \boldsymbol{\mu}\dot{\mathbf{x}}. \qquad (12.36)$$

When $\boldsymbol{\mu}$ is eliminated from the necessary conditions, we obtain

$$-G_{\mathbf{x}} - rG_{\dot{\mathbf{x}}} - \mathbf{u} + G_{\dot{\mathbf{x}}}\ddot{\mathbf{x}} + G_{\dot{\mathbf{x}}\dot{\mathbf{x}}}\dot{\mathbf{x}} = 0, \qquad (12.37)$$

where the $\mathbf{x}$, $\dot{\mathbf{x}}$ subscripts denote derivatives and $\ddot{\mathbf{x}}$ is the second partial derivative with respect to time. The steady-state (long-run) solution satisfies

$$-G_{\mathbf{x}}(\mathbf{w}, \mathbf{x}^*) - rG_{\dot{\mathbf{x}}}(\mathbf{w}, \mathbf{x}^*) - \mathbf{u} = 0, \qquad (12.38)$$

$\mathbf{x}^*$ being unique as long as $|-G_{\mathbf{xx}} - rG_{\mathbf{x}\dot{\mathbf{x}}}| \neq 0$, where * indicates evaluation at $\mathbf{x} = \mathbf{x}^*$ and $\dot{\mathbf{x}} = \mathbf{0}$. Equation (12.38) can be rewritten as

$$-G_{\mathbf{x}}(\mathbf{w}, \mathbf{x}^*) = \mathbf{u} + rG_{\dot{\mathbf{x}}}(\mathbf{w}, \mathbf{x}^*) \qquad (12.39)$$

and interpreted as follows: the left-hand side is the marginal benefit to the firm of changing quasi-fixed inputs (the reduction in variable costs brought about by purchasing energy-efficient capital equipment), while the right-hand side is the marginal cost (user cost plus the marginal adjustment cost) of a change in the amount of capital services at $\dot{\mathbf{x}} = 0$. In equilibrium marginal benefits must equal marginal costs.

The internal cost of adjustment model just outlined is attractive in that it yields clearly defined short-run variable input demand equations (12.32) and is based on explicit dynamic optimization. Treadway has linked this type of model to the flexible accelerator, or partial adjustment, literature by showing that $\dot{\mathbf{x}}$ can be generated from (12.37) and (12.38) as an approximate solution (in the neighbourhood of $\mathbf{x}^*(t)$) to the multivariate linear differential equation system

$$\dot{\mathbf{x}} = \mathbf{M}^*(\mathbf{x}^* - \mathbf{x}) \qquad (12.40)$$

where $\mathbf{M}^*$ is determined from the solution to the quadratic form

$$-G_{\dot{\mathbf{x}}\dot{\mathbf{x}}}^* \mathbf{M}^{*2} - rG_{\dot{\mathbf{x}}\dot{\mathbf{x}}}^* \mathbf{M}^* + G_{\mathbf{xx}}^* + rG_{\mathbf{x}\dot{\mathbf{x}}}^* = 0. \qquad (12.41)$$

In the special case of only one quasi-fixed input Treadway has shown that

$$\dot{x}_1 = M_1^*(x_1^* - x_1), \tag{12.42}$$

where at the stationary point when $G_{xx}^* = 0$,

$$M_1^* = -\frac{1}{2}\left[r - \left(r^2\,\frac{4G_{x_1 x_1}^*}{G_{\dot{x}_1 \dot{x}_1}^*}\right)^{1/2}\right]. \tag{12.43}$$

It should be noted that M_1^* varies inversely with r and is not constrained to be constant, as is the case with typical partial adjustment models. However, if G were quadratic, so that $G_{x_1 x_1}^*$ and $G_{\dot{x}_1 \dot{x}_1}^*$ were constant parameters, and if the discount rate r were relatively stable, M_1^* would also tend to be quite stable.

Once we specify a functional form for G and alter the continuous time model into a discrete time specification, we can obtain short-run demand equations for variable inputs (utilization equations), using (12.32) and net accumulation equations for the quasi-fixed inputs using (12.38) and (12.40). From these demand equations expressions for short-, intermediate-, and long-run price and output elasticities can be derived that completely summarize the dynamic time paths of factor demands. In particular, following the Marshallian tradition, short-run elasticities can be defined as those obtained when $\mathbf{x}$ is fixed, intermediate run as the impact when $\mathbf{x}$ has adjusted partially as determined by $\mathbf{M}^*$, and long run as the response when $\mathbf{x}$ has adjusted fully to $\mathbf{x}^*$ and $\dot{\mathbf{x}} = \mathbf{0}$.

First steps toward implementing this type of explicit dynamic model were made by F. P. R. Brechling and Dale T. Mortenson who specified quadratic costs of adjustment, a Cobb-Douglas production function, and constant $\mathbf{M}^*$. Their approach was generalized considerably to flexible form profit and dual cost functions by M. A. Fuss (1976) and has since been developed and discussed extensively by E. R. Berndt, M. A. Fuss, and Leonard Waverman (1977, 1979, 1980). Recent applications and variations of this basic model include C. J. Morrison and E. R. Berndt, Michael Denny, M. A. Fuss and Leonard Waverman (1979a, b) and E. R. Berndt, C. J. Morrison, and G. Campbell Watkins.

To illustrate the attractive features of third generation models in the analysis of short- and long-run demand for energy, we now briefly present the model employed by C. J. Morrison and E. R. Berndt. In their model there are three variable inputs—unskilled (production) labor, U, aggregate energy, E, and nonenergy intermediate materials, M—and two quasi-fixed inputs—skilled (nonproduction) labor, S, and physical capital, K. The functional form adopted for G incorporates long-run constant returns to scale and a diagonal adjustment matrix $\mathbf{M}^*$; all prices are normalized by P_U (the price of unskilled labor):

$$G = U + P_E E + P_M M = Y(\alpha_0 + \alpha_{0t} t + \alpha_E P_E + \alpha_M P_M$$

$$+ \frac{1}{2}(\gamma_{EE} P_E^2 + \gamma_{MM} P_M^2) + \gamma_{EM} P_E P_M + \alpha_{Et} P_E t + \alpha_{Mt} P_M t)$$

$$+ \alpha_K K_{-1} + \alpha_S S_{-1} + \frac{1}{2}\left[\gamma_{SS}\frac{S_{-1}^2}{Y} + \gamma_{KK}\frac{K_{-1}^2}{Y}\right] + \gamma_{EK} P_E K_{-1} \quad (12.44)$$

$$+ \gamma_{MK} P_M K_{-1} + \gamma_{ES} P_E S_{-1} + \gamma_{MS} P_M S_{-1} + \alpha_{Kt} K_{-1} t$$

$$+ \alpha_{St} S_{-1} t + \frac{1}{2}\left(\frac{\gamma_{\dot{S}\dot{S}} \dot{S}^2}{Y} + \frac{\gamma_{\dot{K}\dot{K}} \dot{K}^2}{Y}\right)$$

Using (12.32), we obtain the short-run energy output demand equation as

$$\frac{E}{Y} = \alpha_E + \alpha_{Et} t + \gamma_{EE} P_E + \gamma_{EM} P_M + \frac{\gamma_{EK} K_{-1}}{Y} + \frac{\gamma_{ES} S_{-1}}{Y}. \quad (12.45)$$

Hence the short-run energy input-output coefficient is affected by prices of the variable inputs, output quantity, stocks of the quasi-fixed inputs K and S, and the state of technology.

Equation (12.45) can be rewritten as

$$\frac{E}{K_{-1}} = \left(\frac{Y}{K_{-1}}\right)(\alpha_E + \gamma_{Et} t + \gamma_{EE} P_E + \gamma_{EM} P_M) + \gamma_{EK} + \frac{\gamma_{ES} S_{-1}}{K_{-1}}, \quad (12.46)$$

which more clearly indicates its utilization interpretation. In particular, if we interpret the amount of energy consumed divided by the fixed (in the short run) capital stock as a measure of capital utilization, in this model short-run capital utilization would be endogenous and affected by output level, stocks of the quasi-fixed inputs, prices of variable inputs, and technical change as represented by t.

Another interesting interpretation can be obtained by multiplying (12.45) through by Y:

$$E = Y(\alpha_E + \alpha_{Et} t + \gamma_{EE} P_E + \gamma_{EM} P_M) + \gamma_{EK} K_{-1} + \gamma_{ES} S_{-1}. \quad (12.47)$$

This equation looks very much like equation (12.15) obtained in the Balestra-Nerlove model, which distinguished captive and free demand. Ignoring for the moment the quasi-fixed input S_{-1}, we could impose on (12.47) the interpretation that $Y(\alpha_E + \alpha_{Et} t + \gamma_{EE} P_E + \gamma_{EM} P_M)$ represents flexible demand for energy and that $\gamma_{EK} K_{-1}$ represents captive demand, where $\gamma_{EK} = (1 - \delta)\bar{u}_i$. However, (12.47) does not necessarily need to be interpreted in this way; as we have pointed out, an alternate interpretation is given by the form (12.46), a short-run capital utilization equation derived from explicit dynamic optimization, and not based on the

Balestra-Nerlove assumption of constant capital utilization and constant technical efficiency. Interestingly, what (12.45) does suggest is that a Balestra-Nerlove type energy demand equation (12.15) model could be generated from an explicit dynamic model with certain restrictions imposed, rather than simply being based on the two identifies (12.12) and (12.13).

An additional insight into utilization measurement based on the restricted variable cost functions is one of capacity rather than capital utilization. Let us define short-run capacity utilization as the ratio of actual output Y to that level of output, denoted Y^*, which minimizes the short-run average total costs of production.[18] Using the form (12.44) for G, we can solve for Y^*:

$$Y^* = -(\gamma_{SS}S^2_{-1} + \gamma_{KK}K^2_{-1} + \gamma_{\dot{S}\dot{S}}\dot{S} + \gamma_{\dot{K}\dot{K}}\dot{K}^2)$$
$$/(\alpha_K K_{-1} + \alpha_S S_{-1} + \alpha_{Kt}K_{-1}t + \alpha_{St}S_{-1}t + \gamma_{EK}P_E K_{-1} + \gamma_{ES}P_E S_{-1}$$
$$+ \gamma_{MK}P_M K_{-1} + \gamma_{MS}P_M S_{-1} + u_K K_{-1} + u_S S_{-1}). \tag{12.48}$$

Hence it is possible with this type of model to develop a measure of capacity utilization based on economic theory rather than based on typical peak-to-peak interpolations or interview methods.[19]

Earlier we noted that net accumulation equations for quasi-fixed inputs in the neighbourhood of $\mathbf{x}^*$ turn out to be of the flexible accelerator form $\dot{\mathbf{x}} = \mathbf{M}^*(\mathbf{x}^* - \mathbf{x})$. In the case of K, based on (12.44) we have

$$\dot{K} = K_{t+1} - K_t = M^*_{KK}(K^*_t - K_t), \tag{12.49}$$

where

$$K^* = \left(\frac{-Y}{\gamma_{KK}}\right)(\alpha_K + \gamma_{EK}P_E + \gamma_{MK}P_M + \alpha_{Kt}t + u_K) \tag{12.50}$$

and

$$M^*_{KK} = -\frac{1}{2}\left[r_t - \left(r_t^2 + \frac{4\gamma_{KK}}{\gamma_{\dot{K}\dot{K}}}\right)^{1/2}\right]. \tag{12.51}$$

Short-run own price elasticities for energy in this model turn out to be

$$\varepsilon^{SR}_{EE} = \left(\frac{P_E}{E}\right)\left\{\frac{\partial E}{\partial P_E}\bigg|_{K=\bar{K}, S=\bar{S}}\right\} = \left(\frac{P_E}{E}\right)\gamma_{EE}Y, \tag{12.52}$$

where $\bar{K}$ and $\bar{S}$ denote fixed levels of quasi-fixed inputs. The corresponding long-run price elasticity is

$$\varepsilon_{EE}^{SR} = \left(\frac{P_E}{E}\right)\left\{\frac{\partial E}{\partial P_E}\bigg|_{K=\bar{K}, S=\bar{S}} + \frac{\partial E}{\partial K^*}\frac{\partial K^*}{\partial P_E} + \frac{\partial E}{\partial S^*}\frac{\partial S^*}{\partial P_E}\right\}$$

(12.53)

$$= \frac{P_E}{E} \cdot Y \cdot \left(\gamma_{EE} - \frac{\gamma_E^2}{\gamma_{KK}} - \frac{\gamma_{ES}^2}{\gamma_{SS}}\right).$$

Hence the difference between short- and long-run price elasticities is

$$\varepsilon_{EE}^{LR} - \varepsilon_{EE}^{SR} = -\left(\frac{P_E}{E}\right) \cdot Y \cdot \left(\frac{\gamma_{EK}^2}{\gamma_{KK}} + \frac{\gamma_{ES}^2}{\gamma_{SS}}\right),$$

(12.54)

which depends on the technological relationships among the variable input E and the quasi-fixed inputs S and K but not on M_{KK}^* or M_{SS}^*. In particular, if E and K, as well as E and S are independent, so that $\gamma_{EK} = \gamma_{ES} = 0$, then there is no difference between short- and long-run own price elasticities. In such a case the quasi-fixed inputs no longer constrain responses in energy consumption to changes in energy prices, even though M_{KK}^* and M_{SS}^* may be considerably less than unity. Incidentally the third generation model permits testing whether an input is fixed or variable simply by examining whether the appropriate elements of $\mathbf{M}^*$ are close to unity.

Although the third generation dynamic models illustrated here have numerous attractive properties, they constitute a very recent development and undoubtedly will undergo further evolution and generalization. Nonetheless, it should be clear that these explicit dynamic approaches provide a better understanding of short- and long-run energy substitution and capital utilization.

12.4 Comparison of Empirical Estimates

Having reviewed and assessed the theoretical merits and shortcomings of first, second, and third generation dynamic models, we now turn to an empirical comparison using a common body of data for U.S. manufacturing from 1952 to 1971.

In table 12.1 we report energy elasticity estimates based on a variety of first generation models. The partial adjustment equation estimated is the log-linear equation (12.7) with the homogeneity restrictions (12.3) imposed. As seen in the top row of the table, when this partial adjustment equation is estimated, the partial adjustment coefficient is quite large ($\hat{\lambda} = 0.887$), indicating that about 90 percent of the adjustment to long run takes place in the first year. The short-run own price elasticity estimate is -0.653, while the corresponding long-run estimate is -0.739.

Table 12.1
Alternative estimates of energy short- and long-run substitution elasticities U.S. manufacturing, 1952 to 1971

		Elasticity				
		ε_{EE}	ε_{EK}	ε_{EL}	ε_{EM}	ε_{EY}
First generation models						
Partial adjustment, log-linear:	SR	−0.653	−0.158	1.076	−0.263	0.141
($\hat{\lambda} = 0.887$)	LR	−0.739	−0.179	1.214	−0.297	0.159
Partial adjustment with long-run constant returns to scale imposed, log-linear:	SR	−0.944	−0.020	0.831	0.133	0.360
($\hat{\lambda} = 0.260$)	LR	−3.630	−0.077	3.196	• 0.511	1.000
Partial adjustment with long-run constant returns to scale imposed, zero cross-price elasticities, log-linear:	SR	−0.623	0.000	0.000	0.000	0.250
($\hat{\lambda} = 0.250$)	LR	−2.492	0.000	0.000	0.000	1.000
Balestra-Nerlove model, linear:	SR	−0.670	−0.128	0.859	−0.061	0.140
($\hat{\delta} = 0.835$)	LR	−0.803	−0.153	1.030	−0.074	0.168
Balestra-Nerlove model, mixed:	SR	−0.689	−0.185	1.104	−0.230	0.141
($\hat{\delta} = 0.915$)	LR	−0.754	−0.202	1.208	−0.251	0.154
Balestra-Nerlove model, mixed, long-run constant returns to scale imposed, δ constrained to 0.10	SR	−6.808	0.264	−0.324	6.868	0.100
	LR	−68.084	2.645	−3.244	68.684	1.000
Second generation models						
Translog share equations with Nadiri-Rosen adjustment matrix (1971 elasticities)[a]	SR	−0.69	−0.23	0.49	0.42	
	LR	−0.70	−0.36	0.40	0.66	
Generalized Leontief input-output equations with Nadiri-Rosen adjustment matrix (1971 elasticities)[b]	SR	−1.17	−0.14	0.72	0.59	
	LR	−4.24	−0.04	0.81	3.46	

[a] Taken from Berndt, Fuss, and Waverman (1977, table III-3, p. 55) based on U.S. manufacturing data, 1948 to 1971.
[b] Taken from Berndt, Fuss, and Waverman (1977, table III-6, p. 63) based on U.S. manufacturing data, 1948 to 1971.

In terms of other elasticities, E and K are complements, E and L are substitutes, and E and M are complements. The short-run elasticity of demand for energy with respect to output is 0.141, and the corresponding estimate in the long run is a surprisingly small 0.159. In the second row we constrain a priori that the elasticity of demand for energy with respect to output in the long run be unity (consistent with long-run constant returns to scale for all inputs). This specification alters the partial adjustment coefficient considerably, decreasing its estimated value to 0.260. There are no sign changes on elasticities, but several of the long-run elasticity estimates become unreasonably large: ε_{EE}, for example, is -0.944 in the short run and -3.630 in the long run, while corresponding ε_{EL} estimates are 0.831 and 3.196. The reason for this large long-run estimate is the combination of a small λ and a quite large ε_{EE}^{SR}.

In the third row we present energy own price elasticity estimates when long-run constant returns to scale is imposed and when in addition all cross-price elasticities are constrained to be zero. This simple, but highly restrictive, specification also yields unacceptably large ε_{EE} estimates: -0.623 in the short run and -2.492 in the long run. The estimated partial adjustment coefficient $\hat{\lambda}$ remains relatively stable at 0.250.

In summary the single-equation, partial adjustment equations yield elasticity estimates that appear unacceptably large in the long run. Moreover, as pointed out in section 12.1, it is difficult to interpret these elasticity estimates unambiguously, since the estimating equation is basically one of long-run statics and ad hoc dynamics. In particular it does not make clear what is held constant during the transition from short to long run.

In the fourth row we present elasticity estimates based on a linear version of the Balestra-Nerlove flexible and captive energy demand equation (12.20):

$$E_t = \alpha_0 + \alpha_1 \left(\frac{P_E}{P_M}\right)_t + \alpha_2 \left(\frac{P_L}{P_M}\right)_t + \alpha_3 \left(\frac{P_K}{P_M}\right)_t + \alpha_y Y_t + (1 - \delta)E_{t-1},$$

$$(12.55)$$

where E_t is total energy demand, $(1 - \delta)E_{t-1}$ is captive demand, and the remainder is flexible demand. Note that equation (12.55) is indistinguishable from a linear version of the partial adjustment model, except that in the case of the Balestra-Nerlove approach the coefficient on the lagged dependent variable ostensibly represents $(1 - \delta)$, or one minus the rate of depreciation on energy-using equipment. As seen in this row, the Balestra-Nerlove approach is not supported empirically, for the implied estimate of the rate of depreciation is 0.835, which is much too large.

Interestingly enough, elasticity estimates based on this Balestra-Nerlove specification are very similar to those based on the log-linear partial adjustment equation summarized in the top row of table 12.1.[20]

An alternative specification in the spirit of Balestra-Nerlove is the following mixed multiplicative-additive equation discussed by Berndt-Watkins (1977):

$$E_t = \alpha_0 P_{Kt}^{\alpha_K} P_{Lt}^{\alpha_L} P_{Et}^{\alpha_E} P_{Mt}^{\alpha_M} Y_t^{\alpha_Y} + (1 - \delta)E_{t-1}, \tag{12.56}$$

where homogeneity requires that $\alpha_K + \alpha_L + \alpha_E + \alpha_M = 0$. when this equation is estimated by nonlinear least squares, the estimate of δ still remains unacceptably high at 0.915. Elasticity estimates, as shown in the fifth row of table 12.1, remain basically unchanged from the corresponding linear specification. Finally, in the sixth row of the table we present elasticity estimates with the restrictions imposed that $\alpha_Y = 1$ (long-run constant returns to scale) and that $(1 - \delta) = 0.9$ (that the rate of depreciation per year is 10 percent). There it is seen that elasticity estimates become incredulous: short- and long-run estimates of ε_{EE} are -6.808 and -68.084, respectively, while corresponding estimates of ε_{EM} are 6.868 and 68.684.

In summary, elasticity estimates and estimates of depreciation based on the single-equation Balestra-Nerlove model are implausible a priori.[21] Hence empirical results for U.S. manufacturing based on both types of first generation models are not very encouraging.

We now turn to a brief discussion of the Nadiri-Rosen type of second generation models, which differ from first generation models principally in that systems of demand equations are specified. Elasticity estimates for both translog and generalized Leontief cost functions are presented in the bottom two rows of table 12.1; these estimates are taken directly from Berndt-Fuss-Waverman (1977, ch. 3), which also provides a more detailed discussion. Again the short- and long-run elasticity estimates are difficult to interpret, since there is no economic optimization subject to constraints in the adjustment process. With the translog specification there is short-run overshooting for $\varepsilon_{EL}(\varepsilon_{EL}^{SR} = 0.49$ while $\varepsilon_{EL}^{LR} = 0.40)$, and little difference between short-and long-run for energy: $\varepsilon_{EE}^{SR} = -0.69$ while $\varepsilon_{EE}^{LR} = -0.70$. However, with the generalized Leontief specification for energy, the difference between short- and long-run is very large (-1.17 to -4.24); the -4.24 estimate is implausible. Energy-capital complementarity is greater in the short (-0.14) than in the long run (-0.04). In summary elasticity estimates based on the Nadiri-Rosen type of second generation models exhibit the property of short-run overshooting but imply unacceptably large long-run energy elasticities.

Table 12.2
1961 energy elasticities based on a third generation model of U.S. manufacturing data, 1952 to 1971

	ε_{EE}	ε_{EK}	ε_{ES}	ε_{EU}	ε_{EM}	ε_{EY}
Short run	−0.239	0	0	0.693	−0.454	0.225
Intermediate run	−0.270	−0.035	−0.138	0.737	−0.294	0.386
Long run	−0.440	−0.101	−1.154	1.032	0.663	1.000

Note: Taken from C. J. Morrison and E. R. Berndt (1980, table 6, p. 41). Estimates of M_{SS}^{*} and M_{KK}^{*} in 1961 are 0.142 and 0.221, respectively.

Energy demand elasticity estimates based on a third generation dynamic model—that of C. J. Morrison and E. R. Berndt—are also available. The Morrison-Berndt model, discussed in section 12.3, specifies three variable inputs (unskilled labor, U, energy, E, and nonenergy intermediate materials, M) and two quasi-fixed inputs (skilled labor, S, and physical capital, K). The 1961 energy short- (within one year), intermediate- (one to two years), and long-run elasticities based on this model are presented in table 12.2. There it is seen that the energy own price elasticity increases (absolutely) from -0.239 in the short run to -0.440 in the long run. Inputs E and K are independent in the short run, when K is fixed, but become increasingly complementary in the long run. This $E - K$ complementarity finding is quite important and will be discussed in greater detail. Input E and unskilled labor, U, are substitutes, while E and skilled labor, S, are complements; in this way energy price increases raise demand for U and decrease demand for S.[22] The short-run elasticity of demand for energy with respect to output is 0.225, indicating substantial short-run increasing returns to energy.

We noted above that a result of the Morrison-Berndt dynamic model is that E and K become increasingly complementary in the long run. Previous $E - K$ complementarity findings based on static models have been somewhat controversial, and at times even the interpretation of $E - K$ complementarity has been at issue.[23] In an attempt to illustrate and clarify $E - K$ complementarity, we now turn to dynamic simulations of the third generation Morrison-Berndt dynamic model.

It is of course possible to simulate this model in various different ways under alternative assumptions. To establish a base case—hereafter called case I—we specified that over the 1972 to 1996 time period the relative prices of P_K, P_U, P_S, P_E, and P_M would remain fixed at their 1971 levels. Output growth is set at 4 percent per year during 1972 and 1973 but 1 percent per year from 1974 to 1996. Predicted dynamic demands for E and K are listed in the first two columns of table 12.3. There it is seen that under this base case E demand increases from 1.000 in 1971 to 1.484 in 1996,

Table 12.3
Simulated dynamic time paths of demand for E and K based case (case I) and 50 percent energy price increase case (case II) for U.S. manufacturing, 1971 to 1966

Year	K(case I)	E(case I)	K(II)	E(II)	E/K (II), E/K (I)	L/K (II), L/K (I)
1971	1.000	1.000	1.000	1.000	1.000	1.000
1972	1.024	1.025	1.024	0.913	0.890	1.057
1973	1.054	1.043	1.031	0.926	0.908	1.069
1974	1.087	1.058	1.061	0.918	0.889	1.075
1975	1.114	1.079	1.087	0.910	0.865	1.073
1976	1.141	1.144	1.089	0.915	0.894	1.070
1977	1.144	1.093	1.090	0.908	0.872	1.066
1978	1.152	1.099	1.095	0.093	0.865	1.057
1979	1.164	1.108	1.101	0.901	0.860	1.050
1980	1.179	1.120	1.109	0.901	0.855	1.045
1981	1.196	1.134	1.118	0.902	0.852	1.042
1986	1.305	1.228	1.168	0.924	0.841	1.033
1991	1.438	1.347	1.227	0.961	0.837	1.032
1996	1.558	1.484	1.289	1.006	0.835	1.031

Note: In case I all relative input prices remain at 1971 levels, output growth is 4 percent per year in 1972 and 1973 but 1 percent per year thereafter through 1996. In case II the conditions are the same as in case I except that relative price of energy increases by 50 percent in 1972 and stays at this higher level through 1996.

while demand for K rises from 1.000 to 1.588. This implies of course that in the base case, the ratio of E to K is predicted to fall from 1.0 in 1971 to 0.935 in 1996.

To illustrate the dynamic effects of energy price increases, we then increases the relative price of energy in 1972 by 50 percent and maintain P_E at this new level through 1996, but we keep output growth as in the base case.[24] We refer to this energy price increase simulation as case II. As seen in the third column of Table 12.3, the simulated effect of the 50 percent increase in the relative energy price is to reduce the capital stock in 1996 to 1.289 from what it would otherwise have been (a base case value of 1.588); it is in this sense that E and K are complementary inputs, for an increase in P_E and the associated reduction in E reduces the optimal level of the capital stock. The fourth column indicates that the 50 percent increase in P_E causes demand for energy to drop considerably and that the predicted energy decrease is larger in the long than in the short run; for example, the ratio of E(II) to E(I) is 0.891 in 1972 but falls to 0.678 by 1996.

The ratio of predicted E to K during the dynamic path is of particular interest. Even though E and K are complementary inputs, the predicted ratio of E to K should be smaller when P_E increases by 50 percent as compared to the base case: even though E and K are complements, energy price increases should induce use of more energy-efficient capital. This phenomenon is illustrated in column 5 where the E/K ratio in case II relative to the E/K ratio in the base case is seen to be less than unity. Hence $E - K$ complementary implies that, as P_E increases, the levels of both E and K decrease; however, the ratio of E to K also falls relative to the base case, since E and K are substituted one for another.[25]

In the last column of table 12.3 we take the ratios of aggregate labor L to K in case II relative to case I.[26] This relative set of ratios is greater than unity, indicating that as a result of the increase in P_E labor-capital ratios increase as labor is substituted for utilized capital. The decline in these ratios over time reflects attrition of the overshooting effect of unskilled labor and the consequent increasing relative importance of energy-skilled labor complementarity.

Earlier we noted that restricted variable cost functions provide the basis for constructing a measure of capacity utilization, defined as the ratio of actual output Y to that level of output Y^* which minimized the short-run average total cost of production, conditional on stocks of the quasi-fixed factors and prices of the variable inputs. In the second column of table 12.4 we present estimates of capacity utilization based on (12.48) and parameter estimates of the Morrison-Berndt, MB, third generation model. For purposes of comparison we also list in the third and fourth columns of table 12.4 the well-known Wharton, W, and Federal Reserve Board, FRB, indexes of capacity utilization in U.S. manufacturing for the same 1952 to 1971 time period.

The first point to notice when comparing these capacity utilization measures is that the MB index is above unity in all years except 1958, whereas the W and FRB indexes are always less than unity. To some extent this phenomenon can be viewed as simply a scaling convention. But there is an economic interpretation of why the MB index is greater than unity. In particular, since Y/Y^* is greater than unity, actual output was being produced at a level to the right of the minimum point of the short-run average total cost curve in all years except 1958; this reflects the fact that in all years except 1958 the MB model predicts there was a backlog of investment, that is, $(K^* - K) > 0$, so that $Y > Y^*$.

A second interesting point is that the three measures of capacity utilization are quite highly correlated: $r_{MB,W} = 0.660$, $r_{MB,FRB} = 0.891$, and $r_{W,FRB} = 0.876$. Moreover each index reaches a trough in the recession year 1958, each shows relative peaks in the expansive years of 1953 and 1965 to 1966, and each index drops in the years 1954 and 1970 to

Table 12.4
Capacity utilization in U.S. manufacturing, 1952 to 1971

	Morrison-Berndt measure, MB^a	Wharton index, W^b	Federal Reserve Board index, FRB^b
1952	1.138	0.884	0.854
1953	1.167	0.924	0.892
1954	1.052	0.829	0.801
1955	1.146	0.914	0.870
1956	1.113	0.908	0.861
1957	1.067	0.879	0.836
1958	0.974	0.775	0.750
1959	1.047	0.840	0.816
1960	1.065	0.821	0.801
1961	1.059	0.791	0.773
1962	1.120	0.825	0.814
1963	1.143	0.840	0.835
1964	1.155	0.868	0.857
1965	1.167	0.924	0.895
1966	1.162	0.966	0.911
1967	1.120	0.935	0.869
1968	1.104	0.950	0.870
1969	1.122	0.952	0.862
1970	1.040	0.878	0.792
1971	1.033	0.864	0.780

Note: Simple correlations are $r_{MB,W} = 0.660$, $r_{MB,FRB} = 0.891$, $r_{W,FRB} = 0.876$.
[a] The MB index is computed as the ratio of actual to economic capacity output, based on their estimated model with two quasi-fixed inputs, 1948 to 1971.
[b] Source of the W and FRB data is the 1979 *U.S. Economic Report of the President*, table B-42, p. 231.

1971. This favorable comparison of third generation with conventional peak-to-peak interpolation and survey-based measures of capacity utilization provides some confidence in the ability of the third generation approach to model cyclical variations in capacity utilization.[27]

12.5 Concluding Remarks

This chapter has surveyed three generations of dynamic models for analyzing Marshallian short-and long-run aspects of energy demand. Each generation of models has introduced more complexity into the modeling effort and involves estimation of a greater number of parameters but also provides a richer and clearer economic interpretation of the energy substitution process. Since researchers often face the trade-off of data availability and model complexity, we believe that models of all three generations will continue to be used.

Although our focus in this chapter has been on energy, the various dynamic models analyzed can also be used to trace time paths of demand for other inputs. The phenomenon of cyclical variation in the productivity of labor, for example, merits much additional attention. Dynamic models of the cost-production process could be used to examine empirically the output-pricing process and its relationship to short- and long-run average and marginal costs and to capacity utilization.

Finally, although in our judgment the third generation models constitute a substantial improvement over those of the first and second generations, there is no reason to believe that the third generation is the last. A number of important problems remain that should be addressed in future research. Among these are (1) the incorporation of alternative expectations formulations into the profit-maximizing or cost-minimizing process, (2) the development of empirically implementable models recognizing the differential features of various vintages of capital and other quasi-fixed inputs, (3) the construction of alternative representations of adjustment costs and rationales for the existence and movement of quasi-fixed inputs, (4) the specification of rental price formulas for quasi-fixed inputs explicitly incorporating costs of adjustment, (5) further disaggregation of the K, L, E, and M inputs, and (6) estimation of endogenous economic depreciation rates and technical change.

Notes

Research support from the Program in Natural Resource Economics (supported by a grant from the Social Science and Humanities Research Council of Canada) and the Graduate School of the University of British Columbia is gratefully acknowledged, as are the helpful comments of Barry Field, Melvyn Fuss, Robert Halvorsen, Larry Lau, Knut Mork, Ross Preston, David Stapleton, and David Wood.

1. Such an emphasis was suggested in the recent energy demand modeling survey by Raymond S. Hartman.

2. For a more complete discussion and critique of partial adjustment specifications of energy demand, see E. R. Berndt, M. A. Fuss, and Leonard Waverman (1977, ch. 2).

3. It follows that long-run own price elasticities are larger in absolute value than short-run own price elasticities. Hence as long as $0 < \lambda \leq 1$, this particular implication of the Le Chatelier principle is satisfied by the partial adjustment specification.

4. For further discussion of the Balestra-Nerlove model, see G. C. Watkins.

5. However, this raises the issue of how to construct degree-day adjusted data. See E. R. Berndt and G. C. Watkins for discussion and alternative treatment.

6. See Balestra, especially footnote 14, pp. 57–58, and Berndt and Watkins, p. 100, footnote 6.

7. In the Balestra model price effects relate primarily to substitution between fuels. An income effect on total energy demand is not directly specified, although changes in the energy-using characteristics of the new capital stock can be accomodated.

8. Some of these problems in empirical implementation have been overcome by David J. Faurot.

9. This time duration dependence of the returns to scale concept has been discussed by Nicholas Georgescu-Roegen.

10. A major difference between the Nadiri-Rosen and Brechling-Mortenson results is that the former find short-run decreasing returns to labor, while the latter obtain the more common and much documented short-run increasing returns to labor. Nadiri-Rosen attribute their unconventional finding to the fact that they take account of capital (actually, capacity) utilization, which earlier studies did not do. The Brechling-Mortenson results using the same capacity utilization data imply that Nadiri-Rosen's unique findings are due to their failure to take into account the overidentifying restrictions and are not related to the capacity utilization issue. See Frank Brechling (1975, ch. 6) for further discussion.

11. An exception to this is the dynamic application to energy demand by J. Randolph Norsworthy and Michael Harper based on a translog cost function (see chapter 9).

12. For a brief survey of alternative functional forms for variable or restricted cost and profit functions, see W. Erwin Diewert (1973, 1974).

13. For further discussion of various economic and engineering notions of capacity utilization, see L. R. Klein (1960). The approach taken here generalizes considerably the procedure developed by Bert G. Hickman. For a production function approach see L. R. Klein and R. S. Preston, and Gary Fromm et al.

14. See, however, Bert G. Hickman and Bert G. Hickman and Robert M. Coen (pp. 79–85) for an application based on a related procedure.

15. One possibility might be to use the relationship (12.28) based on estimated parameters and test whether for a particular observation the predicted shadow cost of a fixed input is statistically significantly different from its actual rental price; this approach might be generalized to models with more than one fixed input.

16. This utilization interpretation also emerges from the second generation short-run demand equations (12.27).

17. For an intuitive discussion of internal adjustment costs, see F. Brechling and Dale T. Mortenson; also see Michael Rothschild and S. J. Nickel (ch. 3).

18. Recall that the functional form (12.44) incorporates the assumption of long-run constant returns to scale.

19. For a review of currently used capacity utilization measures, see George L.

Perry, Lawrence R. Klein, and Virginia Long and the classic article by Lawrence R. Klein (1960).

20. The elasticity estimates in the linear Balestra-Nerlove vary with the data; the estimates reported in table 12.1 are for 1961, the approximate midpoint of the sample.

21. We have also estimated more complex versions of (12.55) and (12.56) that incorporate new output (see E. R. Berndt and G. C. Watkins for further discussion), but the results obtained were no better than those reported in table 12.1.

22. For a static analysis of this income redistribution issue, see E. R. Berndt and C. J. Morrison.

23. See, for example, E. R. Berndt and David O. Wood (1975a, 1979), M. A. Fuss (1977), E. R. Berndt and D. W. Jorgenson, E. A. Hudson and D. W. Jorgenson (1974), J. M. Griffin and P. R. Gregory, Robert S. Pindyck (1979) and Barry Field and Charles Grebenstein.

24. This simulation procedure is confined to the model, as specified, and does not include broader macroeconomic effects that could be generated by some of the more comprehensive models.

25. See E. R. Berndt and David O. Wood (1979) for a further interpretation of energy-capital complementarity.

26. The L is computed as a price-weighted index of U and S, where the weights are the constant 1971 prices P_U and P_S.

27. It is also of interest to note that the FRB and W indexes suggest a greater fall in capacity utilization over the controversial 1959 to 1961 time period than does the MB measure. For a discussion of this controversy, see the congressional testimony of L. R. Klein (1962).

Bibliography

Allen, R. G. D. *Mathematical Analysis for Economists.* London, 1956.

Anderson, R. G. "Energy Conservation and Factor Substitution in U.S. Manufacturing, 1947–1971." Ph.D. dissertation. Department of Economics, MIT, 1980.

Arrow, K. J. "The Measurement of Real Value Added." In P. A. David and M. W. Reder, eds., *Nations and Households in Economic Growth.* New York, 1974.

Arrow, K. J., et al. "Capital-labor Substitution and Economic Efficiency." *Rev. Econ. Statist.* 63 (August 1961): 225–247.

Atkinson, S. E., and R. Halvorsen. "Interfuel Substitution in Steam-Electric Power Generation." *J. Polit. Econ.* 84 (October 1976): 959–978.

Ayres, R. U. *Resources, Environment and Economics.* New York, 1978.

Balestra, P. *The Demand for Natural Gas in the United States: A Dynamic Approach for the Residential and Commercial Market.* Amsterdam, 1967.

Balestra, P., and M. Nerlove. "Pooling Cross Section and Time Series Data in the Estimation of a Dynamic Model: The Demand for Natural Gas." *Econometrica* 3 (July 1966): 585–612.

Barnett, H., and C. Morse. *Scarcity and Growth.* Baltimore, 1963.

Ben-Zion, Uri, and Vernon W. Ruttan. "Aggregate Demand and the Rate of Technical Change." In H. P. Binswanger and V. W. Ruttan, eds., *Induced Innovation.* Baltimore, 1978.

Berndt, E. R. "Reconciling Alternative Estimates of the Elasticity of Substitution." *Rev. Econ. Statist.* 63 (February 1976): 59–68.

Berndt, E. R., and L. R. Christensen. "The Translog Function and the Substitution of Equipment, Structures and Labor in U.S. Manufacturing, 1929–68." *J. Econometrics* 1 (March 1973): 81–114.

Berndt, E. R., and L. R. Christensen. "Testing for the Existence of a Consistent Aggregate Index of Labor Inputs." *Amer. Econ. Rev.* 64 (June 1974): 391–404.

Berndt, E. R., M. Fuss, and L. Waverman. *Dynamic Models of the Industrial Demand for Energy.* Rept. EA-580, Electric Power Research Institute, Palo Alto, Calif., 1977.

Berndt, E. R., M. A. Fuss, and L. Waverman. "A Dynamic Model of Costs of

Adjustment and Interrelated Factor Demands, with an Empirical Application to Energy Demand in U.S. Manufacturing." Discussion paper 79–30. Univ. of British Columbia, 1979.

Berndt, E. R., M. A. Fuss, and L. Waverman. *Empirical Analysis of Dynamic Adjustment Models of the Demand for Energy in U.S. Manufacturing Industries, 1947–74.* Final report. Electric Power Research Institute, Palo Alto, Calif., 1980.

Berndt, E. R., R. E. Hall, and J. A. Hausman. "Estimation and Inference in Non-linear Structural Models." *Annals of Economic and Social Measurement* 3 (October 1974): 653–65.

Berndt, E. R., and D. Jorgenson. "Production Structure." In D. Jorgenson et al., eds., *U.S. Energy Resources and Economic Growth.* Final report to the Ford Foundation Energy Policy Project, Washington, D.C., October 1973.

Berndt, E. R., and M. Khaled. "Parametric Productivity Measurement and Choice Among Flexible Functional Forms." *J. Polit. Econ.* 87 (December 1979): 1220–1245.

Berndt, E. R., and C. J. Morrison. "Income Redistribution and Employment Effects of Rising Energy Prices." *Resources and Energy* 2 (December 1979): 131–150.

Berndt, E. R., C. J. Morrison-White, and G. C. Watkins. "Energy Substitution and Capital Utilization in a Dynamic Context." Discussion paper. Dept. of Economics, Univ. of British Columbia, 1979.

Berndt, E. R., C. J. Morrison, and G. C. Watkins. "Short and Long Run Demand for Aggregate Energy in Canadian Manufacturing," forthcoming.

Berndt, E. R., and N. E. Savin. "Estimation and Hypothesis Testing in Singular Equation Systems with Autoregressive Disturbances." *Econometrica* 43 (September–November 1975): 937–957.

Berndt, E. R., and G. C. Watkins. "Demand for Natural Gas: Residential and Commercial Markets in Ontario and British Columbia." *Canadian J. Econ.* 10 (February 1977): 97–111.

Berndt, E. R., and D. O. Wood. "Technology, Prices, and the Derived Demand for Energy." *Rev. Econ. Statist.* 57 (August 1975a): 376–384.

Berndt, E. R., and D. O. Wood. "Technical Change, Tax Policy and the Derived Demand for Energy." Mimeographed. Univ. of British Columbia, 1975b.

Berndt, E. R., and D. O. Wood. *Consistent Projections of Energy Demand and Aggregate Economic Growth: A Review of Issues and Empirical Studies.* Energy Laboratory working paper MIT EL 77-024WP. MIT, January 1977a.

Berndt, E. R., and D. O. Wood. "Engineering and Econometric Approaches to Industrial Energy Conservation and Capital Formation: A Reconciliation." Energy Laboratory working paper 77-040. MIT, 1977b.

Berndt, E. R., and D. O. Wood. "Engineering and Econometric Interpretations of Energy-Capital Complementarity." *Amer. Econ. Rev.* 69 (June 1979): 342–54.

Bever, R., J. Marsden, V. Salas, and A. Whinston. *Interim Report on Methodology of Process Models.* Purdue University, May 1978.

Binswanger, H. "A Cost-Function Approach to the Measurement of Elasticities of Factor Demand and Elasticities of Substitution." *Amer. J. Agr. Econ.* 56 (May 1974a): 377–86.

Binswanger, H. P. "Induced Technical Change: Evolution of Thought." In H. P. Binswanger and V. W. Ruttan, eds., *Induced Innovation*. Baltimore, 1978c.

Binswanger, H. P. "Issues in Modeling Induced Technical Change." In H. P. Binswanger and V. W. Ruttan, eds., *Induced Innovation*. Baltimore, 1978.

Binswanger, H. P., and V. W. Ruttan, eds. *Induced Innovation*. Baltimore, 1978.

Binswanger, H. P. "The Measurement of Technical Change Biases with Many Factors of Production." *Amer. Econ. Rev.* 64 (December 1974b); 964–976.

Binswanger, H. P. "A Microeconomic Approach to Induced Innovation." *Econ. J.* 84 (December 1974c): 940–958.

Blackorby, C., D. Primont, and R. Robert Russell. *Duality, Separability, and Functional Structure: Theory and Economic Applications*. New York, 1978.

Blackorby, C., and E. R. Russell. "The Morishima Elasticity of Substitution: Symmetry, Constancy, and the Relationship to the Hicks and Allen Elasticities." *Rev. Econ. Stud.*, in press.

Bower, B. T. "Studies in Residuals Management in Industry." In E. S. Mills, ed., *Economic Analysis of Environmental Problems*. New York, 1975.

Brechling, F. *Investment and Employment Decisions*. Manchester, England, 1975.

Brechling, F., and D. T. Mortenson. "Interrelated Investment and Employment Decisions." Mimeographed. Northwestern Univ. and Univ. of Sussex, 1971.

Brobst, D. A. "Fundamental Concepts for the Analysis of Resource Availability." In V. K. Smith, ed., *Scarcity and Growth Revisited*. Baltimore, 1979.

Brown, G. M., and B. C. Field. "Possibilities of Substitution for Natural Resources in U.S. Manufacturing." Working paper. Dept. of Economics, Univ. of Washington, 1980.

Brown, R. S. *Productivity, Returns, and the Structure of Production in U.S. Agriculture, 1947–1974*. Ph.D. dissertation. Dept. of Economics, Univ. of Wisconsin, 1977.

Castle, E. N. "The Economics of Agriculture and Agricultural Economics," *Amer. J. Agr. Econ.* 59 (December 1977): 824–833.

Caves, D. W., and L. R. Christensen. "Modeling the Structure of Production in the U.S. Railroad Industry." Mimeographed. Univ. of Wisconsin, 1975.

Caves, D. W., L. R. Christensen, and J. A. Swanson. "Technical Progress, Scale Economics, and Capacity Utilization in U.S. Railroads, 1955–1974." *Amer. Econ. Rev.*, forthcoming.

Christensen, L. R., and W. H. Greene. "Economies of Scale in U.S. Electric Power Generation." *J. Polit. Econ.* 84 (August 1976): 655–676.

Christensen, L. R., and D. W. Jorgenson. "Measuring the Performance of the Private Sector of the U.S. Economy, 1929–1969." In M. Moss, ed., *Measuring Economic and Social Performance*. New York: NBER, 1973b.

Christensen, L. R., and D. W. Jorgenson. "U.S. Income, Saving and Wealth, 1929–1969." *Rev. Income Wealth* 19 (December 1973): 329–362.

Christensen, L. R., and D. W. Jorgenson. "U.S. Real Product and Real Factor Input, 1929–1967." *Rev. Income Wealth* 16 (March 1970): 19–50.

Christensen, L. R., D. W. Jorgenson, and L. J. Lau. "Conjugate Duality and the Transcendental Logarithmic Production Function." *Econometrica* 39 (July 1971): 255–256.

Christensen, L. R., D. W. Jorgenson, and L. J. Lau. "Transcendental Logarithmic Production Frontiers." *Rev. Econ. Statist.* 55 (February 1973): 28–45.

Clapp, J. M. "The Substitution of Urban Land for Other Inputs." *J. Urban Econ.* 6 (January 1979): 122–134.

Cobb, C. W., and P. H. Douglas. "A Theory of Production." *Amer. Econ. Rev.*, 18 (Suppl. 1928): 139–165.

Cowing, T. G., and V. K. Smith. "The Estimation of a Production Technology: A Survey of Econometric Analyses of Steam Electric Generation." *Land Econ.* 54 (May 1978): 156–186.

Creamer, D., et al. *Capital in Manufacturing and Mining.* Princeton, N.J., 1960.

Dasgupta, P., and G. Heal. *Economics of Exhaustible Resources.* Cambridge: Cambridge Univ. Press, 1979.

David, P. A., and Th. van de Klundert. "Biased Efficiency Growth and Capital Labor Substitution in the U.S., 1899–1960." *Amer. Econ. Rev.* 55 (June 1965): 357–394.

Denny, M., and M. A. Fuss. "The Use of Approximation Analysis to Test for Separability and the Existence of Consistent Aggregates." *Amer. Econ. Rev.* 67 (June 1977): 404–418.

Denny, M., M. A. Fuss, and L. Waverman. *Energy and the Cost Structure of Canadian Manufacturing Industries.* Tech. paper 12. Institute for Policy Studies, Univ. of Toronto, 1979a.

Denny, M., M. A. Fuss, and L. Waverman. "An Application of Optimal Control Theory to the Estimation of the Demand for Energy in Canadian Manufacturing Industries." In *Proceedings of the Ninth IFIP Conference on Optimization Techniques.* Berlin, 1979b.

Dent, W., and J. Geweke. "On Specification in Simultaneous Equation Models." SSRI discussion paper 7823. Univ. of Wisconsin, September 1978.

Diewert, W. E. "Applications of Duality Theory." In M. D. Intrilligator and D. A. Kendrick, eds., *Frontiers of Quantitative Economics, Vol. 2.* Amsterdam, 1974.

Diewert, W. E. "Aggregation Problems in the Measurement of Capital." In D. Usher, ed., *The Measurement of Capital.* Chicago, 1980, pp. 433–528.

Diewert, W. E. "Exact and Superlative Index Numbers." *J. Econometrics* 4 (May 1976): 115–146.

Diewert, W. E. "Functional Forms for Profit and Transformation Functions." *J. Econ. Theory* 3 (June 1973): 284–316.

Douglas, P. H. "The Cobb-Douglas Production Function Once Again: Its History, Its Testing, and Some Empirical Values." *J. Polit. Econ.* 84 (October 1976): 903–916.

Duncan, R. C., and H. P. Binswanger. "Energy Sources: Substitutability and Biases in Australia." *Austral. Econ. Pap.* 15 (December 1976): 289–301.

Eisner, R., and R. H. Strotz. "Determinants of Business Investment." In D. B. Suits et al., eds., *Impacts of Monetary Policy.* Englewood Cliffs, N. J., 1963.

Epstein, L. "Duality Theory and Functional Forms for Dynamic Factor Demands." Revised working paper 7915. Institute for Policy Analysis, Univ. of Toronto, 1980.

Epstein, L., and M. Denny. "The Multivariate Flexible Accelerator Model: Its Empirical Restriction and an Application to U.S. Manufacturing." Working Paper 8003. Institute for Policy Analysis, Univ. of Toronto, 1980.

J. Faucett Associates, Inc. *Data Development for the I–O Energy Model: Final Report.* Washington, D.C., May 1973.

J. Faucett Associates, Inc. *Development of 35 Order Input-Output Tables, 1958–1974, Final Report.* Washington, D.C., 1977.

Faurot, D. J. "Interrelated Demand for Capital and Labour in a Globally Optimal Flexible Accelerator Model." *R. Econ. Statist.* 60 (February 1978): 25–32.

Ferguson, A. R. "An Airline Production Function." *Econometrica* 18 (July 1950): 217–235.

Field, B. C. "Land-Structures Substitution and the Urban Density Gradient." *Land Econ.* 56 (November 1980): 447–450.

Field, B. C., and P. G. Allen. "A General Measure for Output-Variable Input Demand Elasticities." *Amer. J. Agr. Econ.* 63(August 1981), forthcoming.

√ Field, B. C., and C. Grebenstein. "Substituting for Energy in U.S. Manufacturing." *Rev. Econ. Statist.*, 62 (May 1980): 207–12.

Fisher, F. M. "Aggregate Production Functions and the Explanation of Wages: A Simulation Experiment." *R. Econ. Statist.* 53 (November 1971): 305–326.

Fisher, F. M., P. H. Cootner, and M. N. Baily. "An Econometric Model of the World Copper Industry." *Bell J. Econ. Man. Sci.* 3 (Autumn 1972): 568–609.

Fisher, F. M., and C. Kaysen. *A Study of Econometrics: The Demand for Electricity in the United States.* Amsterdam, 1962.

Fisher, F. M., R. Solow, and J. Kearl. "Aggregate Production Functions: Some C.E.S. Experiments." *Rev. Econ. Stud.* 44 (June 1977): 305–320.

Fisher, I. *The Making of Index Numbers.* Boston, 1922.

Foss, M. F. "The Utilization of Capital Equipment: Postwar Compared to Prewar." *Survey of Current Business.* 43 (June 1963): 8–15.

Fraumeni, B. M., and D. W. Jorgenson. "The Role of Capital in U.S. Economic Growth, 1948–1976." In G. M. von Furstenberg, ed., *Capital, Efficiency and Growth,* forthcoming.

Frisch, R. "The Principle of Substitution: An Example of Its Application in the Chocolate Industry." *Nordisk Tidsskrift for Teknisk Okonomi* 1 (1935): 12–27.

Fromm, G., L. R. Klein, F. C. Ripley, and D. Crawford. "Production Function Estimation of Capacity Utilization." Presented at Econometric Society Meetings, Atlanta, 1979.

Fuss, M. A. "Dynamic Factor Demand Systems with Explicit Costs of Adjustment." mimeographed. Stanford Univ., 1976 (appeared as chapter 4 in Berndt, Fuss and Waverman, 1977).

Fuss, M. A. "The Demand for Energy in Canadian Manufacturing: An Example of the Estimation of Production Structures with Many Inputs." *J. Econometrics* 5 (January 1977): 89–116.

Fuss, M. A., and D. McFadden. "Flexibility versus Efficiency in Ex Ante Plant Design." In M. Fuss and D. McFadden, eds., *Production Economics; A Dual Approach to Theory and Applications, Vol. I.* Amsterdam, 1978b.

Fuss, M. A., and D. McFadden. *Production Economics: A Dual Approach to Theory and Applications,* 2 vol. Amsterdam, 1978a.

Fuss, M. A., D. McFadden, and Y. Mundlak. "A Survey of Functional Forms in the Econometric Analysis of Production." In M. A. Fuss and D. McFadden, eds., *Production Economics: A Dual Approach to Theory and Applications, Vol. 1.* Amsterdam, 1978.

Gander, J. P. *Technological Change and Raw Materials.* Bureau of Economic and Business Research, Univ. of Utah, 1977.

Gapinski, J. H. "Putty-Clay Capital and Small Sample Properties of Neoclassical Estimators." *J. Polit. Econ.* 18 (January/February 1973): 145–157.

Gapinski, J. H., and T. K. Kumar. "Nonlinear Estimation of the CES Production Parameters: A Monte Carlo Study." *R. Econ. Statist.* 56 (November 1974): 563–567.

Georgescu-Roegen, N. "Comments on the Papers by Daly and Stiglitz." In V. K. Smith, ed., *Scarcity and Growth Revisited.* Baltimore, 1979.

Georgescu-Roegen, N. "The Economics of Production." *Amer. Econ. Rev.* 60 (May 1970): 1–9.

Geraci, V. J. "Estimation of Simultaneous Equation Models with Measurement Error." *Econometrica* 45 (July 1977): 1243–1266.

Geweke, J. "Testing the Exogeneity Specification in the Complete Dynamic Simultaneous Equation Model." *J. Econometrics* 7 (April 1978): 163–185.

Geweke, J., R. Meese, and W. Dent. "Comparing Alternative Tests of Causality in Temporal Systems: Analytic Results and Experimental Evidence." SSRI discussion paper 7928. Univ. of Wisconsin, Madison, October 1979.

Goeller, H. E. "The age of Substitutability: A Scientific Appraisal of Natural Resource Adequacy." In V. K. Smith, ed., *Scarcity and Growth Revisited.* Baltimore, 1979.

Gold, B. "Tracing Gaps between Expectations and Results of Technological Innovations: The Case of Iron and Steel." *J. Indust. Econ.* 25 (September 1976): 1–28.

Gollop, F. M., and D. W. Jorgenson. "U.S. Productivity Growth by Industry,

1947–1973." In J. Kendrick and B. Vaccara, eds., *New Developments in Productivity Measurement and Analysis.* Chicago, 1980, pp. 17–136.

Goodman, L. A. "On the Exact Variance of Products." *J. Amer. Statist. Assn.* 55 (December 1960): 708–713.

Gorman, W. M. "Measuring the Quantities of Fixed Factors." In J. N. Wolfe, ed., *Value, Capital and Growth: Papers in Honor of Sir John Hicks.* Edinburgh, 1968, pp. 141–172.

Grebenstein, C., and B. C. Field. "Substituting for Water in U.S. Manufacturing." *Water Resources Research* 15 (April 1979): 228–232.

Green, H. A. J. *Aggregation in Economic Analysis.* Princeton, N.J., 1964.

Griffin, J. M. "The Effects of Higher Prices on Electricity Consumption." *Bell J. Econ. Man. Sci* 5 (Autumn 1974): 515–539.

Griffin, J. M. "Engineering and Economic Interpretations of Energy Capital Complementarity: A Comment." Mimeographed. Dept. of Economics, Univ. of Houston, 1979.

Griffin, J. M. "Joint Production Technology: The Case of Petrochemicals." *Econometrica* 46 (March 1978a): 379–398.

Griffin, J. M. "Long-Run Production Modeling with Pseudo-Data: Electric Power Generation." *Bell J. Econ.* 8 (Spring 1977): 112–127.

Griffin, J. M. "Pseudo-Data Estimation with Alternative Functional Forms." Paper presented at the 1978 annual meeting of the Southern Economic Assoc., Washington, D.C., November 1978b.

Griffin, J. M., and P. R. Gregory. "An Intercountry Translog Model of Energy Substitution Responses." *Amer. Econ. Rev.* 66 (December 1976): 845–857.

Griliches, Z. "Estimates of the Agricultural Production Function from Cross-Section Data." *J. Farm Econ.* 45 (May 1963): 419–428.

Griliches, Z., and V. Ringstad. *Economies of Scale and the Form of the Production Function.* Amsterdam: North-Holland, 1971.

Griliches, Z., and V. Ringstad. "Error-in-the-Variables Bias in Nonlinear Contexts." *Econometrica* 2 (March 1970): 368–370.

Guilkey, D. K. "Alternative Tests for a First-Order Vector Autoregressive Error Specification." *J. Econometrics* 2 (January 1974): 95–104.

Guilkey, D. K. and C. A. K. Lovell. "On the Flexibility of the Translog Approximation." *Internat. Econ. Rev.,* 21 (February 1980): 137–147.

Guilkey, D. K. and P. Schmidt. "Estimation of Seemingly Unrelated Regressions with Vector Autoregressive Errors." *J. Amer. Statist. Assn.* 68 (September 1973): 642–647.

Halvorsen, R. "Energy Substitution in U.S. Manufacturing." *Rev. Econ. Statist.* 59 (November 1977): 381–388.

Halvorsen, R., and J. Ford, "Substitution Among Energy, Capital, and Labor Inputs in U.S. Manufacturing." In R. S. Pindyck, ed., *Advances in the Economics of Energy and Resources, Vol. 1; The Structure of Energy Markets.* Greenwich, Conn., 1980.

Hartman, R. S. "Frontiers in Energy Demand Modeling." *Annual Review of Energy.* Vol. 4, Palo Alto, Calif. 1979.

Hazilla, M. "The Use of Economic Theory in Econometric Estimation: Inference in Linear Constrained Models." Ph.D. dissertation. State Univ. of New York at Binghamton, 1978.

Heady, E. O., and J. L. Dillon. *Agricultural Production Functions.* Ames, Iowa, 1961.

Heady, E. O., and L. G. Tweeten. *Resource Demand and the Structure of the Agricultural Industry,* Ames, Iowa, 1963.

Hexem, R. W., and E. O. Heady. *Water Production Functions for Irrigated Agriculture.* Ames, Iowa, 1978.

Hickman, B. G. "On a New Method of Capacity Estimation." *J. Amer. Statist. Assn.* 59 (June 1964): 529–549.

Hickman, B. G., and R. M. Coen. *An Annual Growth Model of the U.S. Economy.* Amsterdam, 1976.

Hicks, J. R. "Elasticity of Substitution Again: Substitutes and Complements." *Oxford Econ. Pap.* 22 (November 1970): 289–296.

Hicks, J. R. *The Theory of Wages,* 2nd ed. London, 1963.

Hildebrand, J. R. "Some Difficulties with Empirical Results from Whole-Farm Cobb-Douglas Type Production Functions." *J. Farm Econ.* 42 (November 1960): 897–904.

Hildebrand, G. H., and T. C. Liu. *Manufacturing Production Functions in the United States, 1957.* Geneva, N.Y., 1965.

Hoch, I. *Energy Use in the United States by State and Region.* Washington, D.C., 1978.

Hogan, W. W. "Capital Energy Complementarity in Aggregate Energy-Economic Analysis." *Bell J. Econ.,* in press.

Hogan, W. W., and A. S. Manne. "Energy-Economic Interactions: The Fable of the Elephant and the Rabbit?" Energy Modeling Forum report. EMF 1.3. Institute for Energy Studies, Stanford Univ., 1977.

Houthakker, H. S. "New Evidence on Demand Elasticities." *Econometrica* 33 (April 1965): 277–288.

Houthakker, H. S. "The Pareto Distribution and the Cobb-Douglas Production Function in Activity Analysis" *Rev. Econ. Stud.* 23 (1955–1956): 27–31.

Houthakker, H. S., and L. D. Taylor. *Consumer Demand in the United States.* Cambridge, Mass., 1966.

Hudson, E. A., and D. W. Jorgenson. "The Economic Impact of Policies to Reduce U.S. Energy Growth." Discussion paper 644. Harvard Institute of Economic Research, Harvard Univ. August 1978b.

Hudson, E. A., and D. W. Jorgenson. "Energy Prices and the U.S. Economy."

Discussion paper 637. Harvard Institute of Economic Research, Harvard Univ. July 1978a.

Hudson, E. A., and D. W. Jorgenson. "Tax Policy and Energy Conservation." In D. W. Jorgenson, ed., *Econometric Studies of U.S. Energy Policy*. Amsterdam, 1976.

Hudson, E. A., and D. W. Jorgenson. "U.S. Energy Policy and Economic Growth, 1975–2000." *Bell J. Econ. and Man. Sci.* 5 (Autumn 1974): 461–514.

Humphrey, D. B. "Estimates of Factor-Intermediate Substitution and Separability." *Southern Econ. J.* 41 (January 1975): 531–534.

Humphrey, D. B., and J. R. Moroney. "Substitution among Capital, Labor and Natural Resource Products in American Manufacturing." *J. Polit. Econ.* 83 (February 1975): 57–82.

Humphrey, D. B., and B. Wolkowitz. "Substituting Intermediates for Capital and Labor with Alternative Functional Forms: An Aggregate Study." *Applied Econ.* 8 (March 1976): 59–68.

Jacobs, R. L., E. Leamer, and M. Ward. "Difficulties with Testing for Causation." *Econ. Inquiry* 17 (July 1979): 401–413.

Jensen, H. R. "Farm Management and Production Economics, 1946–70," in L. R. Martin, ed. *A Survey of Agricultural Literature, Vol. 2*, Minneapolis, 1977.

Jevons, W. S. *The Coal Question*. First edition, 1865; third edition reprinted by Augustus M. Kelley, New York, 1965.

Johansen, L. *Production Functions*. Amsterdam, 1972.

Joreskog, K. G. "A General Method for Estimating a Linear Structural Equation System." In A. S. Goldberger and O. D. Duncan, eds., *Structural Equation Models in the Social Sciences*. New York, 1973.

Jorgenson, Dale W. "Technology and Decision Rules in the Theory of Investment Behavior." *Quart. J. Econ.* 87 (November 1973): 523–543.

Jorgenson, D. W., and Barbara M. Fraumeni. "Substitution and Technical Change in Production." Discussion paper no. 752, Harvard Univ. March 1980.

Jorgenson, D. W., and Z. Griliches. "The Explanation of Productivity Change," *Rev. Econ. Stud.* 34 (July 1967): 249–283.

Jorgenson, D. W., and J. J. Laffont. "Efficient Estimation of Non-Linear Simultaneous Equations with Additive Disturbances." *Annals of Social and Economic Measurement* 3 (October 1975): 615–640.

Jorgenson, D. W., and L. J. Lau. "The Structure of Consumer Preferences." *Annals of Social and Economic Measurement* 4 (Winter 1975): 49–101.

Jorgenson, D. W., and L. J. Lau. *Transcendental Legarithmic Production Functions*, forthcoming.

Kang, H., and G. Brown, Jr. "Elasticity of Substitution and Elasticity of Demand When There Are Many Factors of Production." Discussion paper, Dept. of Applied Econ., Cambridge Univ., 1978.

Katzner, D. *Static Demand Theory*. New York, 1970.

Kennedy, C. "Induced Bias in Innovation and the Theory of Distribution." *Econ. J.* 74 (September 1964): 541–547.

Klein, L. R. *A Textbook of Econometrics*. Evanston. Row, Peterson, 1956.

Klein, L. R. "Some Theoretical Issues in the Measurement of Capacity." *Econometrica* 28 (April 1960): 272–286.

Klein, L. R. "Testimony." In *Measures of Productive Capacity*. Hearings before the Sub-committes on Economic Statistics of the Joint Economic Committee, U.S., Congress, 87th Congress, 2nd Session, May 1962. Washington, D.C.: Government Printing office, 1962, pp. 43–46.

Klein, L. R., and R. S. Preston. "Some New Results in the Measurement of Capacity Utilization." *Amer. Econ. Rev.* 57 (March 1967): 34–58.

Klein, L. R., and V. Long. "Capacity Utilization: Concept, Measurement and Recent Estimates." *Brookings Papers on Economic Activity* 3 (1973): 743–756.

Kloek, T. *Indexcijfers: Enige methodologisch Aspecten*. The Hague, 1966.

Kmenta, J. "Some Problems of Inference from Economic Survey Data." In M. K. Namboodiri, ed., *Survey Sampling and Measurement*. New York, 1978.

Kmenta, J., and R. Gilbert. "Small Sample Properties of Alternative Estimators of Seemingly Unrelated Regressions." *J. Amer. Stat. Assn.* 63 (December 1968): 1180–2000.

Koenker, R. "An Empirical Note on the Elasticity of Substitution between Land and Capital in a Monocentric Housing Market." *J. Regional Sci.* 12 (August 1972): 299–305.

Kohn, R. "On the Relative Efficiency of the Two Methods of Estimating a Dynamic Simultaneous Equation Model." *Internat. Econ. Rev.* 20 (February 1979): 237–252.

Koizumi, T. "A Further Note on Definition of Elasticity of Substitution in Many Input Case." *Metroeconomica* 28 (January–December 1976): 152–155.

Kopp, R. J., and V. K. Smith. "Capital-Energy Complementarity: Further Evidence." Mimeographed. Washington, D.C., Resources for the Future, 1978.

Kopp, R. J., and V. K. Smith. "Capital-Energy Complementarity: Further Evidence." Paper presented at the annual meeting of the Southern Economic Assn., Atlanta, Georgia, November 1979.

Kopp, R. J., and V. K. Smith. "The Perceived Role of Materials in Neoclassical Models of the Production Technology." In V. K. Smith and J. V. Krutilla, eds., *Explorations in Natural Resource Economics*. Baltimore, 1981.

Kuga, K., and T. Murota. "A Note on Definitions of Elasticity of Substitution in Many Input Case." *Metroeconomica* 24 (September–December 1972): 285–290.

Kuh, E. "The Validity of Cross-Sectionally Estimating Behavior Equations in Time Series Applications." *Econometrica* 27 (April 1959): 197–214.

Kuh, E., and J. R. Meyer. "How Extraneous Are Extraneous Estimates?" *Rev. Econ. Statist.* 39 (November 1957): 390–393.

Lau, L. J. "Applications of Profit Functions." In M. Fuss and D. McFadden, eds., *Production Economics: A Dual Approach to Theory and Applications, Vol. I.* Amsterdam, 1978a.

Lau, L. J. "A Characterization of the Normalized Restricted Profit Function." J. Econ. Theory 12 (February 1976): 131–163.

Lau, L. J. "On the Measurement of Raw Materials Inputs." In V. K. Smith, and J. V. Krutilla, eds., *Explorations in Natural Resource Economics.* Baltimore, 1981.

Lau, L. J. "Testing and Imposing Monotonicity, Convexity, and Quasi-Convexity Constraints." In M. Fuss and D. McFadden, eds., *Production Economics: A Dual Approach to Theory and Applications, Vol. I.* Amsterdam, 1978b, pp. 409–453.

Lau, L. J., and P. A. Yotopoulos. "Profit, Supply and Factor Demand Functions with Application to Indian Agriculture." *Amer. J. Agric. Econ.* 54 (February 1972): 11–18.

Lau, L. J., and P. A. Yotopoulos. "A Test for Relative Efficiency and Application to Indian Agriculture." *Amer. Econ. Rev.* 61 (March 1971): 94–109.

Lau, L. J., and P. A. Yotopoulos. "A Test of Relative Efficiency: Some Further Results." *Amer. Econ. Rev.* 63 (March 1973): 214–223.

Lawley, D. N., and A. E. Maxwell. *Factor Analysis as a Statistical Method.* New York. 1971.

Leontief, W. "Composite Commodities and the Problem of Index Numbers." *Econometrica* 4 (January 1936): 39–59.

Lerttamrab, P. *Liquidity and Credit Constraints: Their Impact on Family Household Consumption, Output Supply, and Factor Rewards: A Case Study of Modern Thailand.* Ph.D. dissertation. Stanford Univ., 1975.

Levhari, D. "A Note on Houthakker's Aggregate Production Function in a Multi-firm Industry." *Econometrica* 36 (January 1968): 151–154.

Lucas, R. E., Jr. "Adjustment Costs and the Theory of Supply." *J. Polit. Econ.* 75 (August 1967b): 321–334.

Lucas, R. E., Jr. "Labor-Capital Substitution in U.S. Manufacturing." In A. C. Harberger and M. J. Bailey, eds., *The Taxation of Income from Capital.* Washington, D.C., 1969.

Lucas, R. E., Jr. "Tests of a Capital-Theoretic Model of Technological Change." *Rev. of Econ. Stud.* 34 (April 1967): 175–180.

Lucas, R. E., Jr. "Optimal Investment Policy and the Flexible Accelerator." *Internat. Econ. Rev.* 8 (February 1967a): 78–85.

Maddala, G. S., and B. Roberts. "An Evaluation of the Pseudo-Data Approach." Final report EA 1108. Electric Power Research Institute, Palo Alto, Calif., July 1979.

Magnus, J. R. "Maximum Likelihood Estimation of the GLS Model with Unknown Parameters in the Disturbance Covariance Matrix." *J. Econometrics* 7 (June 1978): 281–312.

Magnus, J. R. "Substitution Between Energy and Non-Energy Inputs in the Netherlands, 1950–1974." *Internat. Econ. Rev.* 2 (June 1979): 465–484.

Mangasarian, O. L. "Sufficient Conditions for the Optimal Control of Non-Linear Systems." *J. SIAM Control* 4 (February 1966): 139–152.

Marsden, J. D., D. Pingry, and A. Whinston. "Engineering Foundations of Production Functions." *J. Econ. Theory* 9 (October 1974): 124–140.

Marsden, J. D., D. Pingry and A. Whinston. "Production Function Theory and the Optimal Design of Waste Treatment Facilities." *Applied Econ.* 4 (December 1972): 279–290.

Marshall, A. *Principles of Economics*, 8th ed. London, 1920.

McFadden, D. "Constant Elasticity of Substitution Production Functions." *Rev. Econ. Stud.* 30 (June 1963): 78–83.

McFadden, D. "Costs, Revenue and Profit Functions." In M. Fuss and D. McFadden, eds., *Production Economics: A Dual Approach to Theory and Applications, Vol. 1.* Amsterdam, 1978.

Meadows, D. "A Critique of the Short-Term Perspectives Implicit in Most Resource Models." In W. A. Vogely, ed., *Mineral Materials Modeling.* Washington, D.C.: Resources for the Future, 1975.

Meadows, D., et al. *The Limits to Growth.* New York. Universe Books, 1974.

Mohr, M. F. *A Quarterly Econometric Model of the Long-Term Structure of Production, Factor Demand, and Factor Productivity in 10 U.S. Manufacturing Industries.* Bureau of Labor Statistics staff paper no. 9, Washington, D.C., 1978.

Morishima, M. "Danryokusei Rison ni Kansuru Ni-san no Teian ('A Few Suggestions on the Theory of Elasticity')." Translated by T. Murota. *Keizai-Hyoron* ("Economic Review") 16 (1967): 144–150.

Mork, K. A. "The Aggregate Demand for Primary Energy in the Short and Long Run for the U.S., 1949–1975." Energy Laboratory report MIT-EL 78-007WP. MIT, May 1978a.

Mork, K. A. "Aggregate Technology, Biased Productivity Growth, and the Demand for Primary Energy in the U.S., 1949–75." *1978 Business and Economics Section Proceedings of the American Statistical Assoc.* Washington, D.C. 1978b, pp. 482–486.

Moroney, J. R. *The Structure of Production in American Manufacturing.* Chapel Hill, N.C., 1972.

Moroney, J. R., and A. Toevs. "Factor Costs and Factor Use: An Analysis of Labor, Capital, and Natural Resources," *Southern Econ. J.* 44 (October 1977): 222–239.

Moroney, J. R., and A. Toevs. "Input Prices, Substitution, and Product Inflation." In R. Pindyck, ed., *Advances in the Economics of Energy and Resources, Vol. I: The Structure of Energy Markets.* Greenwich, Conn., 1980.

Morrisett, I. "Some Recent Uses of Elasticity of Substitution: A Survey." *Econometrica* 21 (January 1953): 41–62.

Morrison, C. J., and E. R., Berndt. "Short-Run Labour Productivity in a Dynamic Model." *J. Econometrics*, forthcoming.

Mortenson, D. T. "Generalized Costs of Adjustment and Dynamic Factor Demand Theory." *Econometrica* 41 (July 1973): 657–66.

Mundlak, Y. "Elasticities of Substitution and the Theory of Derived Demand." *Rev. Econ. Stud.* 35 (April 1968): 225–239.

Murota, T. "On the Summetry of Robinson Elasticities of Substitution: A Three-Factor Case." *Rev. Econ. Stud.* 44 (February 1977): 173–176.

Muth, R. *Cities and Housing*. Chicago: Univ. of Chicago Press, 1969.

Muth, R. "The Derived Demand for Urban Residential Land." *Urban Studies* 8 (October 1971): 243–254.

Nadiri, M. I., and S. Rosen. "Interrelated Factor Demand Functions." *Amer. Econ. Rev.* 59 (September 1969): 457–471.

Nadiri, M. I., and S. Rosen. *A Disequilibrium Model of Demand for Factors of Production*. New York. 1973.

Nerlove, M. "Notes on the Production and Derived Demand Relations Included in Macroeconometric Models." *Internat. Econ. Rev.* 8 (June 1967a): 223–240.

Nerlove, M. "Recent Empirical Studies of the CES and Related Production Functions." In M. Brown, ed., *The Theory and Empirical Analysis of Production*. New York, 1967b.

Nerlove, M. "Lags in Economic Behavior." *Econometrica* 40 (March 1972): 221–251.

Nerlove, M. "Returns to Scale in Electricity Supply." In C. Christ, ed., *Measurement in Economics: Studies in Mathematical Economics and Econometrics in Memory of Yehuda Greenfeld*. Stanford: Stanford Univ. Press, 1963.

Nickell, S. "The Flexible Accelerator Model with Non-Static Expectations. Mimeographed. London School of Economics, 1977.

Nickell, S. *The Investment Decisions of Firms*. Cambridge, England, 1978.

Nordhaus, W., and J. Tobin. *Is Growth Obsolete?* NBER 50th Anniversary Colloquium V. New York, 1972.

Norsworthy, J. R., and M. J. Happer. "Productivity Growth in Manufacturing in the 1980's Labor, Capital and Energy." Proceedings of the Business and Econ. Section of the Amer. Statistical Assn., 1979, pp. 17–26.

Norsworthy, J. R., and M. J. Harper. "The Role of Capital Formation in the Recent Productivity Slowdown." In A. Dogramaci and A. Nabil, eds., *Productivity Analysis at the Macro Level*, forthcoming.

Norsworthy, J. R., M. J. Harper, and K. Kunze. "The Slowdown in Productivity Growth: Analysis of Some Contributing Factors." *Brookings Papers in Economic Activity* (Fall 1979): 387–421.

Oberhofer, W., and J. Kmenta. "A General Procedure for Obtaining Maximum Likelihood Estimates in Generalized Regression Models." *Econometrica* 42 (May 1974): 579–590.

Ozatalay, S, S. Grubaugh, and T. V. Long, III. "Energy Substitution and National Energy Policy." *Amer. Econ. Rev.* 69 (May 1979): 369–371.

Parks, R. W. "Responsiveness of Factor Utilization in Swedish Manufacturing, 1870–1950." *Rev. Econ. Statist.* 53 (May 1971): 129–139.

Perry, G. L. "Capacity in Manufacturing." *Brookings Papers on Economic Activity* 3 (Fall 1973): 701–742.

Peterson, W. "Fuel Use in the U.K.: A Study of Substitution Responses." In A. Astrub, ed., *Energy Models for the European Community.* An Energy Policy Special. Guildford, U.K., 1979, pp. 48–55.

Pindyck, R. S. *The Structure of World Energy Demand.* Cambridge, Mass., 1979a.

Pindyck, R. S. "Interfuel Substitution and the Industrial Demand for Energy: An International Comparison." *Rev. Econ. Statist.* (May 1979b): 169–179.

Plaxico, J. S. "Problems of Factor-Product Aggregation in Cobb-Douglas Value Productivity Analysis." *J. Farm Econ.* 37 (November 1955): 664–675.

Pollak, R. A. "Conditional Demand Functions and Consumption Theory." *Quart. J. Econ.* 83 (February 1969): 60–80.

Robinson, J. *Economics of Imperfect Competition.* London, 1933.

Rothschild, M. "On the Cost of Adjustment." *Quart. J. Econ.* 85 (November 1971): 604–622.

Russell, C. S., and W. J. Vaughan. *Steel Production: Processes, Products and Residuals.* Baltimore, 1976.

Ruttan, V. "The Contribution of Technological Progress to Farm Output: 1950–75." *Rev. Econ. Statist.* 38 (February 1956): 61–69.

Samuelson, P. A. "Prices of Factors and Goods in General Equilibrium." *Rev. Econ. Stud.* 21 (October 1953): 1–20.

Samuelson, P. A. "Relative Shares and Elasticities Simplified: Comment." *Amer. Econ. Rev.* 63 (September 1973): 770–771.

Samuelson, P. A. "A Theory of Induced Innovation along Kennedy-Weizsacker Lines." *Rev. of Econ. Statist.* 47 (November 1965): 343–356.

Samuelson, P. A. "Two Generalizations of the Elasticity of Substitution." In J. N. Wolfe, ed., *Value, Capital and Growth; Papers in Honor of Sir John Hicks.* Edinburgh, 1968, pp. 467–480.

Sato, K. *Production Functions and Aggregation.* Amsterdam, 1975.

Sato, K., and T. Koizumi. "On the Elasticities of Substitution and Complemenatarity." *Oxford Econ. Pap.* 25 (March 1973): 44–56.

Schmookler, J. *Invention and Economic Growth.* Cambridge, Mass., 1966.

Shepard, R. W. *Cost and Production Functions.* Princeton, 1953.

Shih, J. T., et al. "The Validity of the Cobb-Douglas Specification in Taiwan's Developing Agriculture." *Amer. J. Agric. Econ.* 59 (August 1977): 554–558.

Sirmans, C. F., and A. L. Redman. "Capital-Land Substitution and the Price

Elasticity of Demand for Urban Residential Land." *Land Econ.* 55 (May 1979): 167–176.

Smith, V. K., and J. V. Krutilla. "Resource and Environmental Constraints to Growth." *Amer. J. Agric. Econ.* 61 (August 1978): 395–408.

✓ Solow, J. "A General Equilibrium Approach to Aggregate Capital-Energy Complementarity." *Econ. Letters* 2 (1979): 91–94.

Solow, R. M. "The Economics of Resources or the Resources of Economics," *Amer. Econ. Rev.* 64 (May 1974): 1–14.

✓ Solow, R. M. "Resources and Economic Growth." *Amer. Econ.* 22 (Fall 1978): 5–11.

Stapleton, D.C. "Unobserved Variable Methods in the Presence of Symmetry Restrictions." Discussion paper. Univ. of British Columbia, 1981.

Stigler, G. *Capital and Rates of Return in Manufacturing Industries.* Princeton, N.J., 1963.

Stigler, G. "Production and Distribution in the Short Run." *J. Polit. Econ.* 47 (June 1939): 305–327.

Stiglitz, J. E. "A Neoclassical Analysis of the Economics of Natural Resources." In V.K. Smith, ed., *Scarcity and Growth Reconsidered.* Baltimore, 1979.

Theil, H. "The Information Approach to Demand Analysis." *Econometrica,* (January 1965): 67–87.

Theil, H. *Principles of Econometrics.* New York, 1971.

Tinbergen, J. *Econometrics.* London 1951.

Tornquist, L. "The Bank of Finland's Consumption Price Index." *Bank of Finland Monthly Bulletin,* no. 10, (1936): 1–8.

Treadway, A. B. "On Rational Entrepreneurial Behavior and the Demand for Investment," *Rev. Econ. Stud.* 36 (April 1969): 227–239.

Treadway, A. B. "On the Rational Multivariate Flexible Accelerator," *Econometrica* 39 (September 1971): 845–856.

Treadway, A. B. "The Globally Optimal Flexible Accelerator." *J. Econ. Theory,* 7 (February 1974): 7–39.

Tweeten, L. G. "Theories Explaining the Persistence of Low Resource Returns in a Growing Farm Economy." *Amer. J. Agric. Econ.* 51 (December 1969): 798–817.

U.S., Bureau of the Census. *Annual Survey of Manufactures.* Washington, D.C., annual volumes, 1947–1974.

U.S., Bureau of the Census. *Census of Manufactures.* Washington, D.C., 1954, 1958, 1963, 1967.

U.S., Bureau of the Census. *Statistical History of the U.S. from Colonial Times to the Present.* New York: Basic Books, 1976.

U.S., Department of Agriculture. *Agricultural Statistics.* Washington, D.C., annual volumes, 1947–1974.

U.S., Department of Agriculture. "Farm Real Estate Historical Series." ERS Bulletin 570. Washington, D.C., 1973.

U.S., Department of Agriculture. *Farm Real Estate Market Developments*. Washington, D.C., annual volumes, 1965–1974.

U.S., Department of the Interior, Bureau of Mines. *Minerals Yearbook*. Washington, D.C., annual volumes, 1954–1974.

U.S., Department of Treasury, Internal Revenue Service. *Tax Information on Depreciation*. Washington, D.C., 1972.

Uzawa, H. "Duality Principles in the Theory of Cost and Production." *Internat. Econ. Rev.* 5 (October 1964): 291–299.

Uzawa, H. "Production Functions with Constant Elasticity of Substitution." *Rev. Econ. Stud.* 29 (October 1962): 291–299.

Von Weizäcker, C. C. "A New Technical Progress Function." Unpublished paper. Department of Economics, Massachusetts Institute of Technology, Cambridge, Mass., 1980.

Walras, L. *Elements of Pure Economics*. Translated by W. Jaffe. Homewood, Ill., 1954.

Walters, A. A. "Production and Cost Functions: An Econometric Survey," *Econometrica* 31 (January–April 1963): 1–66.

Watkins, G. C. "Canadian Residential and Commercial Demand for Natural Gas." Discussion paper series no. 30. Univ. of Calgary, May 1974.

Wills, J. "Technical Change in the U.S. Primary Metals Industry." *J. Econometrics* 10 (February 1979): 85–98.

Wold, H. *Demand Analysis*, New York, 1953.

Woodworth, R. C. "Agricultural Production Function Studies." In L. R. Martin, ed., *A Survey of Agricultural Economics Literature, Vol. 2*. Minneapolis, 1977.

Zellner, A. "An Efficient Method of Estimating Seemingly Unrelated Regressions and Tests for Aggregation Bias." *J. Amer. Statist. Assn.* 58 (June 1962): 348–368.

Index

(Italicized page numbers denote references to material in tables and figures.)